Lecture Notes
in Business Information Process

T0237840

Series Editors

Wil van der Aalst
Eindhoven Technical University, The Netherlands
John Mylopoulos
University of Trento, Italy
Norman M. Sadeh
Carnegie Mellon University, Pittsburgh, PA, USA
Michael J. Shaw
University of Illinois, Urbana-Champaign, IL, USA
Clemens Szyperski
Microsoft Research, Redmond, WA, USA

Ingo M. Weber

Semantic Methods for Execution-level Business Process Modeling

Modeling Support
Through Process Verification
and Service Composition

 Springer

Author

Ingo M. Weber
University of New South Wales
School of Computer Science and Engineering
Sydney, NSW 2052, Australia
E-mail: ingo.weber@cse.unsw.edu.au; imweber@imweber.de

Dissertation, angenommen von der Fakultät für Wirtschaftswissenschaften
der Universität Karlsruhe (TH).
Tag der mündlichen Prüfung: 8.6.2009
Referent: Prof. Dr. Rudi Studer
Korreferentin: Prof. Dr. Birgitta König-Ries

Library of Congress Control Number: 2009938724

ACM Computing Classification (1998): H.3.5, J.1, D.2.12, I.2.4

ISSN   1865-1348
ISBN-10   3-642-05084-0 Springer Berlin Heidelberg New York
ISBN-13   978-3-642-05084-8 Springer Berlin Heidelberg New York

springer.com

© Springer-Verlag Berlin Heidelberg 2009
Printed in Germany

Typesetting: Camera-ready by author, data conversion by Scientific Publishing Services, Chennai, India
Printed on acid-free paper   SPIN: 12780020   06/3180   5 4 3 2 1 0

Foreword

Enterprises today act in an environment of continuously accelerating change. Since nearly all of an enterprise's activities are supported through IT, the adaptation of IT applications is necessary in a similarly quick fashion. Hereby Service-Oriented Architectures (SOA) and business processes play an important role, which thus have to be either re-designed or adapted accordingly.

This is where the work of Ingo Weber adds to the field, by creating new approaches for the development and adaptation of business processes, focused on an implementation-oriented point of view. Key questions are raised by the verification of specific properties of the processes as well as by the automatic composition of processes out of pre-defined components. The presented work hereby combines formal approaches with real evaluations in an impressive manner.

The work is structured in seven chapters, as follows. The introductory chapter puts forward the motivation for the study, the research questions, and an overview of the work and its central contributions. Subsequently, chap. 2 is concerned with the foundations of the work, where three areas are discussed: business process management, service-oriented computing, and semantic technologies.

Chapter 3 develops a detailed requirement analysis, presenting a total of 19 requirements. Since the breadth of the requirements is too large, the subsequently developed conceptual approach does not cover all of them. The developed approach distinguishes itself primarily by enriching process models with semantic annotations: this way, so-called annotated process models are created, which allow the specification of preconditions and postconditions. For the approach, a component-based architecture is introduced and complemented with a methodology giving targeted instructions on how to systematically use the offered components.

Chapter 4 introduces one of the central technical contributions of the presented work: the verification of annotated process models. Hereby, methods are developed which allow checking of the semantic annotations for consistency – in particular four verification tasks are addressed: (1) "effect conflict": are there activities which can be executed in parallel and whose postconditions are inconsistent; (2) "precondition conflict": are there parallel activities such that the postcondition of one is inconsistent with the precondition of the other; (3) "reachability": are there activities which are never reached in any process execution; (4) "executability": are there activities whose preconditions are not fulfilled albeit they are scheduled for execution; In a first step toward the solution, so-called annotated process graphs are formally defined in terms of syntax and execution semantics. Building on top of these definitions, the above-mentioned verification tasks are formalized, the computational complexity is analyzed, and algorithms for tractable cases of the above tasks are developed.

In chap. 5, new solutions for the composition of services are developed. Hereby, the typical trade-off between expressivity of the formalisms and the efficiency of the solution algorithms is taken into account. Substantial contributions of the developed approaches are according heuristics which make use of the domain knowledge presented in the ontologies, as well as methods for approximate reasoning. The developed solution approaches are first presented in an overview and then detailed step by step. Among others, the Web Service Composition problem is formalized for this purpose, and complexity results are introduced which depend on the expressivity of the formalisms for modeling domain knowledge.

Chapter 6 addresses the evaluation of the developed approaches. Five different prototypical scenarios are presented and illustrated with screen shots. In addition, empirical evaluations for the composition of services are discussed. The chapter ends with the presentation of evaluations based on several case studies.

The work concludes with a short summary and an outlook in chap. 7. Elaborate appendices include detailed proofs to the theorems formulated throughout the work.

The work presented by Ingo Weber contains original methodical contributions for the modeling and formal analysis of implementation-oriented process models. As such, the work impresses with the combination of strictly formally substantiated solution approaches and evaluations in practical application scenarios.

Karlsruhe, Germany
August 2009   Rudi Studer

Preface

The pace of change in the current economical world increases continuously. With respect to information technology (IT), there are currently two main trends with the goal of enabling organizations to adapt to changing circumstances On the one hand, software applications are being altered such that they offer Web services interfaces. This way, the business logic and the functionality become accessible from the outside in a standardized way. On the other hand, organizations increasingly apply methods from business process modeling. The vision is to create executable process models in very short time frames, which orchestrate the usage of Web services, and thus to enable the swift implementation of changed processes. However, the software tools offered today have difficulties to fulfill the demands that arise from the combination of the two technologies.

This monograph aims at the advancement of scientific knowledge on the implementation of business processes in organizations' IT systems. For this purpose, the monograph investigates if and how modelers of processes at the execution level can be supported using semantic technologies. Execution-level processes abstract from the technical details of Web services. Thus, they remain comprehensible for non-technicians. At the same time they reflect which Web services are available. We first analyze the requirements of process modeling support at this level. On this basis, we construct a conceptual framework supporting the majority of the requirements. For two of the components from the framework there were no sufficient solutions available. Therefore, we design detailed solutions for these: Firstly, we investigate the verification of annotated process models. As early as at design time, this type of verification can unveil conflicts arising from various sources such as an incorrect ordering of activities in a process model – e.g., when two activities are scheduled as parallel, but their parallel execution would lead to undefined results. Secondly, we investigate the problem of automatically composing semantically annotated Web services. This is relevant for finding an activity implementation made up of Web services. For both approaches we investigate trade-offs between expressivity and scalability, with an emphasis on scalability. Several prototypical implementations enable the evaluation of the above components with respect to process models from practice.

The monograph was originally written as a PhD thesis with the Universität Karlsruhe (TH) while I worked at SAP Research in Karlsruhe, Germany. This environment allowed me to interact with many great researchers from academia, in particular from the AIFB institute, Universität Karlsruhe (TH), the IPE group at the Forschungszentrum Informatik (FZI), and several publicly funded projects, especially the EU-funded Integrated Project *SUPER*. People that were particularly influential in the creation of this monograph are: Anupriya Ankolekar, Sudhir Agarwal, Nenad Stojanovic, Tomasz Kaczmarek, James Scicluna, and Wil van der Aalst.

Special thanks go to my PhD supervisor Prof. Rudi Studer, who gave me the freedom to pursue my visions, yet guided me with insightful criticism and encouragement. I am also very grateful to Prof. Birgitta König-Ries, the second reviewer of my thesis, for her time and highly valuable feedback. Further I want to thank the other two members of my committee for their support, Prof. Andreas Oberweis and Prof. Christof Weinhardt.

My project leader, Christian Brelage, as well as my managers at SAP, Orestis Terzidis and Elmar Dorner, were extremely supportive by giving me substantial freedom in my work and by allowing me to participate in many international conferences and workshops. My research visit to SAP Research in Brisbane in early 2008 was also very fruitful, allowing me to collaborate with Alistair Barros, Marek Kowalkiewicz, Uwe Kylau, and Julien Vayssière, as well as with Shazia Sadiq and Guido Governatori from the University of Queensland, and Jan Mendling, at the time with Queensland University of Technology.

Further influential feedback came from Michael Altenhofen, Daniel Oberle, Roger Kilian-Kehr, Wasim Sadiq, Matthias Born, Ivan Markovic, Christian Drumm, and many more colleagues and students at SAP Research and from SAP product development groups. Jörg Hoffmann deserves special mention; as co-author on many of my publications he showed me how to apply formal methods to applied problems, and worked with me on many of the topics presented in this monograph.

Finally, I would like to thank my family, friends, and my partner, Susanne, for their patience and endurance during this intense time. Without their support, it would not have been possible to complete this work.

Sydney, Australia
August 2009   Ingo M. Weber

Contents

Part I

Foundations

1

Introduction

This chapter starts with a general motivation and overview of the monograph. The work attempts to verify a main hypothesis which is presented and refined in Section 1.2. For this purpose we follow the methodology described in Section 1.3. A glance on the details of the solution approaches and the contributions is presented in Section 1.4, before we outline the structure of the book in Section 1.5.

1.1 Motivation and Overview

Today's economy suffers under and benefits from an ever-increasing pace of change [103, 127, 62, 265]. In order to adapt to changes such as a changing competitive situation or to leverage new opportunities, organizations need to alter their operational business processes. Since many processes are facilitated by or implemented in Information Technology (IT) systems, i.e., in software, changing the processes often implies changing the implementation. As a result, the speed with which IT can change dictates the speed with which changes required by business can be realized [127], and there is broad consensus that shorter delays in process adaptation are indispensable [62, 265].

In order to enable organizations to adapt their processes more quickly, there is an increasing interest in the Service-Oriented Architecture (SOA) paradigm as well as Business Process Management (BPM). As a predecessor of BPM and one means to ease the burden of changing the process logic, traditional workflow management offers a way to separate the process logic from the implementation of individual activities. However, since workflow management focused on processes with mostly (or exclusively) human activities, the way in which interfaces from workflow management tools to software applications are exposed and consumed has effectively not been standardized[1]. In contrast,

---

[1] From the workflow management side, the interfaces have been standardized – but near to none of the application solution vendors implements these standards.

the SOA paradigm offers encapsulating business functionality in the form of services with standardized interface technology, e.g., Web service standards. Part of the SOA stack is a process layer, where standards for executable processes are placed.

In the near future it is envisioned that business processes are composed over services provided by SOA, enabling the required flexibility on the business level [103]. "BPM is a major reason for turning to SOA" [113], leading to the expectation that the market for BPM Suites will be among the fastest growing software markets at least until 2011 [113]. According to [113], "BPM wins the 'triple crown' of saving money, saving time and adding value." Besides all the promising outlooks, creating executable processes with Web services as activity implementations still is a complex task. As such, it is sometimes also referred to as "visual programming" and not particularly suitable for professionals without a technical background.

Conceptual business process models[2] [178], as opposed to executable processes, focus on depicting processes on the level of activities, subprocesses, and the control flow between them. The target group comprises professionals with business knowledge who typically do not have a strong technical background. The level on which we focus in this work, *execution-level business process modeling*, can be seen as the most technical and detailed level of conceptual process modeling: while still at the conceptual level, an execution-level process model captures the process as it should be executed by a software system, without yet giving all details that are needed for execution. These details are subsequently entered when moving the process from the conceptual to an executable level. In terms of the classification of business processes in [320], execution-level process models are between models of operational business processes and process implementation – we see them as a means to get from the former to the latter level. In order to gain a competitive edge, enterprises are encouraged to widely adopt a process-oriented way of thinking, and to align BPM and SOA initiatives [265], which is exactly the goal of execution-level process modeling.

When an organization changes a process, this change is usually triggered by business professionals. The process owner on the business side, whom we refer to as business analyst, creates the "to-be" conceptual process model, i.e., a model of the process how it should ideally be performed. If this process should be supported by IT, the process model is then refined into an execution-level business process model, by either the business analyst alone, or in cooperation with a process architect. Process architect is an IT role; still, process architects have enough domain knowledge to closely cooperate with the lines of business in order to implement processes in the intended way. Subsequently, the execution-level process model is to be further refined into an executable process model. Thus, it is important that this model represents an agreement between the business world and the IT world. That is, it is still

---

[2] The different process layers are discussed in detail in Section 2.1.3.

comprehensible and acceptable for business, while being consistent and fine-grained enough such that it can be implemented in IT. The problem with this approach is that business analysts' to-be models rarely meet the requirements of the implementation level. Therefore, several iterations of feedback between the business analyst and the process architect are necessary.

With a traditional BPM approach, many of these specification steps can neither be handled automatically nor facilitated by appropriate tools, since the *meaning* of process artifacts is not captured in the process model. The Semantic BPM (SBPM) approach[3] attempts to solve a number of challenges in BPM through the annotation of semantic descriptions for process artifacts and techniques that make use of the annotations. That is, the assumption is that it is helpful to express the meaning of process artifacts in a way that is available for machine reasoning. The annotations usually link the process artifacts to an *ontology*. As detailed in Section 2.3 we herein adopt the definition from [276]: "An ontology is a formal, explicit specification of a shared conceptualisation." The formal and explicit nature allow us to construct tools to ease a business analyst's job by facilitating various BPM tasks. And the application of the tools requires that the ontology is a shared conceptualization, since it is the common model that is reused by many process modelers – the community which must share the understanding with the modeler(s) of the ontology. If the ontology is not shared, the modeler will not understand the vocabulary; if it is not a conceptualization, then the vocabulary does not describe the relevant entities, or not at the right level of granularity. However, if these prerequisites are fulfilled, we can – to some degree – express the meaning of process artifacts. The additional semantic information in the models then allows us to construct new tools and methods for supporting process modelers, as follows.

The goal of this work is to present techniques and methodological guidance for supporting the modeler in the creation of execution-level process models. The business analyst should be enabled to design execution-level process models which satisfy the above-listed requirements while being aware of the execution possibilities. For this purpose we propose to semantically annotate processes at the level of individual activities, enabling us to leverage this additional information for modeler support. We start with analyzing the requirements – e.g., to be able to determine if the ordering of process activities is correct according to meaningful criteria; or being able to discover services which can implement a process activity; etc. On the basis of 19 such requirements, we construct a generic conceptual solution to support a majority of them. The conceptual solution comprises a structural architecture which arranges a number of components as well as a methodology. A subset of these components are state-of-the-art, and we describe the specific role the components take in our framework. The methodology further specifies how the components can be used to achieve the purposes addressed here. There are two flavors of the methodology: one for manual and one for automatic control.

---

[3] Cf. Section 2.3.5 for more details.

As a main contribution of this work, two technical core problems of this conceptual solution are investigated in formal detail: the composition of execution-level artifacts and the verification of semantically annotated process models. The verification can determine, if an annotated process model is consistent by itself and with a domain ontology[4]. The composition can find matching implementation-level artifacts[5] for the process activities and determine a valid execution order of those. The practicability of the solutions is assessed based on prototypical implementations and process models from practical application scenarios.

In Section 1.4, we give a first glance at the details of the two technical core topics. Prior to that, we state the hypotheses that are verified in this work, and the methodology we pursue.

1.2 Hypotheses

This work verifies the hypothesis stated and explained below.

Main hypothesis:

H0. Execution-level process modeling can be supported by enriching the process models with formal change semantics at the level of process activities.

In more detail, by support we mean that (i) modelers with experience in today's tools are facilitated in process modeling at the execution level, and (ii) new groups of users are enabled to model processes at the execution-level. The second part of the hypothesis hints at our approach: attaching semantic annotations to individual process activities for the purpose of stating the change semantics of the process activities explicitly in a machine-accessible way. The change semantics describe which logical states the world may be in when the activity is executed, and how the activity changes these states. This main hypothesis supported by the following sub-hypotheses.

Sub-hypotheses:

H1. Creating and adapting process implementations is a challenge for businesses today; reducing time and money needed for it is a relevant problem which can be addressed by support for execution-level process modeling.

H2. Many of the most common requirements of execution-level process modeling support can be fulfilled by a careful combination of few components.

---

[4] The domain ontology captures the vocabulary used in the domain at hand, as well as a logical theory that models relations and constraints over domain entities. Creating such a domain ontology is not in the scope of this work.

[5] By implementation-level artifacts we mean pre-defined building blocks for which it is known how they can be executed. They can, e.g., take the form of Web services, workflow tasks with a defined user interface, or even recurring manual tasks that are not controlled by an IT system.

H3. It is possible to algorithmically verify the consistency of semantically annotated process models.

H4. It is possible to automatically find and compose pre-existing artifacts for the realization of process activities.

H1 states that the problem addressed by this work is a relevant problem in organizations today, and that execution-level process modeling support is a direction towards solving it. H2 describes the first part of our solution approach: we first conduct a requirements analysis; on this basis we then create a high-level framework with few components[6] which together fulfill the majority of the most common requirements. In H3 the semantic consistency of process models is addressed. What we mean by that is that the combination of the process model, its annotation, and the domain ontology is consistent. H4 deals with finding and composing pre-existing artifacts for the implementation of process activities. The focus is exclusively on artifacts which offer a defined functionality, such as Web services or workflow tasks. While H3 and H4 describe the details of the previously missing or less developed components, H2 states that these and few other components can jointly fulfill the defined requirements. H1 states that the addressed problem is indeed relevant. Together, these four sub-hypotheses give evidence towards the main hypothesis, H0. We outline below how the evaluation of the hypotheses is addressed.

1.3 Methodology

The suggested methodology, depicted in Figure 1.1, is structured in two dimensions: the levels with a focus on particular points of view – namely the business level, the implementation level, and the formal level; and the phases of problem analysis, solution, and evaluation. The complete picture addresses the main hypothesis H0. In contrast, H3 and H4 are dealt with on the formal level, while H1 and H2 cover the business level. The results are discussed in the respective evaluation phases on all levels.

Initially, a business-level requirement analysis is conducted. The sources for relevant coarse-grained problems on this level are mainly market research and analysis (e.g., by Gartner and Forrester) as well as SAP Product Definition departments, who conduct studies with customers and other stakeholders for internal use. Based on the outlined requirements, a conceptual framework is created. This framework is a generic high-level solution to a specified subset of the high-level problem. The conceptual framework lists the required building blocks and their interactions, but leaves out how the building blocks are to be filled: it is a conceptual solution on the business level. Only a subset of the related open research challenges from the requirement analysis can be covered by the framework. The conceptual solution is accompanied by a suggestion

---

[6] Note that component here is meant in the sense of a logical constituent, not necessarily a software component.

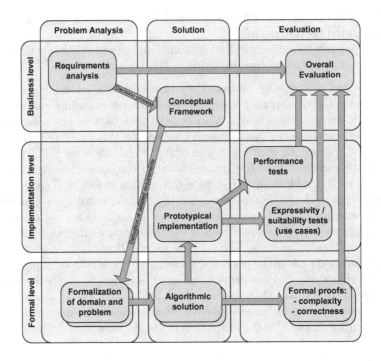

Fig. 1.1. Methodological structure of the work

how to fit the added techniques into Business Process Management (BPM) methodologies. In the scope of this work, choices had to be made regarding which parts of the conceptual framework to actually cover in detail, where the required parts of the framework have a priority over the optional parts.

For the parts to be covered and where a formal approach is promising, we first formalize the domain and the exact problem to be solved. Next, we investigate whether existing solutions can be utilized. If not, we develop algorithmic solutions, e.g., in pseudo-code, where we build on the formalization. Certain properties of the problems and algorithms are then proven formally, such as computational complexity or correctness in the sense that (i) the algorithms give deterministic answers, (ii) the answers given are correct, and, where applicable, (iii) all answers are found – again, with respect to the formalization of the problem. The formal approach is pursued for the parts dealing with the verification of annotated process models and service composition.

The solutions from the formal level are then implemented in a number of prototypes. The prototypes serve two purposes: on the one hand, scalability in practical settings is investigated; and on the other hand, the suitability of the expressivity of the formal basis is evaluated through use case studies.

Finally, an overall evaluation takes the results from all levels into account and discusses in how far the initial hypotheses are supported by the presented solutions.

1.4 Details of the Solution Approach

For the two technical core contributions – verification (H3) and service composition (H4) – the problems are defined through precise formalization. On this basis, algorithms are developed that solve the problems. It is then proven formally that each algorithm solves the defined problem, respectively. An integrated prototypical implementation for these two techniques is developed as an extension to standard BPM tools. H3 and H4 are subsequently evaluated on the basis of this prototype, the initial requirements, and the formal results. The technical details are discussed below.

1.4.1 Verification of Annotated Process Models

In the presented context the question arises whether the combination of a given process model, its semantic annotation, and the respective domain ontology is consistent. The criteria for consistency may, e.g., include the following: are activities presented in the correct ordering in the process model? Or: given the knowledge modeled in the domain ontology, are there parallel activities with conflicting outcomes?

The goal is to make use of the semantic annotations and to verify the consistency of the semantically annotated process model algorithmically. For this purpose, we define suitable verification tasks along with algorithms that can determine flaws in process models of realistic size in an adequate time frame. As the common denominators representing a larger set of possible modeling errors, there are two specific properties which we evaluate over the preconditions and effects of each task:

- *Executability*, where we require the precondition of a task to be satisfied any time the task may be executed.
- *Conflicting parallel construction*, where two tasks which may be enacted in parallel, given the control flow of the process, have annotations which are in conflict with each other.

In a nutshell, we address executability checking in terms of propagating a set of known facts over the process nodes, where all literals in the set of a given node are guaranteed to hold every time the respective node is activated. For conflicting parallel constructions, we devise a method which maintains a matrix over the edges in the process, and performs propagation steps ending in a matrix where parallelism of two nodes can be read off directly from the matrix entries. Given this information, conflicting annotations may be checked in a straightforward manner.

Both propagation algorithms run in time polynomial in the size of the process. Their limitation is that they do not consider edge conditions, i.e., annotations directing the control flow at exclusive-OR-branchings based on properties of the current situation. If such edge conditions are introduced, then, as we show, executability checking becomes computationally hard. Another limitation of these methods is that they work only with limited expressivity of the control flow of a process model – methods suitable for more expressive process formalisms would differ in their very nature from the propagation algorithms devised here and constitute interesting future work.

1.4.2 Composition of Execution-level Artifacts

With composition we address the problem of automatically finding a set of pre-existing artifacts for the realization of individual process activities: when executed in the order determined by our composition approach, this set of artifacts can functionally implement the process activity. This work is based on results in AI planning and related to current works in Semantic Web service composition. By modeling the relevant domain as an ontology that captures the potential states of the world, particularly state-based composition approaches (e.g., [214, 273, 4, 242]) can be employed. The output of the composition of Web services is then expressed as an orchestration of Web service calls, e.g., in the Business Process Execution Language (BPEL) [11].

The goal is to find a valid composition of artifacts that – based on the precondition of an activity – is able to establish the desired effect. In order to suit the context of process modeling, the approach must have an emphasis on scalability and response time. Also, we want to be able to make use of a domain ontology. Thus, the contribution is to adapt an existing planning technique such that it can deal with implicit effects, i.e., facts that are implied given the explicit effect of an action and the domain ontology; and to design a suitable heuristic function for guiding the search. The latter is only addressed by one other work [206], but their heuristic function ignores ontological constraints and their reasoning takes exponential time in the worst case. In contrast, our approach works on the basis of restricted expressivity of the ontology, resulting in polynomial time reasoning behavior, and thus higher scalability.

1.5 Structure of This Book

The book is structured according to the chosen methodology, with an emphasis on the requirements, the conceptual framework, and the two technical core topics. To give an overview, the structure of the monograph in terms of parts and chapters is depicted in Fig. 1.2 and shows, where applicable, references to publications covering contributions of the respective chapters.

Subsequent to the introduction, the background in the fields of Business Process Management, Web services, and Semantic Web is explained in

Chapter 2. Chapter 3 provides our analysis of the requirements for the problem addressed in this work and discusses our conceptual framework. The next two chapters contain the core technical contributions: our methods for the verification of annotated process models (Chapter 4) and task composition (Chapter 5), respectively. The work is evaluated in Chapter 6, and Chapter 7 concludes.

I   Foundations
　　1.   Introduction
　　2.   Background
II   Modeling Support with Verification and Composition
　　3.   Requirements Analysis & Conceptual Framework [311, 316, 317, 318]
　　4.   Verification of Annotated Process Models [314, 315]
　　5.   Task Composition [144, 141, 194]
III   Finale
　　6.   Evaluation [41, 42, 143, 312, 319]
　　7.   Conclusions & Outlook
　　　 Appendix A: Proofs
　　　 References

Fig. 1.2. Book structure

For increased legibility all formal proofs can be found in the appendix. The appendix starts with a paragraph clarifying how the formal results relate to contributions from co-authors of the publications.

Where applicable, we will refer to a set of additional works that build on the results presented in this monograph: compliance checking can be addressed with parts of the given framework [115, 313]; the question how to semantically annotate process models in the required form has also been investigated [40]; the proposed methods also allow the suggestion of promising services to be added during modeling, which we refer to as "auto-completion" [39]; finally, the relation between the roles of workflow tasks, flexible human tasks, and fully automated Web services in semantically annotated process models is discussed in [252].

2

Background

In this chapter we introduce the foundations on which this work builds and position our contributions in the bigger context. The presented work mainly offers improvements to current Business Process Management (Section 2.1) by using technologies from the Semantic Web (Section 2.3). The improvements help, among others, in relating process activities to services (Section 2.2).

2.1 Business Process Management

After giving a brief intuition of what BPM is about we discuss its historical roots. Subsequently, more details on BPM are given: a set of definitions, layering, phases and life-cycles, perspectives, patterns, and finally current challenges.

Roughly speaking, a business process is a set of activities performed by an organization to achieve a certain goal. Business process management (BPM) is a field of research and an industry which aim at understanding business processes, modeling processes, configuring and implementing them – oftentimes in the form of information technology (IT) systems – monitoring and analyzing implemented processes, and finally redesigning them. The objectives for BPM projects in enterprises can vary strongly, but often include documentation of the processes, IT-based control and execution, and efficiency gains.

The focus of this monograph is on business process modeling, which serves as an abstraction of the way enterprises do business. Hereby threads of work are noted down as human-comprehensible business process models. While notations such as the Event-driven Process Chains (EPCs) [157] received much attention in the past, the Business Process Modeling Notation (BPMN) [222] is gaining momentum and support. Figure 2.1 shows an example of a BPMN process model.

A more complete view on the various aspects relevant to BPM will be given after explaining its origins.

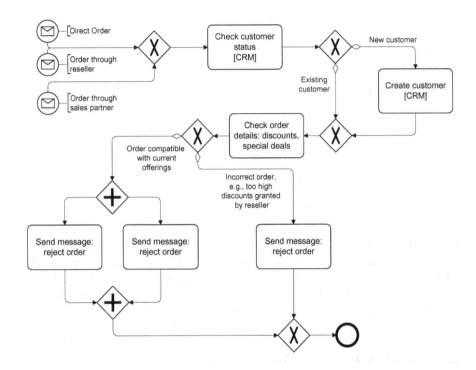

Fig. 2.1. Order-to-provisioning process from the Telecommunications domain, depicted in BPMN. Thin circles correspond to start events, thick circles to end events. The rectangles with rounded corners are tasks, i.e., atomic activities. The diamonds correspond to control-flow gateways, where "X" stands for exclusive OR (XOR) and "+" for parallel execution.

2.1.1 The Path to Business Process Management

Historically, business process management is an offspring of *Business Process Reengineering (BPR)* [122] as well as a broader and more modern version of *Workflow Management (WfM)*. Process re-engineering advocates the complete redesign of business processes; in contrast, workflow management originally aimed at supporting office automation, such as document handling. We first discuss the latter, before addressing BPR in more detail.

Workflow Management

The Workflow Management Coalition (WfMC), a global organization of consultants, academics, and over 200 vendors engaged in workflow and BPM, defines a *workflow* as:

> "the automation of a business process, in whole or part, during which documents, information or tasks are passed from one participant to another for action, according to a set of procedural rules." [172]

In other words, a workflow is a description of a process that involves tasks which are to be executed by information workers, along with the ordering of the tasks and the rules that govern optional behavior. E.g., a workflow for handling insurance claims may start with the claim being entered into the system; a subsequent check if the claimed damage is insured through the products the customer purchased; then a fraud prevention check; and so forth. Optional behavior may include a different treatment for preferred customers.

Further, the WfMC gives the following definition of a *Workflow Management System (WfMS)*:

> "a system that defines, creates and manages the execution of work-flows through the use of software, running on one or more workflow engines, which is able to interpret the process definition, interact with workflow participants and, where required, invoke the use of Information-Technology (IT) tools and applications." [172]

A workflow description can be interpreted by a workflow engine, which controls the execution of instances of the workflow, i.e., to use the above example, the processing of a particular insurance claim. Due to its nature, a WfMS is especially well suited for office environments with processes that are repeated often, and which include work performed by information workers. Thus, WfMSs were most successful in industrial sectors such as banking, insurance, and public administration.

Instead of focusing on the design and enactment of human-centric work-flows for automating the control of the work carried out, BPM aims at addressing end-to-end business processes in organizations. Havey [125] states that the name "workflow" is rather used for processes with a focus on human actions. Controversially, Havey argues that the word "workflow" is just not modern anymore, although according to him it better hints at the meaning than "business process". While this argument can hardly be disproved, the research under the term BPM in fact is broader in its scope, sometimes extending into the space of processes at a strategic level. In contrast, WfM focuses on (partial) operational processes. Further, the emphasis of WfM is on the design and execution of processes, not on discovering how a process is actually carried out in an organization at a given point in time [321].

To understand the origins of BPM, it is of interest to know the background of WfM. Jablonski and Bussler [155] argue that workflow management originates from office automation and BPR, mostly. Office automation pursued the idea of automating individual tasks in an office [86], as opposed to the goal of WfM to control the execution order and data flow between information workers. Other influential works for WfM were [155]:

- Software Process Management [153] – supporting the process of software development by modeling it, analyzing the model, and structuring the development according to it.
- Enterprise Modeling and Architecture [306], as the root of thinking about processes instead of individual work tasks.
- Database systems, email, and document management systems.

Business Process Reengineering

Business Process Reengineering (BPR) was a highly influential trend in the 1990ies, and is mostly credited to Hammer [121, 122]. The core idea is that, in order to realize efficiency gains, companies re-think the ways in which they work – they redesign their business processes. Teng et al. [282] define BPR as "the critical analysis and radical redesign of existing business processes to achieve breakthrough improvements in performance measures."

High efficiency gains were assumed to be possible because the tools available to organizations changed – e.g., traditionally it was a high effort to copy (paper-based) files of customers or cases, and even more costly to integrate concurrent changes. This often left no option but to sequentialize all tasks that had to do with a particular file. With the advent of software applications the costs for copying, concurrent handling, or communicating files have become negligible in many cases.

A basic pillar for achieving a radical redesign of processes is to start with a *clean slate*, i.e., to design the new *to-be processes* (the processes as they should ideally be executed from the business point of view) from scratch with an empty sheet of paper. Thus, the *as-is process* (the process as it is executed so far) is not taken into account.

While the practicability in principle has been demonstrated through highly successful projects [122], the promise of cutting costs by more than 60 % was in many cases overly optimistic. Malhotra [185] concludes: "70% of the BPR projects fail. Biggest obstacles that reengineering [faces] are: (i) Lack of sustained management commitment and leadership; (ii) Unrealistic scope and expectations; and (iii) Resistance to Change."

On the basis of interviews with over 200 companies and analysis of 35 reengineering initiatives, Davenport and Stoddard [64] identify seven myths about reengineering, resulting from popular management literature and the hype around BPR. One of these myths, the "Myth of the Clean Slate", entails that starting from a "blank sheet of paper" requires a "blank cheque" for implementing the resulting process [64]. In order to keep the cost for implementation in realistic boundaries, Davenport and Stoddard propose Clean Slate Design – designing the new to-be process without considering the as-is process, but taking the as-is process into account when implementing the changes. This is of particular interest here, since the methodology suggested in this work builds on this notion.

After having introduced the roots of BPM, we now provide a few definitions around BPM.

2.1.2 Definitions

In the following we give a number of relevant definitions for BPM in chronological order.

Davenport and Short [63] define a business process as: "a set of logically related tasks performed to achieve a defined business outcome for a particular customer or market. [...] a specific ordering of work activities across time and place, with a beginning, an end, and clearly identified inputs and outputs. Business processes have customers (internal or external) and they cross organizational boundaries, i.e., they occur across or between organizational subunits." Business processes therefore comprise tasks, i.e., units of work, and their ordering, inputs, and outputs. Davenport and Short put an emphasis on the cross-organizational aspect of processes, which we do not adopt in this work.

Hammer and Champy [122] give the following definition of a business process: "a collection of activities that take one or more kinds of input and create an output that is of value to the customer." In addition to the previous definition, the aspect of adding value is emphasized.

More recently, Weske, van der Aalst, and Verbeek [321] give the following definition for Business Process Management: "Supporting business processes using methods, techniques, and software to design, enact, control, and analyze operational processes involving humans, organizations, applications, documents and other sources of information." They continue with a definition of a business process management system (BPMS): "A generic software system that is driven by explicit process designs to enact and manage operational business processes."

In the following, the definitions around business processes, business process management, and business process models from Weske [320] are presented. We will adopt these definitions for this work.

Definition 2.1. *A business process consists of a set of activities that are performed in coordination in an organizational and technical environment. These activities jointly realize a business goal. Each business process is enacted by a single organization, but it may interact with business processes performed by other organizations.*

Weske emphasizes the goal-driven aspect of processes. However, the latter point is in contrast to Davenport and Short [63]: there, a process always crosses organizational boundaries. We here adopt the view of Weske, since the focus on intra-organizational processes fits the theme of this work better. He gives the following definitions for BPM and business process models [320]:

Definition 2.2. Business process management *includes concepts, methods, and techniques to support the design, administration, configuration, enactment, and analysis of business processes.*

Definition 2.3. *A business process model consists of a set of activity models and execution constraints between them. A business process instance represents a concrete case in the operational business of a company, consisting of activity instances. Each business process model acts as a blueprint for a set of business process instances, and each activity model acts as a blueprint for a set of activity instances.*

We herein will focus on the creation of business process models, rather than dealing with their instances.

The abbreviation BPM is used to refer to business process management, business process modeling, and business process models depending on the context. Herein, we use BPM as abbreviation for business process management, since this is the most common usage.

The above definitions provide the ground for going into more details about BPM.

2.1.3 Overview and Methodology for BPM

For organizations that want to benefit from BPM, it is crucial to know how to approach the topic. Practitioners regularly ask for a methodology for incorporating process management tools in their day-to-day lives. In this section, we will give an overview over BPM, including methodological aspects, by describing layers and purposes for process modeling and management, perspectives on BPM, a BPM life-cycle for structuring the work around BPM efforts, and roles that should ideally be involved.

Layers in BPM

Business processes exist on and are influenced by various layers. Weske [320] proposes the layers depicted in Figure 2.2, which we describe below.

The *strategy* of a company, e.g., to offer the most innovative products in a certain industry domain, can be broken down into operational *goals*, e.g., developing a specific innovative product. These levels are influential to the *organizational processes* – high-level processes, typically informally described in textual form, presentation slides or the like. Organizational processes capture abstractly how to interact with business partners, which dependencies on other organizational processes exist, and which goals can be achieved.

Multiple *operational processes* contribute to an organizational process. An operational business process describes how the work is to be carried out, in terms of activities, their ordering, and the roles involved. Operational processes can therefore be expressed as business process models. Various notations exist on this level, most prominently the EPC and BPMN notations.

Fig. 2.2. Layering in BPM. Source: [320].

Processes at the operational level do however not address implementation details[1].

In this work we will thus also refer to processes at the operational level as conceptual process models [178]. We further argue that this layer contains a sub-layer, which we refer to as *execution-level process models*: conceptual process models which are refined for the purpose of implementation, but still reside at a conceptual level. Not all technical details required for execution are addressed by an execution-level process model – the purpose is to find a process model which can be implemented. That is, the implementation imposes no constraints on the process which would require a process instance to deviate from the modeled control flow – but the process model is still understandable for non-technical personnel. Execution-level processes are mentioned in [332], although they refer to processes that can actually be executed by a process execution engine. In contrast, we refer to the latter type of processes as executable or implemented processes.

An *implemented business process* is a process that can be executed – regardless of whether it is implemented in static program code, policies in the

---

[1] In terms of layers in Model-Driven Architecture (MDA), this corresponds to implementation-independent models.

organization, or as a process model that can be interpreted by an execution engine. If the latter is the case, we call the respective process model an *executable process model*. The executable process model differs from the execution-level process model in that the former also contains technical details, such as specific data types for messages, technical endpoints at which application programs accept certain messages, and the like.[2] Separate languages are used to represent executable processes, such as the Web Services Business Process Execution Language (WSBPEL, cf. Section 2.2.4).

The reason why we make these subtle differences explicit is that it is necessary to understand these levels for following the motivation and usage scenarios of the core parts of this work. In particular, the levels of main concern here are operational, execution-level, and implemented business process models. Naturally, on which level a process is modeled largely depends on the purpose which is pursued.

Purposes of Process Modeling

The reasons due to which organizations model their processes differ. The scope of a process model should include all relevant aspects, and leave out everything that is irrelevant – where the question of relevance is strongly linked to the purpose for which the process model is created. Reijers [247] summarizes the following purposes for process modeling:

- Training and communication – communicating to employees how a process is (or should be) conducted.
- Simulation and analysis – to simulate the behavior of an as-is or a new process, and to analyze this behavior.
- Costing and budgeting – activity-based costing (ABC) [156] is the idea to determine the price for a service or good on the basis of the costs of activities.
- Documentation, knowledge management, and quality – for people involved in the process execution to know how they contribute to a process; it can be required for quality purposes or compliance with regulations to document processes explicitly.
- Enactment, i.e., execution of the models – where an IT system, such as a WfMS, controls the execution of process instances.
- System development – as input to the development of IT applications to support changed or new processes.
- Organizational design – based on process models it can be analyzed which boundaries of organizational sub-units form more natural splits than others.
- Management information – key mile stones or performance indicators can be specified on a process model, allowing to measure their respective achievement in process instances.

---

[2] This layer corresponds to implementation-specific models in MDA.

We herein mostly deal with process models that are created for the purpose of enactment; however, many of the techniques apply for various other purposes as well.

Perspectives on BPM

For a good understanding of BPM, it is necessary to know which viewpoints on process models exist. Jablonski and Bussler [155] describe already in 1996 a highly general workflow meta-model, which gives the following set of perspectives on a process.

- Function perspective: the hierarchy of subprocesses and tasks – how can subprocesses be decomposed into tasks?
- Operation perspective: which operations and applications support which parts of the process?
- Behavior perspective: the execution order of activities, also referred to as *control flow*.
- Information perspective: how and which data is consumed, forwarded, and produced by the process?
- Organization perspective: which roles are responsible for which activities?
- Causality perspective: why the process is executed.
- Integrity perspective: which constraints have to be adhered to?
- Quality perspective: time and costs consumed by process executions.
- History perspective: logging instance executions for later auditing.
- Security perspective: who is allowed to do what (authorization)?
- Autonomy perspective: independence aspects.

While the requirement analysis in Chapter 3 addresses all but the last three perspectives, the rest of the work focuses on the behavior, operation, and information perspectives. Weske adds the following characteristics to distinguish types of processes [320]:

- Intra-organizational processes versus process choreographies: intra-organizational processes focus on a single organization, which matches well with the definition of a business process by the same author. In contrast, a choreography describes how the processes of multiple partners interact in order to achieve a common goal. Besides being of potential use in intra-organizational settings, choreographies often express collaborative or cross-organizational processes. See also Section 2.2.2 for the use of choreographies in Service-Oriented Computing (SOC).
- Degree of automation: processes and their activities can be automated to various degrees, from no automation up to full automation. The appropriate subject and degree of automation strongly depends on the process at hand. Approval remains an example for a task that is rarely automated; however, multi-level approval processes are often implemented as workflows.

- Degree of repetition: the question how often a process is executed. The higher the degree of repetition, the more attractive a process becomes for partial or full automation, or automated control (i.e., implementation as a workflow).
- Degree of structuring: this dimension distinguishes processes with a rigid control flow (structured) from more flexible (unstructured) processes. In *ad-hoc processes*, the information worker can decide more or less freely which activity to pursue next. Many notations for process modeling are based on an explicit model of the control flow, thus imposing stricter constraints on the process execution. Sadiq et al. [260] suggest a hybrid model by enriching explicit control flow structures with so-called *pockets of flexibility:* inside such a pocket, the (otherwise structured) process behaves like an ad-hoc process.

Leymann and Roller [173] focus on structured processes with a high degree of repetition – which, as they claim, are of high value to the executing organization. They call these *production workflows.*

The work presented in this book is particularly applicable for intra-organizational processes with a high degree of structure and medium to high levels of repetition.

BPM Life-Cycle

In order to structure the work phases in project management efforts, various BPM life-cycles have been proposed. Without going into the details of these approaches, we refer to zur Muehlen [331], who presented an integrated and extended view on the previous approaches. Mendling [201] made a minor revision to the life-cycle of zur Muehlen. The life-cycle proposed by Mendling is shown in Figure 2.3. The phases in BPM are depicted as boxes, while the artifacts carried from one phase to the next are annotated to the arrows connecting the phases. Typical phase transitions are shown as regular arrows, while dashed arrows depict atypical feedback. Below, the phases are described in more detail.

- **Analysis.** Before a process is modeled, there is typically a phase of analyzing the goals of the project as well as the organizational and system context in which the new process will exist. The outcome of this phase are requirements on the process, including e.g., key performance indicators (KPIs) such as maximum execution time.
- **Design.** Based on the requirements from the analysis phase, the new process is modeled. Three common approaches are: creating the process from scratch (cf. the *clean-slate* approach from BPR, Section 2.1.1), starting from a reference model, or improving or creating a variant of an existing (as-is) process model [167]. In the design phase, process activities and their ordering are identified, resources are assigned, and the data flow is modeled

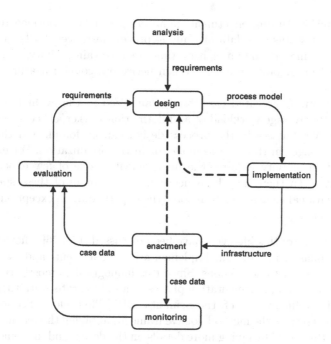

Fig. 2.3. The BPM life-cycle. Source: [201].

(cf. the perspectives above). The outcome is usually a to-be process model that reflects the modeler's view on how the process should be conducted. The behavior of this model can be simulated, and a preliminary assessment whether the model meets the requirements can be made.

- **Implementation.** Subsequently, this process model is implemented, i.e., all steps necessary before enactment are taken. This can mean that developers write new software applications or adapt existing implementations; that existing software is configured to match the new process; that the process model is enriched with all information that is necessary to make it executable in a process engine; that the new implementation is tested; and that staff is trained regarding the changes, if necessary. In an organization that employs the Service-Oriented Architecture (SOA) paradigm, there are specific flavors of executable process languages – we will address these in the respective section on SOA.
- **Enactment.** In this phase, process models are executed in their implementation. If the implementation comprises an executable model deployed in a process engine, instances from the model are created each time the starting condition (often in the form of a dedicated event) is met. Each instance is executed according to the executable model. The data that is produced by each instance, the case data, can be used for the following two phases.

- **Monitoring.** During enactment, monitoring can be performed to assess the current status and data of running process instances. KPIs as current execution time, maximum waiting time for a certain activity, etc. can be measured in ongoing processes. When necessary, countermeasures can be taken.
- **Evaluation.** Aggregated case data is analyzed in the evaluation phase, such as the average workload of an information worker, success rates, and the like. Weaknesses in the process design can be found, and these can lead to changes in the process model or in the organization. For example, if a certain activity requires the involvement of one of few experts in a company, then there may be a decision to hire more of these specialists (organizational change); or to involve the experts only in exceptional cases (process change).

Simpler versions of this life-cycle have been discussed [173, 76] – however, the four main phases, i.e., design, implementation, enactment, and evaluation, are still covered in these versions. Since this monograph is mostly concerned with the design and implementation phases, it also integrates with these other versions of the life-cycle – cf. the Semantic BPM life-cycle in Section 2.3.5. Section 3.6 describes the methodological frame for applying the techniques put forward in this work, by giving more details on the design and implementation phases.

User Types in BPM

In the following we give an overview of the user categories involved in BPM and their interests, and relate their involvement to the phases in the life-cycle.

- An **executive manager** is typically interested in KPI achievement, analytics about processes, and major phases of BPM projects.
- The **LoB**[3] **manager** is additionally interested in a high-level process view. Typically being the sponsor of BPM projects, she is involved in the analysis phase for specifying the KPIs.
- **Business analyst / business process analyst:** A process specialist from the business side,[4] the business analyst is often the process owner. She is interested in non-technical details of the process – but has to deal with technical details to a degree, in order to get a good understanding of the feasibility of implementing a certain process model in budget and time. The business analyst is the driver of the analysis phase, but the main occupation is the process design phase. She creates the initial to-be process model on the conceptual level, which captures how the process should be executed from the business point of view. In the implementation phase, when

---

[3] Line of Business (LoB), e.g., the organizational sub-unit responsible for a product.
[4] For more details, see International Institute of Business Analysis (IIBA), http://www.theiiba.org/

the process model is refined into an executable process model, the process may have to be changed in order to make sensible use of existing implementations. The business analyst's role is then to review the changes and specify which ramifications are acceptable for the business. She is usually not involved in enactment or monitoring, but in the evaluation phase.

- **Process architect:** The process architect is the counterpart of the business analyst from the IT side. In addition to the regular process flow, the process architect is also interested in exception handling, details of conditions (e.g., branching conditions), and implementation-level artifacts. He is usually involved in the process design phase of processes with the goal of execution, drives the implementation phase, and might be involved in monitoring and evaluation.
- **Case worker:** The information worker who completes tasks in process instances. In particular, workflow tasks are pre-specified activities which can be added to the worklist of an information worker. Worklist items are tasks that are to be done by the respective information worker, and can be displayed, contain links to further information, and allow for giving feedback to the system (e.g., approve, reject, mark as completed). The case worker in charge of a task is required to match the role assigned to the task in the process or workflow model – e.g., approval of vacation of an employee is usually done by the employee's manager.
- **System administrator:** Involved in the enactment and monitoring phases. Resolves issues such as "hanging" (dead-locked) workflows, unforeseen exceptions, etc.

Leymann and Roller [173] see the roles of the business analyst and the process architect as a single role. If we mean superset of these two roles, we simply refer to the *process modeler* in the following.

2.1.4 Process Formalisms

The behavioral perspective of a process, i.e., the ordering relations between the activities, can be captured in formal models with well-defined execution semantics. The *execution semantics* of a process model type describe the behavioral meaning of the language constructs, e.g., the process branches that are subsequent to a "parallel split" element are executed concurrently.

Various formal models can be employed for this purpose. The two main formal directions include token-flow semantics and grammars. Petri Nets, described below, are defined over the flow of tokens. In contrast, π-calculus [208, 207] as a representative for the grammar-based approach, is a Turing complete algebraic language that describes control flow based on communication channels in a formal way. The control flow is described using constructs for sequences, conditional branching, concurrency, repetition, and more. The defined grammar allows to check certain properties, such as the absence of deadlocks. While this is of value to process modelers, and many process languages claim to be based on the π-calculus, van der Aalst [297] criticizes that for most languages which claim to build on π-calculus the mapping to the formalism is not specified, and that near to no commercial tooling exists which actually offers any functionality based on the formal model.

As for token-flow-based formalisms, *Petri Nets* [231, 249, 248, 250, 251, 69], have a long-standing history in workflow and business process modeling [301, 293, 1, 87, 221]. Petri Nets have a graphical model, clearly defined semantics and a strong mathematical backing. Certain graph-theoretic results can be employed for analyzing nets and their status. Classic Petri Nets consist of places, transitions, arcs, and tokens, where places and transitions are nodes. *Places* can in general contain any non-negative number of tokens. The *arcs* are directed links connecting transitions to places or places to transitions, but never places to places or transitions to transitions. A *transition* may 'fire', if all of the places that have inbound arcs to it have at least one *token* in it. When a transition fires, one token is removed from every place linked to the transition by an inbound arc, and one token is added to every place that is connected to the transition via an outbound arc. The *state* of the Petri Net, referred to as its *marking*, is the location and number of all tokens in it.

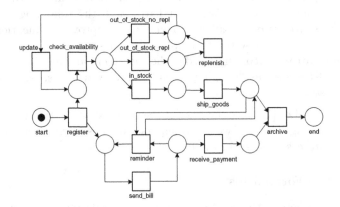

Fig. 2.4. A Petri Net depicting a process for handling orders. Source: [296].

Figure 2.4 shows a Petri Net (circles depict places, squares are transitions, and the only token is the smaller, filled black circle in the start place) with textual annotations for expressing the business meaning of the transitions. Using Petri Nets, processes with sophisticated synchronization mechanisms and mutual exclusion can be modeled and formal properties of them can be checked. Formal properties include [296]: lifeness – each transition can fire; boundedness – the maximum number of tokens in a place is bounded; safeness – the maximum number of tokens in a place is 1; well-formedness – if nets are both live and bounded; free-choice – any pair of transitions with an overlapping pre-set[5] has equal pre-sets. Note that the Petri Net shown in Figure 2.4 is safe and live, but not free-choice (because the transitions labeled "archive" and "reminder" have overlapping pre-sets which are not the same).

Many subsets and extensions of Petri Nets have been proposed and investigated. For process models, *WorkFlow nets (WF-nets)* [292, 296] are of particular interest. A Petri Net is a WF-net iff (i) it has one source and one sink place, and (ii) all other nodes are on a path from the source to the sink. For the correctness of a WF-nets, *soundness* [292] is an important property. A WF-net is said to be sound iff (i) every state of the net that is reached from the start node can complete properly (option to complete); (ii) in every state where the sink contains a token, there is no other token in the net (proper termination); and (iii) for every transition in the net, there is an execution of the net where this transition fires (no dead transitions). Note that the Petri Net shown in Figure 2.4 is a sound WF-net. The soundness property can be verified with Petri Net analysis tools such as Woflan [305].

In the part of this work which deals with the correctness of process models (Chapter 4), we build on the notion of token flow, safeness, free-choice nets, and soundness.

2.1.5 Workflow Patterns

For the sake of completeness, a background section about business process management needs to mention the *Workflow Patterns*. In 1999-2003, 20 workflow patterns were identified [300], i.e., control flow constructs which are recurring in various tools and notations are described on an approach-independent and a formal level. Approaches, notations, and tools in BPM have since been evaluated with respect to their ability to express the patterns. The basic patterns, as sequence, split/join, and the like cause no issues to the most approaches, but for more challenging patterns as "Multiple Instances Without Runtime Knowledge", elegant solutions are rare. If process technology is to be employed in a project, the project team can first determine the requirements of the project in terms of workflow patterns that need to be supported, and then consider this aspect when deciding which tooling best matches the needs.

Subsequent to the original workflow patterns, the resource [255], data [254], service interaction [21], and exception handling patterns [256] were identified. Finally, the original set of control flow patterns has been revised and extended [257]; at the time of writing, 43 workflow patterns were identified.

2.1.6 Current Challenges in BPM

After stating what has been addressed in the field of BPM, we now give a brief outlook on unsolved problems. Bandara et al. [20] identified major challenges

---

[5] The pre-set of a transition is the set of places that have an outgoing arc which ends at the transition.

through interviews with 14 BPM experts, from either a technical or a business background. The outcomes are split up into three levels:

- Strategic level: Lack of governance, employee buy-in, and common mind share of BPM; broken link between BPM efforts and organizational strategy.
- Tactical level: Lack of standards, BPM education, and methodology; weaknesses in process specification.
- Operational level: lack of tool support for process visualisation; miscommunication of tool capabilities; *perceived gaps between process design and process execution – i.e., lack of tools that link process design to process execution.*

The last point is exactly the one that is addressed in this work. We want to strengthen the link between process design and execution by proposing to model processes at the execution level (cf. Section 2.1.3), to annotate them with information about the business meaning of the activities, and to use this information when relating the conceptual process models to the implementation level.

2.2 Service-Oriented Computing

Service-oriented computing is the umbrella term for various aspects of a new paradigm for distributed computing based on services. In the present context, service-oriented architectures, Web services, service-orientation design principles, and service composition are of interest.

2.2.1 Service-Oriented Architecture

Despite being an overused term these days, service-oriented architecture refers to a distinct architectural paradigm. We here adapt the definition of Papazoglou [226]:

Definition 2.4. Service-oriented architecture (SOA) *is a logical way of designing a software system to provide services to either end-user applications or to other services distributed in a network, via published and discoverable interfaces.*

This definition gives the main ingredients of SOA: services are provided, their interfaces are described and published, and they are consumed over a network by programs.

Papazoglou continues [226]: "To achieve this, SOA reorganizes a portfolio of previously siloed software applications and support infrastructure in an organization into an interconnected collection of services, each of which is

discoverable and accessible through standard interfaces and messaging protocols." The above-mentioned service interface descriptions and the messaging
are conducted in a standardized way. This enables to connect applications
which were so far isolated, and makes it easier to connect new applications in
the future.

In the words of Borges et al. [37]: "Service-oriented architecture is the
architectural style that supports loosely coupled services to enable business
flexibility in an interoperable, technology-agnostic manner. SOA consists of a
composite set of business-aligned services that support a flexible and dynamically re-configurable end-to-end business processes realization using interface-
based service descriptions." The additional aspect here is that services are
loosely coupled, and that they package business logics. However, the dynamic
re-configuration of business processes today still is more a vision than practical
reality.

2.2.2 Web Services

SOA is most often implemented using Web services standards and technology.
A Web service is a piece of software that can be accessed in a standardized,
platform-neutral way. Ideally, a Web service is independent, self-contained,
stateless, and modular. Web services are the building blocks on which an SOA
can be constructed – the term Web service however is often used synonymously
with a specific set of standards and technologies. For the meaning as a building
block, we again adopt the definition of Papazoglou [226]:

Definition 2.5. *A* Web service (WS) *is a self-describing, self-contained software module available via a network, such as the Internet, which completes tasks, solves problems, or conducts transactions on behalf of a user or
application.*

A Web service thus performs a certain action, is available via a network.
Further, a Web service is said to be self-describing (as stated above, using
description standards) and self-contained, i.e., knowing the Web service's interface is completely sufficient for using it. Note, however, that a Web service
may call other Web services to complete its tasks.

For capturing the aspects relevant to Web services, standards on several
layers are necessary. Figure 2.5 shows the *Web Services Stack*[6], which consists of six layers, each of which builds on the underlying layers: transport,
messaging, description, discovery, quality of service, and business processes.
It is noteworthy that, in contrast to the stacks with strict layering, e.g., the
OSI Reference Model in networking, where each layer uses solely the functions of the layer on which it is placed, the Web Services Stack's layers are

---

[6] Many versions of this diagram exist, e.g., [226, 309]. Figure 2.5 is nearly equal to
[226], but differs from [309] by focusing on the upper layers instead of the lower
ones.

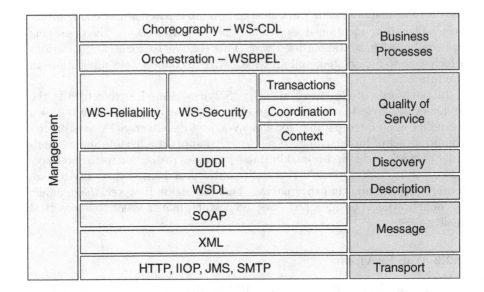

Fig. 2.5. The Web Services Stack depicts various layers of protocols and standards around Web services

permeable. E.g., the orchestration layer directly references elements specified in the description layer.

The main standards in the WS Stack are the following. The WS interface is described by a WSDL[7] document. Messages exchanged with a Web service comply to the SOAP[8] standard, and Web services may be advertised in UDDI[9] registries. All the three standards are based on XML[10] and have a clearly stated meaning. Therefore, Web service technology offers a high degree of interoperability – at the cost of higher bandwidth usage due to (yet) uncompressed XML messages.

The business process layer of the WS Stack is divided into orchestration and choreography, both of which are in this context of a rather technical nature. Thus we see them as instances of implemented processes in terms of the BPM layers (cf. Section 2.1.3). An *orchestration* of WSs is the "inside-out view" [229] on an implemented business process of an organization – while containing the information how to interact with business partners, it also describes how and when to invoke WSs of the organization itself. An orchestration can also focus on either one of these views only. The control and data flow between

---

[7] Web Service Description Language (WSDL), see [310].

[8] Originally the abbreviation meant Simple Object Access Protocol, but this meaning is no longer intended. Different versions exist, e.g., SOAP 1.2 [308].

[9] Universal Description, Discovery and Integration (UDDI), see [220].

[10] Extensible Markup Language, see http://www.w3.org/XML/

WS interactions are an integral part of an orchestration. The activity "service composition" refers to the task of combining Web services, i.e., of creating an orchestration. The outcome is sometimes also called a "service composition". In contrast, a *choreography* "defines the sequence and conditions under which multiple cooperating independent agents exchange messages in order to perform a task to achieve a goal state" [309]. That is, the difference is that the choreography offers a global view on the WS interactions of multiple parties, and is not concerned with internal aspects of service delivery. A choreography model cannot be executed, but resembles a design artifact, a contract to which the process execution of the participants needs to adhere to. At the technical level of WSs, the choreography relates to message data types and the like, in addition to specifying the control and data flow. For the goals of this work, choreographies play a minor role. WSBPEL[11] as the default orchestration language is discussed in Section 2.2.4.

Another initiative of interest is the *Web Services Architecture (WSA)*, being "intended to provide a common definition of a Web service, and define its place within a larger Web services framework to guide the community" [309]. It thus aims at specifying the interplay of the numerous standards and languages around Web services, such as reliable messaging, discovery, and many more. However, it is focused on the basic Web services technologies and only touching the business process level.

For the purposes of this work, it is less important how a service is provided – i.e., whether it is available as a Web service, a workflow task, or behind a proprietary technical interface. What is however of relevance, is that the services follow the paradigm of service-orientation, which we discuss next.

2.2.3 Service-Orientation Design Principles

The goals of SOA include providing value for the organizations applying it. This is to be achieved through re-use of functionality, easier integration of different software applications, both within the organization and with other organizations, and through allowing business processes and process changes to be implemented with less effort. However, just wrapping existing software interfaces of applications with WS technology rarely does the trick, as argued by Papazoglou [226] and Erl [88, 89]. In order to realize the potential benefits of SOA, the question which services to offer should only be answered after going through a thorough design process, referred to as *service-orientation design (SOD)*.

Erl [89] provides an in-depth exploration of the SOD paradigm, and proposes to follow a set of eight design principles[12] (all quotes are from this source).

---

[11] Web Services Business Process Execution Language, see [8].

[12] Discussed more briefly also in [88] and at http://www.soaprinciples.com/

- Standardized Service Contracts – the public interfaces of a services make use of contract design standards.
- Service Loose Coupling – to impose low burdens on service consumers.
- Service Abstraction – to "hide as much of the underlying details of a service as possible".
- Service Reusability – services contain agnostic logic and "can be positioned as reusable enterprise resources".
- Service Autonomy – to provide reliable and consistent results, a service has to have strong control over its underlying environment.
- Service Statelessness – services should be "designed to remain stateful only when required."
- Service Discoverability – "services are supplemented with communicative meta data by which they can be effectively discovered and interpreted."
- Service Composability – "services are effective composition participants, regardless of the size and complexity of the composition."

Erl further mentions *interoperability of services* as the fundamental requirement of service-orientation: "...stating that services must be interoperable is just about as evident as stating that services must exist."

For the purposes of this work, *service composability* is of particular interest. Papazoglou [226] defines composability as "a feature of a service that allows it to be consumed in a composite process." I.e., according to the argumentation of both Erl and Papazoglou, the burden of allowing for services to be consumed is on the design phase – proper service design results in services which can be consumed in a composition. Erl [89] further states: "The ability to effectively compose services is a critical requirement for achieving some of the most fundamental goals of service-oriented computing. Complex service compositions place demands on service design that need to be anticipated to avoid massive retro-fitting efforts. Services are expected to be capable of participating as effective composition members, regardless of whether they need to be immediately enlisted in a composition."

In the words of Papazoglou [226]: "The reality is that an SOA has limited value unless it encompasses disparate applications and platforms, and, most importantly, it moves beyond technology and is orchestrated and controlled in the context of business processes." Thus, services should be composable, both from the business and technology points of view. In the remainder of the work we assume that available services have been designed such that they are adhere to the design principles. In the evaluation, Chapter 6, we will revisit this assumption shortly.

We now introduce a language for expressing service compositions.

2.2.4 An Orchestration Language: WSBPEL

As mentioned above, service composition is the task of combining the functionality of multiple Web services to yield a composition with higher utility. A composite service can be expressed as an orchestration in a language such as WSBPEL [8][13], which we discuss below. An orchestration expresses control flow over calls to various Web services and guarantees a predefined execution order. In BPEL, the orchestration itself is exposed as a Web service.

There are structuring and basic activities in BPEL. Structuring activities contain themselves one or more activities, which in turn can be basic or structuring again. This "nesting" of structuring activities allows for expressing control flow with the required behavior in the style of the π-calculus (cf. Section 2.1.4). Control flow structures include parallel or conditional branching, looping, and more. At the same time, acyclic control flow can be expressed in a graph-based manner, within "flow" structures.

A BPEL process has variables and potentially event, fault, and compensation handlers. Variables can be of a user-defined XML Schema type, of a message data type, or of simple types. Event handlers are a central point of reacting to incoming messages or timeouts, fault handlers catch a single specified fault or all faults, and compensation handlers are intended to be used as the location for the partial 'roll-back' of a long-running business process.

WSBPEL distinguishes between *abstract* and *executable* processes. Abstract BPEL processes are also referred to as *business protocols*. They describe the externally observable behavior of a process by setting the control flow around all interaction-related activities. Such *behavioral interfaces* are also referred to as a *public view* on a process – as opposed to a *private view*, which also concerns internal procedures and often is treated as confidential. Take the interactions between a supplier and a customer in manufacturing as an example: how a production process is executed is highly confidential information for the supplier; in contrast, the steps for ordering goods, delivery, and billing involve the customer as well and are thus part of the supplier's behavioral interface to its customers. Executable processes, as the name suggested, can be executed by a process execution engine. Inherently, they contain more detail, namely data handling, termination, and the like, in addition to the internal parts.

It should be noted that there is no standard graphical notation for BPEL. Tool vendors as Active Endpoints[14] and Oracle[15] provide modeling tools with proprietary graphical notations. In contrast, Intalio[16] uses BPMN symbols for depicting BPEL elements.

Automatic service composition, i.e., automatically determining a composition of multiple Web services, is a big challenge and opportunity for the SOA paradigm. In order to tackle this and other problems, methods for describing the meaning of services, i.e., their semantics, were developed on the basis of Semantic Web technologies. These methods are described in the next section.

---

[13] We here refer to version 2.0. Previous versions were named BPEL4WS, [11]. Often, just the term BPEL is used.

[14] http://www.active-endpoints.com/

[15] http://www.oracle.com/

[16] http://bpms.intalio.com/

2.3 Semantic Technologies

The Web today is mostly made up of HTML[17] documents, which contain information (often in textual form) and a description how to display the information to a user. A machine renders the content such that a user can see it and possibly interact with it. However, the machine is generally unaware of the information in and the capabilities of the Web site. This limits the opportunities in the Web, e.g., since a machine can rarely decide whether a site that refers to another site criticizes or supports the referenced site. Berners-Lee et al. thus proposed the Semantic Web (SW) as an extension of the traditional Web in which machines can become aware of the meaning of Web artifacts they are dealing with [28]: "The *Semantic Web* is not a separate Web but an extension of the current one, in which information is given well-defined meaning, better enabling computers and people to work in cooperation."

In the Semantic Web, the meaning of artifacts becomes accessible to machines. This vision drove the development of *Semantic Technologies*, enabling not only the machine-accessible representation of the meaning of things, but also creating the techniques and algorithms for using this information. In the Semantic Web vision [28], a number of aspects such as knowledge representation, unique resource identification, and ontologies were mentioned. In order to build a Semantic Web system, (a subset of) these aspects may have to be taken into account. The *Semantic Web Stack* illustrates the relation between and the standards for Semantic Web systems in the so-called *layer cake* diagram. Figure 2.6[18] shows the most recent incarnation of it. The layers are described in the following.

- Uniform Resource Identifier (URI) / Internationalized Resource Identifier (IRI): unique, unambiguous names for things.
- XML: see Section 2.2.2
- Data interchange – Resource Description Framework (RDF)[19]: serves to describe the relations between entities (identified through URIs/IRIs) as triples. Typically takes one of two forms: (subject, predicate, object) or (subject, property, value).
- RDF Schema (RDFS)[20]: the vocabulary description language for RDF. Provides constructs for specifying classes or resources, a class hierarchy, and restrictions on property domains (allowed "subjects") and ranges (allowed "values").
- Ontology – Web Ontology Language (OWL) [325]: allows to model a domain of discourse by representing classes and instances of entities in this domain, their attributes and the relations between the classes, as well as

---

[17] HyperText Markup Language, see http://www.w3.org/MarkUp/
[18] Previous versions have more resemblance with an actual layer cake.
[19] http://www.w3.org/TR/rdf-primer/
[20] http://www.w3.org/TR/rdf-schema/

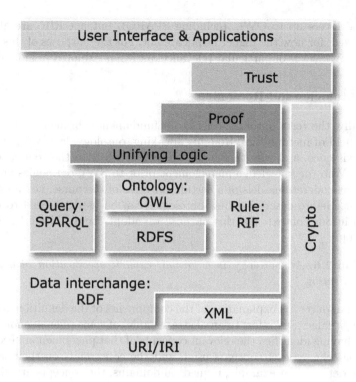

Fig. 2.6. The most current version of the Semantic Web Stack. Source: http://www.w3.org/2007/03/layerCake.svg, accessed 19 September 2008.

constraints on the sets of valid instances. Ontologies in general are discussed in more detail in the next section.

- Query – SPARQL[21]: querying RDF data sources.
- Rule – Rule Interchange Format (RIF)[22]: an interchange format for different rule languages.
- Unifying Logic: a logic layer that unifies the underlying logics for ontologies, rules, queries, and RDFS. Logical reasoning is used to establish the consistency and correctness of data sets and to infer implicit facts.
- Proof: to explain the steps that lead to logical conclusions.
- Trust: authentication and trustworthiness of statements and agents.
- Cryptography (Crypto): to make sure the statements are coming from the intended source and have not been changed.
- User Interfaces and Applications: to enable people and application programs to make use of the underlying layers.

---

[21] A recursive acronym for SPARQL Protocol and RDF Query Language, see http://www.w3.org/TR/rdf-sparql-query/

[22] http://www.w3.org/2005/rules/

While the layers up to OWL, including SPARQL but not RIF, are already standardized, for now the higher layers are not. For the purposes of this work, the ontology layer is of particular relevance, and thus explored in more detail.

2.3.1 Ontologies and Reasoning

Historically, the term ontology refers to a fundamental branch of the philosophical field of metaphysics. Roughly speaking, ontology deals with the reasons of existence, and why things can be said to exist. In the context of the Semantic Web (or knowledge management prior to SW), ontologies are usually seen as concrete models of a certain universe of discourse, i.e., a domain of interest. Before describing how ontologies can be used we need to define the term in our context. For this purpose we adopt the definition by Studer et al. [276][23]:

Definition 2.6. *An* ontology *is a formal, explicit specification of a shared conceptualisation.*

In the same source, an explanation of the components of the definition is given: "A 'conceptualisation' refers to an abstract model of some phenomenon in the world by having identified the relevant concepts of that phenomenon. 'Explicit' means that the type of concepts used, and the constraints on their use are explicitly defined. For example, in medical domains, the concepts are diseases and symptoms, the relations between them are causal and a constraint is that a disease cannot cause itself. 'Formal' refers to the fact that the ontology should be machine readable, which excludes natural language. 'Shared' reflects the notion that an ontology captures consensual knowledge, that is, it is not private to some individual, but accepted by a group." [276]

An ontology often models static knowledge about the concepts within the domain of discourse and the relationships between those concepts, their instances, properties and so forth. Ontologies often include (synonymous expressions in brackets):

- Concepts (classes): types of objects.
- Individuals (objects): instances of classes, entities.
- Relations (properties): relation types between concepts; relations between individuals.
- Attributes (properties[24]): parameter types of classes; parameters of individuals.
- Axioms: additional rules or restrictions on the classes and relations.

---

[23] This is a more precise variation of the widely cited definition by Gruber [118, 119]: "An ontology is an explicit specification of a conceptualization."

[24] The attentive reader may have noticed that properties can be modeled as both, attributes and relations. This depends on the ontology language as well as the particular context.

Axioms can be used to infer implicit facts about concepts and individuals, and to check the consistency of an ontology. The superset of these tasks is called *reasoning*.

In the following, we shortly introduce the two most popular logic formalisms in the Semantic Web and Semantic Web services realms, namely the Description Logics (DL) and Frame Logic (F-logic), which we refer to in the technical chapters.

2.3.2 Frame Logic

F-logic [158] was developed as a solid theoretical foundation for the object-oriented paradigm, and has its strengths in modeling objects and their relations, attributes, and methods. Rules can define logical consequences, and queries can be used to retrieve (explicit or implicit) knowledge. It is a logic with an object-oriented syntax and a model theoretic semantics, and a complete and sound resolution-based proof procedure. Certain aspects of a higher-order syntax are provided, but the underlying semantics can be represented in first-order logic. The work has initially been based on frame-based knowledge representation systems, such as [209].

In F-logic [158], everything is an object – i.e., there is no distinction between an instance and a class. In fact, an object can be both. Every object has an identifier, the *oid*. Canonical modeling primitives include:

- Subclass and instance-of relations
- Facts and their property values, scalar (single-valued) or set-valued
- Classes with named attributes and methods
- Typing (also conjunction of types)
- Methods that take multiple (typed) (sets of) inputs and return ((power-) sets of) outputs
- Deductive rules
- Queries
- Logical connectives and quantifiers

Type errors can be detected, and unknown values are allowed. Inheritance of attributes, methods and values can be specified in a fine-granular way and is thus tightly controllable. Multi-inheritance is allowed, i.e., a class can inherit from multiple super-classes and an object is allowed to be an instance of many classes. Polymorphism can also be modeled, i.e., a method name can be used in different ways – e.g., a method may be defined differently for different classes or for different (arities of) inputs. Comparatively efficient reasoners for variants of F-logic have been developed and are commercially available, e.g., as part of the OntoBroker [95] suite from ontoprise[25].

---

[25] http://www.ontoprise.de

2.3.3 Description Logics

Description Logics [18] are a family of logics with varying expressivity and semantics that use a common Tarski-style syntax. The first description logic KL-ONE [43] was introduced to address the vague and imprecise semantics of semantic networks [240] and frame-based knowledge representation systems [209][26]. The description logic formalism was devised as an attempt to giving knowledge representation mathematically-founded model-theoretic semantics. Most constructs from various description logic dialects can be represented as first-order logic (FOL) expressions [38]. In the context of this work, we use a first-order syntax for logical statements to accommodate for readers without prior experience in description logics. Thus, only the main concepts are introduced here; see [18] for an extensive overview and particularities of the semantics.

In DL, a distinction is made between the *terminology* (TBox), i.e., the concepts, roles, etc. and the assertional part (ABox) which specifies the membership of individuals in concepts and the membership of pairs of individuals in roles, respectively. A DL TBox consists of concepts (unary predicates in FOL) and roles (binary predicates in FOL).

To give an example for the syntax, consider $\mathcal{ALC}$, the "smallest" DL that is closed under all Boolean connectives [262][27]. Concepts can be atomic (enabling the representation of membership in a named class of individuals) or complex (giving the conditions for membership). Say, A is an atomic concept, C, C_1, C_2 are concepts, and R is a role. Then, concepts in $\mathcal{ALC}$ can be defined using the following syntax: $C := A \mid \neg C \mid C_1 \sqcup C_2 \mid C_1 \sqcap C_2 \mid \forall R.C \mid \exists R.C$

Roughly speaking, the semantics is given by interpreting the concepts as the sets of individuals they represent. Then, $\neg C$ is the (possibly infinite) complement of the (possibly infinite) set of individuals that are members of C; $C_1 \sqcup C_2$ ($C_1 \sqcap C_2$) represent the individuals that are members of C_1 or (and) C_2; and $\forall R.C$ ($\exists R.C$) are the individuals for which all (at least one) individual(s) that conform to role R are members of concept C.

Other DLs extend the syntax and / or the semantics. The features supported by a specific DL are given through a unified naming scheme. E.g., $\mathcal{S}$ extends $\mathcal{ALC}$ with transitive roles; $\mathcal{SI}$ extends $\mathcal{S}$ with inverse roles (I); $\mathcal{SI}$ extended with role hierarchies (H) and qualifying number restrictions (Q) yields the DL $\mathcal{SHIQ}$, whereas full qualifying number restrictions (F) yields $\mathcal{SHIF}$ [287]. Various complexity results have been investigated; e.g., reasoning in $\mathcal{SHIQ}$ is ExpTime-complete [287].

Subsumption axioms for concepts and for roles can also be expressed, e.g., for concepts C_1, C_2, the syntax is $C_1 \sqsubseteq C_2$. To give a more concrete example: a car is a kind of vehicle – thus, any car x is also a vehicle. In DL, this can be

---

[26] Note that, although initially based on frame-based representation, F-logic does not suffer from these deficiencies.

[27] We here concentrate on the syntax; for the semantics and a sound and complete algorithm for subsumption reasoning see [262].

expressed as $Car \sqsubseteq Vehicle$ (where Car and $Vehicle$ are concepts); in FOL, the same can be expressed as $\forall x : Car(x) \Rightarrow Vehicle(x)$. Historically, concept subsumption is the most important reasoning task: i.e., does the TBox imply that $C_1 \sqsubseteq C_2$? Meanwhile, other queries (such as retrieving all instances of a concept) have also become important.

With the standardization of OWL [325], two specific DLs basically became W3C recommendations – for details see e.g., [150].

On the basis of Semantic Web technologies, Semantic Web services technologies were developed, which we discuss next.

2.3.4 Semantic Web Services

With the emergence of SOA and Web services as the dominant paradigm for making pieces of software functionality available in a standardized way, the issue how to efficiently find Web services in large repositories came up. In order to find a solution, a research branch focused on using semantic technologies to ease the handling of Web services. The result of these efforts is referred to as Semantic Web services (SWS). Figure 2.7 depicts this development. A Web service interface can now be described semantically so as to enable machine reasoning over it. E.g., the similarity of an available and a requested Web service can be assessed, which enables informed Semantic Web service discovery – as opposed to purely syntactic techniques. While there are multiple initiatives to SWS (OWL-S[28], WSMO[29], and SAWSDL[30] are the most prominent approaches), there is usually a common denominator on which we will focus below, before briefly describing the three approaches.

In order to ease the discovery and composition of SWSs, the states before and after the successful execution of a service are described through *preconditions* and *effects* (also called *postconditions*), respectively. The preconditions and effects are formulated as factual statements with respect to the *inputs* and *outputs* of a service. The combination of inputs, outputs, preconditions, and effects is referred to as IOPE, and has already been researched in the field of Artificial Intelligence [258]. A service can be executed whenever its precondition is met, and if so, it changes the world according to its postcondition. The *functional* aspect of a service's behavior can be formalized with respect to IOPE, and is known as *change semantics*.

In addition, *non-functional properties* (NFPs) can capture further aspects (how the service provides its functionality), such as quality of service (QoS) parameters, cost, security aspects and the like. NFPs are mostly orthogonal to change semantics; they are usually used to evaluate if a service satisfies the required QoS parameters, or to find the preferred service out of a set of

---

[28] OWL-S: Semantic Markup for Web Services, see
http://www.w3.org/Submission/OWL-S/

[29] Web Services Modeling Ontology, see http://www.wsmo.org/

[30] Semantic Annotations for WSDL, see http://www.w3.org/2002/ws/sawsdl/

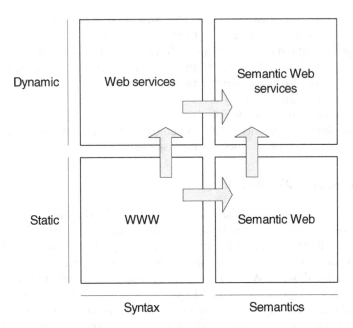

Fig. 2.7. The nature of Semantic Web services. Source: [50].

functionally similar services. However, the boundary between functional and non-functional aspects is sometimes thin, depending on the specific context and purpose. Furthermore, NFPs such as price can sometimes only be determined dynamically – e.g., shipper services for parcels often charge different rates for a national ground delivery and for international air mail.

Further, there may be a need to reason about behavioral interfaces. Besides the general functionality of a service, the order in which service operations should be invoked can be exposed. In order to capture formal execution semantics in addition to functional and non-functional aspects, there are SWS approaches to describe the behavioral interfaces with process algebras, e.g., the μ-calculus [2] or the π-calculus [3] mentioned in Section 2.1.4.

WSMO

In the example of WSMO, the NFPs can be represented directly in the the Web service description while the pre and postconditions are described in the so-called service *capability*. WSMO distinguishes between the statements about the information space of a service and the state of the world: the latter is addressed in terms of assumptions and effects, while the former is subject to WSMO's pre and postconditions. It should be noted that, in the remainder of the work, we ignore assumptions (they refer to conditions that cannot be checked at design time), and we include effects into the postcondition because, from the perspective of our formalisms, there is no difference between WSMO postconditions and effects. We thus use the terms postcondition and effect synonymously throughout the work.

WSMO also allows the specification of a service's behavioral interface in terms of choreography and orchestration. A WSMO choreography describes the interface the service provides to its potential consumers, whereas orchestration describes how this service acts as a consumer of other services. It is worthwhile noting that what is called choreography in WSMO is usually referred to as a public process or the public view on a process in the BPM literature – in contrast to a global view on a collaborative business process, which is meant by choreography in BPM literature, cf. Section 2.1.3. Similarly, an orchestration in BPM also includes the public view on the process, which is excluded in WSMO's orchestration. The split between WSMO's choreography and orchestration can be a source of problems: if the relation between a WSMO choreography and an orchestration are not made explicit, asynchronous messaging between two services cannot be modeled appropriately (cf. the Send-Receive pattern, case 2, in the service interaction patterns [21]).

In WSMO, services are requested explicitly through the notion of a *WSMO goal*, which again specifies a capability and optionally an interface. WSMO further comes with its own ontology model and provides top-level support for mediation, i.e., for handling heterogeneity between services, ontologies, and goals. The Web Services Modeling Language (WSML) is a family of languages in which WSMO entities can be expressed.

OWL-S

OWL-S describes rather similar aspects: the *Service Profile* is based on IOPE, and the *Service Model* describes the behavioral interface. Input and output descriptions in the Service Profile refer to the type of messages, whereas preconditions and (conditional) results deal with changes of the state of the world. To clarify the difference, the following example is given in the OWL-S specification [284]: "[...] to complete the sale, a book-selling service requires as input a credit card number and expiration date, but also the precondition that the credit card actually exists and is not overdrawn. The result of the sale is the output of a receipt that confirms the proper execution of the transaction, and as effect the transfer of ownership and the physical transfer of the book from the warehouse of the seller to the address of the buyer." Naturally, OWL-S makes use of OWL as ontology language. In OWL-S, a service is typically requested through a description of the desired service.

SAWSDL

Much in line with its name, SAWSDL defines how semantic annotations can be added to WSDL. SAWSDL is agnostic with regard to the language for representing the semantic models; it only specifies how to refer to semantic resources from other sources. In particular, there are three extension points: the *model reference* specifies an association from a WSDL entity to a semantic entity, e.g., a concept in an ontology, or an OWL-S service; two schema mapping types can be used for *lifting* XML instance data to a semantic format, and for *lowering*, i.e., mapping in the opposite direction. SAWSDL is thus a non-intrusive extension mechanism for Web service technology – however, if two services provide SAWSDL descriptions of their interface, it may not be the case that the same software can process both.

2.3.5 Semantic Business Process Management

Facilitating Business Process Management with the benefits offered by semantic technologies, especially SWS technology, is the broad vision of *Semantic Business Process Management (SBPM)* – cf., e.g., the SUPER IP(EU-funded Integrated Project, http://www.ip-super.org), the Semantic Business Process Management Working Group (http://www.sbpm.org), the SBPM workshop [129], or a vision paper by Hepp et. al. [130]. In order to enable this vision, semantic information is attached to artifacts used in BPM and specialized reasoning techniques are developed to make use of it. If every (relevant) activity, conditional control flow link, and data entity in a process model is semantically annotated, manifold new opportunities are opened up.

For example, based on this information, repositories of existing process models could be accessed much more easily, e.g., through queries that display all processes that have to do with data-related contracts in telecommunications (and thus, by semantics-enabled subsumption reasoning, all contracts for fixed-line, cable, or mobile connections). In contrast to the status quo, the relationships between the conceptual business process models and the executable processes could become observable from the models. Based on the observability, it may be possible to implement a (partial) projection of changes from one of the layers to the other.

These tasks can be addresses by (i) providing notations and tools for adding semantic information to business process models, and (ii) developing suitable algorithms and methodologies for applying this information successfully. This work makes contributions in both of these directions.

Below, we showcase some of the opportunities based on a specialized life-cycle for the SBPM approach.

SBPM Life-Cycle

As described in Section 2.1.3, several versions of the BPM life-cycle have been presented in the literature. The SBPM life cycle has been introduced in the context of the above-mentioned SUPER project [94], as an extension to [76], and is depicted in Fig. 2.8.

Note that the SBPM life-cycle contains the *modeling* and *configuration* phases. In our context, these two phases directly correspond to the *design*

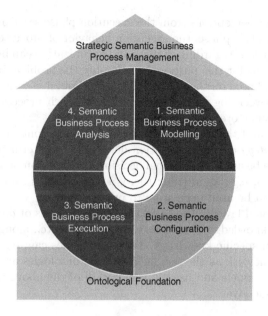

Strategic Semantic Business
Process Management

4. Semantic
Business Process
Analysis

1. Semantic
Business Process
Modelling

3. Semantic
Business Process
Execution

2. Semantic
Business Process
Configuration

Ontological Foundation

Fig. 2.8. Semantic BPM life-cycle. Source: [94].

and *implementation* phases from the life-cycle of [331], which is described in
Section 2.1.3. As argued there, the extensions to the life-cycle that we present
in the course of this work only modify these two phases; and since they are
part of most of the life-cycle models that exist in literature, the adoption of
our extensions is not bound to a specific life-cycle.

We now give a brief overview of the parts of the life-cycle, without further
mentioning our own work. The overall SBPM life-cycle depicted in Fig. 2.8
identifies four principal phases: semantic business process modeling, configuration, execution, and analysis – typically performed in this order.

As before, the *modeling phase* comprises the creation or adaptation of a
business process model. Semantic annotations can be used during modeling
e.g., for automatic suggestion of related process fragments [148, 149, 162]; or
explicit querying for such fragments [186, 187]; or for determining the compliance of a desgined process [212, 213, 84, 85].

The *configuration phase* deals with refining a conceptual process model into
an executable form, traditionally by implementing it. The *execution phase*
is concerned with how process instances are executed in an organization's
IT systems. Both of these phases can be supported using a semantically extended process execution language, such as BPEL for Semantic Web Services
(BPEL4SWS) [217, 219]. Being an extension to BPEL 2.0 [8], BPEL4SWS allows to include calls to SWSs, to base conditions in an executable process on
ontology queries, and the like. However, in order to execute such a BPEL4SWS
process, an appropriate execution environment (such as [302]) is required.

Logs and other perceptions from the execution phase serve as input to the *analysis phase*. In this phase, the execution behavior of processes is inspected and recommendations regarding changes and optimization can be made. Using semantic extensions for this purpose can simplify the problem in a number of ways [10, 9]: e.g., based on the additional information, it is easier to determine the relations between log entries (such as, from which process activity they originate); further, more informed queries are enabled.

The strategic and the foundational layer define the context for these four phases. The *strategy* of an organization defines its long-term business goals, and serves as the basis for operational decisions. The notion of a business goal can be formalized, e.g., as in [189]; there, a suggestion is also made on how business goals can be used in relation to process models.

The foundational layer in the SBPM life-cycle consists of *ontologies* which capture generic knowledge about processes, services, etc., along with domain and organization-specific knowledge. These ontologies can, e.g., be based on an ontology framework as the one in [190]. The ontologies are referenced in business process models and used in some or all of the above phases, as well as on the strategic layer.

2.4 Chapter Summary

This chapter introduced to business process management, service-oriented computing, and semantic technologies with a focus on concepts and aspects relevant to this book. Whenever applicable, the relation to contents of this work were stated. In the next part, the main contributions from this work are described, making use of the background information provided here.

Part II

Modeling Support through Verification and Composition

3

Requirements Analysis and Conceptual Framework

On the basis of the background in the previous chapter, we here describe the problem of composition in business process modeling in more detail. Subsequent to the problem statement in Section 3.1, Section 3.2 presents the outcome of our broad requirements analysis. Fulfilling all the requirements in this broad view would exceed the scope of this work. Thus, Section 3.3 discusses which of the requirements are pursued in the course of this work. Subsequently, we introduce the conceptual framework. We start by refining the problem – given the requirements – in Section 3.4. The main part of the conceptual framework is described in Section 3.5, where an architecture with the required components is presented and the most important functions, namely discovery, task composition, auto-completion, mediation, and validation are described in more detail. Section 3.6 states when and how the individual components and further activities should be carried out as part of a more holistic BPM methodology. Finally, Section 3.7 presents an algorithm which automates the interplay between the components. Related work can be found in Section 3.8. The chapter closes with a discussion and summary. While the architecture and most of the components on this level of detail are largely state of the art, the requirements, the methodology, and the automatic algorithm are contributions.[1]

3.1 The Problem of Supporting Composition in BPM

The focus of this work is on determining if it is helpful to employ semantic technologies during the design of execution-level process models. As stated in the previous chapter, the word composition has different meanings in the domains of Semantic Web services and business process modeling.

- Composing Semantic Web services refers to either of two problems: (i) finding a composition of services out of a potentially large pool of available

---

[1] Parts of this chapter have been published: [311, 316, 317, 318].

services with relatively simple interfaces, such that the composition reaches a defined goal state when starting in a given start state; or (ii) finding out if and how a fixed set of behavioral (complex) service interfaces can be combined, e.g., by composing a mediator process. Both problems can be addressed by a user or an automated tool.

• Composing a business process model, in contrast, means designing the control and data flow of the process – typically a task for a process modeler.

Besides the differences, there is a substantial overlap between the meanings. Thus the first problem addressed in this chapter is to *analyze the requirements* for all three problems, since all of them exist in the realm of designing an execution-level process model. These requirements are described in the subsequent section. The second problem addressed in this chapter is how to *support the requirements*. Once the requirements are laid out, we refine the problem statement in this way, and present a conceptual framework for the refined problem.

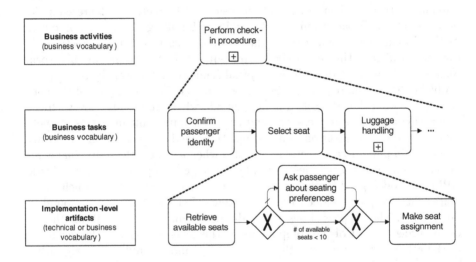

Fig. 3.1. Activity and task layers relevant to the requirements

The requirements described herein are relevant on three different levels of process activities, as depicted in Figure 3.1: business activities, business tasks, and implementation-level artifacts. As suggested in the figure, we assume that the higher the level on which an activity is, the more coarse-grained and business-relevant it typically is; the lower the level, the more technical.

In our context, a *business activity* refers to an aggregate economic activity of an organization; a business activity can even comprise a complete business process. In contrast, a *business task* is a single activity with business relevance which, from a business point of view, is not further decomposable.

Implementation-level artifacts in turn are activities for which it is known how they can be conducted. For example, a Web service or a workflow task are instances of implementation-level artifacts.

Artifacts on all of these three levels can be modeled, annotated semantically, and stored in repositories for later re-use – the advantage being that process modelers are equipped with building blocks that have been created and described by people with an expertise of the artifact. For example, we have seen cases in practice where hundreds of business tasks are pre-modeled and stored in repositories. Similarly, Web services are created in many SOA projects or on top of existing software products. The creators of the services often have to specify pre and postconditions of the services, but today still mostly in the form textual documentation. In summary, if the up-front effort is invested, activities on the business and technical levels can be re-used during process modeling.

Any of the before-mentioned activities – i.e., the business activities, business tasks, and technical artifacts – can be depicted by an activity or task symbol in the BPMN notation. In other business process modeling notations, the respective matching concepts are sometimes called functions. We will use the term activity as the general term for all these concepts. In contrast, tasks are atomic on their respective level. In the following, to avoid clumsy language, we will further refer to implementation-level artifacts, services, and the like synonymously – exceptions will be clearly marked.

It should be noted that the vocabulary can reside in one or more domain ontologies. In order to enable reasoning over artifacts in multiple layers, there has to be some notion of mapping between the vocabularies. There are several possible settings:

- **Same vocabulary:** in the simplest case, the vocabularies are the same. E.g., SAP develops on the basis of the model-driven development (MDD) paradigm, where the implementation-level models essentially make use of business vocabulary. If these models are used for the basis of a the domain ontology for the implementation level, then the vocabulary is potentially the same as on the higher levels. (We do exactly that in a part of the evaluation, Chapter 6.)
- **Explicit mapping:** the relations between the vocabularies may be modeled as a mapping. There is support for the (semi-)automatic generation of ontology mappings [75, 91], which can largely reduce the burden of generating such a mapping. An alternative would be **Ontology Merging:** before performing an operation that requires a unified or mapped vocabulary, the ontologies may be merged. There is research on automated support for this approach [264].
- **Manual mapping:** before a support function on a different level of vocabulary is enacted, the user has to manually express the input of the support function in the respective vocabulary used by it. Apparently, this may hinder or forbid the usage of certain functions, like the below-discussed

auto-completion mechanism – however, it can be used in basically any situation.

Having explained the problem, the relevant layers, and the vocabularies, we now present the actual requirements.

3.2 Requirements for Composition Support in Business Process Modeling

A list of the most important requirements is depicted in Figure 3.2 and discussed below. The thin black lines depict for which of the above layers (business activity, business task, implementation-level artifact) a requirement is of particular relevance. This list is divided into modeling extension requirements, fundamental, non-functional, and situational requirements. In addition to the requirements for traditional process modeling, dealing with the semantic aspects caters for some extra requirements – the modeling extensions. Fundamental requirements serve for defining the functionality of the basic composition technology in terms of service and resource combination. Non-functional requirements are expected to arise regularly in the instances of the problem described here, and capture aspects such as cost, quality, and more. Situational requirements point at specific situations in an enterprise application world that are more business-driven.

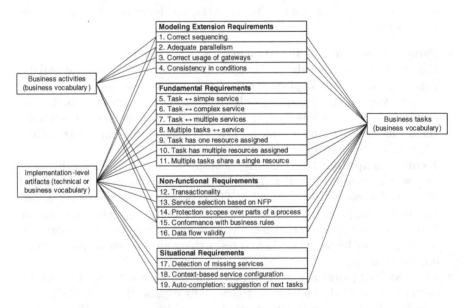

Fig. 3.2. Requirements overview

The requirements are described as a wish list for process modeling support, i.e., they list features which should be provided by an ideal solution approach – given their need. The requirements were derived from the following sources: scientific publications; unstructured discussions with practioners and researchers; standard specifications and tools; and the list has been evolved through many discussions over the duration of two years. Thus, we do not claim completeness of the list, but believe to have captured the most important requirements. Note also that in this section we do not make a decision how the features are consumed: in Sections 3.6 and 3.7 we describe a manual and an automated approach, respectively, where the features described below must be handled in different ways. Thus, the requirement descriptions present situations where a feature is desired, but do not go into the details of how the functionality is consumed.

Each requirement is showcased with an example; we often use a running example of what a passenger does at the airport between arriving there and boarding an aircraft. We use this example as most readers are likely to be familiar with air travel. Where a requirement is better explained with a different example, we deviate from this running example. Further, we describe how the requirement can be addressed in an implementation part. Note that the implementation description is focused on each requirement individually – the combination of the requirements induces the need for combining the implementations, which introduces another level of complexity and is not addressed here in detail.

3.2.1 Modeling Extension Requirements

1. **Requirement:** *Correct sequencing* of tasks and activities, in that the order in which the activities appear in the process is correct with respect to their meaning. The business semantics of each activity must be in line with the ordering of activities as given by the process model.
   Example: The activity "Board airplane" cannot be performed before "Check in". This can be directly captured by including "have Boarding Pass" as a precondition of "Board airplane" and as an effect of "Check in". There may be multiple variants of "Check in", namely the check in at a counter or the self-check in at the airport, via the Internet, the phone, or via text messaging ("SMS").
   Implementation: Whether this requirement is met can be checked by considering all possible execution paths of a process model and checking whether the ordering of the activities matches the desired relation in each of the execution paths. The desired relation can be modeled explicitly [183] or declaratively through pre and postconditions of the tasks, as described in the verification part of this work (Chapter 4).

2. **Requirement:** *Adequate parallelism.* As in the previous requirement, we require that the process is correctly composed – here with respect to parallel activities: activities with conflicting semantics should not be scheduled

for parallel execution. Conflicting semantics may involve the manipulation of a resource, such as occupying the only sales manager, or overlapping pre and postconditions, e.g., when a task relies on a fact which another, parallel, activity may falsify.

Example: Say, two passengers fly together, but during check in have not been seated adjacently to one another. After going through security screening, one of the passengers wants to change their seats, while the other one wants to buy some presents in a duty-free shop; they want to conduct both activities in parallel. The problem with that is that duty-free shopping requires the second passenger to present his boarding pass, and the first passenger needs to have both boarding passes for the seat adjustment. Note that only some of the possible execution paths of this process are problematic, i.e., the problem does not necessarily arise in each instance, but it may.

Implementation: The parallelism relation between all pairs of activities and gateways in a process model can be computed efficiently for a class of processes (cf. Chapter 4). If there exists a means of checking the correctness for parallel tasks, e.g., with respect to resource assignments or pre and postconditions, then this check can be performed for each pair of parallel process elements.

3. **Requirement:** *Correct usage of gateways*[2], in that the right routing structures in the control flow are used at any point in the process. Counterexamples include parallel routing where the subsequent process branches are in part mutually exclusive in their execution. A certain overlap with the previous requirement exists, although it may be very hard to determine automatically when two branches should be synchronized versus when the gateways are incorrect. Also, there is an overlap with Requirement 1, since an activity positioned for execution after two mutually exclusive branches may rely on the outcome of both of them at the same time.

Example: Say, the process is modeled with a parallel split after security screening, where one branch is to go to the airline lounge and the other one is to shop duty-free; subsequently, the branches are synchronized (parallel join) and the passenger boards the aircraft. There are two errors in this model: (i) not every passenger must (or can) do both; and (ii) both activities cannot be carried out by the same person at the same time, only one after the other.

Implementation: Part of the question can be answered with the basic techniques from the previous two requirements: inadequate parallelism or sequencing can hint at incorrect routing constructs. However, determining when which case is present may be out of the scope of an automated tool. It may already help a user to be able to visualize the relation of a part of the process to other parts, e.g., which branches of a process are sequential, mutually exclusive, or potentially parallel.

---

[2] Gateways are the routing constructs, such as XOR split or parallel join.

4. **Requirement:** *Consistency in conditions* of branches and loops, where the conditions can be checked for satisfiability – in the process and in the combination of multiple conditions. There may be modeling errors when it is clear that a loop will never be executed or repeated, or when the conditions of a split gateway never allow a branch to be taken, or when there will be cases where no branch matches the state of the process.
   Example: If an XOR split is followed by two branches, one having the condition "have Boarding Pass" and the other one "be inside Secure Area", and there is a process execution where neither is true, then this execution will get stuck at the XOR split.
   Implementation: The mentioned checks can be performed as a combination of satisfiability (SAT) solvers and a method that determines the "logical" states of the process during its executions, as above. Thus, in the example we could detect if there is a process execution where none of the conditions would apply.

3.2.2 Fundamental Requirements

5. **Requirement:** A *task* can be performed as one *single pre-existing implementation-level activity*. This means, the functionality desired for a given task has already been specified, i.e., it has been implemented as a single service operation or it is another pre-existing, pre-modeled activity for which it is typically well-known how it can be performed. The requirement is that the composition approach needs to be able to find the pre-existing implementation-level artifact. In this case, the process task and the found artifact can be linked, or the artifact can replace the task in the process.
   Example: Say, at check-in the passenger information must be compared with the entries of a government database of criminal suspects and terrorists. If this functionality is available as a pre-implemented service, then this service can be found and used during the check-in process.
   Implementation: (Semantic) Web service discovery based on pre and postconditions. Pre-existing research results for service discovery [25, 117, 274] can be adapted for the purpose of finding the best match for a desired functionality. After the service operation has been found, it must be included in the process flow and data formats of the messages must be adjusted accordingly, e.g., through techniques of data mediation.
6. **Requirement:** A *task* can be implemented by a *complex service with multiple operations*. There may be constraints on the circumstances of an invocation to the service, e.g., in terms of the order in which the operations may be invoked; or a service's effects may be overlapping with constraints on the execution of other services. Among other issues, process mediation between different complex services in the process model may arise. The requirement is that the composition approach should be able to find and include such a service while satisfying the constraints, if possible.

Example: The comparison of the customer data and the governmental database from the previous example may require an authentication invocation prior to the actual request. This authentication can be implemented as a separate service operation.

Implementation: This requirement induces the need for appropriate modeling of behavioral interfaces of services. In terms of the above example, it must become clear for the service consumer that the authentication step is required before the actual request. Constructing a process that is able to interact with the behavioral interface of multiple services has been the subject of various works, such as [233, 100].

7. **Requirement:** A *task* can be implemented by orchestrating *multiple services*. It is assumed that the control flow relations between the services are not specified. Then, these relations need to be inferred from the available service descriptions. The need for a particular service may arise from dependencies that are only indirectly related to the objectives of a certain task. The requirement is that the composition approach should be able to find and correctly orchestrate the needed services. In contrast, the previous requirement aims at a single service with a complex interface.

   Example: In the case of the above-mentioned comparison of customer data with governmental databases for criminals and terrorists, the data may have to be compared with more than one database, e.g., the database of the originating country of the flight and the destination country, and these databases may have to be accessed through different Web services.

   Implementation: Given suitable annotation of the task to be implemented, state-based approaches to automatic Web service composition can suggest possible sequences of services. Our own work in Chapter 5 addresses this problem, being a composition technique which can scale up to a large number of services, even in the presence of a domain ontology.

8. **Requirement:** *Multiple tasks* may be implemented by *a service*. This case may arise, when the granularity of the tasks is smaller than that of the service. Since executable processes, e.g., in BPEL, can be exposed as Web services again, the case can be of relevance. The requirement is to find the mapping between the multiple tasks and the service.

   Example: Reconsider the comparison of customer data with governmental databases. Say, the modeler created a task for communicating with the federal police database, and another one for communicating with the anti-terror database. If now a composite service exists that already combines the relevant communication with the various databases, then this service can be made available to the airport behind a single service operation.

   Implementation: This requirement can be implemented by bundling multiple tasks in a process and attempting to discover services for the bundles. The questions are (i) which tasks to bundle, and (ii) how to compute the semantics of a task bundle. (i) can be addressed by a suitable similarity measure, i.e., it is attempted to bundle similar tasks earlier. This may be particularly appealing when the tasks are in close proximity within the process. For (ii), [204] offers a first step towards a solution. Also, our verification algorithms from Chapter 4 may be helpful. However, situation-specific solutions may be required.

9. **Requirement:** A *task has a resource* attached to it. E.g., an approval task may be associated with a manager-role, meaning that during the execution of the process a specific manager needs to be assigned to play the role. The term *resource* is used not only for roles, but also for machinery, physical goods, and the like. The notion of a resource can also be used to model the relation of a process task to a business partner. The requirement on the composition approach is to take resource assignments into account in the composition, and the requirement on the runtime environment is to resolve the assignments correctly.

   Example: In the airport example, a secondary security screening of a passenger with physical contact between the passenger and the security officer must be performed by a security officer that has the same sex as the passenger.

   Implementation: Traditional role assignment can be resolved by today's workflow tools, given the role affiliation of each person is correctly and completely specified. On the basis of semantic annotations, however, some properties can be expressed more directly; in the above example, a statement like *SecurityOfficer.sex* $\equiv$ *Passenger.sex* (i.e., the *sex* property of the *SecurityOfficer* and the *Passenger* objects should be equivalent) could directly express the desired constraint. Many more flexible queries for role assignments can be thought of, e.g., a preference of people with more years of experience for certain tasks, or the requirement of a certain level of security clearance for others.

10. **Requirement:** A *task has multiple resources* attached to it. In the same way as in Requirement 9, during the process execution, the abstract resources assigned to a task must be instantiated with concrete resources. If multiple resources are attached to a single task, it is likely that the classes of these resources differ – e.g., role A performs the task using machine B. As in the previous requirement, the composition approach has to deal properly with assigned resources, and the execution environment has to be able to resolve them.

    Example: For a number of passengers the distances one has to walk inside the airport buildings are challenging, and they are frequently shuttled to the gates with a kind of electrical motor vehicle. For these shuttle services, a suitable employee and a suitable vehicle have to be made available. By using semantic annotations to express resource assignments, the process modeler could specify that (i) a vehicle that can seat x passengers is required, and (ii) a member of the role "airport support staff" with training for operating the chosen vehicle is required. As mentioned above, the type of the two resources (vehicle and driver) differ.

    Implementation: When the resource assignments are independent of each other, they can be resolved as in Requirement 9. If there are dependencies, however, then the resource resolution needs to process the resources in an order that reflects the dependencies.

11. **Requirement:** A *set of tasks shares a resource assignment*. This entails that a resource assignment is made once and there is subsequent interaction with this resource. It may not be clear when the resource needs to be assigned, since multiple parallel tasks may each be the first to use a resource. As above, the composition approach has to handle the resource assignments correctly, and the execution environment has to be able to resolve the assignments.

    Example: In our airport check-in example, say, the passenger wants to change the seat assignment at the counter at the gate. This can only be done by a representative of the airline with which the booking and the check-in has been made.[3] More generally speaking, whenever there is a reference to "the airline", then it is the role that has been chosen once and maintained from there on.

    Implementation: The resource resolution can be made as in the previous cases, whenever it is first needed. The resolution just needs to be kept in memory.

It may be noted that Requirement 5 can be fulfilled by Requirements 6, 7, or 8 as a side effect. Requirement 9 relates to Requirements 10 and 11 in the analogous way. This is a deliberate choice, allowing us to describe in a more fine-granular way to which degree the requirements are supported by an approach later on.

Note further that the combinations of these requirements are likely to occur. E.g., the combination of multiple services (Requirement 7) with multiple operations each (Requirement 6) may together implement multiple tasks from the high-level process (Requirement 8).

3.2.3 Non-functional Requirements

12. **Requirement:** *Transactionality*. Especially in cross-organizational processes, transactional behavior can specify how the outcomes of multiple activities, often at multiple partners, must be interrelated. If transactional behavior is specified for parts of the business process model, it must be dealt with correctly on all levels.

    Example: In the often-cited travel booking example, e.g., [234], the goal is to book a hotel, a flight, and a rental car for the same dates and location, but if one of the bookings fails, all other existing bookings must be canceled.

    Implementation: A number of works exist on the topic. According to [200], a service can have the following transactional properties: *retriable*, *compensatable*, and *pivot* (i.e., undoable), or a combination of them

---

[3] We here abstract from flight code sharing and see airport employees in certain roles as airline representatives.

(where no service can be both compensatable and pivot). If a composition of services with such properties should have atomic behavior (i.e., succeed / fail for all involved services), then there can only be a single non-compensatable service – namely the last one. In a different stream of work, [278] investigates how desired transaction policies can be attached to service descriptions using existing standards from the Web services domain exclusively. As for specifying transactional needs over behavioral interfaces and automatically composing so-called mediator processes with respect to transactional aspects, there are many existing approaches, e.g., [234, 100].

13. **Requirement:** *Service selection based on NFP* at design or run-time. Out of a class of functionally similar services, a concrete service has to be selected. This is often done on the basis of non-functional properties like price, estimated execution time, location, and the like. This can be done at design time, in which case it is desirable to support the modeler in making the choice; or, the modeler can specify in a suitable way *how* the choice is to be made, and leave it to the run-time system to resolve this specification in the selection.

    Example: For the run-time aspect, take e.g., the delivery of parcels: it may be achieved with one out of a set of available carriers. The business activity in the process model may only specify that the goods are shipped to the receiver. The carrier choice for a particular parcel at runtime may depend on size, weight, value, and such parameters of the goods to be shipped, as well as on the current pricing schemes of the carriers and the source / destination, as possibly not every shipper offers transport into, e.g., crisis zones. In contrast, the modeler could choose a specific carrier already at design time, e.g., for a specific type of goods for a certain region.

    Implementation: Service selection on the basis of non-functional properties has been studied extensively [307], also specifically as the design-time choice in business process modeling [190]. An apparent requirement is that the non-functional properties have to be modeled in a way that the selection can be made. If available, usage history (such as user reviews) can be taken into account. Run-time service selection has also been addressed [101, 99], although it remains an open point whether there can be guarantees of making the right selection. In closed domains, the impact of picking not the optimal service may be very limited; e.g., in the carrier example above, delivery may take longer or be slightly more expensive – none of which is fatal. In other settings, the risks of automatic run-time selection may be more severe and design-time selection is preferable.

14. **Requirement:** *Protection scopes over parts of a process*, i.e., in a part of process certain constraints are required to hold. The respective part of the process is marked by a so-called scope, over which conditions can be expressed.

Example: Reconsider the airport example. During security screening and passport control the usage of cell phones is often prohibited. This can be expressed through a protection scope. Another example from the business domain is when a customer complains about his invoice, and the respective department has not answered him yet – then the customer should not get a dunning letter before his complaint was processed.

Implementation: Firstly, the constraints on the execution of a scope have to be available for description in an appropriate way. Then, appropriate checking mechanisms need to make sure that the constraint is not already scheduled to be violated in the process model. Next, at run-time, the constraint needs to be enforced if the execution environment allows for enough flexibility such that it enables the process execution to potentially violate the constraint. It may be noted that, in terms of the workflow patterns [300], this requirement can lead to the need for the pattern "interleaved parallel routing"; the language used must then be expressive enough to allow for modeling and executing this pattern.

15. **Requirement:** *Conformance with business rules.* Business rules can be used to express aspects like corporate policies, business logic, and legal requirements in a way that allows machine-reasoning. By using a compatible vocabulary in expressing the rules and annotating the process model, checking techniques become possible for determining if the process will be compliant with the constraints. Also, an approach to automatic composition should take the rules into account and only come up with composite processes that conform with the business rules.

    Example: The approval of insurance claims which exceed a certain cost threshold must follow the four-eye principle, i.e., they need to be approved by two independent insurance representatives. Any process that does not take that into account may lead to compliance violations and illegal behavior.

    Implementation: Automatic composition tools can be extended to proper handling of rule bases – previous work in this direction was mostly conducted by the AI Planning community [104]. As for checking the compliance of the overall process, this can in part be addressed on the basis of the logical states through which the process traverses: these states can be compared with the rules in the rule base. For certain forms of rules, such a mechanism will be suitable – where this is not the case, other techniques are necessary. Existing solutions are e.g., based on SWRL [211, 212], or on our verification technique [313, 115] from Chapter 4.

16. **Requirement:** *Data flow validity.* If a process has a data flow, be it implicit or explicit, it needs to satisfy correctness criteria[4]. To pick one possible aspect, all data variables that are used as input of a certain activity should contain the data when the activity is executed. Checking

---

[4] A thorough definition of data flow correctness is outside the scope of this work.

this aspect can get tricky, e.g., when data is only provided by an optional branch in a process which precedes the activity where it is needed. Checking at design-time if there are issues with the data flow is what this requirement is about.

Example: Reconsider the airport check-in process. When the passenger wants to proceed to the departure gate after the first security screening, he needs to know *which* gate to go to. Today, the departure gate is usually known at check-in (at the airport) or before security screening, and can be looked up on screens – however, this is not true for all airports. At some airports the gate assignment is not available to the passenger until 20-45 minutes before scheduled departure time[5]. Thus, the process is blocked until the information becomes available to the passenger.

Implementation: This requirement partially overlaps with Requirements 1 and 2; however, the data aspects from this requirement reside at a slightly finer level of granularity. The propagation mechanisms suggested as implementations of Requirements 1 and 2 may be refined to check the data flow correctness.

Note that the above requirements can also have an impact on functional aspects of process models. However, their focus lies on quality assurance, such as not violating constraints (in the form of rules, protection scope, etc.) and other non-functional aspects. Still, all of these requirements can influence the control flow of a process – e.g., when one composition has a lower maximal duration, then adopting it may change the functional side of the process model at hand.

3.2.4 Situational Requirements

17. **Requirement:** *Detection of missing services*, as suggested in [166]. If a certain service is required but not available, it is desirable to have support for the modeler to take appropriate means to still compose the process as a whole. This can, e.g., be achieved by supporting the development of a new service or a solution in which a user performs the task.

    Example: Reconsider the check-in of flight passengers in need of assistance. Say, a driver with a cart should pick up the passenger from the check-in counter, and assume that requesting and scheduling drivers with carts should be supported by a respective service implementation. If the service does not exist, it may be decided that a new piece of software for handling these requests and the scheduling needs to be implemented. If so, a software developer is assigned to this task, and he might find it helpful to be provided with information about the process in which the service will be used.

---

[5] At the time of writing this is the case in at least one of London Heathrow's terminals.

Implementation: If a business task directly corresponds to a service which has to be created, then the need for the service is indicated by a failure of service discovery and composition. However, if the missing service would, if available, be part of a complex composition inside a business task (cf. Requirement 7) – ie., partial compositions exist, but any complete composition requires the missing service – then detecting which service is missing may be very hard. It may in fact be best to let an expert of the system landscape at hand decide which service to add. Providing the software developer who has to implement the service with the context and with a list of related services (if any) may be feasible and helpful. Besides implementing a missing service in software, there are other ways: part of our own work [252] that is not in the scope of this book discusses the relation between processes, services, workflow tasks, and flexible tasks. If it is infeasible or not desired to implement a software service, a user may be able to perform the task. In [252], we suggest means of supporting the creation of workflow tasks or flexible tasks on the basis of the process context, which is to be performed by a user.

18. **Requirement:** *Context-based service configuration.* If a service is configurable[6] and it is necessary or beneficial to the composite process to exploit this fact, then the composition approach should make use of it. E.g. if there are two mutually exclusive branches in a subprocess, the branching condition is configurable, and the only way to achieve a goal is to take one of the branches, then the composite process should call a respectively configured variant of the subprocess such that it always takes the desired branch.

    Example: In the airport check-in example, there are certain aspects of check-in which are relevant only for flights to specific countries. For example, passengers traveling to the USA nowadays have to answer a set of questions during check-in. If check-in is available as a pre-modeled and implemented subprocess, then an airport from which no flights to the US leave does not have to deal with this part of the subprocess at all.

    Implementation: If a service is configurable, and if the conditions under which a given part of it is relevant are specified in a suitable form, then part of the configuration can potentially be done automatically. This requires that the configuration conditions can be evaluated automatically – which may be doable through respective queries to the organizational context of the process. If the service has a complex interface, it may be possible to only use parts of the functionality which the service provides.

19. **Requirement:** *Auto-completion as the suggestion of next tasks* during modeling. Based on the process modeled so far, the modeling tool suggests possible successor activities (e.g., from a repository) for currently

---

[6] The configuration of a service may comprise a number of possible configuration settings which can change the externally visible behavior, such as variants for handling business cases in different contexts.

selected activities. The suggestion may be based on (i) the context in which a process resides, e.g., the industrial sector or the part of an enterprise's strategy which the process supports, (ii) the current logical state, e.g., in terms of data availability, of the process and the pre and post-conditions of available activities, or (iii) non-functional properties. These different matching degrees can also be combined.

Example: Say, the airport check-in process is modeled up to the point where the passenger went through security screening. Then, based on this information (passenger is inside secure area), the next possible steps are: proceed to departure gate; duty-free shopping; leave the secure area; etc. In order to enable the tool to suggest these activities, they have to pre-exist and be modeled accordingly.

Implementation: The above-mentioned matching degrees, their combination, and related approaches are discussed below in Section 3.5.4 and, in more detail, in [39]. Essentially, these mechanisms rely on existing semantic matching mechanisms between various concepts in ontologies.

As services may be heterogeneous in terms of the data structures used in their input and output messages, automated tooling may face the hardship of having to deal with data mediation. The first simplifying assumption we make in the remainder of this work is that only a single source of vocabulary is used. This is clearly a limiting choice, but enables us to make stronger contributions in the addressed areas. Further, the assumption may be realistic, e.g., in the following settings: in a given industrial sector, a standard ontology may exist; or all software services from a single vendor may be annotated using the same ontology. In terms of the three mapping types in Section 3.1, we assume that either the same vocabulary is used, or that ontology merging has taken place. As a result, there is a single, common domain ontology – it can be seen as a shared frame of reference for all involved parties. With respect to the data mediation issue, we assume that if a term is used in two different contexts – e.g., in the messages of two different services – then a data mapping can be found.

Note that parts of processes may have to be executed, even when they are not related to a subgoal, in order to meet transactional requirements of a process. E.g., when goods are ordered from a supplier, then the subgoal of having the goods is fulfilled as soon as they are delivered. However, the supplier process still foresees a payment, which is necessary before any process instance can terminate successfully. Thus, although it is not part of the goal, the payment to the supplier has to be made. This situation may arise as a side effect of the above requirements, in particular Requirements 6 or 12.

If the approach is extended towards larger domains (e.g., cross-organisational, to service marketplaces or ecosystems, or even the Internet), where presented information is more likely to be incomplete, knowledge gathering techniques as in [170, 199] can be re-visited. Also, adapters for differing artifact description methods may be required.

3.3 Requirements Discussion

Given the breadth of the requirements, addressing all of them in depth is infeasible within the scope of this work. In the remainder of this chapter we describe a generic high-level solution in the form of an extensible framework. The solution can be operated in a manual way (a process modeler operating a tool), or in an automated way (a process composition algorithm is executed). In the subsequent chapters, detailed technical solutions are investigated using a formal methodology. These solutions cover the verification of annotated process models (Chapter 4) as well as service composition (Chapter 5). A majority of the requirements presented here are addressed by the framework and the technical solutions, specifically the following ones:

- The verification of annotated process models addresses Requirements 1 and 2.
- Service composition focuses on Requirement 7.
- Fully addressed by the conceptual framework are Requirements 5, 6, 12, 13, 15, 16, and 19.
- Partially addressed by the conceptual framework are Requirements 3, 4, 8, and 14.
- Further work by the author that is not part of the scope of this book provides solutions for Requirement 15 [313, 115] and Requirement 19 [39].
- Consequently, not further addressed are Requirements 9, 10, 11, 17, and 18.

The discussion of the reasons for this coverage is presented at the end of this chapter, Section 3.9. We believe it is possible to extend the framework for achieving most of the above-listed requirements by including their respective implementations. As already mentioned, great care must be taken in order to adequately combine these implementations.

3.4 Conceptual Framework Overview

In the remainder of this chapter we present a high-level solution to the requirements: the conceptual framework. The framework serves as an extensible base structure on which solutions to the individual requirements from Section 3.2 can be combined. It comprises an outline of the most important components as well as two specifications to make use of the components: (i) a detailed view on the two corresponding phases from the BPM life-cycle; and (ii) an algorithm that can automate the interplay of the components. The most relevant functions span from the discovery of artifacts, their composition, the compatibility of the data exchange between the artifacts (handled through mediators), the suggestion of process activities, to the verification and validation of the composed annotated process. The idea is to formulate on an abstract level how the different techniques can be brought together in order to realize the larger vision. While the description of the components is on a high level and rather describes the state of the art, our contributions are the requirements and (i) and (ii) from above.

In order to construct the framework, we first need to refine the problem addressed. Since the goal is to use SOA services in business processes, and since currently the main technology for implementing SOA is the Web service technology, we herein put more emphasis on technical services than on execution-level artifacts that are executed by users. Thus, we neglect the requirements that deal with resource assignment in the following. The focus lies on the modeling extension requirements and the service-related fundamental requirements, where we also cater for a number of the non-functional requirements. For each individual component we state which requirements it can fulfill. The discussion at the end of the chapter then analyzes the coverage of the requirements in a centralized way.

The conceptual framework addresses the question how changes can be propagated from the conceptual process modeling level to the execution level. That is, if a new process model is created or an existing model is changed, then the respective implementation has to be created or modified to reflect the changes in the executable process model that is ready for execution in the IT infrastructure.

An executable business process model has to specify not only the control flow, but also data flow, interfaces to the services that implement the activities, and run-time binding to service implementations. When modeling a business process with traditional BPM approaches, many of these specification steps cannot be handled automatically or facilitated by appropriate tools, since the meaning of process artifacts is not captured in the process model. We herein follow the SBPM approach, cf. Section 2.3.5, to address these challenges by annotating semantic descriptions to process artifacts, yielding the opportunity to ease a business analyst's job by providing tools that facilitate various parts of the BPM lifecycle. We now provide a semi-formal overview on the form we envision for a functional annotation of processes, which serves as a more solid basis for the framework and components below.

3.4.1 Semantics of Annotated Process Models

In the following, we semi-formally define what we refer to as *annotated process models* from here on: process structures with explicit control flow (execution semantics) together with functional semantic annotations (change semantics) for the process activities. The execution semantics of a business process model are defined using common token-passing mechanisms, as in Petri Nets (cf. Section 2.1.4). The definitions used here are adapted from [304]. The change semantics are described by preconditions and effects of tasks. Whenever we refer to a (semantically) annotated process or process model, the definitions here are meant. Without going into details, we assume that further non-functional aspects and the business context of the process (e.g., the industry domain or the strategy) can be linked to the process model, but these links do not have to be present in an annotated process model. We explicitly state it when this information is needed. A more formal treatment of the terms introduced below is given where this is required, namely in Chapter 4.

A process model is seen as a graph with nodes of various types (a single start and end node, task nodes, XOR split/join nodes, and parallel split/join nodes) and directed edges (expressing sequentiality in execution). The number of incoming (outgoing) edges is restricted as follows: start node 0 (1), end node 1 (0), task node 1 (1), split node 1 (>1), and join node >1 (1). The execution semantics are specified as a token game, as in Petri Nets. Hereby, the control flow is handled by token passing from the start towards the end node. The tokens are carried by the edges. A node which passes a token from (one or all of) its incoming edges to (one or all of) its outgoing edges is said to be executed. Task nodes are executed when a token on the incoming link is consumed and a token on the outgoing link is produced. The execution of an XOR (Parallel) split node consumes the token on its incoming edge and produces a token on one (all) of its outgoing edges, whereas an XOR (Parallel) join node consumes a token on one (all) of its incoming edges and produces a token on its outgoing edge.

The location of all tokens, referred to as a *marking*, manifests the state of a process execution. An execution of the process starts with a token on the outgoing edge of the start node and no other tokens in the process, and ends with one token on the incoming edge of the end node and no tokens elsewhere. The workflow literature defines *soundness* of control flow as the standard criterion for its correctness, as described in Section 2.1.4. In fact, the presented formalism is a subset of WF-nets in terms of expressivity.

As for the semantic annotations, we assume there is a domain ontology[7] Ω out of which two parts are used: the vocabulary as a set of predicates P, and a logical theory $\mathcal{T}$ as a collection of formulae based on literals over the predicates. Further, there is a set of process variables, over which logical statements can be made, again as literals over the predicates. The logical theory is basically interpreted as a rule base, stating, e.g., that all cars are vehicles, or that every motorized vehicle has at least one motor. These rules can then be applied to the concrete process variables, e.g., a particular car or vehicle. Further, the task nodes can be annotated using preconditions (pre) and effects (eff, also referred to as postconditions, post), which are also formulae over literals using the process variables. The change semantics are as follows. A task can only be orderly executed if its precondition is met, then changing the state of the world according to its postcondition. The postcondition states the explicit effects, and together with the current state and the theory we may derive implicit effects. The question to which degree an explicit effect triggers implicit effects, i.e., further changes the state of the world, yields

---

[7] The domain ontology captures the vocabulary used in the domain at hand, as well as a logical theory that models the relations between domain entities.

the well-understood frame and ramification problems. We deal with them by following Winslett's possible models approach [322] from the artificial intelligence actions & change literature. This approach establishes a notion of minimal changes, which can be described as a kind of local stability: if there is no indication that something changed, then we assume it did not change. Further, we assume that all changes (unless explicitly inconsistent with the theory) trigger all applicable implications from the theory directly.

The question now is how these annotations can be added in a way suited for business analysts. We address this question next.

3.4.2 Annotating Preconditions and Effects

In this subsection, we give a short intuition of the form in which semantic annotations can be made. When a business analyst wants to refine a conceptual process model into an execution-level model and semantically annotate it, forcing him to write logical expressions in a language such as OWL-DL is rarely an option. One question thus is: in which form can a tool "disguise" the modeling of semantic annotations, such that the meaning is not changed?

As one possible option, our own approach for user-friendly semantic annotation [40] allows to define preconditions and postconditions through status models of business objects – e.g., after a business object *supplier invoice* has been posted it is in the state *posted*. For SAP's products, this allows us to re-use existing models of business objects and their life-cycles from product development, reducing the effort to model respective ontologies significantly. More details are given in Chapter 6. However, also for other contexts we found that thinking in objects and their states is a natural way for people to think about annotations and changes caused by activities. There are also other works using a similar approach, e.g., [259].

In the approach described in [40], the process modeler can select one or more business objects and describe in which state an object must be before a process activity can be executed (giving us the precondition), and how the state is changed by the respective process activity (the postcondition). All of this can be done graphically, and linguistic matchmaking can heavily simplify the task of finding a suitable business object and state [40]. Chapter 6 evaluates among others the fitness of such annotations for a set of practical use cases.

3.4.3 Refined Problem Description

Traditionally, a change in a process is implemented as follows. First, a business analyst creates a to-be process model, i.e., the model reflects the business expert's view on how the process *should* be conducted in the future. Then, this conceptual process model is implemented by IT experts – e.g., by mapping its control and data flow to implemented artifacts in information systems. The relationship between the business-level model and its IT-level implementation oftentimes is weak.

One of our suggestions is that, as an intermediate step, the to-be process model is refined into an execution-level business process model, by either the business analyst alone[8] or in cooperation with a process architect. It is important that the execution-level model represents an agreement between the business world and the IT world. That is, it is still comprehensible and acceptable for business, while being fine-grained and consistent enough that it can be implemented in IT. The problem so far with this approach is that business analysts' to-be models rarely meet the requirements of the implementation level. Thus, several iterations of feedback between the business analyst and the process architect are necessary.

In this chapter we further propose an approach to automated composition, which attempts to partially automate the projection from a modeled to-be process to its implementation. This goal is achieved by identifying executable artifacts which can be used for the implementation of a process model and defining their usage in an executable process model. We thus assume that executable artifacts and process tasks are annotated with formalizations of their respective functionalities as well as optional quality requirements. The semi-formal model introduced above can capture the functionality as far as this is expressible in terms of change semantics.

There is a notable difference between recent related work addressing service composition and this work: we are looking at composition from the viewpoint of an enterprise, not an end user. While business processes in business-to-consumer scenarios can be a point of contact with end users, service composition on the consumer's end is not the focus of our work. Our work is rather placed in the context of enterprise software and enterprise application integration. An exemplary difference is that, in the scope of this work, the final results must be correct and compliant with both organization-internal policies and external regulations such as the Sarbanes-Oxley Act. Thus, the focus is on design-time composition in a known domain, which, while being inherently complex, also simplifies the problem in two ways:

- Firstly, design-time composition can always be checked and approved manually before deploying and enacting it. Thus, unanticipated side effects can be avoided as in the manual control step decisions from the automated composition can be overruled.
- Secondly, in our known domain – the enterprise – we can assume to have full control over the artifacts and can thus enforce a uniform way and formalism of their description.

On the above basis, the problem addressed here can be restated in the following way: given a conceptual process model and a set of previously modeled

---

[8] There is an increasing trend to move such traditional IT responsibilities to the business level [62].

artifacts in a repository, all of which are semantically annotated, a composition approach should come up with the required set of artifacts from the repository and orchestrate these artifacts in a way that reflects the business process model's structure and business semantics – it should *compose the execution-level process model automatically.*

It should be noted that we explicitly encourage applying only parts of this vision. In particular, achieving the whole vision may be hard in the near-term future, and it may be problematic in terms of the modeling effort required, or the user acceptance if too much of a process model is changed at once. However, we believe that, by targeting the whole vision in this chapter, we can learn more about its parts and how they can be used in isolation.

3.5 High-Level Architecture and Components

In this section we address the vision described above. For this purpose, we present the structural architecture for the conceptual framework, depicted in Fig. 3.3. Subsequently, we describe the components in more detail, with particular emphasis on the usage in the framework.

3.5.1 Component Overview and Explanation

The **Process Modeling Tool** is used for designing process models and serves as the graphical user interface (GUI) to the rest of the architecture. In this modeling tool, the user must be provided with a convenient way to attach semantic annotations to his process models, e.g., [163, 40], which are part of the necessary input for the approach presented here. At any point during the modeling phase or after finishing the design of the process, the user may request the functionality of one of the other components. E.g., the request for composition of executable artifacts for an individual process task triggers an interaction between the modeling tool and the Task Composition Component.

The **Executable Artifact Repository** stores descriptions of the available artifacts. For each artifact this repository contains the description of its functionality, its non-functional properties and how it can be accessed.

The **Discovery Component** serves as an interface to the Executable Artifact Repository, in that it answers simple and complex requests for artifacts by matching requests to semantic descriptions of artifacts in the repository.

The **Data Mediation Component** provides a simple querying interface for the **Mediator Repository**. It enables the other components to retrieve the available mediators for a given mediation problem. The Mediator Repository contains the available mediators as well as descriptions of their functionality.

The **Task Composition Component** provides the composition of executable artifacts for single tasks in the process model. We refer to this functionality as "task composition" (since it operates on a given task) in order

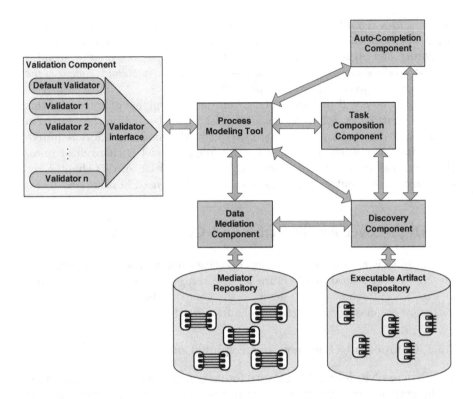

Fig. 3.3. Structural component architecture and interactions for manual control, where arrows correspond to data exchange

to differentiate from the composition of the whole process ("process composition") as described in Section 3.7.

The **Auto-Completion Component** can make suggestions how to continue a partially modeled process. As task composition, it relies on the discovery to retrieve executable artifacts.

The **Validation Component** comprises the **Validator Interface** and the required **Validator Plug-Ins**. Validation is desired in order to provide an achievable degree of automatic assertion. The suggested structure allows for flexibly plugging in validators with respect to the current context of the application. A default validator makes sure that the process flow is consistent with its functional annotation.

One technique that is required by a number of components is the so-called *information gathering* [194]. Its aim is to determine the fitness of the artifacts in the process context. Information gathering aims at asserting that the artifacts used for the implementation of a process task do conform to the properties that are checked by the default validator. That is, if information gathering succeeds for a particular task, then the implementation that is suggested for it by discovery, auto-completion, or composition imposes no conflicts on the process. This is achieved by gathering the information on the process context of a task, and, for the components which suggest implementations, that they make use of this information. Information gathering is performed by the default validator, and is implicitly requested by the modeling tool before discovery, composition, and auto-completion. The details on information gathering are presented in Section 5.6.1.

3.5.2 Discovery

One of the obstacles when creating an executable process from a to-be process is finding out if and how the tasks in the process model can be implemented in the specified way. For a process task which should be performed by an IT system there may be an existing service, there may be services at a different level of granularity, or there may be no implementation at all. In the activity of finding suitable existing services, the process designer can be supported by an intelligent software tool for automatic discovery and composition, which in term makes use of reasoning techniques over domain ontologies.

In discovering existing artifacts for a given process activity, the tool searches in the executable artifact repository to check whether an existing artifact can implement that task. This check involves *matching* the services against the requirements of the task. To be able to do so, both the services and the task are annotated with a semantic description of the provided or requested functionality, respectively. Matchmaking then is comparing the semantic descriptions of artifacts against the semantic descriptions of process tasks. The matching artifact descriptions are then ranked according to their relevance with respect to the goal. This fulfills Requirement 5. For this task it is sufficient to adapt and extend the Semantic Web service discovery techniques to find single artifacts that implement process tasks [188]. Vast literature is available on discovery – e.g., on overviews [238, 288], case studies [116], as well as concrete approaches using preconditions and effects [25, 117, 274], inputs and outputs [152, 174, 225], or non-functional criteria [171, 307].

If no single service can implement the chosen process activity, then it may be tried to find a composition of services that matches the task based on the semantic annotations, e.g., by the task composition component described below. This component makes use of the discovery functionality as well: a set of candidate artifacts for composition must be discovered before the actual composition may start (cf. Section 5.6.2).

By discovery we mean the search for an activity which matches a user goal best. Discovery relies on the following input: (1) a domain ontology Ω with $\mathcal{T}$ and P as introduced in Section 3.4.1, (2) a set of services S, also referred to as the service pool, with their preconditions and postconditions being formulae over the predicates in P, (3) a search request Q for a set of services which is described through its preconditions and postconditions just as the services and has additional non-functional criteria, e.g., execution time, availability, and the like. Given this input, discovery returns a ranked set of artifacts R that match the search request Q given ontology Ω, and is ordered according to the functional and non-functional criteria. The ranking can be based on, e.g., the widely used degrees of match introduced in [225] and [174], or on fine-grained notions of preferences, policies, and the according matchmaking techniques [171]. If a single artifact with the required functionality cannot be found, the set of invocable artifacts can be reused as an input for task composition.

Note that this type of discovery can find rather general matches, i.e., artifacts which match what is required for a task implementation in a comparatively fuzzy way. It is an open question how to find multiple process tasks that match the artifact's functionality in this case, i.e., to fulfill Requirement 8. In principle, it could be tried to determine if, for the annotation of any pair (or, more generally speaking, any set) of tasks, there is an executable artifact which can satisfy the goal of the combined tasks – given this combined goal is consistent in itself. However, this may be a costly test, since the possible combinations are exponential in the number of available tasks.

Further, we can make use of the information gathering technique mentioned above. This way, the logical state arising from the process can be taken into account, and services that would lead to conflicts can be filtered out preemptively. In a similar fashion, protection scopes (cf. Requirement 14) can be taken into account – given that potential violations can be detected on the basis of single artifacts.

The business context of a process may be modeled in a suitable ontology framework, such as [190]. There, the functional, behavioral, organizational, informational and intentional perspectives are seen as relevant to adequately organize information about a process. For each of these perspectives, a specialized ontology is proposed. In the presence of annotations from this ontology framework, the Business Functions Ontology and the Process Resources Ontology can be used to pre-filter the service pool S. E.g., services from the functional area in which the process resides may be more promising candidates; or if a specific enterprise application is mentioned as a resource, then the services provided by it should ideally be used.

In the business domain, besides discovering the artifacts meeting the functional requirements and match in terms of their context, it can be important to discover artifacts which best meet the non-functional (quality) requirements of a process task [307]. The desired NFP, if specified, are also part of the search request Q. We envision that the before-mentioned functionality-based discovery will take place at design time. A ranking of the artifacts can be determined based on an annotation of desired non-functional requirements (e.g., price, execution-time, availability, etc.). This can already be of help at design time. However, it may be more interesting to make the decision during process execution, using the current values for the NFPs which may not be known at design time. Both options together correspond to Requirement 13.

In case that only a single artifact fully matches the desired goal, the top ranked artifact is selected for process task implementation. If there are multiple similarly good matches, the discovery component returns a set of artifacts that both provide the desired functionality and comply with the non-functional requirements. If no single service matches, either in terms of functionality or in terms of the NFP, we search for a composition of multiple activities that is a better match.

3.5.3 Task Composition

Task composition, in contrast to discovery, tries to find a *combination* of executable artifacts which jointly satisfy the goal of a task, given such a combination exists. In many cases task composition will be performed when discovery cannot find a single service; however, it may be that the composition is a better match to the request than any service individually. Often, composition is only applicable for less fuzzy matches than discovery: the fuzziness of each match in a service chain can make the overall result in a composition less reliable than in discovery. Figure 3.4 depicts discovery and composition as a combined functionality – the difference is mainly in the result. Of course, the choice which technology to use can also be left to the user.

Several algorithms for service composition exist and can be integrated into our framework. All of them[9] have in common that they find a sequence (or a different control flow structure) of services $S_{i1}, S_{i2}, \ldots, S_{in}$ for a user request (i.e., the annotation of task T_i, and/or the result of information gathering) where the following conditions hold: (1) the precondition of each Web service is fulfilled at the point where this service is to be executed (in particular, in the context here the precondition of T_i enables the execution of the first service); (2) the postcondition of task T_i is satisfied by the state after the last service.[10] By using the discovery, the filters used there are applied for composition, too – i.e., information gathering and the ontology framework.

For task composition, we build on existing approaches to Web service composition, such as AI Planning[11]. The applicability of this technology for service composition has been examined, e.g. in [206, 60, 241, 242] – these approaches could in principle be adapted for the usage in our context. However, the existing approaches have either no support for domain ontologies to express constraints on the entities in the domain of interest, or their efficiency severely limits the number of services they can deal with. Thus, our own work in Chapter 5 seeks a novel trade-off between scalability and expressivity of a

---

[9] Note that there is another notion of service composition as mentioned above, namely the composition of complex behavioral interfaces of a small number of known services.

[10] Note that for the special case of $n = 1$ the composition result is a subset of the result of discovery.

[11] An overview over Artificial Intelligence (AI) planning can be found in [258], recent work in the area is often published at the ICAPS conferences, e.g., [111].

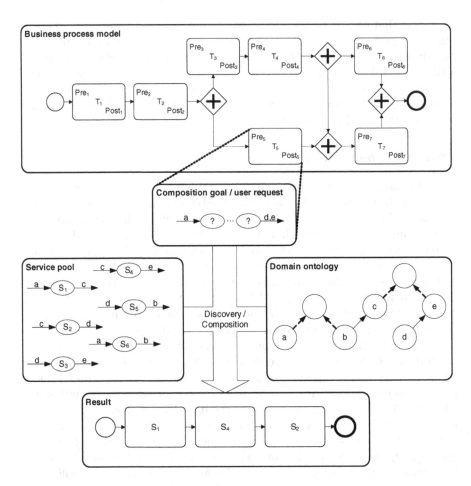

Fig. 3.4. Task composition (adapted from [144]): a user need for implementing a task (here: T_5) in the process is fulfilled by composing services from a service pool, while respecting an ontology Ω. The letters on top of the incoming and outgoing arrows of the user request and the services in the pool denote preconditions and effects and refer to concepts in the domain ontology.

domain ontology. It includes specifying and implementing a modification of forward search AI planning guided by heuristics. The approach builds on the Fast-Forward (FF) planning algorithm developed by Hoffmann [133], an algorithm that has received high attention due to its outstanding efficiency. We investigate the usage of domain ontologies with restricted expressive power as background theories in planning. These characteristics, i.e., the combination of a (restricted) domain ontology with practical efficiency, make it especially appealing in the context of this work. More details on the relation to related work can be found in Section 5.7. The Task Composition Component thus addresses requirements 7 and 6, and can also cater for Requirement 5. However, the latter is best addressed directly by discovery, as outlined before.

Another key difference to other approaches is that the task composition only supports the assignment of services to tasks at design time, and that discovery and composition are performed *per task*. More ambitious approaches, like e.g. [234], try to compose the entire process. While such a technology would be nice to have, composing entire processes is essentially a form of automatic programming, which is a notoriously hard problem. Apart from the obvious severe challenges regarding the computational complexity of such a general problem, there is the practical difficulty of formulating the "goal" for such a composition. Such a goal must be a specification of what the process must fulfill in order to be suitable. Providing such a specification is often more difficult for the modeler than just formulating the process itself.[12] In that sense, our approach trades some generality for pragmatics: for a single task, specifying a goal is often quite easy, and it is tedious to manually search for appropriate services.

The context of the process in which the chosen task is situated can be taken into account through the information gathering technique mentioned in Section 3.5.1. This technique can also make sure that no effects of the composed services are in conflict with other parts of the process.

3.5.4 Auto-completion

Discovery and composition are well-known techniques for finding services based on the precondition and postcondition of a semantic goal. We further suggest a technique which we call auto-completion for finding and proposing services to the modeler of an executable business process on the fly during modeling. I.e., while the modeler creates the model, new tasks are suggested to him by the system – based on the current state of the process and its context information. The suggestions may be presented in one of several ways, e.g., as tasks when the modeler moves the mouse cursor over an already modeled activity of the process as depicted in Figure 3.5. (Note, that this is only a mockup, i.e., the feature is not yet implemented.)

The approach we pursued in [39] uses three different sources, namely the process context, preconditions and effects, and non-functional properties. These sources provide sets of possible successor activities and a combined analysis can be used to improve the overall quality of the suggestions.

As with discovery before, it can be helpful if the process context is modeled by its annotations referring to the ontologies in the framework of [190]. In particular, the Business Function Ontology provides a structural breakdown

---

[12] The unconvinced reader is invited to think about the last computer program he wrote, and then think about how he would have explained to the computer what that program is supposed to do.

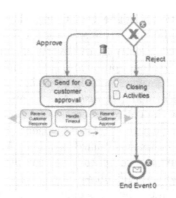

Fig. 3.5. Auto-completion makes suggestions for successors of "Send for customer approval". Mockup screenshot.

of the organization's business functions. It does so by splitting the domain in two dimensions, namely vertical (industry domain-specific, e.g., telecommunications) and horizontal (industry domain-independent, e.g., finance or human resources). Concepts from this ontology classify processes by their functionality with respect to these two dimensions. Furthermore, business goals[13] indicate what processes need to achieve from the business perspective and provide answers to why processes exist in the organization. The Business Goal Ontology models a hierarchy of business goals and provides a set of relations between them. Examples for business goals are "achieve and maintain internationally recognized quality standards" or "increasing the operative margin by 2 percent in consumer markets".

With the context-based approach we can ensure that the proposed services fit the specific context of the process. However, there is no indication that the proposed services can be executed as the current state of the process might not fulfill the requirements of the service. By applying the information gathering technique mentioned in Section 3.5.1, we can derive a summary of the logical state of the process at any point. This state summary can then be matched against the preconditions of the services in the repository, allowing us to find the list of invocable artifacts for the current point in the process, solely based on the prior annotation of the process.

Finally, the user may specify his preferences in terms of non-functional criteria in the modeling tool. By taking into account the quality of service properties when proposing follow up activities, we increase the level of precision of the suggestions and achieve a more refined ranking according to user preferences.

The three different techniques are used to identify appropriate services from a repository and the results of these three independent techniques are weighted

---

[13] Business goals are operational goals to implement an organization's strategy and are not related to the functional goals that are frequently mentioned in this work.

and consolidated. The resulting list of proposed services is presented to the user within the process modeling tool. This component directly addresses Requirement 19.

Related work in this area is mostly concerned with suggesting partial process models which are also referred to as process fragments [149, 162, 148, 190]. However, the weakness of these more ambitious approaches is that the fragments rarely fit the needs of the modeler perfectly, and near to always need further adaptation [148]. That is, a modeler needs to fit a fragment into place in his particular process context – a fragment that in general was created by another modeler. Our own work [39], in contrast, suggests only single artifacts. While the potential benefits from single artifacts may be lower, the need for adaptation is avoided.

Note that the described discovery, composition, and auto-completion techniques can be employed in a straight-forward manner only if the goals and artifacts are annotated using the *same* ontology. If this is not the case, a mediator for translating between different ontologies is required, as described in the next section.

3.5.5 Data Mediation

Mediators play a role in two areas of our framework. Firstly, they may be required in order to compose different independently developed Web services in one executable process. In this context it is necessary to mediate between the different message formats used by these services. Secondly, the discovery component needs mediators to cope with artifacts annotated using different ontologies. In the context of this framework we do not focus on how necessary mediators are developed. Instead, we assume that the mediators have already been defined beforehand and, furthermore, have been deployed and published in a mediator repository [49]. In relation to the distinction between "same vocabulary", "explicit mapping", and "manual mapping" we made in Section 3.1, a mediator represents an explicit mapping. Depending on the context, a mediator can also be defined during process modeling. This case is discussed in Section 3.6.2. We further assume that a mediator is available through a standard Web service interface.

In our framework two types of mediators are necessary:

- Mediators capable of translating between syntactic message formats of Web service and ontology instances.
- Mediators capable of mediating between ontologies.

Depending on the type of the mediator, invoking the associated Web service interface requires different input data. Invoking a mediator of the first type will, for example, require an instance of an XML message as an input. In contrast to that, invoking a mediator of the second type will require instances of concepts according to a given ontology. Note that our notion of mediators is broader than the one used by WSMO [70]. WSMO mediators are only concerned with the mediation on the ontology level, whereas our notion of mediators also takes the mediation between syntactic message formats and ontologies into account.

Based on these assumptions we are now able to differentiate between two possible usage scenarios of our framework. In the first scenario we assume that all artifacts are annotated using the same ontology. In the second scenario we assume that the artifacts are annotated using different ontologies, which are not integrated. Each of these scenarios results in a different set of requirements on the integration of mediation and is detailed in the following.

Annotation using a single ontology: If all artifacts are annotated using a single ontology, no mediators need to be executed during the composition of the process. In addition, the task composition does not necessarily need to insert any ontology mediation steps into the process. However, in order to execute the composed process, mediators of the first type might need to be inserted before and after calls to the Web services implementing tasks or parts of them. The necessary calls to the mediators therefore need to be inserted into the process before it is deployed to the runtime environment – however, this can easily take place after functional discovery, auto-completion, or composition.

Annotation using different ontologies: If all artifacts are annotated using different ontologies the situation becomes considerably more complex. In order to discover artifacts capable of implementing a given task, the discovery component needs to execute mediators of the second type as the tasks and each of the artifacts might be annotated using different ontologies. Therefore the discovery needs to interact with the mediator repository in order to locate the required mediators, given they exist. However, this approach might result in the execution of a very large number of mediators. Therefore a pre-selection might be necessary in order to identify promising candidates before executing the mediator. How such a pre-selection is performed efficiently is currently an open research question and out of scope for this work. We thus assume from here on that this scenario, i.e., annotations using different ontologies, is *not* given (or that the ontologies have been merged).

After the discovery component has identified a suitable artifact for a given task it will return this artifact as well as the mediator necessary for mediating between the ontology used for the process annotation and the data formats used by the artifact. The component receiving this information can then use this mediator to create the composed process by inserting calls to it before and after the discovered artifact, as stated above. Note that this approach results in the usage of the ontology in which the tasks are described as a central hub format. If this is not desired it would also be possible to query the mediator repository for mediators suitable for pair-wise translation between the formats used by artifacts with a data flow connection.

3.5.6 Validation

In this section we briefly discuss validation and verification techniques in the framework. After sketching the default validation, we provide a sample of further validator plug-ins.

Default validation – verification of annotated process models

The default validation checks if the process flow is consistent with the preconditions and effects of the tasks in a process. We refer to the default validation as *verification of annotated process models*: it deals with detecting inconsistencies in the functional annotations of tasks and essentially extends traditional criteria like deadlock freeness to annotated processes. Since the annotations allow for expressing the intended behavior of a process to a certain degree, we sometimes also refer to it as semantic business process validation [315]. This type of verification can answer two questions: is the precondition guaranteed to be fulfilled for every task in a semantically annotated process model? And are there tasks that may be executed in parallel but may cause a conflict (e.g., because the effects of a task T_1 executed in parallel to another task T_2 may violate T_2's precondition)?

Two properties are evaluated by the verification, based on the process' annotation and the domain ontology:

- Detection of conflicting parallel tasks. Two parallel tasks T_i and T_j are in *precondition conflict* if there is a literal in pre_i and its negation is in eff_j, and they are in *effect conflict* if there is a literal in eff_i and its negation is in eff_j.
- Determining if the preconditions will always hold. By propagation over the process model it is possible to compute a summary of the logical states which may exist while an edge e is activated (i.e., a token resides on the edge). Say, T_i is the task node whose incoming edge is e. Then we can check if the precondition of T_i will always hold when T_i may be executed, based on the computed state summaries. We refer to this property – i.e., the fact that a task's precondition is guaranteed to be fulfilled – as *executability*.[14]

The result of consistency checking can then highlight inconsistencies in the process, as depicted in Figure 3.6. The most related prior work on this topic is based on model checking techniques, e.g., on the basis of linear temporal logic (LTL) [236] or using the SPIN model checker [13]. However, due to the exponential number of possible execution paths of a process model together with further sources of exponential growth of the possible process states induced by the semantic annotations, the practical applicability of model checking

---

[14] When establishing executability for the tasks, as we will see in Chapter 4, *reachability* follows. A task is reachable if there is an execution of the process that allows the task to execute.

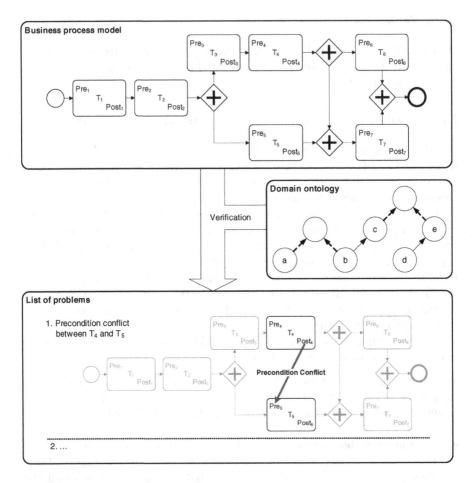

Fig. 3.6. Verification of annotated process models determines potential flaws stemming from the functional annotation of process tasks. The list of problems in the bottom here shows a precondition conflict between $Post_4$ and Pre_5.

techniques is limited, even *without* considering restrictions from domain ontologies. Thus, this problem has been investigated in depth, and is addressed in Chapter 4. There, we also evaluate other possible approaches in more detail. The presented solution approach works on a restricted process formalism and domain ontology, as introduced in Section 3.4.1. The advantage is that the time spent on verifying a process is polynomial to the number of activities and control flow links in the process.

Since this component checks if annotated process models are consistent with themselves and the domain ontology, it can be seen as the default validator. This component addresses the Requirements 1, 2, and in part 3 and 4.

A sample of further validators

The following three examples of validators show possible validator plug-ins, as depicted in Figure 3.3. Note that these validators correspond to common requirements from Section 3.2.

- *Validation w.r.t. policies and regulations.* Organisations typically have internal policies and are subject to laws or other regulations. If these policies and regulations are expressible in a machine-accessible way, e.g., in Business Rule Engines or specialized languages such as FCL [114], they can potentially be used to evaluate in how far the composed executable process is compliant with them. Our own work [313, 115], which is not further described in this book, addresses this topic. This corresponds to Requirement 15.
- *Taking into account transactional requirements.* A certain set of artifacts might have an interrelation with respect to a joint outcome, e.g., either all artifacts achieve a positive outcome or the effects of all artifacts' executions have to be undone [234]. Such a setting would require (i) an understanding for the joint outcome, i.e., which outcomes denote success and which ones represent failures; (ii) using services that provide cancellation actions (cf. Requirement 12 in Section 3.2); and (iii) case-based cancellation policies, depending on which actions actually have to be undone in which cases. Detecting such situations, evaluating and correcting the process could be achieved by a validator. Also, besides atomic behavior (yes-or-no outcomes only), more complex transactional properties could be represented and handled. This corresponds to Requirement 12.
- *Validation of the data flow of the composed business process model.* The framework can benefit of data flow analysis in a couple of different ways: the available data can be checked before the composition and the correctness of the data flow of the composed process model can be checked after the process design and further composition. Note that data flow validation may, at least in part, be realized as a variant of default validation, e.g., by expressing required input data availability as a precondition. This corresponds to Requirement 16.

3.6 Methodological Guidance for the Semantic BPM Life-Cycle

In this section we describe a methodology which structures the usage of the above described components when creating an execution-level or an executable process model. By methodology we mean "a documented approach for performing activities in a coherent, consistent, accountable, and repeatable manner" [290]. In contrast to the perspective so far, we here take a slightly broader view and describe what is necessary to really make a process model executable.

That is, we start from a to-be process model on the conceptual modeling level[15], derive an execution-level model from it, and now further refine this model into an executable process model. This last step is where the difference lies: up to this point, we most often stopped our consideration with the execution-level model. However, it is necessary to expand the view for a moment, in order to understand what needs to be contained in the execution-level model such that it can actually be made executable. The focus still remains on the modeling phase, and we do not discuss which additional components might be needed for configuration.

The methodology presented here describes how a modeler can use the functionality from the individual components of the conceptual framework. In contrast, the next section presents a process composition algorithm, which triggers the components' usage automatically. The aim of this section is not to give a complete discussion containing all aspects that may ever arise in relation to a methodology for SPBM, but to provide methodological guidance with respect to the new opportunities. After an overview of our approach we discuss the modeling and configuration phases from the BPM life-cycle and close with a brief discussion. The outcome of the modeling phase is an execution-level process model; the goal of the configuration phase is to arrive at an executable process specification.

3.6.1 Overview

We here demonstrate how isolated functionality from the components described above can be used in the modeling and configuration phases of the BPM life-cycle. For this purpose, we relate established activities and new activities as follows. Firstly, we suggest combining existing control flow verification techniques and semantic process validation. Second, discovery, composition, and auto-completion techniques can be used to find implementations for process activities at modeling time. The discovered implementations allow for mapping the process steps to the IT infrastructure according to several strategies during process configuration, which helps clearly separating modeling from configuration concerns. Furthermore, a novel way of testing executable process models is suggested.

Several versions of the BPM life-cycle have been presented in the literature – cf. Section 2.1.3. However, the life-cycles always remain on a rather abstract level, such that they provide only limited methodological guidance for the implementation of executable process models. Other approaches such as [126, 98] focus on partial aspects of BPM design and do not cover implementation details. This section takes the Semantic BPM life-cycle from [94] (cf. Section 2.3.5) as a starting point and describes our proposal of a methodology for semantic business process modeling and configuration. While the life-cycle of [94] is followed in this section on the high level, the *content* of the modeling

---

[15] The layering of process models is discussed in Section 2.1.3.

and configuration phases described here is quite different. To mention just one difference: composition per process task is described in [94] as an activity of the configuration or execution phase, while we argue below that this activity should be part of modeling.

Fig. 3.7 gives a more detailed view of the modeling and configuration phases and shows the activities we identified for each of them. The goal of the modeling phase is to create an execution-level process model. Therefore, beyond conceptual modeling (M.1) and discovery and composition of tasks (M.4), it is important to consider control flow verification (M.2) and semantic validation (M.3) to guarantee the necessary level of correctness. In the configuration phase, the process model is translated to an executable language (C.1), yielding an executable model. After the service binding (C.2) the executable process is tested (C.3) and finally deployed (C.4). The process designer conducts each of these four plus four activities and is supported by respective tools. In many cases there will be two process designers with partially overlapping expertise (cf. Section 2.1.3): a business analyst being responsible for the activities of the modeling phase, and a process architect in charge of the configuration phase.

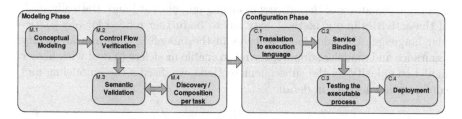

Fig. 3.7. Detailed view of the Modeling and Configuration phases in the BPM life-cycle. The arrows depict a suggested usage of the various activities in the absence of problems.

Section 3.6.2 describes the steps for the modeling phase, section 3.6.3 respectively for the configuration phase. A short overview follows, highlighting the particularities of the semantics. During the actual conceptual modeling, the control flow is created, depending on the notation at hand data flow and further aspects of the business processes are modeled, and semantic information is annotated; after the control flow has been checked, annotated process verification makes sure the annotations and the control flow do not contradict each other, while other validators ensure that policies and regulations are being adhered to; if this check has a positive result, composition and discovery may be used to find out if services can be found for the creation of an executable process on the basis of the conceptual process model; when the right granularity of annotations is established, semantic process validation checks again if the semantics of the process activities form a consistent picture, and that, given the composition and discovery results, still no policies or regulations are violated, etc. All of these activities are performed on the execution-level process model. The configuration phase starts with translating the execution-level process model from the modeling phase to the execution language; following one of the possible strategies, the process activities can be bound to services at design time, or this point can be left open for run time; before the executable process is deployed and enacted in a productive setting, it should first be tested thoroughly; for deployment, the executable model and potentially supporting deployment information is needed.

Note that the activities related to quality assurance (M.2, M.3, C.3) are optional, and the arrows show one possible recommended order of their execution. However, if a process model is created for execution in an industry setting, model quality and correct execution are of crucial importance. Accordingly, it is strongly recommended to consider control flow verification (M.2), semantic validation (M.3), and testing (C.3) before deploying an executable process model.

Since we aim at a generic methodology, a number of the suggested activities must be tailored to a specific notation or language in order to provide a thorough solution. For instance, the control flow verification depends on the execution semantics of the process modeling language at hand. Basically, each of the activities in our methodology has to be further refined for any particular language. The additional features in the modeling time aim at quality assurance and modeler support, trying to enable modelers to deal with higher model complexity. In the subsequent sections, we discuss each modeling and configuration activity in detail.

3.6.2 The Modeling Phase

The goal of the modeling phase is to create an execution-level process model that represents a good trade-off between the ideal structure of the to-be process on the one hand and the constraints given through the available executable artifacts on the other hand. As the components supporting the various activities have already been introduced, we here focus on the particularities of using the components within the methodology.

Conceptual Modeling (M.1)

Business Process Modeling can serve various purposes ranging from documentation to reorganization and workflow automation (cf. Section 2.1.3). Before starting the actual modeling the process designer has to carefully decide for a suitable modeling language, a respective tool to facilitate the modeling, and required perspectives on the process [22]. The choice for a *modeling language* can hardly be made without considering potential *tool support* since industry-scale modeling projects require sophisticated management features such as multi-user support or persistent storage in a database. Several languages are used for modeling business processes including EPCs, Petri Nets, YAWL, UML Activity Diagrams, and BPMN – see e.g., [76] for an overview. The *required perspectives* on the process depend on the purpose of modeling. Since our goal is to finally arrive at executable processes we need to not only model the control flow, but also the data flow between the activities. Furthermore, in the case of SBPM the user has to annotate references to ontologies to the model. In [40] we present an approach towards user-friendly annotation of semantic information.

SBPM offers content-aware process model auto-completion as further modeling support. As discussed above, the auto-completion component in this framework suggests possible next artifacts. Note that this makes the discovery or composition for implementations unnecessary for the respective resulting tasks. As described in discovery/composition (M.4) the semantic annotation of the artifact can be added to the new task, and a link to the suggested artifact is kept.

Control Flow Verification (M.2)

It is an important design goal for an executable process model that no matter which decisions are taken at run-time the process will always complete properly without deadlocking. The *soundness* property, cf. Section 2.1.4, is often used for asserting the absence of such potential problems. Petri Net analysis techniques are not directly applicable for other languages, but need to be adapted to the routing elements these languages provide. The OR-join that is included in EPCs, YAWL, and BPMN has been a challenge from a verification perspective for quite a while. One solution in this context is to use the notion of relaxed soundness instead of soundness. A process is *relaxed sound* if every transition in a Petri Net representation of the process model is included in at least one proper execution sequence [68]. A problem though is that this relaxed soundness notion does not guarantee that the process always completes properly. As a consequence, dedicated verification techniques have recently been defined for the verification of EPCs including OR-joins [203] and for YAWL nets including cancellation regions [326]. Since these languages cover most of the control flow features of other languages, these verification techniques can easily be adapted for UML Activity Diagrams or BPMN. This way the process designer can make sure that a process model will not deadlock at run-time.

Semantic Process Validation (M.3)

Once the process control flow is sound[16], we can use the validators from Section 3.5.6 to check if the model satisfies other desired properties for which

---

[16] The work on verification of annotated process models presented in Chapter 4 explicitly requires the control flow to be sound before it can be applied.

validators exist. In particular, it is advisable to execute the default validator before discovery and composition (M.4), since otherwise these steps would try to discover/compose for a potentially ill-defined process model. As in classical logics[17], if the assumption (the process is well-defined in terms of the semantics used) is not met, discovery and composition may lead to undefined results.

However, since discovery and composition may not be able to take into account all the properties that can be checked by the various validators, M.3 should be executed *after M.4 again*. The steps M.2 and M.3 can be seen as quality assurance criteria, and can help to detect potential problems early in the design process – often saving a lot of time during deployment and testing.

Discovery/Composition per Task (M.4)

Discovery and composition, cf. Sections 3.5.2 and 3.5.3 respectively, find executable artifacts for tasks in a process model, based on the functional and non-functional properties specified in the annotation of the task at hand. The question that now needs to be addressed is how to fit these techniques into the methodology presented here. The information gathering technique makes sure the discovered/composed artifacts fit into the process context. The remaining aspect we describe here is, what happens with the results of these techniques.

As for the consumption of the results from discovery/composition, there may be a found implementation or there may be no fitting (set of) artifacts for the chosen task. If an implementation has been found, the goal of a task may be refined with the semantic annotations of the found services. In the case of discovery this is straight-forward. In case the result is a composition of artifacts, the original task may be replaced with a container holding the tasks that relate to the services which were composed together, i.e., the tasks in the newly created container are annotated with semantic goals that correspond to the composed services and are ordered as specified by the composition. This way, the granularity of the process tasks can be adapted to the granularity of the available services, which is usually a challenge in process modeling. Further, the ambiguity in the execution-level model is reduced this way.

Discovery/composition may change the process model as such, since the implementation of a task can easily introduce further constraints on the control flow. A constraint may be of a technical nature and/or specific to the particular service implementing the task; there does not have to be a correspondence to a constraint from the business point of view. The semantic process validation (M.3) can further relate the constraints of the implementation of a single task to the other process activities. That way, deviations from the to-be process model may be necessary after M.3 and M.4. Thus, we argue that these activity should be performed as part of the modeling phase. In contrast, if such changes are made during configuration, the original process designer with the business knowledge may be excluded from the decision.

---

[17] In Latin: *ex falso sequitur quodlibet*, i.e., from falsehood follows anything. Also known as the "principle of explosion".

Importantly, the discovered/composed "services" are identified with their semantic descriptions. Having such a semantic description in a task means that we can, later on in the configuration phase, replace this description with any service that satisfies it. In other words, we can separate the discovery from the *binding* of artifacts – links to the found services may be kept, but during modeling no particular implementation of a service is chosen. This is advantageous because in this way we do not force a premature decision on what the actual implementation technology will be: the semantic task description can be mapped onto all sorts of technologies whichever is available and suits best the requirements of the particular deployment scenario. Further, it may be assumed that the process architect in charge of the configuration phase is more knowledgeable with regard to the available artifacts than the business analyst modeling the process. Leaving the decision on the specific implementation to use to the process architect is arguably a good choice.

If discovery/composition reports that there is no implementation, then according action must be taken by the process designer. Possible actions in such a situation include changing the process model; marking the particular task such that it is clear that an implementation for it must be created during the configuration phase; or creating a so-called "task pattern" [252] for manual execution, where a task pattern is like a generic workflow task without a specific implementation, and can be used in extremely flexible ways. In contrast, if discovery/composition succeeds, the results should be displayed to the process designer for checking, if only for safety reasons. E.g., the semantic descriptions might be flawed, or not precise enough to obtain a fully implemented process.

In the sense outlined here, discovery/composition can be seen as a further quality assurance activity, in that it can provide feedback if a process model is implementable or not: if discovery/composition succeeds, the modeler knows that there is at least one service for each task to implement it. As such it is even available to a modeler who is not trained in IT or the system landscape. If no artifacts are found, then the implementation of the process may take more time and budget. Knowing these implications early in the design process can be of high value, and may even lead to deviation from the to-be process as the ideal process from the business point of view.

3.6.3 The Configuration Phase

The configuration phase aims at mapping a semantically annotated execution-level process model to an executable model that is bound to a particular IT infrastructure. That is, the process model has to be translated from the formalism used by business experts to a formalism that can be executed for instance by an execution engine. Further, the semantic descriptions of tasks have to be mapped to concrete implementations, e.g. services. Given the execution-level model is sufficiently well described, required tests have been pre-specified, and no errors occur, the configuration phase could be automated.

Where necessary, we exemplify steps in this phase by using particular technologies in describing the configuration phase for reasons of increased tangibility. Nevertheless, most of the concepts can be easily ported to other concrete technology.

Translation to executable processes (C.1)

The modeling phase leads to a process model that is both sound regarding its control flow and validated against domain constraints using reasoning techniques. In the translation phase this process model is mapped to an executable language such as BPEL. There are several challenges for the transformation exercise since executable languages are often more restrictive in the way they represent control flow [244]. Still, there are some standard solutions to automate the transformation if there are no unstructured loops in the conceptual models [202]. For the transformation of BPMN to BPEL there are several implementations of a transformation, among others the one defined in [224].

Service Binding (C.2)

During discovery and composition per task (M.4) it is tried to find at least one implementation for any given task. When binding to the infrastructure the discovery is used to discover the most appropriate implementations out of the available ones. Given this setting there are several strategies for binding implementations to executable process models during configuration:

1. Web services as activity implementations
   A task may be bound to a concrete Web service. This configuration strategy results in a conventional executable process model (e.g., in BPEL) that runs on a conventional execution engine which invokes conventional Web services. Thus, the semantic extensions can be kept entirely inside the modeling and configuration phases, and no specialized tooling is required for the execution. Note that, in case of asynchronous bi-directional communication to the Web service, the executable process model has to expose a Web service interface as well [218].
   The static binding to a concrete Web service limits the flexibility of the executable process model, because this means using a specific WSDL description for an activity's implementation. Thus, this strategy sacrifices the option to use functionally equal services that implement different WSDL interfaces. The actual implementation, i.e. endpoint, can be either extracted from the discovered service and determined during deployment or discovered during runtime. In the latter case, multiple implementations may be used, given their interface is the same and they only differ in their endpoint.

2. Semantic goals as activity implementations

   Using a semantic goal description, such as a WSMO goals, as activity implementations implies the existence and usage of a semantically enhanced
   middleware (in the case of WSMO, e.g., WSMX (Web Service Modeling
   eXecution environment) [120]) and execution engine [302]. Goals can be
   used with and without a restriction on the set of services that might be
   used. The restriction might be a single service (which corresponds to design time binding of Web services with respect to flexibility) or a (ranked)
   list of functionally equal services that were discovered during design time.
   Even more flexibility is achieved by using a goal without any restrictions
   on services that might be used. In this case any Semantic Web service that
   meets the functional requirements can be discovered and invoked during
   runtime. However, this flexibility comes at the price of uncertainty: at
   design time it cannot be predicted which service is selected at runtime,
   especially since new services may become available over time, while others may cease to exist. Depending on the specific setting, the risk that
   comes with this flexibility may not be tolerable for critical processes in
   the enterprise domain.

If a specific service has been selected for (possible) execution, there may
be a need for mediating between the data formats used by the service and
the process. Potentially, new mediators have to be created. Note that, if two
services refer to the same ontology element, we act on the assumption that a
mediator *can* be created between the actual data formats that correspond to
the referred ontology element (if any). If this is not the case, the implementation may have to be changed – in the extreme cases requiring to go back to
the modeling phase and change the execution-level process model.

Testing the executable process (C.3)

Creating correctly executing processes is a cumbersome task, due to the fact
that the precision of the process then is the same as the precision of a programming language. Practical experience shows that producing correctly executing
BPEL code for non-trivial processes even with state of the art tools requires
several attempts and hours. Therefore, even though control flow and semantic
validity have been checked, it is necessary to test an executable process before
deployment.

For this purpose, [175] presents an approach to BPEL testing through "unit
tests", which is related to traditional white box tests from software engineering. While this work is focused on BPEL exclusively, the methodology
presented in this chapter is independent of a specific format for executable
processes. The approach from [175] should be adaptable to other languages
and is certainly worthwhile considering. Two alternative ways for testing an
executable process are mentioned below. Both of these testing scenarios require some additional infrastructure.

The first additional option is inspired by traditional software engineering, where a replication of the productive systems is made available as a test infrastructure. Within a single organization, this approach may be extended to executable processes in the obvious way. For cross-organizational processes, a dummy replication of the remote systems within the own testing infrastructure may be required.

The second additional option requires an abstract communication layer, e.g. in form of an *Enterprise Service Bus (ESB)* [51]. This bus can then be extended with a test mode, such that it reacts to messages with a "test" flag with one of a set of predefined test replies, e.g., chosen by random. The test reply messages for a particular service are stored in the ESB when this service is deployed, and may be updated over time. With this mechanism, the test message never reaches the productive application systems, and the tested executable process may only make use of the services which are available through the ESB. However, there are a few pitfalls to this approach, e.g., when a process relies on instance-related replies the predefined test answers may not be sufficient. Although this approach aims at a lean and elegant testing infrastructure with minimal overhead, the practical applicability remains yet to be shown.

Regardless of the particular approach chosen, as soon as a process is critical and non-trivial to the least extent, testing an executable process before deploying it to productive systems is a must.

Deployment (C.4)

Deployment is the step of making an executable process available for productive use. Processes are deployed to the infrastructure and registered, e.g., as a service. In case a service binding strategy other than static binding (in our scenario, design time binding to Web services or a semantic goal that is restricted to exactly one concrete service are forms of static binding) has been chosen, additional NFP parameters like cost, duration, etc., can be applied to make the (runtime) discovery of services more precise.

3.6.4 Discussion of the Methodology

In this section we described a structured methodological approach to the process modeling and configuration phases from the BPM life-cycle. This methodology easily facilitates reuse of existing process artifacts, and by doing so, aims to bridge between conceptual modeling of business requirement and information system implementation.

Let us briefly discuss our proposed order of activities as per Fig. 3.7 and the motivations behind it. A process model with sound control flow is not invalidated by discovery and composition, but potentially the model grows through these activities. Therefore, control flow verification is best done before discovery/composition, because it is easier for a modeler to correct a smaller model. Moreover, semantic process validation can only be done on the basis of a sound control flow, and, as argued above, semantic validation should happen both before and after discovery / composition. In the configuration phase, the language translation takes place before service binding, because binding mechanisms are language-specific. Testing the executable process is done after service binding, because it of course requires concrete services. Deployment finalizes the configuration phase, and thus is performed last.

The utilization of semantic technologies in this methodology differs from previous approaches in several important aspects. For example, performing composition per task, rather than for an entire process, has a much better chance to yield useful results at a low modeling cost. Semantic validation is an entirely new step. Our arrangement takes the appropriate measures to deal with the subtle interplay between discovery and binding. Composition is best viewed as part of the modeling phase, since getting to the desired IT-level model may require an iteration of human and computer-supported activities; at last, a final approval by the process modeler is needed before a composed process is deployed.

3.7 Automatic Process Composition Algorithm

While the methodology in the previous section described how a modeler can use the components presented in this chapter, this section addresses how parts of this procedure can be automated. In principle, the algorithm suggested here could also be executed with manual control, but the focus here is on automation. More concretely, the automation concerns steps M.3 and M.4 from the previous section – all other parts are not affected.

Firstly, a revised component architecture is required for the desired automation, as shown in Fig. 3.8. The difference to Fig. 3.3 is that a central **Composition Component** serves as the controlling entity of the automatic process composition algorithm. Thus, nearly all interactions between the process modeling tool and other components are passing through the composition component. However, as before, auto-completion takes an exceptional role, and is not affected by the change put forward in the following.

The composition component executes the process composition algorithm described below. This process composition is concerned with finding an implementation for each activity of a sound annotated process model. It should be noted that this goal differs substantially from the goal of task composition as argued in Section 3.5.3. The numbered tasks in the process depicted in Figure 3.9 corresponds to the steps in this algorithm:

1. Identification of existing process parts which are not affected by changes. E.g., during re-engineering, parts of a process may stay unchanged, which implies that the respective executable process does not necessarily have to be changed in those parts either.

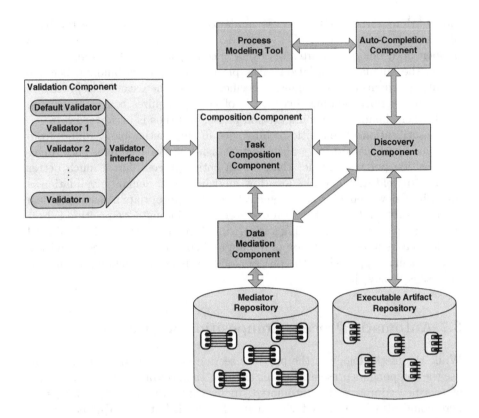

Fig. 3.8. Structural component architecture and interactions for automatic process composition, where arrows correspond to data exchange

2. Semantic process validation (validation component, Section 3.5.6). If a validator detects a problem which can automatically be resolved, then this is done. Otherwise, the unsuccessful outcome is presented to the user. In this case, the parts of the process that are not valid according to one of the validators (e.g., not consistent, violate a policy, or the like) are brought to the user's attention. The user is then asked for a refinement or changes to the process model. Validation here includes:
    2.1. Default validation verifies the correct combination of the control-flow and functional annotations of the tasks in a process. Problems here may be resolved by adding additional ordering links between affected activities. Our work on this topic is presented in Chapter 4.
    2.2. Validation through the validator plug-ins, e.g., in an order given by a prioritization.
3. For each task in a changed part (cf. Step 1) of the source process: derivation of executable artifacts. This is done in an order that resembles the

control-flow, i.e., if task T_1 is always executed before task T_2, then this step considers T_1 before T_2.

3.1. Information gathering (as mentioned in Section 3.5.1 and detailed in Section 5.6.1) derives as much implicit information from the process context as possible for two purposes: (i) to extend the preconditions of tasks, and thus making more services applicable; and (ii) to derive constraint sets to rule out incompatible services. See Section 5.6.1 for the technical details.

3.2. Discovery/composition of artifacts.

    3.2.1. Discovery (discovery component, Section 3.5.2) of single artifacts that implement a task.

    3.2.2. If no single artifact can achieve the required functionality or match the NFP: task composition (task composition component, Section 3.5.3) for implementing a single task.

3.3. Semantic validation (validation component) of the composed artifacts on the level of a single task implementation (data flow, adherence to policies and regulations, etc.). There is potential that this step can be integrated with the previous one, e.g., in order to take policies into account during composition. However, this may also prove infeasible or impractical for certain validators, e.g., when the examined property is rather uncommon and relevant only for the application domain at hand.

4. As in Step 2, process-wide semantic validation (validation component) is performed. Again, potential inconsistencies are reported to the user. Note that additional problems may arise from the implementation choices made by the previous step.

If the final validation step succeeds, the derivation completed. At any point in the algorithms, problems that cannot be dealt with automatically are reported to the modeler.

In order to explain the steps of the algorithm in a more tangible way, Figures 3.10 (a) – (d) depict how the resulting composed process evolves with the steps of the algorithm. Fig. 3.10 (a) shows a BPMN process model with tasks, connectors, and events. Fig. 3.10 (b) presents the same process after discovering single services that can implement a full task in the process (step 3.2.1 in the algorithm). Fig 3.10 (c) shows additionally groups of services that jointly implement tasks (as composed together by step 3.2.2 in the algorithm). Finally, Fig 3.10 (d) depicts the process in terms of only the services after the algorithm's execution.

3.8 Related Work

In the following, we describe the related work for the two main parts of this chapter: the requirements analysis and the conceptual framework.

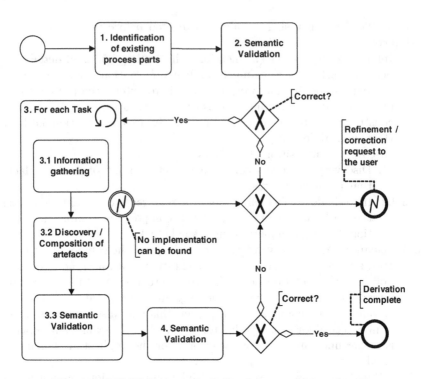

Fig. 3.9. BPMN diagram depicting the composition algorithm

3.8.1 Related Work for the Requirements Analysis

The recent years brought afore a vast number of publications around the service composition topic, just to mention a few: [242, 234, 241, 24]. Amongst them is a collection of surveys on approaches, frameworks, and platforms in the service composition area [169, 77, 228, 243] and more. Some of these surveys formulate needs and motivations for service composition. But, in contrast to our work, those needs and requirements remain rather vague; their main purpose is to categorize different kinds of solution methods.

Requirements on service composition are mentioned in a couple of publications. In [205] a list of requirements for a specific software component, the service composer, is given. Naturally, those requirements are much more specialized than the ones given here. [289] discusses among other aspects how non-functional requirements should be included in service composition. Web Service Composition Management, as described in [90], deals with security, fault, accounting, performance and configuration management aspects of service composition, and addresses these issues by giving requirements for this purpose. To the best of our knowledge, general requirements for composition in the realm of business process modeling as given in this chapter have not been discussed before. Related work that does not focus on requirements only is given in the following.

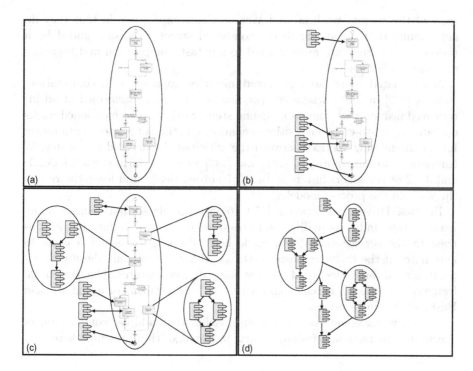

Fig. 3.10. Results from the steps of the composition algorithm

[169] lists a number of problems in current approaches, which partially overlap with the requirements collected here. Additionally, they mention the problem of degrading quality in long service chains: the longer the composition produced by the tool, the less likely that it meets the needs. In the realm of business process models, this problem can e.g., be avoided by composing only smaller parts of the model automatically, and modeling the larger process manually.

[77] defines seven criteria, along which they evaluate existing composition approaches, frameworks, and platforms. Four of those criteria have the characteristics of requirements, and form a subset of our requirements.

Business rules in composition play a role in [223] as well, only there they are not used as constraints to the search space, rather, the composition process is defined through composition rules. The composite service then is a result of evaluating the rules.

3.8.2 Related Work for the Conceptual Framework

Recently service composition has been an active area of research, e.g., [27, 234, 241, 242]. However, Sections 3.5-3.7 address a different problem than most of the current work around Web service composition, in that they do not assume that an automatically composed structure is surrounded by a process. Thus, they are more related to our task composition and therefore discussed in Section 5.7.

More related issues address mixed-initiative approaches to composition, such as [242] or [261], where composition of services is performed in an interleaved fashion with human modeling steps. Still, the two mentioned works operate on end-to-end composition scenarios, i.e., the automated composition fills in the missing services between the anticipated start and end states. In comparison to our approach, [261] and [242] would perform steps 3.1, 3.2.1, and 3.2.2 of the algorithm in Section 3.7 automatically and leave the rest of the work to the process modeler.

Business-Driven Development [159, 167] is also related, but assumes many manual steps and is more directed to traditional software engineering, in contrast to the service-assumption made here. Probably it is not feasible to automate all the tasks in Business-Driven Development, but the use of explicit, formal semantics could provide many desired features. The conceptual framework discussed herein might serve the advancement of automation in Business-Driven Development.

So far, we have not seen other approaches that address composition of executable artifacts in a fashion similar to the algorithm presented here.

3.9 Summary and Discussion

In this chapter, we analyzed the requirements for supporting the composition of business processes with semantic technologies. 19 such requirements are listed in the body of this chapter, illustrating a wide variety of situations with which an ideal solution should be able to cope. Fulfilling all of these requirements is a challenging task, in technical and computational terms. We then described an approach to address the chosen set of these requirements, i.e.: how can we fulfill the chosen requirements to provide support to the process designer? This is achieved by making simplifying assumptions and by providing a conceptual framework as a high-level solution. We introduced the necessary components and described their interactions. Furthermore, we presented two approaches for making use of the components: a methodology for manual control and an automated process composition algorithm. The described components in combination with the information how to use them should allow the implementation of business process models by composing an executable process out of executable artifacts. While most of the basic components on this abstract level are part of the state of the art, the requirements, the methodology that uses the semantic technologies, and the process composition algorithms are contributions of this work.

Together, the components, the methodology, and the algorithm form an extensible framework for the refined problem, as described in Section 3.4.3. The modeling tool serves as the user entry point to the system; the composition component executes the process composition algorithm; the discovery component is used for finding single suitable available artifacts; task composition can combine multiple artifacts; the auto-completion component suggests artifacts that look promising at a given point in the process during modeling; the mediation component bridges heterogeneities; and the validators evaluate whether the composition satisfies a number of properties, such as adherence to policies and regulations.

The framework facilitates reuse of existing executable artifacts, and by doing so, eases the projection from the conceptual modeling level to executable processes. An emphasis is put on activities for quality assurance that benefit from semantic annotations. The increased quality and the further support aim for a shortened effort for process design and implementation, more generally also referred to as *Total Cost of Development (TCD)*.

Table 3.1. Overview over requirements addressed by the conceptual framework. A requirement number is shown in a cell if the respective component addresses this requirement; numbers in brackets signify that the corresponding requirement is only addressed partially.

	Modeling Extension Requirements	Fundamental Requirements	Nonfunctional Requirements	Situational Requirements
Discovery		5, (8)	13, (14)	
Task Composition		6, 7, (5)		
Auto-Completion				19
Default validation	1, 2, (3), (4),		(16)	
Further validation			12, 15, 16	
Not addressed		9, 10, 11		17, 18

With respect to the requirements from Section 3.2, the emphasis is on the modeling extension requirements and the service-related fundamental requirements. Further, all of the NFP requirements are, at least in part, supported through the framework – mostly through the additional validators. With the exception of auto-completion, the situational requirements are not addressed in this framework. In more detail, the components address the requirements as shown in Table 3.1.

Due to the availability and suitability of the available components, we develop detailed solutions for task composition (in particular Requirement 7) in Chapter 5 and verification of annotated processes (specifically Requirements 1 and 2) in the next chapter. For a number of other (partially) addressed requirements (3, 4, 5, 6, 8, 12, 13, 14, 15, 16, 19) we do not go into more detail than the conceptual framework's description. However, our additional work that is not described in more detail within the scope of this book addresses also auto-completion (Requirement 19, [39]) and compliance checking (Requirement 15, [115, 313]).

4

Verification of Annotated Process Models

Semantic annotations in business process models enable additional automatic checks to analyze if the way in which a process arranges the activities is correct – i.e., if the process model is consistent with respect to the control flow, the semantic annotations, and the domain ontology-based background knowledge which is now available. This chapter[1] deals specifically with the latter two kinds of checks, which we term *verification of annotated process models*. This kind of verification assumes that the process is correct in terms of control flow, and proceeds to check whether the process is correct with respect to the semantic annotations and their ontological axiomatization. As such, classical verification techniques become a pre-process to the verification of annotated process models. This form of verification should be able to check questions as the ones raised in the modeling extension requirements from Section 3.2: are there any two activities in the process that may be executed in parallel and that have conflicting effects? If we want to execute a service at a certain point in a process, can we always do that – i.e., is its precondition always satisfied? Given the annotations of conditions, can every activity in the process be reached, i.e., is there a valid execution using that activity in the presence of the annotation?

In relation to the conceptual framework outlined in the previous chapter, the techniques described in this chapter deal with the activity "Semantic Validation" from Figures 3.3, 3.8, and 3.9 – more specifically we see them as the default validator (cf. Section 3.5.6). In order to enable readers to consume this and the next chapter after breaks (or in isolation), we do not base their descriptions completely on the rest of the work. This results in a few redundancies in the explanations, which we try to keep on a minimal level. We now give an overview of the verification techniques discussed in this chapter.

---

[1] Parts of this chapter have been published: [314, 315].

4.1 Overview

Nowadays, the verification of control-flow correctness is well understood as an important step before deploying executable business process models. In this context, the soundness criterion and its derivatives, cf. Section 2.1.4 or, e.g., [292, 68, 239, 203], are typically used to check whether proper completion is possible or even guaranteed. Tools like Woflan [305] provide the functionality to efficiently verify soundness based on Petri Nets theory.

Control-flow soundness is a necessary condition for correctness. However, it covers only the control-flow perspective of the process model. To assure that a process model indeed behaves as expected, it is necessary to take into account what the individual activities in the process – the activities whose order of execution is governed by the process – actually do when they are executed: What are the prerequisites for the activities to execute successfully? How do they affect the state of the world in case they are executed? Traditional workflow models do not contain any information about this, apart from the naming of the activities. Such naming may be sufficient for simple applications in closed domains, where the behavior of the activities is not overly complex and/or known in detail to all persons involved. For more complex applications, however, a more powerful means of describing the semantics of activities is in order. This is particularly true if the individual activities in the process will be executed by different agents (persons or computers) in a heterogeneous and distributed environment. The first question then is: How should we describe the semantics of activities?

Essentially this same question has been addressed, since several years, in the area of Semantic Web services (cf. Section 2.3.4). Approaches such as OWL-S [12, 284] and the Web Service Modeling Ontology (WSMO) [253, 61] are in use. At a particular level of abstraction, called "service profile" in OWL-S and "capability level" in WSMO, Web services are perceived as functions with a single entry and exit point. This corresponds well to the individual activities in a workflow. The profile/capability of a Web service is described in terms of a precondition, a logical formula capturing the prerequisites of the service, as well as a postcondition (which we will also refer to as effect), a logical formula capturing how the service affects the state of the world. The formulas are stated relative to the vocabulary of an ontology, which formalizes the underlying domain, i.e., the "world" in which the service executes. The use of ontologies facilitates the precise formulation of the domain structure and its characteristic properties, through ontology axioms. Such precise domain descriptions are useful for precisely capturing preconditions/effects. Also, they reduce ambiguities in the communication among heterogeneous agents.

Following recent work in the area of Semantic Business Process Management (cf. Section 2.3.5), particularly following [74, 71, 40], we adopt these notions from the Semantic Web services area for making explicit the semantics of workflow activities. For the rest of this chapter, we will assume that semantic annotations have been designed, i.e., we assume a domain ontology formalizing the business domain in which a process executes, and we assume a logical precondition and effect for the activities in the process. We will state further below the precise formalism used for those annotations. The research question we address is that of verification: Does the control flow interact correctly with the behavior of the individual activities? Precisely, we address the following four verification tasks:

- **Effect conflicts:** Are there activities whose effects are in conflict, but that may be executed in parallel?
- **Precondition conflicts:** Are there parallel activities where the effect of one activity is in conflict with the precondition of the other?
- **Reachability:** Are there activities that will never be reached by the execution?
- **Executability:** Are there activities whose respective preconditions are not guaranteed to be true whenever they can be executed?

Note that, in this verification, we go far beyond what is possible based on activity names. We are able to conveniently express and check how particular aspects of the preconditions/effects of some activities affect particular aspects of other activities. For example, activity A may not be reachable because activity B has an effect invalidating the preconditions of activities C and D, if the workflow is such that B must be executed before C and D, and either C or D must be executed before A.

Verification of this kind is particularly natural and relevant in the branch of SBPM that aims at exploiting semantic annotations and Semantic Web services to help bridge the gap between high-level process models and the actual IT infrastructure (c.f. [130, 316] and Section 2.3.5). In that approach, the functions realized by the IT infrastructure are provided as Web services, and the Web services are annotated following the OWL-S/WSMO service profile/capability exactly as above. Then, implementing the process – binding its activities to Web services – corresponds to well-researched notions of Semantic Web service discovery and composition (see the previous or the next Chapter or, e.g., [214, 174, 181, 135]). However, modeling is an error-prone activity, and so this scenario calls for verification techniques. Prior to trying to bind the process, verification should help to ensure that the process model as such makes sense. Also, even after the binding, verification is useful since it may reveal flaws that were not visible at the abstraction level of the original model, as argued in the previous chapter.

Traditional verification techniques, as considered in the workflow community (e.g. [301]) and the model checking community (e.g. [57]), do not deal with ontologies, i.e., they do not allow ontological axiomatizations in the descriptions of the systems to be verified. It is important to note here the particular role that ontology axioms play in our context. Many existing verification techniques are heavily based on logic, i.e., on the manipulation of formulas representing certain properties of the system to be checked, such as the set of states the system can reach within a given number of steps. However, the semantic descriptions considered here formalize the behavior of the system, not its properties. The ontology axioms are part of the execution semantics of the process; they are like "physical laws" in that regard. For example, the ontology might say that a claim can never be accepted and rejected at the same time. Then, if a claim is rejected, by the physical law of the domain it is not accepted. For a more complex example, presume our ontology contains the four-eyes-principle, stating (amongst other things) that a payment is accepted provided it has been accepted by both reviewers. We encode this using the predicates claimAcceptedRevA(x), claimAcceptedRevB(x), claimAccepted(x), and the axiom $\forall x$: claimAcceptedRevA$(x) \land$ claimAcceptedRevB$(x) \Rightarrow$ claimAccepted(x). Presume that, in our current state, x has been accepted by both A and B. Presume we execute an activity that cancels x, with the effect $\neg$claimAccepted(x). What is the outcome state? Certainly, $\neg$claimAccepted(x) will hold. However, due to physical law, this means that either claimAcceptedRevA(x), or claimAcceptedRevB(x), or both, must have been invalidated. Hence there are several possibilities for the state after execution of the activity. Which of those possibilities should we consider?

Closely related questions have been investigated for a very long time in the AI actions and change literature, e.g. [322, 45, 177, 131]. It has been investigated in depth how the outcome of actions (which correspond to the activities in our context) should be defined, and how complex it is to compute that outcome. In our work, we follow the "possible models approach" (PMA) suggested by Winslett [322], which is in wide-spread use and, in particular, underlies most formalisms relating to the execution of Semantic Web services, e.g. [182, 17, 65]. The PMA admits all outcome states that comply with the action effect and the axioms, and that differ from the previous state in a minimal way. Intuitively, "minimality" here ensures that the world does not change without a reason. The most simple example for this is that of a credit card C1, which is of course not affected by a booking made via another credit card C2 – in other words, if the status of C1 was also different in the outcome state, then the change made with respect to the previous state would not be minimal. In the example above, we concede that either claimAcceptedRevA(x) or claimAcceptedRevB(x) are invalidated; but not both, because that would not be a minimal change. Intuitively, since x was canceled, something bad must have happened, namely either A or B must have revoked their acceptance. While, of course, both may be the case, this seems an unnecessarily strong assumption and is hence not considered. Note that it is important to sensibly restrict the outcome states, since otherwise the verification is likely to report flaws where there are none (like, credit card C1 running out of budget as a consequence of booking via credit card C2).

In summary, the workflow community has devised formal machinery dealing with control-flow, and the AI actions and change community has devised formal machinery dealing with logical preconditions and effects in the presence of ontology axioms. Our work combines these two fields of research, hence devising the formal machinery required for dealing with semantic business process models, i.e., the combination of control-flow with logical axioms and preconditions/effects. To the best of our knowledge, ours is the first work considering such a combined formalism. There is a body of related work addressing the validation or verification of business process models extended beyond control-flow, e.g. [30, 214, 260, 245, 246, 183, 160, 184]. Some of those are related to our work. However, apart from other differences, none of those works combines workflows with AI actions and change, encompassing ontology axioms as physical laws, as we do. For the case where there are preconditions/effects, but no ontology axioms, results from Petri Net theory can be re-used to check reachability properties. This has previously been recognized by [214]. A detailed discussion of all these related works will be given in Section 4.8.

Our formalism for semantic business process models (as sketched out in Section 3.4.1) relies on a straightforward token passing semantics for the control-flow, and on the above-mentioned PMA for the semantics of activities. We define formally the set of possible executions of the process, where each state in the execution consists of two parts: the positions of the tokens, as well as a logical state, i.e., an interpretation of the logical propositions from the ontology vocabulary. We consider the following features: parallel and XOR splits/joins; structured loops in the form of subprocesses that may be repeated; preconditions/effects annotated at individual activities; conditions annotated at the outgoing edges of XOR splits, governing which edge is taken; conditions annotated at loops, governing whether a loop is repeated or exited. In this way we consider similar control flow primitives as BPEL and cover the major elements of process modeling languages like EPCs, BPMN, UML Activity Diagrams, and YAWL.

The XOR split and loop conditions, like the preconditions/effects, are logical formulas. For the sake of simplicity, we restrict all these formulas to be conjunctions of literals; richer annotations are a topic for future research.[2] Our ontology axioms take the form of universally quantified clauses, like the axiom $\forall x : \text{claimAcceptedRevA}(x) \land \text{claimAcceptedRevB}(x) \Rightarrow \text{claimAccepted}(x)$ in the example above, which is equivalent to the clause $\forall x : \neg\text{claimAcceptedRevA}(x) \lor \neg\text{claimAcceptedRevB}(x) \lor \text{claimAccepted}(x)$. Clauses can be used to state many typical domain properties, such as subsumption $\forall x : p(x) \implies q(x)$, disjointness $\forall x : \neg p(x) \lor \neg q(x)$, or coverage $\forall x : p(x) \implies q_1(x) \lor \cdots \lor q_n(x)$. The investigation of other kinds of axioms, such as Description Logics (cf. Section 2.3.3 or [18]), is an open topic.

We formalize the verification tasks mentioned above, addressing effect conflicts, precondition conflicts, reachability, and executability. We examine the

---

[2] Note, however, that some extensions can easily be covered by compiling them back into our formalism. For example, an activity with several alternative effects, one of which occurs non-deterministically, is equivalent to an XOR split/join construct containing one activity for each alternative effect.

borderline between classes of processes that can, or cannot, be verified in polynomial time. Apart from the theoretical relevance of this borderline, it is important in settings where the runtime of the verification is a critical issue. We expect this to typically be the case. In particular, we target the application where a modeler uses the verification frequently, during the modeling, to check whether there are any bugs. In that setting, the runtime is bounded by the patience of a human. Hence, for the verification to be useful, its answer should be instantaneous.

For effect and precondition conflicts, the borderline between tractable and intractable verification is the same as that of the logic underlying the ontology axioms. Whether or not two activities are parallel depends only on the control-flow, not on the semantic annotations; control-flow parallelism can be determined in polynomial time.[3] Once parallelism has been determined, checking for precondition/effect conflicts reduces to satisfiability tests. We need to test, for every pair of parallel activities, whether the conjunction of the ontology axioms with the respective precondition/effect is satisfiable. With our particular formalism for axioms, this means that we inherit the well-known tractability/intractability results for clausal formulas. Unrestricted formulas are intractable, but, e.g., Horn formulas [147] (where each clause contains at most one positive literal) and binary formulas [14] (where each clause contains at most two literals) are tractable.

For reachability and executability, matters are more complicated, because those tasks are more tightly linked to the overall behavior of the process. We show that neither can be checked in polynomial time (unless $\mathbf{P} = \mathbf{NP}$) if we allow either of: unrestricted axioms; Horn axioms; XOR conditions; or loop conditions. We further show that, even in the class of what we call *basic* processes, with binary axioms and without XOR/loop conditions, it is $\mathbf{NP}$-hard to test reachability and it is $\mathbf{coNP}$-hard to test whether or not a particular activity is executable. Our positive result is that, for basic processes, we can test in polynomial time whether *all* activities are executable. The proof is constructive, i.e., we devise a polynomial-time verification algorithm. The algorithm performs propagation steps over the process structure, maintaining at every edge in the graph a set of literals that is deemed to be true whenever that edge carries a token. Starting out from all possible literals annotated to each edge, the algorithm deletes some literals in every propagation step – namely those that are known to be possibly untrue in some state where this edge carries a token. E.g., after the algorithm propagates over a task node n with effect $\neg A(c)$, we know that $A(c)$ cannot be true at any time when the outgoing edge of n is active (given the absence of effect conflicts). Once a fixpoint in the propagation is reached, the remaining literals are guaranteed

---

[3] This follows from earlier results in Petri Net theory. [164] devise an algorithm for free-choice Petri Nets that determines concurrency in cubic time. We improve on this result by devising an algorithm that exploits the particular structure of our control-flows, and runs in quadratic time. See Section 4.4 for more details.

to be true. The fixpoint nature of the algorithm stems from possible loops in the process: while $B(c)$ may be necessarily true in the first iteration of a loop, this may not be the case in the second or n^{th} iteration. If any non-executable activities exist, then the remaining literals are potentially a subset of the guaranteed literals, i.e., overly many literals may have been deleted (at any edge, not only at those connected to non-executable activities); if all activities are executable, that cannot happen. Hence all activities are executable iff every precondition literal of every activity remains at the ingoing edge of the respective activity. This can be tested exactly with our methods. Executability of all activities implies reachability of all activities (in a process with sound control-flow), so in this way we can establish correctness for basic processes. The intricate details are described in more detail throughout the chapter.

Once conflicts have been detected, the question how they may be resolved arises. For the purpose of suggesting possible resolutions, we provide a set of initial resolution strategies. We here rely in part on task composition as described in the next chapter, and in part we suggest changing the control flow of the process to avoid a conflicting situation.

The chapter is organized as follows. Section 4.2 introduces our formalism for semantic business process models. Section 4.3 formalizes the four verification tasks we consider, and states a few basic facts about their dependencies. Section 4.4 presents our results for the verification of effect and precondition conflicts. Section 4.5 contains our negative results on the computational complexity of reachability and executability checking. Section 4.6 presents the fixpoint algorithm outlined above, and details its relevant properties. Section 4.7 discusses how conflicts, once detected, may be resolved. Section 4.8 discusses related work, Section 4.9 concludes the chapter. For the sake of readability, the text gives only proof sketches. Full proofs are available in Appendix A.1.

4.2 Annotated Process Graphs

In this section, we introduce our formalism for semantic business process models. As stated, the formalism combines control-flow (adopted from the workflow community) with preconditions/effects (adopted from the Semantic Web service and AI communities). For the sake of readability, we first consider the former in isolation, then enrich it with the latter.

4.2.1 Process Graphs

Our process models are inspired by the control flow elements provided by process modeling languages like UML Activity Diagrams, EPCs, BPMN, BPEL, and YAWL. They cover the most common routing elements (XOR-split and XOR-join, AND-split, and AND-join). They cover a powerful notion of

structured loops, forming sub-graphs within a process graph.[4] Our analysis
methods apply to any process model that can be expressed in terms of these
constructs.

Our formal definition is adopted from [304], with straightforward notions
added to capture structured loops.

Definition 4.1. *There are two kinds of Process Graphs:* atomic *process
graphs, and* complex *process graphs.*

1. *An* atomic process graph *is a directed graph* $P = (N, E)$, *where N is
   the disjoint union of* $\{n_0, n_+\}$ *(start node, stop node), N_T (task nodes),
   N_{PS} (parallel splits), N_{PJ} (parallel joins), N_{XS} (XOR splits), and N_{XJ}
   (XOR joins). For $n \in N$, $in(n)/out(n)$ denotes the set of incoming/
   outgoing edges of n. We require that: P is acyclic; for every split node
   n, $|in(n)| = 1$ and $|out(n)| > 1$; for every join node n, $|in(n)| > 1$ and
   $|out(n)| = 1$; for every $n \in N_T$, $|in(n)| = 1$ and $|out(n)| = 1$; $|in(n_0)| = 0$
   and $|out(n_0)| = 1$ and vice versa for n_+; every node $n \in N$ is on a path
   from the start to the stop node.*
2. *Say $Q_1, \ldots, Q_m$ are process graphs. Then a* complex process graph *is a
   triple $\mathcal{P} = (N, E, \lambda)$, where (N, E) is like an atomic process graph except
   that there is an additional kind of nodes, N_L, called* loop *nodes, where
   $|in(n)| = 1$ and $|out(n)| = 1$ for every $n \in N_L$. λ is a bijection from N_L
   into $\{Q_1, \ldots, Q_m\}$.*

$Q_1, \ldots, Q_m$ *are sub-graphs of $\mathcal{P}$; a sub-graph of any Q_i is (recursively) also
a sub-graph of $\mathcal{P}$. For any process graph Q, we denote by $Sub(Q)$ the set of
graphs containing Q as well as all its sub-graphs. We denote $e_0 := out(n_0)$ and
$e_+ := in(n_+)$. We use superscripts in order to distinguish constructs belonging
to particular sub-graphs; e.g., N^{Q_2} is the node set of sub-graph Q_2. Further,
we use $\mathcal{N}$ to denote the set of all nodes appearing in $\mathcal{P}$ itself or in any of its
sub-graphs, and we use $\mathcal{E}$ to denote the set of all edges appearing in $\mathcal{P}$ itself
or in any of its sub-graphs.*

*We require that the direct sub-graph relation is a tree; precisely, the graph
$(Sub(\mathcal{P}), \{(Q, Q') \mid ex.\ n \in N^Q : \lambda^Q(n) = Q'\})$ is a tree with root $\mathcal{P}$. Further,
we require that, for any $Q, Q' \in Sub(\mathcal{P})$ with $Q \neq Q'$, $N^Q \cap N^{Q'} = \emptyset$, i.e.,
the same node may not be re-used across several sub-graphs.*

If the context is clear, we omit the superscript indicating the process referred
to. We do not distinguish between atomic and complex process graphs unless
necessary, and we assume by convention a void function λ for atomic process
graphs.

Atomic process graphs are (sub-)graphs without loop nodes, whereas complex process graphs can contain loop nodes. A loop node is "implemented" by
a sub-graph, which, again, may be complex or atomic. The λ-function maps

---

[4] BPEL [8] directly enforces such a structure. Recent process graph parsing techniques can be applied to untangle loops and move them into subprocesses [329, 303].

from loop nodes to sub-graphs. We require the compositional sub-graph structure to be a tree. We will generally refer to the root of the tree as the "top-level process", and refer to it with $\mathcal{P}$; subprocesses will generally be referred to with $\mathcal{Q}$. Note the difference between the set of nodes and edges of a single process graph, N, E, and the nodes and edges of all sub-graphs combined, $\mathcal{N}, \mathcal{E}$.

Example 4.2. Figure 4.1 shows our running example, serving to illustrate many of our definitions. The example is based on a process model from the IBM Insurance Application Architecture [154] (a large collection of best practice process models from insurance industry); the model was published in [165]. It defines how a claim is handled by an insurer. For the purpose of our presentation, we slightly adapted and simplified the model.

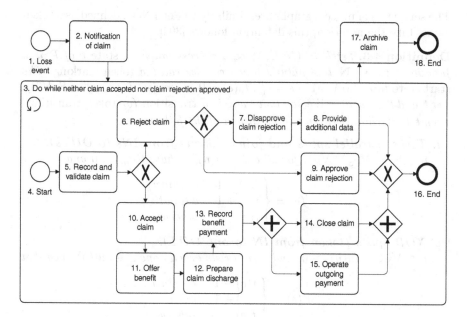

Fig. 4.1. Our running example: a claims handling process, adapted from [165]

The process starts when a loss event occurs (step 1 in Figure 4.1). The insurance company is notified of the claim (step 2). Then a subprocess (step 3) is repeated until either the claim has been accepted, or its rejection has been approved. In the subprocess, first the claim is recorded and validated. Then the insurer chooses to either accept or reject the claim.[5] In the former

---

[5] In the original model, this choice is encoded into a task node with non-deterministic outcome, governing which branch of the XOR split to take. From the perspective of verification, i.e., as far as the possible execution traces are concerned, the two models are equivalent. The model as in Figure 4.1 is more convenient for our illustration purposes.

case, an according benefit is offered and paid, and the claim is closed (steps 10-15). In the latter case, the rejection needs to be either approved (step 9) or disapproved (step 7). If the rejection is disapproved, additional data needs be provided (step 8). Once the subprocess completes, the claim is archived in the final step, number 17 in Figure 4.1. Note that step 14 can be executed in parallel to step 15, due to the parallel split and join nodes.

For illustration purposes, say we write $\mathcal{P}$ for the overall process, $n \in N_L^{\mathcal{P}}$ for the loop node (step 3), and $\mathcal{Q}$ for the subprocess shown as the content of the loop node. Then, the subgraph relation has the root $\mathcal{P}$, and the only subgraph $\mathcal{Q}$ with $\lambda^{\mathcal{P}}(n) = \mathcal{Q}$. The start edge $e_0^{\mathcal{Q}}$ of the subprocess is the edge from the start node (step 4) to "5. Record and validate claim", and the respective end edge $e_+^{\mathcal{Q}}$ is the single incoming edge of node 16, $n_+^{\mathcal{Q}}$.

The semantics of process graphs are, similarly to Petri Nets, defined as a token game. Like the notation, this definition follows [304].

Definition 4.3. Let $\mathcal{P} = (N, E, \lambda)$ be a process graph. A state t of $\mathcal{P}$ is a function $t : \mathcal{E} \mapsto \mathbf{N}$ (the natural numbers); we call t a token marking. The start state t_0 is $t_0(e) = 1$ if $e = e_0^{\mathcal{P}}$, $t_0(e) = 0$ otherwise. Let $\mathcal{Q}, \mathcal{Q}' \in Sub(\mathcal{P})$. Let t and t' be states. We say that there is a transition (or token-transition) from t to t' via n, written $t \xrightarrow{n} t'$, iff one of the following holds:

1. **Tasks, parallel splits and joins (tokens from INs to OUTs).**
   $n \in \mathcal{N}_T \cup \mathcal{N}_{PS} \cup \mathcal{N}_{PJ}$, for all $e_{in} \in in(n)$ we have $t(e_{in}) > 0$ and

$$t'(e) = \begin{cases} t(e) - 1 & e \in in(n) \\ t(e) + 1 & e \in out(n) \\ t(e) & otherwise \end{cases}$$

2. **XOR splits (token from IN to one OUT).**
   $n \in \mathcal{N}_{XS}$, $t(in(n)) > 0$, and there exists exactly one $e' \in out(n)$ such that

$$t'(e) = \begin{cases} t(e) - 1 & e = in(n) \\ t(e) + 1 & e = e' \\ t(e) & otherwise \end{cases}$$

3. **XOR joins (token from one IN to OUT).**
   $n \in \mathcal{N}_{XJ}$ and there exists $e' \in in(n)$ such that $t(e') > 0$ and

$$t'(e) = \begin{cases} t(e) - 1 & e = e' \\ t(e) + 1 & e = out(n) \\ t(e) & otherwise \end{cases}$$

4. **Entering a loop (push token downwards).**
   $n \in N_L^{\mathcal{Q}}$ with $\lambda^{\mathcal{Q}}(n) = \mathcal{Q}'$, $t(in(n)) > 0$, and

$$t'(e) = \begin{cases} t(e) - 1 & e = in(n) \\ t(e) + 1 & e = e_0^{\mathcal{Q}'} \\ t(e) & otherwise \end{cases}$$

5. **Repeating a loop (put token back on start).**
   $n = n_+^{\mathcal{Q}}$, $t(in(n)) > 0$, and

   $$t'(e) = \begin{cases} t(e) - 1 & e = in(n) \\ t(e) + 1 & e = e_0^{\mathcal{Q}} \\ t(e) & \text{otherwise} \end{cases}$$

6. **Exiting a loop (push token upwards).**
   $n = n_+^{\mathcal{Q}}$ with $\mathcal{Q} = \lambda^{\mathcal{Q}'}(n')$, $t(in(n)) > 0$, and

   $$t'(e) = \begin{cases} t(e) - 1 & e = in(n) \\ t(e) + 1 & e = out(n') \\ t(e) & \text{otherwise} \end{cases}$$

An execution path, or token-execution path, is a transition sequence $t_0 \overset{n_1}{\to}$ $t_1 \overset{n_2}{\to} t_2 \dots t_{k-1} \overset{n_k}{\to} t$. A state t is reachable, or token-reachable, if there exists an execution path ending in t. We say t' is reachable from t $(t \to t')$ if there exists a transition sequence such that $t \overset{n_1}{\to} t_1 \overset{n_2}{\to} t_2 \dots t_{k-1} \overset{n_k}{\to} t'$.

The tokens are carried by edges, and the state of the process is given by the position of all tokens, the token marking. $t(e)$ denotes the number of tokens on an edge e for a given token marking t. A node which passes a token from (one or all of) its incoming edges to (one or all of) its outgoing edges is said to be executed. Token passing from edge e to e' and from token marking t to t' is denoted as $t'(e) = t(e) - 1$ and $t'(e') = t(e') + 1$.

Task nodes are executed when a token on the incoming edge is consumed and a token on the outgoing edge is produced. The execution of an XOR (parallel) split node consumes the token on its incoming edge and produces a token on one (all) of its outgoing edges, whereas an XOR (parallel) join node consumes a token on one (all) of its incoming edges and produces a token on its outgoing edge. A loop node consumes a token from its incoming edge and produces a token on the start edge of the sub-graph that is associated with the loop node. The execution of the end node of a sub-graph consumes a token from its incoming edge e_+, and produces a token either on the start edge e_0 of the same process graph (repeating the sub-graph's execution) or on the outgoing edge of the loop node (exiting the loop). Note that this is a "do-while" semantics: the loop is executed at least once.

Soundness, first introduced by van der Aalst in [292], is an important correctness criterion for business process models – cf. Section 2.1.4. The soundness property is defined for workflow nets, i.e., a Petri Net with one source and one sink. A workflow net is sound iff: (1) for every state reachable from the source, there must exist a firing sequence to the sink (option to complete); (2) there is no reachable state which has a token both in the sink and in some other edge (proper completion); and (3) there are no dead transitions, i.e., for every transition there is an execution path that can fire it [292]. We adopt this definition. Van der Aalst shows that soundness of a Workflow net is equivalent to liveness and boundedness of the corresponding short-circuited Petri Net. It follows easily from earlier results [299] that process graphs as per Definitions 4.1 and 4.3 map to free-choice Petri Nets, where no output branch of an XOR split $n \in N_{XS}$ can be disabled by other choices in the process graph.

We will later utilize a property of soundness related to so-called contact situations. A contact situation is a marking in which a node has tokens on its incoming edges as well as on its outgoing edges. Such a situation can never occur in a sound process.

Proposition 4.4. *Let* $\mathcal{P} = (N, E, \lambda)$ *be a sound process graph. Then there do not exist a token-reachable token marking* t, *a node* $n \in \mathcal{N}$, *and edges* $e \in in(n), e' \in out(n)$ *such that* $t(e) > 0$ *and* $t(e') > 0$.

Proof: Assume a sound process graph $\mathcal{P}$ with a node n such that $t(e) > 0$ and $t(e') > 0$ for $e \in in(n), e' \in out(n)$. Since there is a path from n to the sink n_+ and $\mathcal{P}$ is sound, the nodes on the path can propagate the token from e' to n_+. Since $\mathcal{P}$ is free-choice, this firing sequence does not require the token from e. This means that there can still be a token on edge e after the sink n_+ has received a token via the firing from e'. The latter is a contradiction to condition (2) of the soundness assumption. ∎

4.2.2 Semantic Annotations

For the semantic annotations, we use standard notions from logic, involving logical *predicates* and *constants*. Predicates provide the formal vocabulary, referring to properties of tuples of constants. Constants correspond to the entities of interest at process execution time.[6] We denote predicates with G, H, I and constants with c, d, e. *Facts* are predicates grounded with constants, *Literals* are possibly negated facts. If l is a literal, then $\neg l$ denotes l's opposite ($\neg p$ if $l = p$ and p if $l = \neg p$); if L is a set of literals then $\neg L$ denotes $\{\neg l \mid l \in L\}$. We identify sets L of literals with their conjunction $\bigwedge_{l \in L} l$. Given a set P of predicates and a set C of constants, $P[C]$ denotes the set of all literals based on P and C; if arbitrary constants are allowed, we write $P[]$.

A *theory* $\mathcal{T}$ is a closed (no free variables) first-order formula. Given a set C of constants, $\mathcal{T}[C]$ denotes $\mathcal{T}$ with quantifiers interpreted over C. For the purpose of our formal semantics, $\mathcal{T}$ can be arbitrary. For computational purposes, we will consider the following standard restrictions. A *clause* is a universally quantified disjunction of atoms, e.g., $\forall x. \neg G(x) \lor \neg H(x)$. A clause is *Horn* if it contains at most one positive literal. A clause is *binary* if it contains at most two literals. A theory is Horn (binary) if it is a conjunction of Horn (binary) clauses.

---

[6] Hence our constants correspond to BPEL "data variables" [8]; note that the term "variables" in our context is reserved for variables as used in logic, quantifying over constants.

An *ontology* Ω is a pair $(P, \mathcal{T})$ where P is a set of predicates (Ω's formal terminology) and $\mathcal{T}$ is a theory over P (constraining the behavior of the application domain encoded by Ω). For complexity considerations, we will often assume *fixed arity*, i.e., a fixed upper bound on the arity of the predicates P. This is a realistic assumption because predicate arities are typically very small in practice (e.g., in Description Logics the maximum arity is 2). Further, we will sometimes assume *fixed nesting*, i.e., a fixed upper bound on the number of variables quantified over in any single clause. Again, such a restriction appears reasonable based on practical examples.

Definition 4.5. *An* annotated process graph *is a tuple* $\mathcal{P} = (N, E, \lambda, \Omega, \alpha)$ *where* (N, E, λ) *is a process graph,* $\Omega = (P, \mathcal{T})$ *is an ontology, and the annotation* $\alpha = \{pre,\ eff,\ rcon,\ (con, pos)\}$ *is defined as follows (where* Π *denotes the powerset):*

- *pre is a partial function* $pre: \mathcal{N}_T \cup \{n_+^P\} \mapsto \Pi(P[])$ *mapping a task node or global end node to a set of literals (its* precondition*).*
- *eff is a partial function* $eff: \mathcal{N}_T \cup \{n_0^P\} \mapsto \Pi(P[])$ *mapping a task node or global start node to a set of literals (its* effect *or* postcondition*).*
- *rcon is a partial function* $rcon: \mathcal{N}_L \mapsto \Pi(P[])$ *mapping a loop node to a set of literals (its* repetition condition*).*
- *con is a partial function* $con: \{e \in \mathcal{E} | ex.n \in \mathcal{N}_{XS}: e \in out(n)\} \mapsto \Pi(P[])$ *mapping an XOR split's outgoing edge to a set of literals (its* condition*).*
- *pos is a partial function* $pos: \{e \in \mathcal{E} | ex.n \in \mathcal{N}_{XS}: e \in out(n)\} \mapsto \{1, \ldots, |out(n)|\}$ *mapping an XOR split's outgoing edge to an integer (its* position*, encoding the evaluation order of the XOR split).*

We require that:

- *There is no n such that $\mathcal{T} \wedge eff(n)$ is unsatisfiable or $\mathcal{T} \wedge pre(n)$ is unsatisfiable.*
- *There is no n such that $\mathcal{T} \wedge rcon(n)$ is unsatisfiable.*
- *There is no e such that $\mathcal{T} \wedge con(e)$ is unsatisfiable.*
- *$con(e)$ is defined iff $pos(e)$ is defined.*
- *There do not exist n, e, e' such that $e, e' \in out(n)$, $pos(e)$ and $pos(e')$ are defined, and $pos(e) = pos(e')$.*

Any task node, as well as the top-level end node, may have a precondition pre. Any task node, as well as the top-level start node, may have an effect eff. Loop nodes may have a repetition condition rcon, and the outgoing edges of an XOR split may have a condition con and an evaluation position pos. Note here the "may have" – all the annotation functions are partial, capturing the situation where only parts of the process can be sensibly annotated, or where a developer wants to run verification tests on a model whose annotations have not yet been completed.

As stated, the annotation of task nodes – atomic actions that might be implemented by Web service invocations – in terms of logical preconditions and effects closely follows Semantic Web service approaches such as OWL-S [12, 284] and WSMO [253, 61]. As also stated, all the involved sets of literals ($\text{pre}(n)$, $\text{eff}(n)$, $\text{con}(e)$, $\text{rcon}(n)$) will be interpreted as conjunctions.[7] We now formally define the semantics of annotated process graphs and give a more intuitive explanation below.

Definition 4.6. *Let* $\mathcal{P} = (N, E, \lambda, \Omega, \alpha)$ *be an annotated process graph. Let* C *be the set of all constants appearing in any of the annotated* $\text{pre}(n)$, $\text{eff}(n)$, $\text{rcon}(n)$, $\text{con}(e)$. *A state* s *of* $\mathcal{P}$ *is a pair* (t_s, i_s) *where* t *is a token marking and* i *is a logical interpretation* $i : P[C] \mapsto \{0, 1\}$. *A start state* s_0 *is* (t_0, i_0) *where* t_0 *is as in Definition 4.3, and* $i_0 \models T[C]$, *and* $i_0 \models \text{eff}(n_0^P)$ *in case* $\alpha(n_0^P)$ *is defined. Let* $\mathcal{Q}, \mathcal{Q}' \in \text{Sub}(\mathcal{P})$. *Let* s *and* s' *be states. We say that there is a* transition *from* s *to* s' *via* n, *written* $s \xrightarrow{n} s'$, *iff one of the following holds:*

1. **Parallel splits and joins (straightforward; no change of logical interpretation).**
   $n \in \mathcal{N}_{PS} \cup \mathcal{N}_{PJ}$, *for all* $e_{in} \in \text{in}(n)$ *we have* $t_s(e_{in}) > 0$, $i_s = i_{s'}$, *and* $t_s \xrightarrow{n} t_{s'}$ *according to Definition 4.3.*

2. **XOR joins (straightforward; no change of logical interpretation).**
   $n \in \mathcal{N}_{XJ}$, *there exists* $e' \in \text{in}(n)$ *such that* $t_s(e') > 0$, $i_s = i_{s'}$, *and* $t_s \xrightarrow{n} t_{s'}$ *according to Definition 4.3.*

3. **XOR splits (depends on condition; no change of logical interpretation).**
   $n \in \mathcal{N}_{XS}$, $t_s(\text{in}(n)) > 0$, $i_s = i_{s'}$, *and*

   $$t_{s'}(e) = \begin{cases} t_s(e) - 1 & e = \text{in}(n) \\ t_s(e) + 1 & e = e' \\ t_s(e) & \text{otherwise} \end{cases}$$

   where either $e' \in \text{out}(n)$ *and* $\alpha(e')$ *is undefined, or* $e' = \text{argmin}\{\text{pos}(e) \mid e \in \text{out}(n), \alpha(e) \text{ is defined}, i_s \models \text{con}(e)\}$.

4. **Entering a loop (condition not tested due to do-while semantics; no change of logical interpretation).**
   $n \in N_L^{\mathcal{Q}}$ *so that* $\lambda^{\mathcal{Q}}(n) = \mathcal{Q}'$, *with* $t_s(\text{in}(n)) > 0$, $i_s = i_{s'}$, *and*

   $$t_{s'}(e) = \begin{cases} t_s(e) - 1 & e = \text{in}(n) \\ t_s(e) + 1 & e = e_0^{\mathcal{Q}'} \\ t_s(e) & \text{otherwise} \end{cases}$$

---

[7] It is easy to extend our formalism to allow arbitrary formulas for $\text{pre}(n)$, $\text{eff}(n)$, $\text{con}(e)$, $\text{rcon}(n)$. The actual verification involving such formulas, however, is likely to lead to much harder decision problems, and remains an open topic for future work.

5. **Repeating a loop (condition must be true; no change of logical interpretation).**
$n = n_+^Q$ so that $Q = \lambda^{Q'}(n')$, $t_s(in(n)) > 0$, where either $\alpha(n')$ is undefined or $i_s \models rcon(n')$, with $i_s = i_{s'}$, and

$$t_{s'}(e) = \begin{cases} t_s(e) - 1 & e = in(n) \\ t_s(e) + 1 & e = e_0^Q \\ t_s(e) & otherwise \end{cases}$$

6. **Exiting a loop (condition must be false; no change of logical interpretation).**
$n = n_+^Q$ so that $Q = \lambda^{Q'}(n')$, $t_s(in(n)) > 0$, where either $\alpha(n')$ is undefined or $i_s \not\models rcon(n')$, with $i_s = i_{s'}$, and

$$t_{s'}(e) = \begin{cases} t_s(e) - 1 & e = in(n) \\ t_s(e) + 1 & e = out(n') \\ t_s(e) & otherwise \end{cases}$$

7. **Executing a task (affects the logical interpretation, may have ambiguous outcome).**
$n \in \mathcal{N}_T$, $t_s(in(n)) > 0$, $t_s \xrightarrow{n} t_{s'}$ according to Definition 4.3, and either: $\alpha(n)$ is undefined and $i_s = i_{s'}$; or $i_s \models pre(n)$ and $i_{s'} \in min(i_s, \mathcal{T}[C] \wedge eff(n))$ where $min(i_s, \mathcal{T}[C] \wedge eff(n))$ is defined to be the set of all i that satisfy $\mathcal{T}[C] \wedge eff(n)$ and that are minimal with respect to the order defined by $i_1 \leq i_2$ iff $|i_1 \cap i_s| \geq |i_2 \cap i_s|$ – i.e., the number of literals that changed from i_s to i_1 is smaller than the respective number for i_2.

An execution path *is a transition sequence* $s_0 \xrightarrow{n_1} s_1 \xrightarrow{n_2} s_2 \ldots s_{k-1} \xrightarrow{n_k} s$, *where* s_0 *is a start state. A state* s *is* reachable *if there exists an execution path ending in* s. *We say* s' *is reachable from* s ($s \rightarrow s'$) *if there exists a transition sequence such that* $s \xrightarrow{n_1} s_1 \xrightarrow{n_2} s_2 \ldots s_{k-1} \xrightarrow{n_k} s'$. *By* $\mathcal{S}^P$ *we denote the set of reachable states; where the process referred to is clear from the context, we will sometimes omit the superscript* P.

A state s of the process now consists of the token marking t in combination with the logical interpretation i. The interpretation assigns truth values to all logical facts formed from the relevant predicates and constants. To avoid clumsiness of language, we will usually drop the "logical" in "logical interpretations". Also, we will often overload s with i_s, writing e.g. $s \models \phi$ instead of $i_s \models \phi$. Further, we identify i_s with the set of literals that it contains.

An execution of the process starts with a token on the outgoing edge of the start node, and with any interpretation that complies with the start node's effect (if any) and the implications of the logical theory. Parallel splits and joins, as well as XOR joins, remain unaffected by the annotation. An XOR split, in contrast, either non-deterministically selects an outgoing edge without annotation, or it produces a token on the outgoing edge e with lowest position $pos(e)$ whose condition $con(e)$ is satisfied by the current interpretation, i_s. E.g., if an XOR split that is being executed has three outgoing edges e_1, e_2, e_3 with the annotation $pos(e_1) = 1, pos(e_2) = 2, pos(e_3) = 3$ and $con(e_1) = \{A(c) \wedge B(c)\}, con(e_2) = \{B(c)\}, con(e_3) = \{\}$, then we can see the following behavior: if $A(c)$ and $B(c)$ are true, then e_1 receives the token; if only $B(c)$ is true, then e_2 receives the token; otherwise e_3 receives the token; Note that this is a hybrid between a deterministic and a non-deterministic semantics, depending on how many output edges are annotated. If all edges are annotated, then we have a case distinction as handled in, e.g., BPEL, where the first case (smallest position) with satisfied condition is executed (Section 11.2 in [8]). If no edges are annotated, then the analysis must foresee that a case distinction may be created later on during the modeling. No assumptions can be made on the form of that case distinction, so any possibility must be taken into account. Definition 4.3 just generalizes these two extremes in the straightforward way.

Entering a loop node also remains the same as in Definition 4.3, since each loop is executed at least once (do-while semantics). If the annotation of the loop node is undefined, then we can non-deterministically choose whether to repeat or exit the loop. If the repetition condition rcon is defined, then the loop is repeated iff the current state's interpretation satisfies rcon.

The execution of any routing node does not affect the logical interpretation. In contrast, the execution of an annotated task node (which is possible only if the current state satisfies the precondition pre) changes the interpretation according to the effect eff and the implications of $\mathcal{T}$. The tricky bit lies in the definition of the possible outcome states i'. The semantics defines this to be *the set of all i' that comply with $\mathcal{T}$ and $eff(n)$, and that differ minimally from i.*[8] This draws on the AI literature for a solution to the *frame* and *ramification* problems. The latter problem refers to the need to make additional inferences from $eff(n)$, as implied by $\mathcal{T}$. This is reflected in the requirement that i' complies with both. The frame problem refers to the need to not change the previous state arbitrarily – e.g., if an activity makes a payment via a credit card C1, then any other credit card C2 should not be affected. This is reflected in the requirement that i' differs minimally from i, such that there is no i'' which can fulfill the constraints with fewer changes. As explained in the introduction, this semantics follows the so-called possible models approach (PMA) [322], which underlies most formalisms relating to the execution of Semantic Web services [182, 17, 65]. Alternative semantics from the AI literature (see [131] for an excellent overview) could be used in principle; this is a topic for future research.

We next give two examples. The first provides the semantic annotations for our running example.

---

[8] It may be noted that, in a strict mathematical sense, the defined order is neither a partial nor a total order: antisymmetry is not given.

Example 4.7. Consider again Figure 4.1. The semantic annotations of the task nodes are listed in Table 4.1. The ontology specifies the following axioms:

(1) $\forall x : \neg\text{claimAccepted}(x) \lor \neg\text{claimRejected}(x)$

(2) $\forall x, y : \neg\text{benefitOffered}(x, y) \lor \neg\text{benefitPosted}(x, y)$

  $\forall x, y : \neg\text{benefitOffered}(x, y) \lor \neg\text{benefitPaid}(x, y)$

  $\forall x, y : \neg\text{benefitPosted}(x, y) \lor \neg\text{benefitPaid}(x, y)$

(3) $\forall x : \text{claimRejectionDisapproved}(x) \Rightarrow \neg\text{claimRejected}(x)$

Axiom (1) means that no claim may be both accepted and rejected at the same time; in other words, a claim may be in at most one of its possible states. Similarly, axioms (2) mean that no benefit may be in more than one of its possible states. Axiom (3) expresses a somewhat more subtle dependency, namely that a claim is no longer rejected if its rejection has been disapproved.

Table 4.1. Preconditions and effects of all task nodes in the process from Figure 4.1. Node labels abbreviated.

Node	Precondition	Postcondition
1. Loss event		lossEvent(e)
2. Notification	lossEvent(e)	claim(c)
5. Record claim	claim(c)	claimRecorded(c), claimValidated(c)
6. Reject claim	claim(c)	claimRejected(c)
7. Disapprove rejection	claimRejected(c)	claimRejectionDisapproved(c)
8. Additional data	claim(c)	claimChanged(c)
9. Approve rejection	claimRejected(c)	claimRejectionApproved(c)
10. Accept claim	claim(c)	claimAccepted(c)
11. Offer benefit	claimAccepted(c)	benefit(b), benefitOffered(b,c)
12. Prepare discharge	benefitOffered(b,c)	dischargePrepared(c)
13. Record payment	benefitOffered(b,c), dischargePrepared(c)	benefitPosted(b,c)
14. Close claim	claimFinalized(c)	claimClosed(c)
15. Payment	benefitPosted(b,c)	benefitPaid(b,c)
17. Archive claim	claim(c)	claimArchived(c)

The following example illustrates the subtleties of the PMA semantics.

Example 4.8. We first illustrate the ramification problem. We show how ontology axioms may lead to "side effects", i.e., to literals that are not mentioned explicitly in the effect annotation of a task node n, but that change their value nevertheless when n is executed.

  Assume, in the process from Figure 4.1, a hypothetical task n that one can choose to execute after step 10, and that revokes the acceptance of the claim.

Suppose for simplicity that n is annotated with eff$(n) = \{\text{claimRejected}(c)\}$ (rather than with a new fact representing claim revocation as opposed to claim rejection). Say we execute n in a state s where the claim is accepted, i.e., $i_s(\text{claimAccepted}(c)) = 1$. Which are the possible outcome states s', with $s \xrightarrow{n} s'$? By the definition of $min(i_s, \mathcal{T}[C] \wedge \text{eff}(n))$ in Definition 4.6, any such state s' must satisfy the conjunction of effect eff(n) and axioms $\mathcal{T}$. In particular, s' must satisfy $\forall x : \neg\text{claimAccepted}(x) \vee \neg\text{claimRejected}(x)$, c.f. the previous example; we refer to this axiom with ϕ in the following. Together with the effect claimRejected(c), ϕ of course implies that s' must satisfy $i_{s'}(\text{claimAccepted}(c)) = 0$. That is, the value of claimAccepted(c) is changed as a side-effect of applying n. Sloppily formulated, when we apply the effect claimRejected(c) to s, then ϕ is invalidated and we need to "repair" it by switching the value of claimAccepted(c).

To illustrate the frame problem, we now show how ontology axioms may lead to ambiguities in the outcome state, namely to several alternative outcome states depending on how and to what extent the previous state is kept intact. Note first that the clause ϕ is binary (contains only two literals). This means that, whenever one of the literals is invalidated, the other literal follows necessarily. That is, there is only one option to "repair" the clause. For that reason, binary clauses do not lead to ambiguities. This is not so for clauses with more than two literals.

Consider a variant of the process where claim acceptance has to undergo the four-eyes-principle. Two distinct reviewers need to accept the claim. We have the new predicates claimAcceptedRevA(.) and claimAcceptedRevB(.) for the two reviewers, A and B. The ontology contains a new axiom specifying that any claim is accepted provided it has been accepted by both:

$$\forall x : \text{claimAcceptedRevA}(x) \wedge \text{claimAcceptedRevB}(x) \Rightarrow \text{claimAccepted}(x)$$

We refer to this axiom with ϕ' in what follows. Suppose about our state s from above that $i_s(\text{claimAcceptedRevA}(c)) = 1$ and $i_s(\text{claimAcceptedRevB}(c)) = 1$. Upon executing n, as pointed out above, c is no longer accepted. So ϕ' is no longer true and we must "repair" it. Since, in difference to ϕ, ϕ' is not binary, this spawns a non-trivial behavior of the minimal change semantics. There are three options to "repair" ϕ': falsify claimAcceptedRevA(c), falsify claimAcceptedRevB(c), or falsify both.[9] The first two options each yield a resulting state s'; the latter does *not* yield a resulting state s' because that option is not a minimal change. As explained in the introduction, the intuitive meaning of this semantics is that, since c was revoked (by n), something bad must have happened to c. Either of the reviewers must have cancelled her approval. While, of course, both reviewers may have done that, this seems an unlikely assumption and is hence not considered.

---

[9] Making claimAccepted(c) true is not an option because $\neg$claimAccepted(c) follows logically from eff(n) and ϕ.

4.3 Verification Tasks

We now formalize our four verification tasks, relating to precondition conflicts, effect conflicts, reachability, and executability. As a helper notation, we first need to define when two task nodes are parallel.

Definition 4.9. *Let $\mathcal{P} = (N, E, \lambda, \Omega, \alpha)$ be an annotated process graph. For $e_1, e_2 \in \mathcal{E}$, we say that e_1 and e_2 are parallel, written $e_1 \parallel e_2$, if there exists a token-reachable token marking t such that $t(e_1) > 0$ and $t(e_2) > 0$. For $n_1, n_2 \in \mathcal{N}_T$, we say that n_1 and n_2 are parallel, written $n_1 \parallel n_2$, if $in(n_1) \parallel in(n_2)$.*

Definition 4.10. *Let $\mathcal{P} = (N, E, \lambda, \Omega, \alpha)$ be an annotated process graph.*

- *A node n is* reachable *iff either $n = n_0$ or there exist a reachable state s and an edge $e \in in(n)$ so that $t_s(e) > 0$.*
- *A node n is* executable *iff either $n \notin \mathcal{N}_T \cup \{n_+^P\}$ or, for all reachable states s with $t_s(in(n)) > 0$, we have that $s \models pre(n)$.*

$\mathcal{P}$ is reachable *iff all $n \in \mathcal{N}$ are reachable. $\mathcal{P}$ is* executable *iff all $n \in \mathcal{N}$ are executable.*

Let $n_1, n_2 \in \mathcal{N}_T$, $n_1 \parallel n_2$. We say that

- *n_1 has a* precondition conflict *with n_2 if $\mathcal{T} \wedge eff(n_1) \wedge pre(n_2)$ is unsatisfiable;*
- *n_1 and n_2 have an* effect conflict *if $\mathcal{T} \wedge eff(n_1) \wedge eff(n_2)$ is unsatisfiable.*

Consider first precondition and effect conflicts. Such conflicts indicate that the semantic annotations of different task nodes may be in conflict; n_1 may jeopardize the precondition of n_2, or n_1 and n_2 may jeopardize each other's effects.[10] If n_1 and n_2 are ordered with respect to each other, then this kind of conflict cannot result in ambiguities and should not be taken to be a flaw. Hence Definition 4.10 postulates that $n_1 \parallel n_2$. Note that, as an alternative definition, we may want to say that $n_1 \parallel n_2$ if there exists a reachable state – rather than a reachable token mapping – that activates them both. The use of Definition 4.9 in Definition 4.10 is more generous and hence more conservative. Also, it leads to computationally easier verification problems. We get back to this issue in Section 4.4.

It is debatable to some extent whether precondition/effect conflicts represent flaws, or whether they are a natural phenomenon of the modeled process. We view them as flaws, because in a parallel execution it may happen that the conflicting nodes appear at the same time.

Consider now the notions of reachable and executable task nodes n. Reachability is important because, if n is not reachable, then it is superfluous; this

---

[10] For illustration it is useful to consider the special case where $\mathcal{T}$ is empty. Then, a precondition conflict means there exists $l \in eff(n_1) \cap \neg pre(n_2)$. Similarly for effect conflicts.

certainly indicates a problem in the process model.[11] As for executability, if n is not executable then the process may reach a state where n is active – it has a token on its incoming edge – but its prerequisites for execution are not given. If the process is being executed by a standard (non-semantic) engine, e.g. based on BPEL, then the implementation of n will be enacted regardless of the unsatisfied precondition, which may lead to undefined behavior and errors. In general, the possibility to activate a task without establishing its precondition indicates that the process model does not take sufficient care of achieving the relevant conditions in all possible cases.

For illustration, consider our running example, i.e., the process from Figure 4.1 and its annotation as per Table 4.1. The task node "21. Close claim" has a precondition claimFinalized(c), but there is no activity whose effect provides this assertion. Thus, this task will not be able to execute when it is activated during runtime. While this may be due to faulty annotation (e.g., "19. Prepare claim discharge" may have claimFinalized(c) as an additional effect), it may also be the case that another activity "Finalize claim" is actually missing.

Reachability and executability are both temporal properties on the behavior of the process, and of course it may be of interest to allow arbitrary verification properties via a suitable temporal logic (see e.g., [236, 298]). We leave this open for future work. The focus on reachability and executability is, in that sense, an investigation of special cases. Note that these special cases are of practical interest, and perhaps more so than the fully general case allowing arbitrarily complex quantification which may rarely be used in practice.

Reachability can sometimes be established as a side-effect of executability: if there are no conditions that can prevent a sound process from pursuing any given execution path and if, in addition, all nodes are executable, then reachability holds for the whole process. Formally:

Proposition 4.11. *Let* $\mathcal{P} = (N, E, \lambda, \Omega, \alpha)$ *be a sound annotated process graph where* α *is undefined for all edges and loop nodes. If* $\mathcal{P}$ *is executable, then* $\mathcal{P}$ *is reachable.*

Proof: Let $n \in N \setminus \{n_0\}$. By definition, there exists a sequence $\vec{e}$ of edges from n_0 to n. By soundness and executability, and because none of the edges in $\vec{e}$, nor any loop nodes passed by $\vec{e}$, are annotated with a condition, one can easily use $\vec{e}$ to construct an execution path that reaches n.   ■

The overall methodology we propose for debugging a given process model is to first remove any precondition and effect conflicts, and thereafter to ensure the process is executable. Proposition 4.11 then implies that the process is correct with respect to all four verification tasks considered herein – provided

---

[11] To understand our definition of reachability, note that all nodes except parallel joins can be token-executed as soon as one of their incoming edges is active. For parallel joins, this property follows with soundness.

there are no XOR/loop conditions. The latter restriction is of no consequence as far as the identification of tractable classes is concerned, because, as we will see, in the presence of XOR/loop conditions we cannot verify reachability/executability efficiently anyway.

The techniques presented in what follows provide the tests needed, during the debugging, to see whether any bugs remain. Of course, it would be useful to be able to point out bugs/potential bugs, and perhaps to make suggestions for bug fixes. We describe some initial steps in that direction in Section 4.7, but exploring this in full is a topic for future work; we get back to this in Section 4.9.

4.4 Checking Precondition and Effect Conflicts

We devise an algorithm for finding precondition and effect conflicts, consisting of two parts:

(1) We determine which pairs of tasks in the process are parallel.
(2) For each such pair the respective preconditions and effects are tested for conflicts.

Step (1) runs in time polynomial in the size of the process. Step (2) consists of two satisfiability tests of the ontology axioms in conjunction with the preconditions/effects. Hence the overall complexity is the same as that of testing satisfiability in the logic underlying the semantic annotations. We now consider the two steps in detail.

For step (1), one can re-use results from the Petri Net literature. Namely, [164] show that, for free-choice Petri Nets, step (1) can be done in time cubic in the size of the process. In our own work, we devised an algorithm that exploits the particular structure of our control-flows, achieving the same result in quadratic time.

In Petri Nets, the "concurrency relation" is the set of pairs of places that may contain a token at the same time, i.e., for which there exists a reachable marking putting a token on both places. [164] devise an algorithm that computes the concurrency relation in time $O(|\mathcal{E}| * (|\mathcal{E}| + |\mathcal{N}|)^2)$, provided the net is free-choice. The algorithm is initialized with a set of known pairs of parallel nodes (transitions and places). It then performs local propagations based on a candidate set that evolves from this initial set. For example, if a place in the pre-set of a transition t is parallel to some other node n (i.e., a transition or place), then the post-set of t is set to be parallel to n.

Improving over the general result, we devise an algorithm for the specific formalism introduced above, called M-*propagation*. This algorithm has a runtime performance of $O(|\mathcal{E}|^2 + \Sigma_{\mathcal{Q} \in Sub(\mathcal{P})} |N^{\mathcal{Q}}| * |E^{\mathcal{Q}}| * max^{\mathcal{Q}})$, where $max^{\mathcal{Q}}$ is the maximum number of incoming or outgoing edges any node in $\mathcal{Q}$ has. The sum $(\Sigma_{\mathcal{Q} \in Sub(\mathcal{P})})$ comes from the sub-process structure, an explanation for the other terms is given in the proofsketch of Theorem 4.14. Presuming that max^Q (the branching factor in splits and joins) is fixed, this means that our algorithm runs in time quadratic in the size of the process, by contrast to the cubic time taken by [164]'s algorithm. This improvement is possible because our control-flows are less general than free-choice Petri Nets.[12] The enabling property is that our loops are structured. The concurrency relation of the overall process can be constructed directly from the concurrency relations of the individual subprocesses. Within each subprocess, the process graph is cycle-free, which means that we can compute concurrency according to a topological order of the subprocess. We now consider this in detail.

Given a subprocess Q, M-propagation determines pair-wise parallelism for all edges within Q. Parallelism of task nodes can then be read off directly from the parallelism of their respective incoming edges. Since parallelism according to Definition 4.9 is not affected by semantic annotations, M-propagation does not need to consider those; we will get back to this at the end of the section.

Example 4.12. The example process in Figure 4.1 does not contain a lot of parallelism, hence Figure 4.2 introduces a new example for this section.

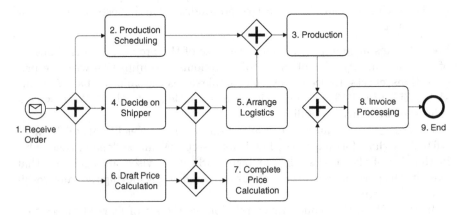

Fig. 4.2. Example of a sales order handling process

We consider a sales order process that is inspired by the BPEL specification [11]. Figure 4.2 shows this process in BPMN. Herein, the receipt of a sales order triggers three concurrent activities: initiating the production scheduling, deciding on the shipper, and drafting a price calculation. Once the shipper has been selected, the price calculation can be completed and the logistics can be arranged. After the latter, the production can be completed. Finally, the invoice is processed. The process model is obviously sound.

---

[12] We are not aware of any work computing concurrency, for general free-choice nets, with a better runtime bound than [164]; neither are the authors of [164] aware of any such work. In personal communication, Javier Esparza conjectured that a faster algorithm does not exist.

The M-propagation algorithm populates a matrix M whose rows and columns correspond to the edges of the process and whose entries are Boolean. M contains a 1 in the ith row and j^{th} column, denoted M_i^j, iff $i \neq j$ and $e_i \parallel e_j$, i.e., e_i and e_j may hold a control flow token at the same time. Note that, by its nature, M is irreflexive and symmetric. The indices i and j here refer to the positions of the edges in a *flow ordering*. A flow ordering is a bijective function $\# : E \mapsto \{0, \ldots |E| - 1\}$, numbering the edges such that (i) every incoming edge of a node has a lower number than any of the node's outgoing edges, and (ii) all outgoing edges of a split node are consecutively enumerated. Flow orderings obviously exist, since (N, E) is acyclic. For example, a flow ordering results from a breadth-first traversal of the process graph. We assume in the rest of the chapter that, for every process graph under consideration, a flow ordering $\#$ is fixed. This is just a simple device to be able to define the order in which M-propagation proceeds. We use the following helper notations. $\#^{-1}$ is the inverse function of $\#$, i.e., $\#^{-1}(i) = e$ iff $\#(e) = i$. If E is a set of edges, then $\#E_{max} := max\{\#(e) \mid e \in E\}$ is the maximum number of any edge in E, and analogously for $\#E_{min}$. For example, given a node n, $\#in(n)_{max} = max\{\#(e) \mid e \in in(n)\}$ is the maximum number of any incoming edge.

We now introduce M-propagation formally. The definition is hard to read at first, but its underlying ideas are straightforward. A detailed intuitive explanation will be given below. To slightly simplify notation, we do not include symmetric updates in the definition, i.e., wherever we write that $M_j'^i$ is assigned a value, we assume that $M_i'^j$ is assigned the same value.

Definition 4.13. *Let* $\mathcal{P} = (N, E, \lambda)$ *be a process graph. A matrix M is a function* $M : \{0, \ldots, |E| - 1\} \times \{0, \ldots, |E| - 1\} \mapsto \{0, 1, \bot\}$. *We define the matrix M_0 as* $(M_0)_j^i = 0$ *if* $i = j$, $(M_0)_j^i = \bot$ *otherwise. Let M and M' be matrices,* $n \in N$. *We say that M' is the* propagation *of M at n iff we have:*

1. *For all* $i, j \in \{0, \ldots, \#out(n)_{min} - 1\}$ *we have* $M_i^j \neq \bot$.
2. *For all* $e \in out(n)$ *and* $j \in \{0, \ldots, |E| - 1\} \setminus \{\#(e)\}$, *we have* $M_{\#(e)}^j = \bot$.

As well as one of the following:

3. $n \in N_T \cup N_L$ *and M' is given by* $M_j'^i = M_{\#(in(n))}^i$ *if* $\#(out(n)) = j$ *and* $i < j$, $M_j'^i = M_j^i$ *otherwise.*
4. $n \in N_{PS}$ *and*

$$
M_j'^i = \begin{cases} M_{\#(in(n))}^i & \#^{-1}(j) \in out(n) \text{ and } i < \#out(n)_{min} \\ 1 & \#^{-1}(j) \in out(n) \text{ and } i \neq j \\ & \text{and } \#out(n)_{min} \leq i \leq \#out(n)_{max} \\ M_j^i & \text{otherwise.} \end{cases}
$$

5. $n \in N_{XS}$ *and*

$$M'^i_j = \begin{cases} M^i_{\#(in(n))} & \#^{-1}(j) \in out(n) \ \text{and} \ i < \#out(n)_{min} \\ 0 & \#^{-1}(j) \in out(n) \ \text{and} \ i \neq j \\ & \text{and} \ \#out(n)_{min} \leq i \leq \#out(n)_{max} \\ M^i_j & \text{otherwise.} \end{cases}$$

6. $n \in N_{PJ}$ and

$$M'^i_j = \begin{cases} 1 & \#(out(n)) = j \ \text{and} \ i < j \ \text{and for all} \ e \in in(n) : M^i_{\#(e)} = 1 \\ 0 & \#(out(n)) = j \ \text{and} \ i < j \ \text{and ex.} \ e \in in(n) : M^i_{\#(e)} = 0 \\ M^i_j & \text{otherwise.} \end{cases}$$

7. $n \in N_{XJ}$ and

$$M'^i_j = \begin{cases} 1 & \#(out(n)) = j \ \text{and} \ i < j \ \text{and ex.} \ e \in in(n) : M^i_{\#(e)} = 1 \\ 0 & \#(out(n)) = j \ \text{and} \ i < j \ \text{and for all} \ e \in in(n) : M^i_{\#(e)} = 0 \\ M^i_j & \text{otherwise.} \end{cases}$$

If M^* results from starting in M_0, and stepping on to propagations until no more propagations exist, then we call M^* an M-propagation result.

Figure 4.3 illustrates the outcome of M-propagation on the example from Figure 4.2. M-propagation propagates parallelism information across the nodes in the process graph. M is initialized with 0 on the first diagonal (i.e., the fields M^i_i), and with the $\perp$ symbol in all other fields, marking all these values as being unknown yet. The propagation then commences at the start node, which is *receive order* in our example. Note here that our processes have a single start node and that this node is not parallel to any other nodes. We perform propagation steps in an order following the flow ordering $\#$, making sure that we only propagate over nodes n whose incoming edges have already been considered (their M-values have been determined) and whose outgoing edges have not yet been considered. Each propagation step derives a new matrix M' from the previous matrix M. The form of M' depends on the type of the node n considered. The cases in the following correspond directly to the cases in Definition 4.13.

Task and loop nodes. For this type of nodes, we copy the M-values up to the outgoing edge from the incoming edge (in Definition 4.13: $M'^i_j = M^i_{\#(in(n))}$). This works because a task or loop node neither synchronizes nor splits the control flow, and thus has no effect on parallelism. So n's outgoing edge is parallel to the same edges as n's incoming edge.

Parallel splits. Here, there are two things to consider. First, similarly as for task or loop nodes, parallelism from the ingoing edge is preserved in the outgoing edges. To account for this, we copy the respective M-values: if e_i is the incoming edge and e_j is the outgoing edge with the lowest number, then we set $M'^i_k = M^j_k$ for all $k < j$. Second, the outgoing edges of a

	Receive Order	Production Scheduling	Decide on Shipper	Draft Price Calculation	Arrange Logistics	Production	Complete Price Calculation	Invoice Processing
Receive Order	0	0	0	0	0	0	0	0
Production Scheduling	0	0	1	1	1	0	1	0
Decide on Shipper	0	1	0	1	0	0	0	0
Draft Price Calculation	0	1	1	0	1	1	0	0
Arrange Logistics	0	1	0	1	0	0	1	0
Production	0	0	0	1	0	0	1	0
Complete Price Calculation	0	1	0	0	1	1	0	0
Invoice Processing	0	0	0	0	0	0	0	0

Fig. 4.3. The matrix M for the process in Figure 4.2, projected to input edges of task nodes

parallel split introduce new parallelism. This is covered simply by setting $M''^i_j = 1$ for all outgoing edges e_i and e_j of n (in Definition 4.13: $\#^{-1}(j) \in out(n)$ and $i \neq j$ and $\#out(n)_{min} \leq i \leq \#out(n)_{max}$). In Figure 4.3 this can be observed at the first parallel split node: *Production Scheduling*, *Decide on Shipper*, and *Draft Price Calculation* are pairwise parallel.

XOR splits. These nodes are handled exactly like parallel splits, except that we set $M''^i_j = 0$ for all pairs of outgoing edges e_i and e_j. This reflects the fact that the outgoing edges of an XOR split can never carry a token at the same time (since we assume the workflow to be safe and sound).

Parallel joins. Here, matters are slightly more tricky. Say e_j is the outgoing edge. For any i with $i < j$, we set M''^i_j to 1 iff there is no incoming edge e_k with $M^i_k = 0$. This is necessary because parallel joins synchronize branches that were previously parallel. If one of the incoming edges is already synchronized with e_i, then the parallel join will transfer this synchronization to e_j as well. This can be observed in Figure 4.3 at the parallel join after *Production Scheduling*. *Production Scheduling* is parallel to *Decide on Shipper* and *Arrange Logistics*, but the latter two are synchronized (i.e., not parallel to one another). Therefore, *Production*, coming after the parallel join, is not parallel to *Decide on Shipper*.

XOR joins. For this node type, we perform an index-wise logical OR: say e_j is the outgoing edge again; for any i with $i < j$, we set M'^i_j to 1 iff an incoming edge e_k exists, with $M^i_k = 1$. The reason is that any incoming edge e_k which carries a token together with e_i may pass that token to the outgoing edge. Note that, in a sound process graph, no two incoming edges of an XOR join may carry a token at the same time. This follows directly from Proposition 4.4.

The algorithm stops when no more propagation steps are possible, which obviously is the case when M has been determined up to the incoming edge of the end node, and hence for all pairs of edges. The resulting matrix is unique, correct, and is computed in polynomial time.

Theorem 4.14. *Let $\mathcal{P} = (N, E, \lambda)$ be a sound process graph, and let $\mathcal{Q} \in Sub(\mathcal{P})$. There exists exactly one M-propagation result M^* for $\mathcal{Q}$. For all $n_1, n_2 \in N^{\mathcal{Q}}_T$ we have $n_1 \parallel n_2$ iff $M^{*\#(in(n_2))}_{\#(in(n_1))} = 1$. The time required to compute M^* is $O(|E^{\mathcal{Q}}|^2 + |N^{\mathcal{Q}}| * |E^{\mathcal{Q}}| * max^{\mathcal{Q}})$, where $max^{\mathcal{Q}}$ is the maximum number of incoming or outgoing edges any node in $\mathcal{Q}$ has.*

Proof Sketch: Consider first correctness, i.e., that $n_1 \parallel n_2$ iff $M^{*\#(in(n_2))}_{\#(in(n_1))} = 1$, for all $n_1, n_2 \in N^{\mathcal{Q}}_T$. This is proved via induction over the process structure, deducing correctness for a node's outgoing edges from correctness for its incoming edges. The arguments used for that are essentially simple, but sometimes tedious in the details. One example is that of a parallel join node, n. Amongst other things, we need to show that, if all $e_i \in in(n)$ are parallel to some edge e, then $out(n)$ is also parallel to e. Our prerequisite is that, for each e_i, there exists a reachable token-marking activating both e_i and e. We need to show that there exists a reachable token marking activating *all* the e_i and e – so that we can execute n and put a token on both $out(n)$ and e. We show in a separate lemma that this can be done, i.e., that every set of pairwise parallel edges can be activated all at once.

Uniqueness follows directly from correctness. As for computation time, initialization of M^* takes time $O(|E^{\mathcal{Q}}|^2)$, since one operation is necessary for each entry in the matrix. Thereafter, one propagation step is performed for every $n \in N$. It is easy to see that each step takes time in $O(|E^{\mathcal{Q}}| * max)$, where max is the maximum number of incoming or outgoing edges any node has: an operation on a row in the matrix takes $O(|E^{\mathcal{Q}}|)$ time, and each step considers either exactly one row or (for a split or a join node) one row per incoming / outgoing edge. Hence overall we get $O(|E^{\mathcal{Q}}|^2 + |N^{\mathcal{Q}}| * |E^{\mathcal{Q}}| * max^{\mathcal{Q}})$. ∎

The following definition captures how the overall parallelism relation can be re-constructed from the parallelism relation of the sub-graphs.

Definition 4.15. *Let $\mathcal{P} = (N, E, \lambda)$ be a sound process graph. For any $\mathcal{Q} \in Sub(\mathcal{P})$, let $M^{*\mathcal{Q}}$ be the M-propagation result M^* for $\mathcal{Q}$. The accumulated*

M-propagation result for $\mathcal{P}$ is the function $M^* : \mathcal{E} \times \mathcal{E} \mapsto \{0,1\}$ which sets $M^{*e}_{e'} := 1$ iff either:

- *$e, e' \in E^{\mathcal{Q}}$ for some $\mathcal{Q} \in Sub(\mathcal{P})$, and $M^{*\mathcal{Q}\#(e')}_{\#(e)} = 1$; or*
- *$e \in E^{\mathcal{Q}}$ and $e' \in E^{\mathcal{Q}'}$ so that there exists $n \in N^{\mathcal{Q}}_L$ with $\mathcal{Q}' \in Sub(\lambda^{\mathcal{Q}}(n))$ and $M^{*\mathcal{Q}in(n)}_{\#(e)} = 1$.*

Definition 4.15 simply says that e and e' are parallel if either they belong to the same subprocess and have been determined to be parallel by M-propagation, or e' appears beneath a loop node which has been determined to be parallel with e. The sub-graph relation (stating which process graphs are beneath which other ones) can be stored as an array, so that look-up takes constant time. Hence the M-propagation result for $\mathcal{P}$ can be constructed from the M-propagation results for the individual sub-graphs in time $O(|\mathcal{E}|^2)$. Overall, we obtain the runtime bound $O(|\mathcal{E}|^2 + \Sigma_{\mathcal{Q} \in Sub(\mathcal{P})} |N^{\mathcal{Q}}| * |E^{\mathcal{Q}}| * max^{\mathcal{Q}})$.

With the information about parallelism in hand, we are ready to detect precondition and effect conflicts.

Corollary 4.16. *Let $\mathcal{P} = (N, E, \lambda, \Omega, \alpha)$ be a sound annotated process graph, and let M^* be the accumulated M-propagation result for $\mathcal{P}$. Then, for any two task nodes $n_1, n_2 \in \mathcal{N}_T$:*

- *n_1 has a precondition conflict with n_2 iff $M^{*in(n_1)}_{in(n_2)} = 1$ and $T \wedge eff(n_1) \wedge pre(n_2)$ is unsatisfiable;*
- *n_1 and n_2 have an effect conflict iff $M^{*in(n_1)}_{in(n_2)} = 1$ and $T \wedge eff(n_1) \wedge eff(n_2)$ is unsatisfiable.*

Using Corollary 4.16, it is obvious how to perform step (2) in our overall algorithm. We detect precondition and effect conflicts simply by performing a loop over all pairs of edges e, e', and executing the described satisfiability tests for every pair where $M^{*in(n_1)}_{in(n_2)} = 1$.

Since the computation of M^* is polynomial, and the number of edge pairs is quadratic, the only source of exponential worst-case complexity is the satisfiability testing. In other words, the borderline between tractable classes and intractable classes is the same as that of the satisfiability tests. When restricting, as we do, the preconditions and effects to be conjunctions of logical atoms, then the borderline is identical to that of the logic used for formulating the ontology axioms. Note that this property does not depend on the particular logic we selected in our framework. That latter logic, clausal formulas, has been investigated in depth in the literature. In our particular setting, where quantification is over a finite set of constants and arity as well as nesting are fixed, the complexity is that of propositional logic. Known tractable classes are, e.g., Horn formulas [147] and binary formulas [14].

One important aspect of precondition and effect conflicts, as handled here, is the underlying definition of "parallelism". Definition 4.9 defines this exclusively based on the control-flow, i.e., two edges are parallel iff there exists a *token-reachable token marking* that puts a token on both. An alternative definition would be to say that two edges are parallel iff there exists a *reachable state* that puts a token on both. We refer in what follows to the former as *token parallelism*, and to the latter as *execution parallelism*. The difference between the two is that execution parallelism, in difference to token parallelism, takes into account the logical states. This can make a difference in the presence of XOR split and loop conditions, and in the presence of non-executable task nodes: such constructs allow traversal only by a subset of the token execution paths, and hence there may be less pairs of parallel edges. If a pair of edges is execution-parallel, then it is token-parallel; but not vice versa.

To some extent, it is a matter of taste which notion of parallelism one uses as the underlying definition for precondition and effect conflicts. Token parallelism has two advantages. First, it is more conservative, not relying on the annotation of XOR splits and loops, or on non-executable task nodes, to prevent the co-occurrence of conflicting preconditions/effects. Second, token parallelism leads to easier verification problems. Determining whether or not two edges are execution-parallel is hard. Namely, it is easy to see that the hardness results reported in Section 4.5 for reachability hold for that problem as well. It remains an open question how to develop verification techniques for dealing with precondition/effect conflicts based on execution parallelism.

4.5 Computational Hardness of Executability and Reachability Checking

Precondition and effect conflicts are "local" in the sense that they concern only the respective pair of nodes; whether or not some pair of nodes has a conflict does not influence whether or not some other pair has. This is not so for reachability and executability. If a node n is not reachable, then neither is any other node that can be reached only on paths through n. If a node n is not executable, then it can be traversed only by a particular subset of the execution paths that reach it, and hence some later node may become unreachable, or may become executable. In that sense, reachability and executability are more "global" phenomena. As we shall see now, this leads to some quite unfavorable properties regarding computational complexity. We consider four different decision problems:

(1) Is $\mathcal{P}$ executable, i.e., are all nodes $n \in \mathcal{N}$ executable?
(2) Is a particular $n \in \mathcal{N}$ executable?
(3) Is $\mathcal{P}$ reachable, i.e., are all nodes $n \in \mathcal{N}$ reachable?
(4) Is a particular $n \in \mathcal{N}$ reachable?

The difference between (1) and (2) is that, for (2), we admit the case where some other node $n' \in \mathcal{N}$ is not executable. Similar for (3) and (4). Most of the time, this difference does not have an impact on computational complexity.

But in one particular case, (2) is **coNP**-hard while (1) is in **P**. That case is the class of what we have termed "basic processes":

Definition 4.17. *Let* $\mathcal{P} = (N, E, \lambda, \Omega, \alpha)$, $\Omega = (P, \mathcal{T})$, *be an annotated process graph.* $\mathcal{P}$ *is* basic *if* α *is undefined for all edges and loop nodes, and* $\mathcal{T}$ *is binary.*

In words, basic processes restrict the ontology axioms to mention at most two literals in each clause, and they restrict the annotations to not define any conditions for choosing XOR branches or for determining whether or not a loop is repeated. As per Definition 4.6, this means that XOR-branches are fully non-deterministic, i.e., the execution is free to choose which branch to take. Likewise, the execution is free to choose whether to repeat a loop or exit it. Intuitively, this simplifies the verification problem because the available choices are the same regardless of what the logical state is. The reason why binary clauses are easier for the verification is that, with axioms consisting only of such clauses, the outcome of an activity – i.e., the logical state after execution of the activity – can be computed in polynomial time. The latter is obviously not the case for general clauses, and neither, as we shall see, is it the case for Horn clauses. We will get back to these issues below. For the moment, note that binary clauses can be used to specify many common ontology properties such as subsumption relations $\forall x : G(x) \Rightarrow H(x)$, type restrictions for attribute ranges $\forall x, y : G(x, y) \Rightarrow H(y)$, and role symmetry $\forall x, y : G(x, y) \Rightarrow G(y, x)$.

All the decision problems (1) – (4) are hard for any sensible generalization of basic processes. Decision problems (2) – (4) are hard even for basic processes. Decision problem (1) for basic processes is in **P**. In that sense, basic processes form a maximal tractable class for this kind of verification. Our focus is exclusively on proving this fact, i.e., for the hard cases we prove only hardness and do not consider membership. Establishing the precise complexity classes of the various problems is a topic for future research.

We will next formally state the negative complexity results, i.e., the hardness results, and explain what the sources of complexity are. Section 4.6 will prove the positive result regarding decision problem (1) for basic processes. We first consider the decision problems relating to executability, then those relating to reachability. Note that the claims hold even when there is no initial state uncertainty, i.e., $\text{eff}(n_0)$ is a complete assignment of truth values to all literals.

Theorem 4.18. *Assume a sound annotated process graph* $\mathcal{P} = (N, E, \lambda, \Omega, \alpha)$ *without effect conflicts, where* $N \setminus \{n_0, n_+\} \subseteq N_T \cup N_{XS} \cup N_{XJ} \cup N_L$, $\text{eff}(n_0)$ *is a complete assignment, all predicates have arity 0, and either* $\mathcal{P}$ *is atomic or for all* $n \in N_L$ *we have* $N^{\lambda(n)} = \{n_0^{\lambda(n)}, n_+^{\lambda(n)}\}$. *The following problem is* Π_2^p*-hard even if* $\mathcal{P}$ *is known to be reachable:*

- *Is* $\mathcal{P}$ *executable, or is* $n \in N$ *executable, given that* $\mathcal{P}$ *is basic except that* $\mathcal{T}$ *may involve arbitrary clauses?*

*The following problems are **coNP**-hard even if P is known to be reachable:*

- *Is P executable, or is $n \in N$ executable, given that P is basic except that T may involve arbitrary Horn clauses?*
- *Is P executable, or is $n \in N$ executable, given that P is basic except that $con(e)$ may be defined for some $e \in E$?*
- *Is P executable, or is $n \in N$ executable, given that P is basic except that $con(n)$ may be defined for some $n \in N_L$?*
- *Is $n \in N$ executable, given that P is basic?*

Proof Sketch: The first two results, $\mathbf{\Pi_2^P}$-hardness when T is unrestricted and **coNP**-hardness when T is Horn, are entirely due to the complexity of computing activity outcomes, i.e., determining whether or not a particular literal is necessarily true after a task node has been executed. The control-flows used in the proof constructions are trivial, with only 3-4 nodes arranged in a sequence. The hardness is proved via the design of a particular set of axioms, and of the task node preconditions and effects. Those constructions are adapted from the proofs given by Eiter and Gottlob [83] to show that "belief update" is $\mathbf{\Pi_2^P}$-hard (**coNP**-hard) for unrestricted (Horn) formulas. In both cases, the axioms take a rather intricate form, assuming as input a Quantified Boolean Formula (QBF) formula $\psi = \forall X . \exists Y . \phi[X, Y]$ for the unrestricted case, and a QBF formula $\psi = \forall X . \phi[X]$ for the Horn case. One task node n_t has a single effect literal t, and the following task node n has a precondition q. The constructions are such that ψ is valid iff q is necessarily true after n_t. The latter is, of course, the case iff n is executable.

Intuitively, the source of complexity in both cases is the need to figure out what is true in all possible "minimal" changes to the previous state. Any candidate for an outcome state can be tested for minimality easily, but the number of candidates is exponential. This complexity combines unfavorably with the complexity of reasoning about the axioms, and hence we get $\mathbf{\Pi_2^P}$ (rather than **coNP**) for unrestricted clauses and **coNP**(rather than **P**) for Horn clauses.

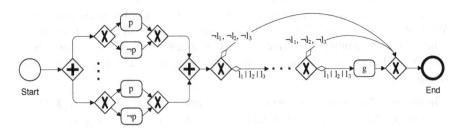

Fig. 4.4. Schematic illustration of 3SAT reduction for Theorem 4.18

For all the other results, essentially the same construction can be used, reducing the complement of 3SAT to the respective decision problem. Figure 4.4

shows an illustration. The construction assumes as input a CNF formula ψ. It starts with a parallel split/join including one XOR split/join for every variable p_i in the CNF formula, allowing the execution to set p to be either true or false. In this way, we allow to generate all possible truth value assignments. Afterwards, we filter those assignments, removing all but those that comply with all clauses in ψ. The construction used for doing so is easiest to understand for the case of XOR splits annotated with conditions. For every clause $C = \{l_1, l_2, l_3\}$ in the formula, we include an XOR split $split(C)$ with four outgoing branches. Three of those are annotated with the condition l_i, for $l_i \in \{l_1, l_2, l_3\}$, and lead to the XOR split for the next clause. The fourth edge is annotated with $\neg l_1 \wedge \neg l_2 \wedge \neg l_3$, and leads directly to a final XOR join just in front of the end node. The node marked g in Figure 4.4 lies at the end of the sequence of XOR splits $split(C)$, and is hence reachable if and only if the CNF is satisfiable. To obtain our proof for executability, we now simply introduce a new variable q, obtain a formula ψ' by inserting q into every clause, perform our construction for ψ', and make q a precondition of the node marked g. Then, g is executable iff q is true in all satisfying assignments to ψ', which is the case iff ψ is unsatisfiable. Note that g is definitely reachable because we are free to set q to be true.

If we are not allowed to annotate the outgoing edges of XOR splits, then we have to find a replacement for those annotations. If we are allowed to annotate loop nodes, then we can replace the XOR edge conditions with loops. Where before we had an outgoing edge annotated with l_i, we now have a loop with condition $\neg l_i$, meaning that the loop will be exited, and hence the path will be traversed, only if l_i is true. For XOR edges annotated with a conjunction of literals, i.e., with $\neg l_1 \wedge \neg l_2 \wedge \neg l_3$, the construction is only slightly more complicated.

Finally, consider the case where we may neither annotate XOR edges nor loop nodes, but our decision problem is to figure out whether some particular node $n \in N$ is executable. This decision problem allows the presence of other task nodes n' that are not executable. We can use such task nodes to filter truth value assignments, much in the same way as we did before. Indeed, wherever previously we had an XOR outgoing edge e annotated with condition ϕ, we replace e with a construction $e' \rightarrow n \rightarrow e''$ where $pre(n) = \phi$. In this way, the execution paths that pass through e are the same as those that pass through e''. The only difference is that, in the new construction, some task nodes are definitely not executable – e.g., the task nodes encoding the conditions of the first clause are not, since any precondition l_i of them may be invalidated by setting the respective variable to the opposite value.

All of the constructions are made so that, trivially, all nodes are reachable. In that sense, the hardness of executability does not depend on the hardness of reachability. All the constructions comply with the restrictions mentioned in the claim (in particular, the parallel split/join in Figure 4.4 can be replaced by a sequence). Except for the result regarding hardness of executability checking

in basic processes, it does not matter to the constructions whether we ask for
executability of a particular node, or of the whole process.   ∎

Note that the last proof argument, i.e., the one regarding executability of a
particular node $n \in N$ in a basic process (decision problem (2) in the above),
does not work if we ask whether *all* nodes are executable (decision problem
(1) in the above). In such a setting, we can no longer use task nodes to "filter" execution paths, like we did here. Indeed, as indicated, decision problem
(1) will turn out to be solvable in polynomial time, for basic processes. Our
hardness results for reachability are closely related to those for executability.

Theorem 4.19. *Assume a sound annotated process graph* $\mathcal{P} = (N, E, \lambda, \Omega, \alpha)$
without effect conflicts, where $N \setminus \{n_0, n_+\} \subseteq N_T \cup N_{XS} \cup N_{XJ} \cup N_L$, $eff(n_0)$
is a complete assignment, all predicates have arity 0, and either $\mathcal{P}$ *is atomic*
or for all $n \in N_L$ *we have* $N^{\lambda(n)} = \{n_0^{\lambda(n)}, n_+^{\lambda(n)}\}$. *The following problem is*
Σ_2^P-*hard:*

- *Is* $\mathcal{P}$ *reachable, or is* $n \in N$ *reachable, given that* $\mathcal{P}$ *is basic except that* $\mathcal{T}$
  may involve arbitrary clauses?

The following problems are **NP**-*hard:*

- *Is* $\mathcal{P}$ *reachable, or is* $n \in N$ *reachable, given that* $\mathcal{P}$ *is basic except that* $\mathcal{T}$
  may involve arbitrary Horn clauses?
- *Is* $\mathcal{P}$ *reachable, or is* $n \in N$ *reachable, given that* $\mathcal{P}$ *is executable, and basic*
  except that $con(e)$ *may be defined for some* $e \in E$?
- *Is* $\mathcal{P}$ *reachable, or is* $n \in N$ *reachable, given that* $\mathcal{P}$ *is executable, and basic*
  except that $con(n)$ *may be defined for some* $n \in N_L$?
- *Is* $\mathcal{P}$ *reachable, or is* $n \in N$ *reachable, given that* $\mathcal{P}$ *is basic?*

Proof Sketch: Like for executability, the first two results, Σ_2^P-hardness when
$\mathcal{T}$ is unrestricted and **NP**-hardness when $\mathcal{T}$ is Horn, are entirely due to the
complexity of computing activity outcomes, i.e., determining whether or not
a particular literal is necessarily true after a task node has been executed.
The constructions are essentially the same as in the proof of Theorem 4.18.
We consider a QBF formula $\psi = \forall X.\exists Y.\phi[X, Y]$ for the unrestricted case, and
a QBF formula $\psi = \forall X.\phi[X]$ for the Horn case. We still have the task node
n_t, and the following task node n. The only difference is that, now, n has a
precondition $\neg q$, rather than q. Then, ψ is not valid iff q is not necessarily true
after n_t, which is of course the case iff $\neg q$ might be true after n_t. Hence at
least one execution path can traverse through n iff ψ is not valid, and so the
node behind n is reachable iff ψ is not valid. Importantly, n is not executable:
irrespectively of the precise form of ψ we can construct a path where n's
ingoing edge is active but $\neg q$ is false. In that sense, this proof of hardness for
deciding reachability relies on the hardness of executability.

If we are allowed to annotate XOR outgoing edges with conditions, then we
can use exactly the same proof argument as used for the respective result of

Theorem 4.18, except that we do not have to introduce the new variable q – as already stated in the proof of Theorem 4.18, the node marked g in Figure 4.4 is reachable iff the CNF formula ψ is satisfiable. If we are allowed to have annotated loop nodes or non-executable task nodes, then, as before, we can use those to simulate XOR conditions. Note here that, in the constructions using XOR/loop conditions, the process is executable, i.e., those results do not rely on the hardness of executability.

All the constructions comply with the restrictions mentioned in the claim. In none of the constructions does it matter whether we ask for reachability of a particular node, or of the whole process.   ∎

As discussed in the proof sketch, for those results where executability is not explicitly mentioned in Theorem 4.19, the proof of hardness for deciding reachability is due to the hardness of deciding executability. This is a necessity, not a coincidence of our proof arguments. If the process in question is executable, then reachability follows trivially. Namely, in the respective classes of processes, no conditions are allowed at XOR splits and at loops. With Proposition 4.11, this means that executability implies reachability. Hence any reduction of a computationally hard problem to these decision problems must make use of non-executable task nodes.

Table 4.2. Overview of our complexity results. The results for deciding whether $n \in \mathcal{N}$ is reachable are the same as those for deciding whether $\mathcal{P}$ is reachable. All results are valid for (only for, in the case of the membership result) processes without effect conflicts. For all hardness results, we can further impose that $N \setminus \{n_0, n_+\} \subseteq N_T \cup N_{XS} \cup N_{XJ} \cup N_L$, that eff($n_0$) is a complete assignment, that all predicates have arity 0, and that either $\mathcal{P}$ is atomic or for all $n \in N_L$ we have $N^{\lambda(n)} = \{n_0^{\lambda(n)}, n_+^{\lambda(n)}\}$. Every hardness result for executability holds even if $\mathcal{P}$ is known to be reachable; the same is true vice versa for the reachability results, except those marked (*), where executability implies reachability by Proposition 4.11.

Class of $\mathcal{P}$	$\mathcal{P}$ exec?	$n \in \mathcal{N}$ exec?	$\mathcal{P}$ reach?
Basic but $\mathcal{T}$ unrestricted	Π_2^P-hard	Π_2^P-hard	Σ_2^P-hard (*)
Basic but $\mathcal{T}$ Horn	coNP-hard	coNP-hard	NP-hard (*)
Basic but con(e) may be def	coNP-hard	coNP-hard	NP-hard
Basic but con(n) may be def	coNP-hard	coNP-hard	NP-hard
Basic	in P	coNP-hard	NP-hard (*)

Table 4.2 provides an overview of our complexity results, including also the positive result. Note that all the hardness results hold even without effect conflicts. The same restriction, however, applies also to our positive result, i.e., our polynomial algorithm works correctly only when there are no effect conflicts. Hence, in the verification, effect conflicts should be found and removed

first, and thereafter executability should be checked. We will now discuss the executability checking in detail.

4.6 Polynomial-Time Executability Checking for Basic Processes

As stated, we now presume that the process under consideration is basic, and that it does not contain any effect conflicts. We design a polynomial-time algorithm determining whether or not the process is executable. Using this verification test as a debugging facility, the process modeler can remove flaws from the process until it is executable. Then, by Proposition 4.11, the process is also reachable, and thus has been established to be correct with respect to all four verification tasks considered herein.

Our verification algorithm computes, for every edge e in the process, what we call e's *intersection literals*: the literals that must hold true whenever e carries a token. Formally:

$$\bigcap e := \bigcap_{s \in \mathcal{S}, t_s(e) > 0} s$$

where a state is written as the set of literals it satisfies, i.e., $s = \{l \in P[C] \mid i_s \models l\}$. Once we know this set of literals, we can check executability simply by testing whether $\mathrm{pre}(n) \subseteq \bigcap in(n)$.

The intersection literals are computed by a fixpoint algorithm that performs propagation steps over the process structure, maintaining for every e a set $I(e)$ of literals. We call the algorithm I-propagation. Like that of M-propagation, its formal definition may be a little hard to read at first, but its underlying ideas are straightforward. A detailed intuitive explanation will be given below. For the remainder of the chapter, given a node n we write $\overline{\mathrm{eff}}(n) := \{l \in P[C] \mid \mathcal{T} \wedge \mathrm{eff}(n) \models l\}$ if $\alpha(n)$ is defined; else we set $\overline{\mathrm{eff}}(n) := \emptyset$.

Definition 4.20. *Let $\mathcal{P} = (N, E, \lambda, \Omega, \alpha)$ be an annotated process graph. Say α uses the constants C. We define the function $I_0 : \mathcal{E} \mapsto 2^{P[C]}$ as $I_0(e) = \overline{\mathrm{eff}}(n_0)$ if $e = out(n_0)$, $I_0(e) = P[C]$ otherwise. Let $I, I' : \mathcal{E} \mapsto 2^{P[C]}$, $n \in N$. We say that I' is the propagation of I at n iff $I' \neq I$ and one of the following holds:*

1. $n \in N_{PS} \cup N_{XS}$ and

$$I'(e) = \begin{cases} I(e) \cap I(in(n)) & e \in out(n) \\ I(e) & otherwise \end{cases}$$

2. $n \in N_{PJ}$ and

$$I'(e) = \begin{cases} I(e) \cap \left(\bigcup_{e' \in in(n)} I(e') \right) & e = out(n) \\ I(e) & otherwise \end{cases}$$

3. $n \in N_{XJ}$ and

$$I'(e) = \begin{cases} I(e) \cap (\bigcap_{e' \in in(n)} I(e')) & e = out(n) \\ I(e) & \text{otherwise} \end{cases}$$

4. $n \in N_T$ and

$$I'(e) = \begin{cases} I(e) \cap (\overline{\mathit{eff}(n)} \cup (I(in(n)) \setminus \neg \overline{\mathit{eff}(n)})) & e = out(n) \\ I(e) \setminus \neg \overline{\mathit{eff}(n)} & e \parallel in(n) \\ I(e) & \text{otherwise} \end{cases}$$

5. $n \in N_L^{\mathcal{Q}}$ so that $\lambda^{\mathcal{Q}}(n) = \mathcal{Q}'$ and

$$I'(e) = \begin{cases} I(e) \cap I(in(n)) & e = e_0^{\mathcal{Q}'} \\ I(e) & \text{otherwise} \end{cases}$$

6. $n = n_+^{\mathcal{Q}}$ so that $\mathcal{Q} = \lambda^{\mathcal{Q}'}(n')$ and

$$I'(e) = \begin{cases} I(e) \cap I(in(n)) & e = e_0^{\mathcal{Q}'} \\ I(e) \cap I(in(n)) & e = out(n') \\ I(e) & \text{otherwise} \end{cases}$$

If I^* results from starting in I_0, and performing propagations until no more changes occur, then we call I^* an I-propagation result. We will show below that there exists exactly one such I^*.

An I-propagation path is a sequence $I_0 \xrightarrow{n_1} I_1 \xrightarrow{n_2} I_2 \ldots I_{k-1} \xrightarrow{n_k} I_k$ so that, for all $0 \le j < k$, I_{j+1} is the propagation of I_j at n_{j+1}.

Figure 4.5 shows the outcome of I-propagation on part of our example claims handling process. Since the literals lossEvent(c), claim(c), claimRecorded(c), and claimValidated(c) are true for all shown edges, they are omitted in the figure. Each propagation step performed by I-propagation updates the annotated $I(e)$ sets according to the type of n. Initially, $I(e)$ is set to $\overline{\mathit{eff}(n_0)}$ for the start node n_0, and to $P[C]$, i.e, the set of all literals for all other nodes. A node may be propagated only if such propagation results in changes. The propagation steps over a node n depend again on the type of n. The cases discussed in the following correspond directly to the cases in Definition 4.20.

Splits: If n is a parallel split or an XOR split, the propagation simply forwards I from the incoming edge to every outgoing edge. This is because splits do not change the state of the world.[13]

---

[13] The reader may notice at this point that the outgoing edges of the parallel split in Figure 4.5, i.e., the ingoing edges of nodes 14 and 15, have different I sets. This is due to the effect of node 15: propagation over that node affects the ingoing edge of node 14 as per the second line of Definition 4.20 case 4; see also the explanation of task nodes below.

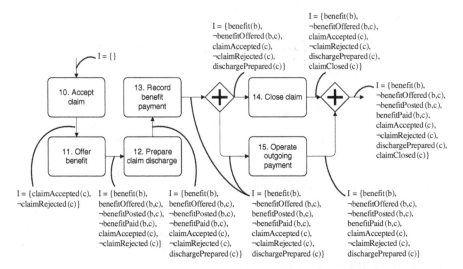

Fig. 4.5. Outcome of I-propagation on a part of the example process from Figure 4.1. The literals lossEvent, claim, claimRecorded, and claimValidated are present in all shown sets, and are omitted.

Parallel joins: Say e' is n's outgoing edge. We intersect $I(e')$ with the union of the sets $I(e)$ for all of n's ingoing edges e. This is justified per the assumed absence of effect conflicts. A parallel join can only fire if there is a token on all of its incoming edges; for all such cases we know that the literals $I(e)$ of these edges hold. Since there are no effect conflicts, the sets $I(e)$ do not contradict each other. Hence, for a literal l to be guaranteed to hold after execution of n, it suffices if l is guaranteed to hold on one of the incoming edges.[14] See the parallel join in Figure 4.5 (subsequent to steps 14 and 15) for illustration: the I sets of the 2 incoming edges are combined, c.f. benefitPaid(b, c) and claimClosed(c).

XOR joins: We set $I(e')$ to the intersection of the sets $I(e)$ for all of n's ingoing edges. This is adequate because a literal l holds after an XOR join only if all paths leading to the join guarantee that l holds (any one of the paths may be executed). Figure 4.6 shows this behavior in two variants, for the part of the process including the sub-graph's end node 16 and the preceding XOR join. On the left-hand side, no literals is in the intersection of the I sets of all three edges, and hence the I set of the outgoing edge is empty. On the right-hand side, for better illustration a variant is shown where the single XOR join has been split up into two XOR joins. In that variant, ¬claimAccepted(c) holds on both incoming

---

[14] In the presence of effect conflicts, the outcome of parallel branches depends on the order of execution.

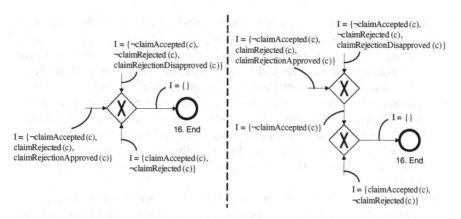

Fig. 4.6. *I*-propagation over an XOR join on a part of the example process from Figure 4.1, showing only the literals for claims in terms of acceptance, rejection, rejection approval, and rejection disapproval. Left: directly on the XOR join of Figure 4.1. Right: Variant, where the original XOR join has been split up to illustrate the behavior at XOR joins.

edges of the first join node, and hence holds also on the outgoing edge of that node.[15]

Task nodes: These are the most complicated propagation steps. By $\overline{\text{eff}(n)}$ we denote n's explicit and implicit effects, containing not only eff(n) but also all its implications together with $\mathcal{T}$. Note here that, if $\mathcal{T}$ consists of binary clauses, then $\overline{\text{eff}(n)}$ can be computed in polynomial time. Say n has the incoming edge e and the outgoing edge e'. Three different actions need to be performed. (1) We write $\overline{\text{eff}(n)}$ into $I(e')$. (2) We copy every literal l from $I(e)$ to $I(e')$, unless $\neg l$ is already present in $I(e')$. (3) We go through the list of all edges e'' that are parallel to e (by M-propagation we know which edges to consider), and remove from $I(e'')$ all literals l where $\neg l$ is contained in $\overline{\text{eff}(n)}$.

(1) and (2) are direct consequences of the semantics of annotated task nodes, c.f. Section 4.2.2. (1) must be done simply because any effect forces a direct change on the world. (2) must be done since the world is required to change minimally, i.e., if a property is true before and is not affected, then it is still true. (3) deals with the case where an edge e'' parallel to e' inherited a literal l which is in conflict with $\overline{\text{eff}(n)}$ (l cannot be established by the effect of a task node connected to e'' since that would be an effect conflict). In this situation, l is *not* guaranteed to hold whenever e'' carries a token: n may be fired, leading to $\neg l$. This is best understood using an example. Consider Figure 4.5. The task node n we consider is step 15, "Operate outgoing payment". The preceding parallel split, let's denote it

---

[15] Note that this is not the case for claimRejected(c), because, due to the ontology axioms in our example, claimRejectionDisapproved(c) implies $\neg$claimRejected(c).

by n', has two outgoing edges. One of those leads to n; the other one, which we denote with e'', leads to step 14, " Close claim". Say n' fires, putting a token on both of the edges. In this situation, we know due to the execution of step 13, "Record benefit payment", that benefitPosted(b, c) holds. Due to $\mathcal{T}$, $\neg$benefitPaid(b, c) is also certain to hold. Accordingly, I-propagation over n' (as explained above) keeps these literals in $I(e'')$. However, say n fires next. Then e'' still carries a token, but both literals have been inverted. Hence benefitPosted(b) and $\neg$benefitPaid(b) may be false when e'' carries a token. The two literals must thus be removed from $I(e'')$. (3) does that. The annotation of e'' in Figure 4.5 shows the outcome.

Loop nodes: For a loop node n with $\lambda(n) = \mathcal{Q}$, we intersect $I(e_0^{\mathcal{Q}})$ with $I(in(n))$. This is adequate because an execution of the process will always enter into a loop, due to the defined do-while-semantics.

End nodes of sub-graphs: At an end node of a sub-graph, the loop can either be repeated or exited. In basic process graphs, this decision is non-deterministic. We thus intersect both $I(out(n'))$ and $I(e_0^{\mathcal{Q}})$ with $I(e_+^{\mathcal{Q}})$, where $\lambda(n') = \mathcal{Q}$.

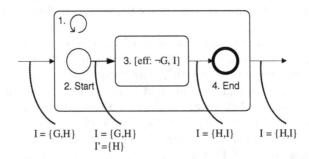

Fig. 4.7. I-propagation across an end node, in an illustrative example

The behavior of this procedure is illustrated with a toy example in Figure 4.7: a loop node $(1, n)$ contains a sub-graph $(\mathcal{Q})$ with only a start (2), task $(3, n')$, and end node (4). $I(in(n))$ comprises two literals G, H, which are copied onto $I(e_0^{\mathcal{Q}})$. The task node (3) has the effect eff$(n') = \{\neg G, F\}$, thus replacing G with $\neg G$ on its outgoing edge, and adding F. The propagation over the end node of the loop then, as described above, copies this I to the outgoing edge of the loop, and yields a changed $I(e_0^{\mathcal{Q}})$ (denoted as I'), where G has been removed. Note how this reflects the behavior of the process. When first entering the loop, both G and H are true. After the execution of the task node, the state is $F, \neg G, H$. Then, if the loop is repeated, we know two states in which $e_0^{\mathcal{Q}}$ carries a token. In one of those we have G, H, in the other we have $F, \neg G, H$. The intersection thus only contains H.

It is important to note here that step (2) for task nodes can be done in such a simple way only because $\mathcal{T}$ is restricted to disjunctions of at most 2 literals. The minimal change semantics as per Definition 4.6 can get quite intricate in the presence of more complex $\mathcal{T}$ – c.f. the proofs of Theorems 4.18 and 4.19. For illustration, reconsider Example 4.8. We execute a task node with effect claimRejected(c) in a state s where both claimAcceptedRevA(c) and claimAcceptedRevB(c) hold. Suppose that the two facts necessarily hold prior to n, i.e., claimAcceptedRevA(c), claimAcceptedRevB(c) $\in I(in(n))$. As discussed in Example 4.8, execution of n invalidates either claimAcceptedRevA(c) or claimAcceptedRevB(c). In particular, after n, neither of the two facts is guaranteed to hold – although their opposites are not implied by $\mathcal{T} \wedge$ eff(n)! Step (2) does not recognize this, and wrongly includes both facts into $I(out(n))$. Situations like this (and other more complicated situations) cannot appear when $\mathcal{T}$ consists of binary clauses only; hence for basic process graphs (1) and (2) suffice.

We now analyze the properties of I-propagation formally. We first observe that I-propagation yields a unique result, terminates in polynomial time, and is correct provided the process is executable. The reader may be alerted at this point since, as stated above, we wish to use I-propagation for testing *whether* the process is executable. We will show below that this is indeed possible. The analysis of I-propagation is more natural, and easier to understand, when first considering the more restricted case where executability holds a priori.

Theorem 4.21. *Let $\mathcal{P} = (N, E, \lambda, \Omega, \alpha)$ be an executable basic sound annotated process graph without effect conflicts. Say we run I-propagation on $\mathcal{P}$. There exists exactly one I-propagation result I^*. For all $e \in \mathcal{E}$, $\bigcap e = I^*(e)$. With fixed arity, the time required to compute I^* is polynomial in the size of $\mathcal{P}$.*

Proof Sketch: The main result is correctness. First, we prove that, provided $\mathcal{P}$ is executable and basic, it does not affect the intersection literals to remove $\mathcal{T}$ and replace each eff(n) with $\overline{\text{eff}(n)}$. The behavior for a single state and task node is the same in both cases because, intuitively, $\overline{\text{eff}(n)}$ captures all forced consequences of $\mathcal{T}$, and with binary clauses every consequence of $\mathcal{T}$ is forced. The claim for the overall process follows because the process structure is not changed, and logical states do not affect the possible token executions when there are no XOR/loop conditions and when all task nodes are executable. We can hence, without loss of generality, assume that $\mathcal{T}$ is empty (we get back to this below the proof).

Our core proof argument focuses on the literals that are "deleted" during I-propagation, i.e., the literals l and edges e for which there exists an I-propagation step so that, after that step, $l \notin I(e)$. We show soundness and completeness of the literal deletion: for soundness, if l is removed at e then there exists a reachable state s with $t_s(e) > 0$ and $s \not\models l$; vice versa for completeness.

Completeness is shown as follows. Given any execution path $s_0 \overset{n_1}{\to} s_1 \dots$ $s_{k-1} \overset{n_k}{\to} s_k$, we construct a sequence $I_1, \dots, I_k$ by performing I-propagation of I_j at n_j if that is possible, i.e., if it results in any changes, and setting $I_{j+1} := I_j$ otherwise. Obviously, a sub-sequence of $I_1, \dots, I_k$ corresponds to an I-propagation path. We show by induction over j that, for all e where $t_{s_j}(e) > 0$, we have $s_j \models I_j(e)$; in particular, if $s_j \not\models l$ then $l \notin I_j(e)$. The proof distinguishes the different kinds of nodes n_j. For example, say n_j is a task node, and $t_{s_{j+1}}(e) > 0$. Then either $e = out(n_j)$, or $e \parallel out(n_j)$. In the former case, we have the induction hypothesis for $in(n_j)$ because we must have $t_{s_j}(in(n_j)) > 0$; in the latter case we have that property for e itself. In both cases, it is easy to see that $s_{j+1} \models I_{j+1}(e)$ because the propagation step over n_j deletes all literals that become false when executing n_j.

Soundness is more tricky to prove. We assume an I-propagation path $I_0 \overset{n_1}{\to} I_1 \dots I_{k-1} \overset{n_k}{\to} I_k$. We prove by induction over j that, for every e and l where $l \notin I_j(e)$, there exists an execution path ending in a state s so that $t_s(e) > 0$ and $s \not\models l$. Again, we distinguish the different kinds of nodes n_j. The most tricky kind are parallel joins. By the definition of I-propagation over parallel join nodes, we either have (a) $l \notin I_j(e)$ or (b) $e = out(n_j)$ and for every $e_i \in in(n_j) : l \notin I_j(e_i)$. In case (a), the induction hypothesis shows the existence of an execution path as desired, so there is nothing to prove. For case (b), we need to construct a reachable state s' where $s' \not\models l$ and $t_{s'}(e_i) > 0$ for all $e_i \in in(n_j)$; in s', we can execute n_j and are done. However, the induction hypothesis gives us such a state only for every *individual* $e_i \in in(n_j)$. For each $e_i \in in(n_j)$, we have a state s_i with $t_{s_i}(e_i) > 0$ and $s_i \not\models l$. We prove in a separate lemma that, for every set of edges e_i that are pairwise parallel and where such states s_i exist, we can construct a state s' as desired. The proof is by induction over the process structure. The lemma makes use of the absence of effect conflicts: if $l \in \mathrm{eff}(n), l \in \mathrm{eff}(n')$ but $l \notin \bigcap out(n), l \notin \bigcap out(n')$ due to effect conflicts, then we may never be able to falsify l at both e and e' together (an example for this is given below this proof sketch).

The soundness arguments for the other kinds of nodes n_j are similar but have a more direct connection between induction hypothesis and claim. For XOR split/end nodes, to construct the desired execution paths we exploit the fact that, in a basic process, an execution path may choose any outgoing edge/may choose to repeat or exit the loop; similar for executability and task nodes.

Uniqueness follows directly from correctness. As for computation time, the main observation consists in an upper bound for the number of propagation steps performed by I-propagation. Denote with $|I|$ the total number of literals annotated by I, at any edge in the process. I-propagation performs a propagation step from I to I' only if $|I| > |I'|$. If $|I'| = 0$, then certainly a fixpoint is reached. Obviously $|I_0| \leq |\mathcal{E}| * |P[C]|$, so this is the desired upper bound. With fixed arity, $|P[C]|$ is $O(|P| * |C|)$, where C is the set of constants mentioned by α. Overall, we can derive that the runtime of I-propagation is $O(|P[C]|^3 + |\mathcal{N}| * |P[C]| * max_{\mathrm{eff}} + (|P[C]| * max_E + |\mathcal{E}| * |P[C]|) * |\mathcal{E}| * |P[C]|)$, where max_{eff} is the maximum number of effect literals any task node has, and max_E is the maximum number of incoming or outgoing edges any node has.   ∎

Note that the runtime is low-order polynomial. If we assume that $|P|$ is fixed, then the runtime is roughly cubic in the size of the process graph.

It may seem odd that we can assume an empty $\mathcal{T}$ without loss of generality. It is important to note here that this holds only for the purpose of executability checking. When removing $\mathcal{T}$ (and accordingly extending effects), the space of reachable states does *not* stay the same, because $\mathcal{T}$ imposes restrictions on how particular pairs of literals can be combined. However, that does not affect the intersection literals.

To illustrate why we need to disallow effect conflicts, consider the following example. We have a parallel split node n_{split}, a parallel join node n_{join}, and four task nodes $n_{1\neg p}$, $n_{2\neg p}$, n_{1p}, n_{2p} where each $n_{i\neg p}$ has the effect $\neg p$ and each n_{ip} has the effect p. The edges are $(n_{split}, n_{1\neg p})$, $(n_{split}, n_{2\neg p})$, $(n_{1\neg p}, n_{1p})$, $(n_{2\neg p}, n_{2p})$, $e_1 := (n_{1p}, n_{join})$, $e_2 := (n_{2p}, n_{join})$. That is, we have two parallel branches, on each of which p is first made false and then made true. Consider the edges going into the join node, e_1 and e_2. Even though e_1 is the outgoing edge of a task node with effect p, we have $p \notin \bigcap e_1$ because $n_{2\neg p}$ may be executed while e_1 still carries a token – note here the effect conflict between n_{1p} and $n_{2\neg p}$. The same is true of e_2, i.e., $p \notin \bigcap e_2$. So for each e_i there exists a reachable state where e_i is active and p is false. However, there does *not* exist a reachable state where *both* e_i are active and p is false! If both e_i are active then either n_{1p} or n_{2p} was executed last, so p is necessarily true. In consequence, $p \in \bigcap out(n_{join})$; since $p \notin \bigcap e$ for any $e \in in(n_{join})$, this means that, in the presence of effect conflicts, the intersection literals of the outgoing edge of a parallel split are no longer a function of the intersection literals of the ingoing edges. It is currently an open issue whether this problem can be overcome by maintaining supplementary information during I-propagation, in addition to the sets $I(e)$; see also the outlook in Section 4.9.

Theorem 4.21 presumes that the process is executable. For checking whether that is the case, of course we cannot make that assumption. The key observation here is that, if the process is not executable, and even if XOR/loop conditions are defined, the outcome of I-propagation is conservative.

Lemma 4.22. *Let $\mathcal{P} = (N, E, \lambda, \Omega, \alpha)$ be an annotated process graph without effect conflicts, which is basic except that α may be defined for edges and loop nodes. Say we run I-propagation on $\mathcal{P}$, and I^* is an I-propagation result. Then, for all $e \in \mathcal{E}$, $\bigcap e \supseteq I^*(e)$.*

Proof Sketch: This is surprisingly easy to show by considering the modified process $\mathcal{P}_0 = (N, E, \lambda, \Omega, \alpha^0)$ which is like $\mathcal{P}$ except that all preconditions and all XOR/loop conditions have been removed. Obviously, Theorem 4.21 applies to $\mathcal{P}_0$ and so in particular we get completeness of literal deletion, i.e., $\bigcap^{\mathcal{P}_0} e \supseteq I_0^*(e)$ for all $e \in \mathcal{E}$, where $\bigcap^{\mathcal{P}_0} e$ are the intersection literals for $\mathcal{P}_0$

and I_0^* is an I-propagation result for $\mathcal{P}_0$. The claim then follows because the execution paths of $\mathcal{P}$ are a subset of those of $\mathcal{P}_0$; hence the intersection literals of $\mathcal{P}$ are a superset of those of $\mathcal{P}_0$; hence $\bigcap e \supseteq \bigcap^{\mathcal{P}_0} e \supseteq I_0^*(e)$.   ∎

Putting Theorem 4.21 and Lemma 4.22 together, we immediately get our two main results regarding executability checking.

Theorem 4.23. *Let* $\mathcal{P} = (N, E, \lambda, \Omega, \alpha)$ *be a basic annotated process graph without effect conflicts. Say we run I-propagation on $\mathcal{P}$, and I^* is an I-propagation result. Then $\mathcal{P}$ is executable iff for all $n \in \mathcal{N}_T \cup \{n_+^{\mathcal{P}}\}$: $pre(n) \subseteq I^*(in(n))$.*

Proof Sketch: First, clearly $\mathcal{P}$ is executable iff, for every $n \in \mathcal{N}_T \cup \{n_+^{\mathcal{P}}\}$: $pre(n) \subseteq \bigcap in(n)$. If $\mathcal{P}$ is executable, then Theorem 4.21 applies, meaning that $I^*(in(n)) = \bigcap in(n)$ and hence $pre(n) \subseteq I^*(in(n))$. If $\mathcal{P}$ is not executable, then Lemma 4.22 applies, meaning that $I^*(in(n)) \subseteq \bigcap in(n)$. So if $l \in pre(n) \setminus \bigcap in(n)$, then $l \in pre(n) \setminus I^*(in(n))$ and hence $pre(n) \nsubseteq I^*(in(n))$.   ∎

Theorem 4.24. *Let* $\mathcal{P} = (N, E, \lambda, \Omega, \alpha)$ *be an annotated process graph without effect conflicts, which is basic except that α may be defined for edges and loop nodes. Say we run I-propagation on $\mathcal{P}$, and I^* is an I-propagation result. If, for all $n \in \mathcal{N}_T \cup \{n_+^{\mathcal{P}}\}$: $pre(n) \subseteq I^*(in(n))$, then $\mathcal{P}$ is executable.*

Proof Sketch: Say that $\mathcal{P}$ is not executable. Then $l \in pre(n) \setminus \bigcap in(n)$, for some l and n. With Lemma 4.22 we have $I^*(in(n)) \subseteq \bigcap in(n)$. Hence $l \in pre(n) \setminus I^*(in(n))$, and $pre(n) \nsubseteq I^*(in(n))$.   ∎

Theorem 4.23 means that, for basic processes, we can use I-propagation for executability checking, as desired. We simply run I-propagation up to its fixpoint and check whether all precondition literals remained at the respective edges. If the process has binary axioms only, but uses XOR/loop conditions, then the verification is weaker, with Theorem 4.24 providing a sufficient but not necessary test for correctness.

Having discussed the techniques for verifying the correctness of annotated process models with respect to our criteria, we now address how processes that do not meet the criteria can be corrected.

4.7 Resolving Inconsistencies

In Sections 4.4 and 4.6 we described techniques that can *detect* inconsistencies in annotated process models. Of course, if an inconsistency is detected, it would be desirable to have a technique for suggesting to the modeler how that inconsistency could be resolved, or to even explore some such resolutions automatically. However, as discussed in Section 3.2, it is hard to devise an automated technique to *guess* the specific source of an inconsistency. Thus, the suggestions made should in most cases serve as a supporting means for a modeler, and rarely make the final decision.

We herein outline some strategies for inconsistency resolution. Exploring these approaches in more detail and investigating alternative approaches is a topic for future work. We first consider the resolution of a conflict due to a non-executable task node; we then consider the resolution of precondition and effect conflicts.

4.7.1 Executability

Assume that, for task node n, executability is not given. I.e., there is a literal $l \in pre(n)$ and an execution of the process leading to a state where there is a token on n's incoming edge, but l is not true.

Assume that we know l, i.e., we know what the faulty precondition is. A straightforward solution for resolving this inconsistency is to compose a set of services that is inserted in front of n, and that achieves l based on the literals that hold immediately prior to n. In detail, say we know the set $I(in(n))$ of literals that are always true in a state where there is a token on n's incoming edge. We add a new task node n' before n, and set the precondition and effect as follows:

- $pre(n') := I(in(n))$
- $eff(n') := pre(n)$

Then, task composition (as described in the next chapter) can be applied to find an implementation for this placeholder task. If such an implementation exists and does not result in any additional conflicts, then task composition should be able to find it. The result is a set of executable artifacts which change the state of the process at the respective point in a way so that the executability of n is guaranteed. Note that we add the full precondition of n as the effect of n'. If we do not do that, then it may happen that the composed services achieve the witness literal l, but are in conflict with some other literal $l' \in pre(n)$. Note further, that information gathering (cf. Section 5.6.1) is required as well, such that the resulting composition does not conflict with any tasks that are parallel to n and n'.

If we are facing a basic annotated process graph without choice, then we can use the algorithms from Section 4.6 to determine the literal l, as well as the set of literals $I(n)$, in polynomial time. In more general situations, determining l and $I(n)$ may be more costly.

However, using the approach outlined above, new inconsistencies may be caused by the composition if there exists a literal l' that is contained in $I(in(n))$, but not in the outcome of the composition. This can be easily avoided by setting $eff(n') := I(in(n)) \cup pre(n)$ instead of $eff(n') := pre(n)$. That is, we can simply require that everything that was previously true at n is again true after the composition was executed. Note that this only works if $I(in(n)) \cup pre(n)$ does not contain both a literal and its negation.[16] If $l \in I(in(n))$ and $\neg l \in pre(n)$, then we can still make n executable by including $\neg l$ in $eff(n')$ – at the cost of possibly introducing some other inconsistency, because the composition has to invert the value of l.

In any case, before making a suggestion to the modeler the suggested change should definitely be checked for new inconsistencies. A tool that contradicts itself jeopardizes the user's trust.

4.7.2 Precondition and Effect Conflicts

If there is a precondition or effect conflict between two task nodes n, n', then it can be resolved by enforcing sequentiality over these nodes. In the case of a precondition conflict, the required ordering is clear: the node whose precondition may be violated has to be the first in the sequential order. In the case of a postcondition conflict, the question remains which of the task nodes should occur last – since the effect of the latter node is the one that will prevail. This question may be answered in the context of other related precondition conflicts or executability violations, or it may even suggest that the two paths on which n and n' reside should not be parallel, but mutually exclusive. In terms of the requirements of Section 3.2, we can only guess whether the issue is related to inadequate parallelism (Requirement 2) or incorrect usage of gateways (Requirement 3).

In case the ordering of parallel nodes is chosen, the two nodes can often be ordered by minimally changing the process model, in that a simple synchronization construct is introduced. Assume that tasks n_3 and n_4 in Figure 4.8 need to be ordered such that n_4 is always executed before n_3. This can be done with little changes, as shown in Figure 4.9.

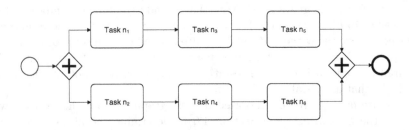

Fig. 4.8. Illustrative example process for task synchronization

However, there may be situations in which a valid ordering cannot be introduced with minimalistic changes to the process model, unless edge conditions

---

[16] Note that such a literal l indicates a particularly strong executability conflict – n is *never* executable in the original process – and hence such a situation should probably be brought to the attention of the modeler anyways.

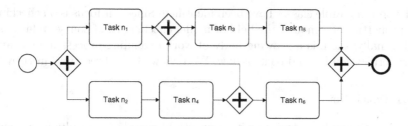

Fig. 4.9. Illustrative example process with task synchronization

are allowed. For an example, consider Figure 4.10. A fix as in Figure 4.9 would result in an unsound process model, and a valid fix would require to duplicate the affected process part – one branch for synchronization and one where this is not required (because n_4 is not included). More elegant fixes require additional control flow constructs.

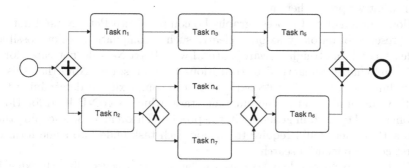

Fig. 4.10. Illustrative example process where task synchronization is not easily established

Note that, because the repair operation reduces the parallelism in the process, it cannot introduce new precondition and effect conflicts. However, executability and reachability may be affected, and, as above, the resolution strategy may introduce new flaws. Again, the changed process model should be checked before it is suggested to the user.

After the presentation of our verification techniques and resolution strategies for detected inconsistencies, we now discuss related work.

4.8 Related Work

In the following overview of related work, we discuss in detail the most relevant technical connections to our work. Such a connection mainly exists to the area of Petri Nets, which has been used as the basis for control-flow verification, and where tractable classes have been identified. Since our focus is on checking the properties of a model, the field of model checking is, of course, related as well. Finally, there is a growing body of work extending process models and their verification beyond control-flow. We review these three areas in turn.

4.8.1 Petri Nets

Petri Net theory has come up with a wealth of complexity results for various classes of Petri Nets, including in particular tractability results for a number of restricted classes. We already discussed in Section 4.4 how one of these results [164] can be exploited to determine parallel task nodes in our framework, which is half of the job of finding all precondition/effect conflicts. Task node parallelism does not depend on the annotation, hence this is an application of Petri Net theory to non-annotated process graphs. We can also obtain an application to annotated process graphs, via compiling such graphs into Petri Nets. However, the results obtainable in this way are substantially weaker than what we proved herein.

How can annotated process graphs be compiled into Petri Nets? First, in the presence of ontology axioms, clearly such a compilation is not possible, at least not in a straightforward/natural way. Petri Nets do not cater for a "minimal change semantics" of transitions between states. Note that this is quite fundamental, as is reflected e.g. by the complexity of determining the truth value of a literal in the outcome state, which is **coNP**-hard for Horn axioms and Π_2^p-hard in general, c.f. the proof of Theorem 4.18. Encoding this into a Petri Net would require to encode each task node into some form of worst-case exponential search.

If there are no ontology axioms (or, as far as executability checking is concerned, if the axioms are binary, c.f. the proof of Theorem 4.21), then a straightforward compilation exists. Encode each task as a transition, and encode edges as places. Joins and splits can then be encoded using the rules defined in [294]. Loops, i.e., transitions into and out of sub-graphs, are encoded in the straightforward fashion. Next, enumerate all facts that can be built from the predicates and constants. Create an additional place for each fact, as well as one for its negation. Add an arc for each precondition/effect literal to the respective place; similarly, encode XOR/loop conditions.

Apart from the process structure, we also need to express our verification tasks in terms of Petri Net queries. Reachability in the annotated process model is equivalent to the question whether the control flow pre-place of a task may ever carry a token. Executability in the annotated process model is equivalent to the question whether, whenever the control flow pre-place of a task carries a token, the precondition pre-places carry a token as well. To ask whether a particular task node n is executable, we need to ask for every precondition p of n whether a state is reachable where the control flow pre-place of n carries a token, but p does not. To ask whether the overall process is executable, we need to ask these questions for every task node.

To test reachability in our annotated process graph, we hence need to be able to test, in a Petri Net, whether a given place can be active. This is a fairly common query for Petri Nets. To test executability, we need to be able to test whether a given place p can be active while another place p' is not. This is a rather unusual query. It corresponds to what has been termed "implicit places" and "implicit place sets". Apart from enumerating all reachable markings or enumerating all markings m with $m(p) > 0, m(p') = 0$, the only known technique to detect implicit places is the detection of "structural implicit places" [29, 295], which can be done in polynomial time. However, structural implicit places are a special case of implicit places, i.e., this technique corresponds to a sufficient but not necessary criterion for executability and is hence not a verification method in our sense. Even for live and safe free-choice nets (corresponding to process graphs without annotations), it is **NP**-complete to check conditions under which the sufficient criterion is also necessary [102]. Summing up, results from Petri Net theory can not be applied to derive non-trivial tractable classes of executability checking.

What we can derive are two tractable classes for checking reachability. A closely related topic was previously investigated by [214], who are concerned amongst other things with a Petri Net based formalization of compositions of Semantic Web services, and with verification of reachability. [214] use a formalism that does not encompass any ontology axioms, but that is otherwise closely related to ours. They use a Petri Net encoding similar to what we sketched above. They state two tractability results, based on restricting the process in a way so that the compiled Petri Net becomes free-choice [69], respectively conflict-free [151]. These results, in the form stated in [214], are slightly flawed – the stated restrictions do not suffice to make the Petri Net free-choice/conflict-free. However, the results can easily be repaired, by imposing more restrictions. We have:

(1) If every literal l appears in at most one task node precondition, XOR condition, or loop condition, then the compiled Petri Net is free-choice.
(2) If the process has no loops and no XOR splits, and for every fact p we have that either p is not made false by any task node, or is contained in the precondition of at most one task node, then the compiled Petri Net is conflict-free.

Both for free-choice and conflict-free Petri Nets, it can be decided in polynomial time whether there exists a reachable marking activating a given place. Hence, (1) and (2) identify tractable classes for checking reachability in annotated process graphs. These tractability results are not implied by our results – we propose to establish reachability as a side-effect of establishing executability, in a class of processes where reachability checking is **NP**-hard. Note that class (2) is a heavily restricted subset of the tractable class we identify[17].

---

[17] There are no ontology axioms; with no loops and no XOR splits, clearly there cannot be any XOR/loop conditions; the restriction on facts implies that there cannot be any effect conflicts.

Hence this class is considerably more impractical than ours. Class (1), on the other hand, could be useful since it allows XOR/loop conditions, albeit in a restricted form. The tractability of reachability in class (1) clearly is complementary to the results proved herein.

4.8.2 Model Checking

Model checking is concerned with checking the properties of some formal model of a piece of software or hardware under consideration; see [57] as an entry point into the vast amount of literature. There are two key differences to our work. First, model checking has not been concerned with ontologies, i.e., with ontology axioms that form part of the model to be checked. Like for Petri Nets, this is a fundamental difference to our approach, and a natural encoding into traditional model checking formalisms is not possible. Hence we can only consider the restricted case where the axioms are empty (or, as far as executability checking is concerned, where all axioms are binary clauses).

The second major difference to model checking is that model checking has traditionally not been concerned with the identification of tractable fragments, which is the core contribution of our work. Model checking is usually concerned with very general formalisms, which are far from tractable. When using model checking for verification tasks in the context of process models, this quickly becomes apparent – e.g., in [13] the runtime of a verification of complex compositions of OWL-S process models increases from 8.77 seconds to more than 7200 seconds as the number of loops is increased from two to three. Instead of tractability, as targeted here, the focus of research on model checking is rather on theoretical analysis of algorithms addressing such formalisms, and on the development of search techniques for enhancing empirical performance, such as symbolic representations (e.g. [46, 48]), constraint propagation (e.g. [191, 56, 275]), search space reduction (e.g. [291, 146]), and clever implementation techniques (e.g. [23]). In our view, the main importance of model checking for our work lies in the potential of applying (adaptations of) these search techniques to the intractable cases identified by Theorems 4.18 and 4.19. We have already performed an initial experiment in this direction; we will get back to this in the outlook, Section 4.9.

4.8.3 Beyond Control-Flow

Verification of process models has been studied for quite a while, mostly from a control flow perspective. In this context, different notions of soundness have been proposed; for an overview see [301]. There is a growing body of contributions beyond pure control-flow verification. Those relate to semantic checks and data flow analysis.

The approach of [183, 184] checks a notion of *semantic correctness* that builds on annotations to tasks as being mutually exclusive or dependent. In the first case they cannot co-occur in a trace, in the second case they must appear in a certain order. For semantic correctness the process must comply with the annotations. This approach provides somewhat similar features as linear temporal logic [298]. This kind of annotations can be simulated using a subset of our framework (using only preconditions/effects, with an empty ontology). In that sense, [183, 184] can be viewed as a special case of our framework.

In the area of *access control* the approach of [30] extends process models with predicates, constants, and variables. The meaning of these constructs relates to constraints on role assignments, while in our model they directly affect the executability of tasks. The work of [212] describes methods to *check compliance* of a process against rules for role assignment. This is related to our approach in that an ontology could (to some extent) be defined to model such rules; but not vice versa since we build on general logic while [212] covers some practical special cases. Paper [259] addresses amongst others *life-cycle compliance* (essentially whether the process model does not violate the constraints expressed in the life-cycles). This can be partly reformulated in terms of preconditions, effects, and ontological axioms. Our running example illustrates some constraints related to the life-cycle of business objects, i.e., when certain actions can only be performed, if the business object is in the required state.

In [204], the preconditions and effects of service compositions are calculated on the basis of atomic services of which the compositions consist. Similar to our approach, the preconditions and effects of the atomic services are formulas, and the processes are assumed to be sound, have a single start and end node, respectively, and the routing constructs are parallel/XOR join/split. However, [204] deals neither with loops nor with ontological axiomatizations. There is no formal discussion of the algorithms or their properties. In particular, there is no proof of correctness and no consideration of complexity. The algorithm is based on computing the reachability graph of the composition's workflow, which is exponential in size of the workflow. This is in contrast to our investigation of polynomial time algorithms.

In [160], based on annotations of task nodes with logical effects, the authors use a propagation algorithm somewhat reminiscent of our I-propagation. There are, however, a number of important differences between the two approaches. [160] allows CNF effects which are considerably more expressive than our purely conjunctive effects. On the other hand, their propagation algorithm is exponential in the size of the process (the size of the propagated constructs multiplies at every XOR join). Further, [160] circumvents the consideration of loops, by assuming that entire subprocesses are annotated with effects. That is, subprocesses are handled as if they were atomic task nodes. This makes the analysis simpler, but, obviously, seriously impedes the ability to model subprocesses at a fine granular level. [160] do not consider preconditions, and they do not consider ontology axioms constraining the domain behavior. Finally, [160] do not provide a formal semantics for their effect annotations, and consequently, in difference to us, do not prove any formal correctness properties for their algorithms.

Another related line of work is data flow analysis, where dependencies are examined between the points where data is generated, and where it is consumed; some ideas related to this are implemented in the ADEPT system [245]. Data flow analysis builds on compiler theory [6] where data flows are typically examined for sequential programs mostly; it does neither consider theories $\mathcal{T}$ nor logical conflicts, and hence explores a direction complementary to ours. To some extent, our concepts can be applied in this area by expressing data dependencies as preconditions, effects, and ontological axioms.

4.9 Chapter Conclusion and Discussion of Open Questions

In this chapter, we presented a verification method exploiting semantic annotations, hence taking into account what the individual activities in the process actually do when they are executed. As the basis for this work, we introduced a formalism for checking certain correctness properties of semantically annotated process models. The formalism is unique in that it combines notions from the workflow community and from the AI literature, resulting in a syntax that integrates control-flow with logical preconditions and effects relative to an ontology, and resulting in an integrated execution semantics able to capture the interaction between the two. We have shown that, based on this formalism, one can detect execution problems in process graphs with sound control flow, hence enabling verification beyond soundness. Our working assumption is that this extended verification ability will lead to fewer errors, and hence to a shorter time span for design and deployment of process models. As the pace of business is ever increasing [265], reducing this time span is a very relevant problem [62].

We expect that verification of process models will typically take place within a process modeling environment, in an online setting where the modeler will frequently want to check for bugs. In order to enable an efficient and user-friendly design support, the answer of the verification should be instantaneous. It is hence important to determine which verification tasks, for which classes of processes, can be performed in polynomial time. For precondition/effect conflicts, we have shown that the hardness of verification is the same as the hardness of reasoning in the logic underlying the ontology axioms. For reachability/executability, we have determined the class of basic processes. In that class, presuming effect conflicts have already been removed, executability of the overall process can be checked in polynomial time using a particular fixpoint algorithm which we devise. We have shown that polynomial time verification is not possible for any of the most relevant extensions of basic processes. In that sense, the class of basic processes is maximal.

Once executability is established for a basic process, reachability follows. So the modeler may debug a basic process by first finding and removing any precondition/effect conflicts, and then removing any bugs leading to non-executable task nodes. The resulting process is correct with respect to all four verification tasks identified herein.

The techniques presented herein provide the tests needed, during the debugging, to see whether any bugs remain. Naturally, it is useful to make suggestions for fixes to bugs/potential bugs. We have made some initial steps in that direction: essentially based on the local information obtained by M-propagation and I-propagation, we suggest (i) how to synchronize conflicting parallel process branches, and (ii) how to compose executable artifacts such that a non-executable task becomes executable. It may further be of interest to provide diagnosis mechanisms to identify/approximate the reason why a particular literal is/is not true. First steps in this direction have been taken as well, based on backchaining from the occurrence of a phenomenon to its source [142], but are not discussed in this work.

The evaluation in Chapter 6 provides first findings based on a set of process case studies regarding the expressivity choices made herein. In short, we found that basic processes are restrictive, but there are cases where this is acceptable. At this stage, we do not yet have insight into user acceptance of the presented techniques. Clearly, this requires an empirical research agenda addressing questions like: How large is the benefit of the extended verification in different application scenarios? Do those benefits make up for the overhead of defining the semantic annotations? Answering these questions requires more detailed case studies in concrete use cases, and is beyond the scope of this work. A technical prototype of our techniques is integrated in multiple front-end prototypes. One of the front-end tools is scheduled for pilot customer evaluation to investigate the usefulness of the verification methods described herein and the composition methods from the next chapter – cf. Section 6.2.

Some details are still open in the technical results presented herein. The most important of those is the question whether executability of basic processes can be verified efficiently also in the presence of effect conflicts. If so, then the debugging facility provided becomes more flexible, allowing to check executability without prior removal of effect conflicts, and allowing to tolerate effect conflicts (to not view them as bugs) in case such behavior is intended. This issue also tightly connects to the approach where, in the definition of precondition and effect conflicts, control-flow parallelism (based on token executions) is replaced with execution parallelism (based on reachable states), c.f. the discussion at the end of Section 4.4. For executable basic processes, one can show that both notions of parallelism are the same. So if we were able to establish executability for basic processes in the possible presence of effect conflicts, then we could arrange the overall verification to (1) remove all flaws leading to non-executable task nodes, and (2) to thereafter remove all flaws leading to precondition/effect conflicts. Once (1) is completed, we can determine efficiently, using the same algorithms as presented herein, whether or not two edges are execution-parallel. Hence we can then perform (2), i.e., find precondition/effect conflicts, exactly as before.

Last but not least, computational hardness is certainly a challenge for verification in an online setting, but is not necessarily a deal-breaker. If the process models are not too large, and if the verification makes use of advanced search techniques (like symbolic representations, constraint propagation, search space reduction, or process decomposition), then the response times may be tolerable. It is hence important to explore the design of verification techniques for the hard cases identified by Theorems 4.18 and 4.19, such as process models with XOR and loop conditions. Indeed, in our view, apart from assessing the practical benefits of the verification, this is the main open line of research. We have made some initial experiments encoding processes with empty ontology (no axioms) for the explicit-state model checker SPIN [145]. The results are not encouraging, taking excessive runtime and/or memory even in fairly small processes. However, certainly that is not the end of the story. The performance of SPIN can possibly be improved by using different encodings, or some algorithmic extensions to SPIN (e.g. [79]). Also, one option we deem particularly promising is the use of SAT solvers (e.g. [210, 80]) for the verification, in the style of the bounded model checking approach [56]. In some cases, a single SAT call suffices for testing whether a particular node is executable. For example, we have already shown that this the case for basic processes without loops.

It should be noted that the techniques presented in this chapter can be useful for task composition, as discussed in Section 5.6.1. In turn, task composition may be used in the resolution of detected inconsistencies (cf. Section 4.7). We present our work on task composition in the next chapter.

5

Task Composition

Automatic Web service composition (WSC) is a key component of flexible SOAs – inside the business process setting investigated in this work and in general. In the specific context of this work, WSC is required for task composition, i.e., automatically composing Web services and other executable artifacts to construct an implementation for a process task.[1] Further, as mentioned in Section 4.7, task composition can make suggestions how inconsistencies in annotated process models may be resolved.[2]

Since the (manifold) previous works were perceived as insufficient for our context (cf. Section 5.7), we addressed WSC as the second technical core topic of this work. In particular, we address WSC at the profile/capability level, where preconditions and effects of services are described in an ontology. The main reasons for choosing preconditions and effects are the following: (i) the understanding that inputs and outputs do not suffice to capture the meaning of a Web service – in practice, hundreds of operations can have the same input types, e.g., purchase orders; and (ii) for preconditions and effects it is possible to define composition semantics – a verb describing an action may be easier to understand for users, but is far harder to formalize. Certainly, it is a deliberate choice that the formalisms of WSC and the verification from the previous chapter fit each other (although they are *not* equal, due to separate requirements). Since WSC is of interest for SOA in general we do not base the presentation of this chapter completely on the rest of the work. As in the previous chapter, this results in a few redundancies in the explanations.

In its most expressive formulation, WSC has two sources of complexity: (A) a combinatorial explosion of the service composition space, and (B) worst-case exponential reasoning is needed to determine whether the underlying ontology implies that a particular composition is a solution. Any WSC technology must

---

[1] In this chapter, we will use Web service as a synonym for executable artifact, whereas the word service will be used to refer to individual Web service calls. A more formal definition follows.

[2] Parts of this chapter have been published: [144, 141, 194].

hence choose a trade-off between scalability and expressivity. We devise new methods for finding better trade-offs. We address (A) by techniques for the automatic generation of heuristics. We address (B) by approximate reasoning techniques for the expressive case, and by identifying a sub-class where the required reasoning is tractable. Finally, we show empirically that our approach scales gracefully to large pools of pre-discovered services, in several test cases.

5.1 Overview

In this chapter, we detail the technology that is used to solve particular WSC *problems*. In a nutshell, a WSC problem is given by a repository of available Web services to compose from, and by a user goal. Our technology then fully automatically composes an orchestration of Web services that satisfies the user goal. That is, the technology we now define implements the *task composition* step of the conceptual framework presented in Section 3.5.3: by solving a WSC problem, we compose services to implement a task from the process model at hand, thus recommending compositions to the process modeler. For this to be successful, the WSC tool must be both sufficiently expressive (for powerful modeling) and sufficiently fast (for good response times).

The WSC problem in the process modeling context is illustrated in Figure 5.1. To enable the automated composition of a set of services (depicted as the composition of S_1, S_4, and S_2 at the bottom of the figure) for a task in the process (T_5 in the figure), WSC requires Web services to be advertised with a description of their functionality. I.e., WSC, in the form we consider here, requires Semantic Web services (cf. Section 2.3.4). In the figure, a pool of such services is assumed to be available, and – as in the verification technique in the previous chapter – a domain ontology formalizes the domain of discourse. At the so-called *service profile* or *capability* level, typical SWS approaches such as OWL-S [12, 284] and WSMO [61, 70] describe SWS akin to AI planning formalisms, specifying their input/output parameters, preconditions, and effects (IOPE)[3]. These attributes of SWS are described within an ontology, which formalizes the underlying domain.

Composition at this level of abstraction is commonly called *functional service composition*. The main simplifying assumption made at this level is that Web services, as well as user goals, are treated as atomic entities that are completely specified by their start and end points; in other words, a Web service or user goal is viewed as a function with a single point of input and a single point of output. One of course obtains a more precise technology if one does not make that assumption, and instead considers the Web services and goals in terms of their detailed behavioral interfaces, i.e., in terms of the interaction behavior they exhibit. This kind of composition is referred to as

---

[3] Note the analogy to the annotation of task nodes in the previous chapter, which was inspired from this kind of formal description.

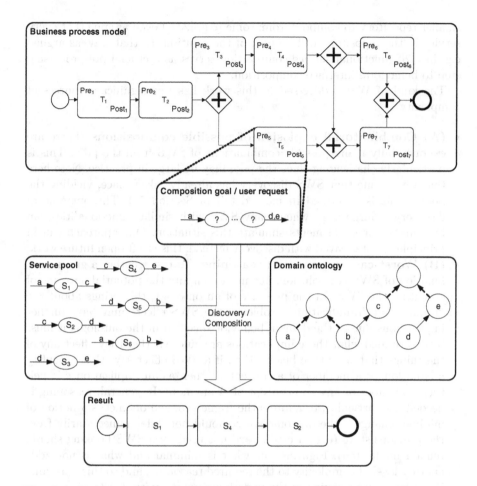

Fig. 5.1. Task composition (adapted from [144]): a user need for implementing a task (here: T_5) in the process is fulfilled by composing services from a service pool, while respecting an ontology Ω. Repetition from Fig. 3.4.

behavioral interface composition (cf. Section 2.2 for an overview of choreography, orchestration, and behavioral interfaces) or process-level composition. Unfortunately, behavioral interface composition is very close to automatic programming, which is a notoriously hard and unsolved task. Functional level composition trades some accuracy for feasibility (although, as we will see, functional service composition is still hard). In that way, functional service compositions may not always be guaranteed to be actually executable. In these cases, they serve to support the process modeler with rich information on what the implementation can be; ideally, minor modifications suffice to correct any remaining inaccuracies. Also, all existing behavioral interface composition techniques benefit significantly from a more concise input, i.e., a smaller repository to compose from; some (e.g. [234]) even assume that every service in the repository will be part of the solution. In that way, as argued e.g. in [32], functional service composition serves as a crucial pre-processing step to behavioral interface composition.

The kind of WSC addressed in this work has two significant sources of complexity:

- **(A) Combinatorial explosion of possible compositions.** There are exponentially many possible combinations of SWS from the pool. This is particularly challenging since the pool may be large in practice. Note here that we assume that SWS discovery has already taken place, yielding the pool – this is described in more detail in Section 5.2. The outcome of discovery is large, e.g., when many SWS with similar functionalities can be found. Our experiments simulate this situation. Our approach can in principle be interleaved with discovery instead; this is left open future work.
- **(B) Worst-case exponential reasoning.** To test whether a given combination of SWS is a solution, one must compute the potential outcome of executing the SWS. In the presence of an ontology, this brings about the "frame" and "ramification" problems: the SWS effects may have further implications due to the domain behavior specified in the ontology; it must be determined what those implications are, and whether they affect any of the things that were true before. E.g., if a SWS effect says that an entity c is no longer a member of a concept A, then as an implication c is neither a member of any sub-concept of A anymore. In general, reasoning is needed. In particular, to address the frame problem one needs a notion of minimal change – the outcome state should not differ unnecessarily from the previous state (e.g., a credit card not used by a SWS booking should remain unaffected). Figuring out what is minimal and what is not adds another level of complexity to the required reasoning, and so this reasoning is harder than reasoning in the underlying ontology itself [83].

Given this complexity, it is clearly important to look for good trade-offs between expressivity and scalability[4]. We address (A) by heuristic search (more below). Regarding (B), this problem is closely related to what AI calls "belief update" (e.g. [322, 83]), and we will henceforth refer to the reasoning required for computing the outcome of SWS execution as *update reasoning*. Many existing approaches to WSC (e.g. [237, 214, 234, 4, 277]) simply ignore the ontology, i.e., they act as if no constraints on the domain behavior were given. Most other approaches (e.g. [81, 267, 206, 181]) employ full-scale general reasoners, and suffer from the inevitable performance deficiencies. The middle ground between these two extremes is relatively unexplored but for

---

[4] Note that another aspect of importance in our context is that of understandability: the process modeler has to be able to understand and define the logics, in part, himself. This aspect is discussed in more detail in the evaluation, Chapter 6.

[60], which devises a method restricting the ontology to be a subsumption hierarchy and [65], which identifies an interesting fragment of description logics (*DL-Lite*) where update reasoning is tractable, but they do not develop an actual WSC approach or tool. In our work, we develop such an approach and a tool for a class of ontologies related to DL-Lite; further, we address the fully general case by devising approximate update reasoning techniques.

Our WSC approach uses heuristic search [227], a well known technique for dealing with combinatorial search spaces. The main algorithm for the composition performs a kind of "forward search", in a space of states s corresponding to different situations during the execution of the various possible compositions. The key functions deal with maintaining the search states and detecting solutions, as well as the heuristic function that estimates which search states and which Web services are promising. The search through the states is ordered by the heuristics (e.g., pursuing a standard method called "best-first search" [227]). The set of most promising services is used for *filtering* the explored SWS calls. We will see that both of the heuristics, and especially their combination, bring huge scalability gains.

We base our work on a natural formalism for WSC, with a semantics following the *possible models approach* (PMA) [322] as in the previous chapter. The PMA addresses the frame and ramification problems via a widely adopted notion of minimal change; it underlies almost all recent work on formal semantics for WSC (e.g. [182, 17, 65]). Our technical contributions are:

- We develop a *heuristic function*, by suitably adapting AI Planning techniques [139].[5] This has been attempted for WSC only in a single research effort [206] as yet. Going beyond that work, and beyond all related work in planning, ours is the first technology that takes domain knowledge, as given in the ontology, into account in the heuristic.
- We show that, if the ontology specifies binary clauses only, then update reasoning is tractable. Note that this is not self-evident from the fact that reasoning over binary clauses is tractable: e.g., it is known [83] that, for Horn clauses, update reasoning is *not* tractable. Binary clauses are related to, but not a subset or superset of, DL-Lite (details in Section 5.7).
- We open up a new way to more fine grained trade-offs between expressivity and scalability: *approximate update reasoning*. Instead of restricting the ontology up to a point where update reasoning is tractable, we propose to approximate the update reasoning itself. We identify certain properties of updates that can be exploited to design techniques for under-approximation and over-approximation. We show how either of soundness or completeness can be guaranteed by interleaving both approximations. Empirical

---

[5] For the reader not familiar with the field of AI Planning, we remark that this kind of heuristic function used in a forward search is since almost a decade by far the most successful method in planning. In particular, in almost all known benchmark domains it is far more efficient than, e.g., approaches based on Graphplan [34] or partial-order planning [230].

exploration of these techniques is beyond the scope of this work, but forms a promising topic for future research.[6]

- Web service outputs are naturally modeled as new ontology instances: e.g., if a service makes a flight reservation, then this is modeled as a new instance of the respective concept. Previous WSC tools (e.g. [206]) have taken the same approach, but were limited to consider pre-fixed sets of "potential" outputs. By contrast, our algorithms keep track of on-the-fly creation of outputs. In particular, while doing this naïvely leads to an exponential blow-up in the heuristic function, we show how this can be achieved with polynomial effort.

The algorithms devised here have been implemented for the case of binary clauses. We ran experiments on three test cases, one of which stems from a case study in the telecommunications sector, and one being based on actual services from SAP. The results show how our heuristic and filtering techniques enable us to scale to large SWS pools. As part of the evaluation chapter, Section 6.3 describes the empirical analysis of the techniques presented in this chapter.

The rest of this chapter is structured as follows. Section 5.2 provides a high-level summary of our approach, explaining at an intuitive level all the design decisions involved, and the reasons for taking them. There, the main search algorithm is discussed in two forms: for deterministic and for non-deterministic service effects. Section 5.3 introduces our formalization of composition. Section 5.4 treats all the issues regarding the computation of search state transitions, including some general observations as well as our treatment of restricted ontologies. Section 5.5 introduces our heuristic function and the filtering technique. Section 5.6 explains the peripheral aspects of our approach, namely the information gathering and discovery pre-processes. The most important connections to related work are explained at the respective points in the text. A broader summary of related work can be found in Section 5.7. Section 5.8 provides a brief summary and outlook. To improve readability, the main text provides only brief proof sketches; full proofs are in Appendix A.2.

5.2 Design and Main Algorithms

In the following, we provide an overview of the design of our approach, and we explain the various decisions underlying this design. We begin with a high-level overview of our approach in Section 5.2.1. We then outline, in Section 5.2.2, the workings of the main loop performing the search for a solution. Since the default main loop can only accurately handle services with deterministic

---

[6] [66] also consider approximation, but in a very different way: instead of using approximation to treat more general ontologies (DL TBoxes) as we do, they use approximation to deal with less general DL ABoxes.

effects, Section 5.2.3 discusses an alternative algorithm that trades the ability to handle non-deterministic services for some scalability.

5.2.1 Overall Arrangement

An illustration of the architecture of our composition approach is given in Figure 5.2.

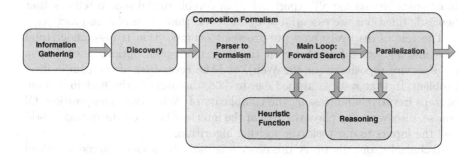

Fig. 5.2. Illustration of the task composition architecture

Our approach starts with the *Information Gathering* step, where the process context for the task to be composed is analyzed. We here gather all available process information for the selected task, in terms of the state of the world at this point in the process as well as on the parallel tasks. Essentially, the information gathering described here makes use of the algorithms from the previous chapter: I-propagation is used to compute a summary of the logical states that may be encountered during any valid execution of the process, i.e., the $I(e)$. In addition, we use M-propagation (or an equivalent technique) to compute the parallelism between the selected task and all other tasks. Based on this information, we construct a constraint set: a set of all facts that should be avoided in a composition for the task at hand, since otherwise the composition creates a precondition or effect conflict with one of the tasks parallel to it. The benefits of this approach are:

- Reduced modeling effort, since the preconditions stemming from tasks that will be executed before the selected task can be derived, rather than having to be manually repeated.
- Improved efficiency of the refinement into an execution-level process, since compositions do not lead to precondition / effect conflicts.
- Potentially higher user acceptance, since the results of composition do not lead to a negative verification – i.e., the different means for modeling support do not lead to contradictions.

More details on information gathering are given in Section 5.6.1.

As the next step in our architecture, discovery is a pre-process to composition. That is, first a set of relevant services is selected from the repository, and then that set is taken as the available services from which to compose the solution. This is a deliberate and important choice. If one interleaves discovery and composition, as explored e.g. by [60, 59], then it is not possible to compute a meaningful heuristic function: without knowing what the available services are, there is no way of estimating how many of them are still needed. Indeed, [60, 59] perform a blind (depth-first) search. This is unlikely to scale in complex situations: all experience from combinatorial search tells us that heuristic functions are essential to obtain tools that are usable in practice.

The role of discovery as a pre-process to composition is best understood as a first relevance filter between the huge number of options offered by a large service repository (or the Web), and the necessities of the composition problem. In that way, as argued e.g. by [32], discovery is the first in a chain of steps iteratively addressing the complexity of Web service composition. Of course, discovery also plays the role of the interface between the outside world and the inputs to our task composition algorithm.

Technically, our discovery pre-process is basically a loop around standard discovery methods, as the ones described in Section 3.5.2 or, e.g., [25, 117, 274]. Namely, these methods look for a single Web service that may help to implement the goal. By contrast, for the composition process we need to find Web services that may help *to help other Web services* to implement the goal. That is, we need to discover Web services that may have no direct connection whatsoever to the goal, as long as they can usefully contribute to/benefit from other already discovered Web services. To discover such indirectly relevant Web services, we use a loop performing a simple forward or backward chaining, where the atomic discovery step in the loop is a standard discovery based on either only precondition matching (in forward chaining) or postcondition matching (in backward chaining). The atomic discovery step can use either so-called "subsumption" or "plug-in" matches, or so-called "intersection" or "partial" matches. Full details on our techniques will be given near the end of this chapter, in Section 5.6.2.

Similar to the verification techniques in the previous chapter, our composition takes place in a formalism following work from the AI actions and change literature [322] and from the update of DL ontologies [180, 65]. WSMO capabilities and OWL service profiles can be naturally formulated in this formalism, for a relevant subset of the respective logics. Hence, once a relevant set of Web services has been discovered, the next step in our architecture (automatically) transforms those Web services into our formalism[7].

The main control loop searching for a solution is a forward searching engine inspired by recent work developing scalable tools for AI Planning, the Fast-Forward (FF) algorithm [139, 137]. The motivation for following this work

---

[7] For WSMO, such a parser has been implemented in our composition prototype – cf. Section 6.3.

is its extreme success in the AI Planning area, winning several prizes at the International Planning Competitions, and inspiring a whole generation of efficient planning tools. This work was conducted in cooperation with the main author of the FF algorithm, Jörg Hoffmann.

The main loop, as described in the next subsection, searches in a space of search *states*. Each of those states corresponds to the situation brought about by a particular combination of Web services. More precisely, each state arises as the result of applying a particular sequence of Web services, where the "result" refers to the possible truth values of logical statements about the objects of interest. The loop calls upon a *reasoning* component to compute the state transitions. To guide the search, the loop calls a *heuristic function* in each state, which returns an integer value estimating the distance to the nearest solution state and a set of the most promising services. In other words, the heuristic function estimates how many Web services need still be added to the current sequence in order to obtain a solution. Further, the heuristic function returns filtering information, in the form of a subset of Web services which should be tried next. The loop stops when a solution has been found. This solution is then a sequence of Web services.

In BPM, it is of importance to exploit parallelism where possible, since it reduces the overall process execution time per instance. Therefore, a final step in the architecture removes unnecessary ordering constraints from the solution. The solution is "parallelized", turning it into a partially ordered subprocess. We emphasis here that this configuration of functionalities is a deliberate choice. An alternative, which was explored by [206], is to use parallel Web services[8] "online" during search already, rather than using a post-processing step "off-line" to remove the unnecessary orderings. While the online approach seems more natural at first sight, the experience from AI Planning (and from [206]) is that parallel state transitions seriously impede performance, due to the much higher branching factor. Further, experience from AI Planning tells us that off-line parallelization techniques can be quite successful [19, 73].

One intricacy of parallelization in our context is that matters are complicated by the presence of background ontologies. In the absence of such an ontology, e.g., in standard AI Planning formalisms, performing two services in parallel yields exactly the same outcome as applying them in either of the two possible orderings, provided the services do not have any direct conflicts between their respective effects and preconditions. This is not so in our context. If background ontologies affect the consequences of the outcome of a service, then it makes a difference whether two things are achieved one-by-one, or whether they are achieved *at the same time*. The latter may allow more deductions. We will give an example for this below, in Section 5.3, when we introduce our WSC formalism. Note that this phenomenon is rather artificial, because in process execution environments one can never (or only in very rare cases) guarantee that two activities are performed at exactly the

---

[8] Sets of services to be executed in parallel, as opposed to single services.

same time. What we really want is that *every possible sequentialization* of a parallel solution is valid. With the phenomenon explained above, such a test in general involves enumerating all the possible sequentializations, which is of course exponential in the size of the solution. This difficulty can be avoided by performing parallelization based on the simplifying assumption that parallel services *can* actually be performed at exactly the same time. The details of parallelization are not discussed in this work; a simple greedy algorithm has been described in [74]. The basic idea is the following: while there are ordering constraints that have not been tested, try if removing one of them still yields a valid solution; if so: remove the ordering constraint and continue.

Following this overview, we now describe the main loop algorithm below.

5.2.2 Forward Search

We next outline the workings of the primary main loop in more detail. The pseudo-code given in Figure 5.3 corresponds to an algorithm for deterministic services, i.e., where the explicit effect of a service is known in advance. For domains where this is not the case, Section 5.2.3 discusses an alternative main loop.

$s_0 := reasoning\text{-}startstate()$
if s_0 is undefined **then return** "start state is inconsistent"
$(h, H) := heuristic\text{-}function(s_0)$
open-list $:= \langle (s_0, h, H) \rangle$
while TRUE **do**
    if open-list is empty **then return** "no solution exists"
    $(s, h, H) :=$ remove-front(open-list)
    if is-solution(s) **then return** path leading to s
    $appl :=$ find-all-services-with-satisfied-precondition(s, H)
    for all $a \in appl$ **do**
        $s' := reasoning\text{-}resultstate(s, a)$
        if s' is undefined **then continue**
        $(h', H') := heuristic\text{-}function(s')$
        insert-queue-ordered-by-increasing-h(open-list,s',h',H')

Fig. 5.3. The main loop, performing forward search.

The overall structure of the algorithm in Figure 5.3 is straight out of the standard AI text books, e.g., [258]. The input to the algorithm is a composition problem. Its output is either a solution to the problem, or a message that no such solution exists, or a message that the start state is inconsistent. The latter implies that the user goal precondition cannot be satisfied, in which case, of course, a solution cannot usefully be composed.

The algorithm performs a search in a space of "search states" s. Each s corresponds to a set of possible configurations of the instances in the background ontology. The possible configurations change as Web services are applied, and the states keep track of this information. The computation needed for this purpose is encapsulated in the *reasoning-startstate* and *reasoning-resultstate* functions, which are supplied by the reasoning component of our approach, c.f. Figure 5.2. The precise form the search states take, and the computation needed to implement *reasoning-startstate* and *reasoning-resultstate*, depends on the allowed ontology modeling constructs. Full details on this will be given in Section 5.4. In a nutshell, *reasoning-startstate* creates the start search state for the search; the input for this computation is the precondition of the user goal, as specified for the composition problem. Computing the start search state involves, amongst other things, reasoning over the background ontology in order to identify its logical consequences, i.e., the literals that follow from user goal precondition and the ontology. Similarly, *reasoning-resultstate* takes a search state s and a Web service a, and returns the corresponding result state, capturing what happens if we apply a to s. Again, this involves reasoning over the background ontology, amongst other things.

Let us assume for the moment that the *reasoning-startstate* and *reasoning-resultstate* functions are available. The basic data structure of the algorithm is the "open-list". This is a list of triples (s, h, H) where s is a search state as explained above, and h and H are the corresponding return values of *heuristic-function*, which takes a search state s and returns h as well as H. The former is an estimate of how many Web service need still be applied to s in order to obtain a solution. In accordance with an algorithm usually referred to as "greedy best-first search" [258], the algorithm orders search states by increasing h. In other words, the search prefers to explore states that appear – according to the estimation done by *heuristic-function* – to be closer to a solution. As for H in (s, h, H), this is a subset of the Web services that are applicable in s; the search is constrained to consider only search states generated by H, and in this way H serves to prune the search space.

Let us consider in detail how the algorithm processes the open list. The list is initialized with the start state, and the corresponding outputs of *heuristic-function*. The algorithm then enters a loop. If the open list is empty, then we have unsuccessfully explored the entire search space and can hence stop. Otherwise, we remove the front element from the list – a search state with minimal h value – and perform some processing for this state. First, the "is-solution" function determines whether s corresponds to a solution, i.e., whether the user goal postcondition is true in every possible configuration of the instances in the background ontology. This test will be easy to do based on the information stored in search states; details are in Section 5.4.

If s is not a solution, then we must continue the search; in AI parlance, we now "expand" s. First, the "find-all-services-with-satisfied-precondition" function determines which services – a subset of the ones contained in H, in the case of filtering – can be applied next. This functionality basically checks the service preconditions; like the solution test, this will be easy to do based on the information stored in search states. After the applicable services have been determined, a simple loop processes each such service a. The outcome s' of applying a to s is determined using the *reasoning-resultstate* function. It may be that applying a causes a contradiction; in that case, s' is undefined and the service is skipped. Else, s' is evaluated with *heuristic-function*, and thereafter inserted into the open list as obvious.

It should be noted that greedy best-first search does *not*, in difference to the more widely known A* algorithm, give any guarantees on the quality of the returned solution, even if h is an admissible heuristic (a lower bound on the actual solution distance from the corresponding state s). The motivation for using greedy best-first search instead of A* is that, in almost all practical cases, greedy best-first search is by far more efficient than A*. Since response time is highly critical in our framework, setting the priorities this way seems more sensible. Note that the algorithm can be changed effortlessly to implement A* instead; also, weighted A* algorithms, where the trade-off between runtime and solution quality can be controlled via a parameter, can easily be used. This can be done by computing a value $f(s)$ for each state s as $f(s) = w \times c(s) + h(s)$, where w is the weight and $c(s)$ is the cost of reaching s (in our case, the number of services to reach s from the start state s_0). The open list is then sorted according to f instead of h. When w is low[9], the emphasis is on the heuristic value, and the behavior is similar to greedy best-first search. In comparison to best-first search, weighted A* trades some scalability for the feature of not pursuing dead ends in the search space that have a promising heuristic value. Depending on the heuristic function used, dead ends can be very unlikely to appear in practice – however, in most cases a dead end situation can be constructed for a known heuristic function.

It should also be noted that most AI text books, and most actual implementations of A* like search, include not only an open list but also a "closed-list". This stores all search states that have been generated so far, i.e., the closed list always contains all search states that have been inserted into the open list as yet (in other words, when the loop picks the first element from the open list, then that state is removed from the open list, but not from the closed list). Before a state s' is inserted into the open list, it is checked whether s' is contained in the closed list; if so, s' is skipped, i.e., excluded from further consideration. Obviously, since s' has already appeared in the open list, this can be done without affecting the completeness of the search.[10]

Closed lists are important if the same search state can be reached on different paths in the search space. This is typical of many search problems, e.g.,

---

[9] In our experiments, 0.2 seemed a useful value for w.

[10] The effect on solution optimality guarantees is much more subtle, see e.g. [227, 258]; one must re-open s' in case it was reached on a less costly path than previously. As stated, we believe that optimality cannot be guaranteed in reasonable time anyway.

those usually encountered in AI Planning. Hence closed lists are of potential relevance in our setting. Still, we do not include an explicit treatment of closed lists in the following. The reason for not doing so is that a naïve implementation – realizing the closed list as a store of already generated search states, with fast membership test via a hashing function – is trivial. More intricate solutions may test membership in the closed list not by identity, but by some measure of when a closed state s is guaranteed to be "better" than the s' which is tested. Exploring such notions in our context is a topic for future work.

5.2.3 A Non-deterministic Search Algorithm

The algorithm described above, as well as the remainder of this chapter, are concerned with deterministic services, i.e., services whose effect is purely conjunctive. When there are services with non-deterministic (optional) effects – i.e., it is a priori not known which (out of a set of possible) effects will occur when invoking the services – matters become slightly more complicated. In AI, these (and related) problems have been studied under the label "planning under uncertainty". A common formalization of the resulting search space is referred to as *And/Or graphs* [216], where And nodes refer to services and Or nodes to states. The naming is due to the fact that a solution in this search space is a sub-graph of the search graph, with all of the services' successor nodes and one of the states' successor nodes. Any path through the tree consists of an alternating sequence of And and Or nodes. A small example is depicted in Fig. 5.4. The meaning in the literature is the following. In a state, one can *choose* which of the applicable services to execute (thus a state is an *Or* node). A service execution leads to a set of possible successor states, and the solution forms a *contingency plan*, where *for each* possible successor state (thus *And* node) of a service a path to a goal state is available. Note that search with only deterministic services is a special case of search in And/Or graphs – cf. e.g., service a_2 in Fig. 5.4, which has only one possible successor state.

For a search space in this form, Nilsson first devised a heuristics-guided search algorithm called AO^* [215] ("AO" for "And/Or"), which found solutions in the form of trees in the search space. This algorithm was later on revised by Martelli and Montanari [192, 193] such that equal nodes in sub-trees are joined. The solution hence becomes a sub-graph of the search space. Nilsson then referred to the graph version as AO* as well [216]. This algorithm is a common foundation for planning algorithms in the presence of non-deterministic actions, cf. e.g., [123, 26, 136] and is referred to as *conformant* [137] or *contingent planning* [136]. The difference is, that in the latter case observation actions are available, which allow us to "sense" aspects of the world (e.g., does literal l hold?) even if they are not connected to an action's outcome.

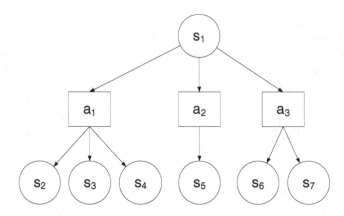

Fig. 5.4. And/Or search space: in a state s_1, the services a_1 through a_3 are applicable, each of which leads to a set of possible successor states.

In Fig. 5.3, the main loop for the deterministic case is shown. The alternative approaches that we use are best-first search, weighted A* search, and (Best-first or weighted) AO* search. All these algorithms can be encoded within a single main loop, as shown in Fig. 5.5.

$s_0 := reasoning\text{-}startstate()$
if s_0 is undefined **then return** "start state is inconsistent"
$(h, H) := heuristic\text{-}function(s_0)$
open-list $:= \langle (s_0, h, H) \rangle$
while TRUE **do**
        if open-list is empty **then return** "no solution exists"
        $(s, h, H) := get\text{-}next\text{-}search\text{-}state(\text{open-list}, s_0)$
        if $is\text{-}problem\text{-}solved(s, s_0)$ **then return** $solution(s, s_0)$
        $appl := find\text{-}all\text{-}services\text{-}with\text{-}satisfied\text{-}precondition(s, H)$
        for all $a \in appl$ **do**
            $S' := reasoning\text{-}resultstates(s, a)$
            if S' is undefined **then continue**
            for all $s' \in S'$ **do**
                $(h', H') := heuristic\text{-}function(s')$
                if h' is undefined **then** $mark\text{-}as\text{-}unsolvable(s')$, **continue**
                if $h' = 0$ **then** $mark\text{-}as\text{-}solved(s')$
                $insert\text{-}queue(\text{open-list}, s', h', H')$
            $update\text{-}service(a)$
        $propagate\text{-}values(s)$

Fig. 5.5. The generic main loop, performing forward search. Generalization over Fig. 5.3.

A* and best-first search can be realized in this combined algorithm by ignoring some of the new functions (*mark-as-unsolvable(s')*, *mark-as-solved(s')*, *update-service(a)*, *and propagate-values*) and by simplifying the remaining functions to deliver the results from the previous algorithm (Fig. 5.3). In more detail:

- *get-next-search-state*(open-list, s_0) is realized as *remove-front*(open-list).
- *is-problem-solved*(s, s_0)) simplifies to *is-solution*(s).
- *solution*(s, s_0) is the path leading to s.
- *reasoning-resultstates*(s, a) is *reasoning-resultstate*(s, a), and returns an array of size 1 – deterministic services have only a single successor state, under the assumption that the ontology axioms do not create non-determinism.
- *insert-queue*(open-list,s',h',H') becomes *insert-queue-ordered-by-increasing-h*(open-list,s',h',H').

Like the deterministic search algorithm, AO* explores paths from a start state to a state that satisfies the goal. Unlike the deterministic algorithms, AO* has to take into account that services can have alternative outcomes. We therefore assume that postconditions have DNF form, i.e., are a disjunction of conjunctions. Hereby, either of the disjuncts (i.e., the conjunctions in the DNF) *will* be the effect of applying the service, and regarding them in isolation is sufficient.

The composition problem then is to find a solution tree as follows: the start state is the root of the tree, each leaf satisfies the goal, and all nodes correspond to search states or services. The search takes place in a (partially determined) And/Or Tree, as described above. We here mostly follow the notion of AO*, except for one deviation: for each successor state in which *the goal can still be reached*, a path to a goal state is known – and there must be at least one successor state where this is the case. The difference is, that not for all successor states there must be a path to the goal – only for those where the goal still can be reached. This change is necessary in the domain of Web services, since there are many services with one positive possible effect (e.g., a succeeded booking, approval, etc.) and many possible negative or erroneous outcomes (a failed booking, rejection, invalid input data, unavailability of the service, etc.).[11] Without the change, frequently there would not be a solution to a WSC problem.

In AO*, each node can be in one of the following states: solved, unsolved, unsolvable, or undetermined (states only). *Unsolvable* means that the goal cannot be reached at all from this state or with this service. *Solved* means that there is a path to a solution from this state / with this service, and that all successor states of services on this path are either solved or unsolvable as well. States can further be *undetermined*, i.e., their successor services have not yet been determined. *Unsolved* means neither of the above. The algorithm

---

[11] This is already specified in the WSDL standard [53], where the reply of a service can be of one defined message type or of one of a set of defined error types.

stops when the root node (i.e., the start state) is marked as either unsolvable or solved. This is checked by the function $solution(s, s_0)$.

Each state s further has a value $f(s)$ associated with it. If the state is undetermined, the function is defined as $f(s) = h(s)$, i.e., the outcome of the heuristic function. That implies that $f(s) = 0$ if s is a goal state (function $mark\text{-}as\text{-}solved(s')$), and that $f(s) = \infty$ when the heuristic function can already determine that this state is unsolvable (function $mark\text{-}as\text{-}unsolvable(s')$).

If s is determined and not unsolvable, then

$$f(s) = min\{w \times c(a) + f(a) \mid a \in A(s)\}$$

where

- $A(s)$ is the set of successor nodes (applicable services) in s which are not marked as unsolvable;
- w is the weight, similar to the weighted A* variant above, and can be set to 0 to obtain a greedy best-first AO* search;
- $c(a)$ is the cost of a service, which, if not further determined, defaults to 1;
- $f(a)$ is the value of a given service, and is determined as the maximum of the successor states: $f(a) = max\{f(s') \mid s' \in S(a)\}$; to be more precise: $S(a)$ is the set of possible successor states of a which are not marked as unsolvable.[12]

The function $propagate\text{-}values(s)$ updates the f-values of s and where else this is needed. I.e., after a state has been determined (starting in the fourth line of the while loop in Fig. 5.5), the values of this state node and all its predecessors must be updated (from the successors of s to s itself and from there on towards the root). When, at a given propagation, no change in f occurs, the propagation can be terminated.

The function $get\text{-}next\text{-}search\text{-}state(\text{open-list}, s_o)$ returns the most promising (lowest f) undetermined state: starting from the start node s_0, the function always selects the next state / service with the minimal f value which is neither unsolvable nor solved. Due to this behavior, it is unnecessary to maintain the open list (i.e., to implement $insert\text{-}queue(\text{open-list}, s', h', H')$).

$reasoning\text{-}resultstates(s, a)$ applies the previous function $reasoning\text{-}resultstate$ for each possible outcome of a service a, i.e., for each conjunct in the DNF effect. It thus yields a set of possible successor states.

The heuristic function can address non-deterministic services in a number of ways. An estimate can be obtained by pretending that we can *choose* which of the possible effects will occur. For this to be the case, a service with an effect in DNF is split up into multiple services, one for each disjunct in the effect. The heuristic estimate is then a guess of the minimal number of necessary services,

---

[12] Note that using the maximum of the successor states' f values is a rather conservative estimate. Other options include the arithmetic mean, or, if the transition probabilities for the successor states are known, a linear combination of those and the f values [123].

basically approximating $f(a) = min\{f(s') \mid s' \in S(a)\}$ (i.e., *min* instead of *max*). This is a relaxation of the problem, and it is easy to construct cases where this relaxation leads to less accurate estimates. Intuitively it seems desirable to have a heuristic function that estimates how many services are required in the contingency plan or in the worst case. Adapting the heuristic function in this way is left for future work.

In contrast to the classic notion of joining equal states in a solution graph, our actual solution is only concerned with the services. We thus construct a solution tree or graph as described in literature [216], remove the state nodes, and merge sub-graphs with equal services. The difference stems from the preconditions: different states can make the same service applicable. A screenshot with an example is shown in the next Chapter, in Fig. 6.3.

5.3 Formalizing Web Service Composition

In this section, we introduce a formalism for Web Service Composition, denoted $\mathcal{WSC}$. While there are commonalities with the formalism for the verification in the previous chapter, there are also various differences like the treatment of inputs and outputs. For this reason, and for enabling a reader to consume this chapter without reading the previous one, we describe the formalisms in isolation.

As stated, the formalism, like all recent work on semantics for WSC (e.g. [182, 17, 65]), follows the possible models approach [322] to address the frame and ramification problems. The input/output behavior of SWS maps to input/output parameters, on which preconditions and effects are specified. This closely follows the specification of SWS at the OWL-S "service profile" level and at the WSMO "service capability" level. We first introduce the syntax, then the semantics.

5.3.1 $\mathcal{WSC}$ Syntax

We use standard terminology from logics, involving predicates G, H, I, variables x, y, and constants c, d, e (ontology "instances"). We treat equality as a "built-in" predicate. *Literals* are possibly negated predicates whose arguments are variables or constants; if all arguments are constants, the literal is *ground*. Given a set X of variables, we denote by $\mathcal{L}^X$ the set of all literals which use only variables from X. If l is a literal, we write $l[X]$ to indicate that l uses variables X. If $X = \{x_1, \ldots, x_k\}$ and $C = \{c_1, \ldots, c_k\}$, then by $l[c_1, \ldots, c_k/x_1, \ldots, x_k]$ we denote the substitution, abbreviated $l[C]$. In the same way, we use the substitution notation for any construct involving variables. By $\neg l$, we denote the inverse of literal l. If L is a set of literals, then $\neg L$ denotes $\{\neg l \mid l \in L\}$, and $\bigwedge L$ denotes $\bigwedge_{l \in L} l$.

An *ontology* Ω is a pair $(P, \mathcal{T})$ where P is a set of predicates and $\mathcal{T}$ is a conjunction of closed first-order formulas. We call $\mathcal{T}$ a *theory*. A *clause* is a disjunction of literals with universal quantification on the outside, e.g. $\forall x. \neg G(x) \vee H(x) \vee I(x)$. A clause is *Horn* if it contains at most one positive literal. A clause is *binary* if it contains at most two literals. $\mathcal{T}$ is Horn/binary if it is a conjunction of Horn/binary clauses. Note that binary clauses can be used to specify many common ontology properties such as subsumption relations $\forall x. G(x) \Rightarrow H(x)$ ($\phi \Rightarrow \psi$ abbreviates $\neg \phi \vee \psi$), type restrictions for attribute ranges $\forall x, y. G(x, y) \Rightarrow H(y)$, and role symmetry $\forall x, y. G(x, y) \Rightarrow G(y, x)$. An example of a property that is Horn (but not binary) is role transitivity, $\forall x, y, z. G(x, y) \wedge G(y, z) \Rightarrow G(x, z)$.

A *Web service* w is a tuple $(X_w, \mathrm{pre}_w, Y_w, \mathrm{eff}_w)$, where X_w, Y_w are sets of variables, pre_w is a conjunction of literals from $\mathcal{L}^{X_w}$, and eff_w is a conjunction of literals from $\mathcal{L}^{X_w \cup Y_w}$. The intended meaning is that X_w are the inputs and Y_w the outputs, i.e., the new constants created by the Web service; pre_w is the precondition, eff_w the effect (sometimes referred to as the *postcondition* in the literature). Before a Web service can be applied (i.e., called), its inputs and outputs must be instantiated with constants, yielding a *service*; to avoid confusion with the search states s, we also refer to services as (Web service) *applications*, and denote them with a. Formally, for a Web service $(X, \mathrm{pre}, Y, \mathrm{eff})$ and tuples of constants C_a and E_a, a service a is given by $(\mathrm{pre}_a, \mathrm{eff}_a) = (\mathrm{pre}, \mathrm{eff})[C_a/X, E_a/Y]$. The Web service's inputs are instantiated with the constants C_a, and its outputs are instantiated with the constants E_a. The E_a thus are the constants that are created by a given service.

$\mathcal{WSC}$ *Problems* are tuples $(\Omega, \mathcal{O}, \mathcal{U})$, i.e., the collection of all aspects relevant to a specific composition request. Ω is an ontology and $\mathcal{O}$ is a set of Web services. $\mathcal{U}$ is the user requirement, a pair $(\mathrm{pre}_\mathcal{U}, \mathrm{eff}_\mathcal{U})$ of precondition and effect. By $C_\mathcal{U}$, we will denote a set of constants corresponding to the variables of the user requirement precondition. These will be the only constants taken to exist initially. In other words, these variables become generic and typeless "constants" about which we know only the user requirement precondition; we want to apply Web services from $\mathcal{O}$ to reach a situation where an appropriate instantiation of the variables in $\mathrm{eff}_\mathcal{U}$ is guaranteed to exist.

5.3.2 $\mathcal{WSC}$ Semantics

In what follows, assume we are given a problem $(\Omega, \mathcal{O}, \mathcal{U})$. The semantics of these problems – the definition of what a solution is – relies on a notion of *beliefs*, where each belief is a set of *models* that are considered possible. A "model" corresponds to a particular situation during the execution of a composition. Now, since the precondition of the user requirement does not completely describe every aspect of the status of the ontology instances, several models are possible initially. Similarly, since Web service effects do not completely describe every aspect of the changes they imply, executing a Web service can result in several possible models. This uncertainty about the actual situation is formalized in terms of beliefs, containing the entire set of models possible at a given point in time.

Formally, a model m is a pair (C_m, I_m) where C_m is a set of constants, and I_m is a C_m-*interpretation*, i.e., an interpretation of the predicates P over the constants C_m. Here, C_m contains the constants that exist in m; this serves to keep track of the creation of new constants. I_m is a truth value assignment to all propositions formed from P and C_m. We write $m \models \phi$ for $I_m \models \phi$, where the quantifiers in ϕ range over C_m.

The *initial belief* b_0 is undefined if $\mathcal{T} \wedge \mathrm{pre}_{\mathcal{U}}$ is not satisfiable; else, $b_0 := \{m \mid C_m = C_{\mathcal{U}}, m \models \mathcal{T} \wedge \mathrm{pre}_{\mathcal{U}}\}$. A *solved belief* is a belief b s.t. ex. a tuple C of constants so that, for all $m \in b$, $m \models \mathrm{eff}_{\mathcal{U}}[C]$. It remains to define how services affect beliefs. This is a rather involved definition, relying on a notion of transitions over models: given a model m and a service a, the result of applying a in m is a set of models, denoted $res(m, a)$. We will formally define $res(m, a)$ below. For the sake of readability, it is convenient at this point to explain how $res(m, a)$ will be used to define belief transitions. Assume a belief b and a service a; the result of applying a in b is denoted with $res(b, a)$. This is undefined if there exists a model $m \in b$ so that $res(m, a)$ is undefined, or so that $res(m, a) = \emptyset$.[13] Else, $res(b, a) := \bigcup_{m \in b} res(m, a)$. The res function is extended to sequences of services in the obvious way. A *solution* is a sequence $\langle a_1, \ldots, a_n \rangle$ s.t. $res(b_0, \langle a_1, \ldots, a_n \rangle)$ is a solved belief.

Note here that the requirement that a is applicable to *all* $m \in b$ corresponds to what is usually called *plug-in matches*: the ontology implies that a is always applicable. A more general notion are *partial matches*, where the requirement is relaxed to state that a must be applicable to *at least one* $m \in b$. We do not consider partial matches because, with those, update reasoning is **coNP**-complete even with empty $\mathcal{T}$.[14]

The last bit missing in the formal semantics is the core definition, which tells us what happens if a service is applied to a model. That is, we now define $res(m, a)$. Given a model m and a service a, a is *applicable in* m if $C_a \subseteq C_m$ and $m \models \mathrm{pre}_a$. That is, we require that the inputs exist and that the precondition is satisfied. If a is not applicable in m, then $res(m, a)$ is undefined. Otherwise, we set $res(m, a) :=$

$$\{(C', I') \mid C' = C_m \cup E_a, I' \in min(m, C', \mathcal{T} \wedge \mathrm{eff}_a)\}$$

---

[13] The former happens if a is not applicable to m, the latter happens in case of unresolvable conflicts between the a's effects and $\mathcal{T}$; more below.

[14] A reduction of DNF validity checking is straightforward.

Here, $min(m, C', \phi)$ is the set of all C'-interpretations that satisfy ϕ and that are minimal with respect to the order[15] defined by $I_1 \leq I_2$ iff $|I_1 \cap I_m| \geq |I_2 \cap I_m|$ – i.e., the number of literals that changed from I_m to I_1 is smaller than the respective number for I_2. In other words, a C'-interpretation is in $min(m, C', \phi)$ iff it satisfies ϕ, and is as close to m as possible. Note that the definition here is basically equal to the change semantics for verification (cf. Definition 4.6 in Section 4.2.2), but adapted to the composition context (i.e., handling variable-constant substitutions, etc.).

This definition of $res(m, a)$ follows the widely used PMA semantics for belief update [322]. As stated, the PMA is used in all recent works on formal semantics for WSC (e.g. [182, 17, 65]). Alternative belief update semantics from the AI literature (see [131] for an excellent overview) could be used in principle; this is a topic for future work.

The intuition behind $res(m, a)$ is as follows. The new set of constants is the old set of constants plus those generated by the service that is applied. The new interpretation must satisfy the theory, and the effect of the service. While this is a "must", we would also like to keep as much of the previous interpretation as possible – in particular if the service affects just one small fraction of the model, then we want the rest of the model to remain unchanged. Normally, what one does is simply to take the previous model, and to change the truth values of the literals as specified in the service effect. However, in the presence of a theory, more changes may be necessary. Consider the following informal example, a simplified version that abstracts from the verification setting of Example 4.8 from the previous chapter.

Example 5.1. Let p, q, r be propositions, $T = \neg p \lor \neg q \lor \neg r$. Let m be a model where $p = 1, q = 1, r = 0$. Let a be a service with precondition $p \land q$ and effect r. What happens if we apply a to m?

If we simply set $r = 1$, the model we get is $p = 1, q = 1, r = 1$. This model is inconsistent with T. The PMA resolves this inconsistency by making changes to what we inherited from m. Namely, p and q are not mentioned by the effect; their values are inherited. Setting one of them to 0 resolves the conflict; if we set both to 0, then the change to m is not minimal. Hence we get two resulting models: $p = 0, q = 1, r = 1$ and $p = 1, q = 0, r = 1$.

5.4 Update Reasoning

We now specify what the search states s from Figure 5.3 (c.f. Section 5.1) are, and how they are maintained. We first explain the basic aspects of our search; then we discuss the difficulties with unrestricted T, and with Horn T; subsequently we show that binary T can be dealt with efficiently; then we summarize our approximations for the general case.

---

[15] Note that, in a strict mathematical sense, this function is neither a partial nor a total order: antisymmetry is not given.

5.4.1 Basic Aspects of the Search

Our approach is based on forward search. We search for a solution in the space of beliefs b that can be reached by chaining services starting from b_0.[16] The elementary steps in such a search are: testing whether a belief b is a solution; testing whether a service a is applicable to a belief b; and computing the outcome $res(b, a)$ of such a service. The question arises: How do we represent beliefs? And even: Which *aspects* of the beliefs do we represent?

A naïve approach is enumeration of models, i.e., to store for each b the set of $m \in b$. This is infeasible due to the sheer number of such m: e.g., b_0 contains all models consistent with $\mathcal{T}$ and the user requirement precondition. In AI Planning, some works have addressed this problem by representing beliefs as BDDs [55] or in terms of CNF formulas [137]. However, those approaches do not consider ontologies – corresponding to an empty $\mathcal{T}$ – and hence deal with a trivial frame/ramification problem. It remains an open question if and how such approaches can be extended to our setting. Herein, we instead focus on methods that maintain only a partial knowledge about the beliefs b.

First, maintaining the information about which constants exist is easy. Since every model $m \in b_0$ has $C_m = C_{\mathcal{U}}$, and since every service adds the same new constants to each model, we have that $C_m = C_{m'}$ for every $m, m' \in b$ for every reachable b. We will hence ignore this issue for the remainder of this section, and concentrate fully on the interpretations, I_m.

The minimum knowledge we need to maintain about each b is *the set of literals that are true in all models of b*, which we refer to as $Lits(b) := \bigcap_{m \in b} \{l \mid I_m \models l\}$. Based on $Lits(b)$, we can determine whether a is applicable, namely iff $pre_a \subseteq Lits(b)$, and whether b is solved, namely iff there exists C s.t. $eff_{\mathcal{U}}[C] \subseteq Lits(b)$. So we define the search states s for the algorithm in Figure 5.3 as pairs (C_s, L_s); if b is the belief reached via the same service sequence, then we want to have $C_s = C_m$ for $m \in b$, and $L_s = Lits(b)$.[17]

5.4.2 General and Horn Background Theory

How do we maintain those s? There are two pieces of bad news. The first of those is that computing $Lits(res(b, a))$ is hard, even if $\mathcal{T}$ is Horn; similar to the proof of Theorem 4.18 in the verification chapter, this can be proved based on earlier work in the area of belief update [83]:[18]

---

[16] One can alternatively, e.g., search backwards or formulate the search problem as an instance of logical deduction; we choose forward search here because that has, in combination with heuristic functions, been found to be quite successful in AI Planning (e.g. [139]).

[17] This is in line with [65, 180], who require updates in DL to be represented in terms of changed ABoxes.

[18] By *fixed arity*, we mean a constant upper bound on predicate arity, on the number of input/output parameters of any Web service, and on the depth of quantifier nesting within $\mathcal{T}$. This is a reasonable restriction in practice; e.g., predicate arity is at most 2 in DL.

Theorem 5.2. *Assume a WSC problem* $(\Omega, \mathcal{O}, \mathcal{U})$ *with fixed arity. Assume a model* m, *a service* a, *and a literal* l *such that* $m \models l$. *It is* $\mathbf{\Pi_2^p}$-*complete to decide whether* $l \in Lits(res(m, a))$. *If* $\mathcal{T}$ *is Horn, then the same decision is* **coNP**-*complete.*

Proof Sketch: Membership: First, with fixed arity and nesting depth, transformation to grounded (propositional) format is polynomial. Second, for any m', in general it can be tested in **coNP** whether $m' \in res(m, a)$; if $\mathcal{T}$ is a conjunction of Horn clauses, then this can be tested in polynomial time. The claim follows from there in both cases with a simple guess-and-check argument.

Hardness for the general case follows by an adaptation of the proof of Lemma 6.2 from [83]. There are two sources of complexity, reasoning in $\mathcal{T}$ and minimization of change, and the proof shows that those complexities combine. More concretely, the proof is by reduction from validity checking of a QBF formula $\forall X. \exists Y. \phi[X, Y]$.

Hardness for Horn clauses follows by an adaptation of the proof of Lemma 7.1 from [83]. The proof shows that the complexity inherent in minimization of change remains harmful even if the ontology is in Horn format. More concretely, the proof is by reduction from satisfiability checking of a propositional CNF formula.   ∎

So, even if we are considering only a single model m, it requires exponential effort to determine $Lits(res(m, a))$. Note here that each decision problem (general/Horn) has worse complexity than reasoning in the respective fragment of logics. Note also that this is due to the frame problem: we have $m \models l$, and we want to know whether l *disappears*. We will see that, if $m \not\models l$, then testing whether $l \in Lits(res(m, a))$ is significantly easier. Before we do so, we deliver the second piece of bad news, which is concerned with belief updates in the Horn case:

Theorem 5.3. *There exist a WSC problem* $(\Omega, \mathcal{O}, \mathcal{U})$ *where* $\mathcal{T}$ *is Horn, a service* a, *and two beliefs* b *and* b' *so that* $Lits(b) = Lits(b')$, *but* $Lits(res(b, a)) \neq Lits(res(b', a))$.

Proof Sketch: A possible model m may disappear by service a', due to a conflict with effects and ontology, and m may not be re-created when the effect of a' is inverted by another service a''. This leads to beliefs b where $b \neq \{m \mid m \models \mathcal{T} \wedge Lits(b)\}$, and hence we can construct b and b' where $Lits(b) = Lits(b')$ but $b \neq b'$. A service a as claimed is then easy to construct.   ∎

This is because it can happen that $b \neq \{m \mid m \models \mathcal{T} \wedge Lits(b)\}$. So, even if we had access to an oracle computing $Lits(res(b, a))$, it would not always do to define search states as (C_s, L_s), because $L_s = Lits(b)$ does not provide enough information to compute $Lits(res(b, a))$.[19]

5.4.3 Binary Background Theory

The good news is: if we consider binary clauses instead of Horn clauses, then the difficulties disappear. We will now show this through a series of technical observations. First, literals $l \in Lits(res(b, a))$ do not appear without a cause:

Lemma 5.4. *Assume a $\mathcal{WSC}$ problem $(\Omega, \mathcal{O}, \mathcal{U})$. Assume a belief b and a service a. Then $Lits(res(b, a)) \subseteq \{l \mid \mathcal{T} \wedge eff_a \models l\} \cup Lits(b)$.*

Proof Sketch: Say $l \in Lits(res(b, a))$ does not follow logically from $\mathcal{T} \wedge$ eff_a. Assume $l \notin Lits(b)$. Then there exists $m \in b$ s.t. $m \not\models l$. Since $\neg l$ is consistent with $\mathcal{T} \wedge eff_a$, we can construct a $m' \in res(m, a)$ s.t. $m' \not\models l$, in contradiction. ∎

This means that, in general, $Lits(res(b, a))$ can be computed in two steps: (A) determine $\{l \mid \mathcal{T} \wedge eff_a \models l\}$; (B) determine which $l \in Lits(b)$ do not disappear, i.e., $l \in Lits(res(b, a))$. Note that, in the light of this, the meaning of Theorem 5.2 is that (B) can be harder than (A): if $l \notin Lits(b)$ then testing whether $l \in Lits(res(b, a))$ is the same as testing whether $\mathcal{T} \wedge eff_a \models l$, which is **coNP** for the general case, and polynomial for the Horn case.

Obviously, (A) is easy (polynomial) for binary clauses. We will now see that – in difference to Horn clauses – (B) is also easy. We first characterize exactly the cases in which $l \in Lits(b)$ disappears:

Lemma 5.5. *Assume a $\mathcal{WSC}$ problem $(\Omega, \mathcal{O}, \mathcal{U})$. Assume a belief b, a service a, and a literal $l \in Lits(b)$. Then, $l \notin Lits(res(b, a))$ iff there exists a set L_0 of literals satisfied by a model $m \in b$, such that $\mathcal{T} \wedge eff_a \wedge \bigwedge L_0$ is satisfiable and $\mathcal{T} \wedge eff_a \wedge \bigwedge L_0 \wedge l$ is unsatisfiable.*

Proof Sketch: Right to left: Let $m \in b$ with $m \models \bigwedge L_0$. We construct a model $m' \in res(b, a)$ by first setting the values following logically from $\mathcal{T} \wedge eff_a$, then filling in the remaining values according to m, then repairing m' until it satisfies $\mathcal{T} \wedge eff_a$. The latter is possible without affecting L_0; in the repaired model, l is necessarily false.

Left to right: Let $m' \in res(b, a)$ so that $m' \not\models l$, and let $m \in b$ so that $m' \in res(m, a)$. We set $L_0 := \{l_0 \mid m \models l_0, m' \models l_0\}$. If $\mathcal{T} \wedge eff_a \wedge \bigwedge L_0 \wedge l$ is satisfiable, then we can construct a model $m'' \in res(m, a)$ which satisfies $m'' \models \bigwedge L_0 \wedge l$ and is hence closer to m than m', in contradiction. ∎

From this, we can conclude that, with binary clauses, a literal disappears only if its opposite is necessarily true:

---

[19] This relates to [180], who show that DL updates can often not be represented in terms of changed ABoxes.

Lemma 5.6. *Assume a WSC problem $(\Omega, \mathcal{O}, \mathcal{U})$ where $\mathcal{T}$ is binary. Assume a belief b, a service a, and a literal $l \in Lits(b)$. If $l \notin Lits(res(b,a))$, then $\mathcal{T} \wedge eff_a \wedge l$ is unsatisfiable.*

Proof Sketch: By Lemma 5.5, there exists a set L_0 of literals such that, in particular: (1) Exists $m \in b$ so that $m \models \bigwedge L_0$. (2) $\mathcal{T} \wedge eff_a \wedge \bigwedge L_0 \wedge l$ is unsatisfiable. From (1) we get that: (3) $\mathcal{T} \wedge \bigwedge L_0 \wedge l$ is satisfiable. Because every clause in $\mathcal{T}$ has at most two literals, we have that, if $\mathcal{T} \wedge \bigwedge_{l' \in L_1 \cup L_2} l'$ is unsatisfiable but $\mathcal{T} \wedge \bigwedge_{l' \in L_1} l'$ is satisfiable, then $\mathcal{T} \wedge \bigwedge_{l' \in L_2} l'$ is unsatisfiable. Hence the claim follows from (2) and (3).   ∎

Putting Lemmas 5.4 and 5.6 together, and from the fact that reasoning in propositional binary theories is polynomial, we have our main result for binary clauses:

Theorem 5.7. *Assume a WSC problem $(\Omega, \mathcal{O}, \mathcal{U})$ with fixed arity, where $\mathcal{T}$ is binary. Assume a belief b, and a service a; let $L := \{l \mid \mathcal{T} \wedge eff_a \models l\}$. Then $Lits(res(b,a)) = L \cup (Lits(b) \setminus \neg L)$. Given $Lits(b)$, this can be computed in time polynomial in the size of $(\Omega, \mathcal{O}, \mathcal{U})$.*

Theorem 5.7 corresponds directly to a way of dealing with the states s from Figure 5.3: each s is a pair (C_s, L_s) as explained above; given a, we test whether $pre_a \subseteq L_s$; if so, we compute $L := \{l \mid \mathcal{T} \wedge eff_a \models l\}$, which can be done in polynomial time, e.g., following a graph-based approach as described in [14]; we then take the successor state to be $(C_s \cup E_a, L \cup (Lits(b) \setminus \neg L))$ where E_a denotes a's output constants; we stop when we found s so that ex. $C \subseteq C_s$ s.t. $eff_{\mathcal{U}}[C] \subseteq L_s$.

5.4.4 Approximate Update Reasoning

Of course, in practice it may be useful to able to handle more general ontologies, e.g., featuring arbitrary clauses. One option is to sacrifice some precision by mapping $\mathcal{T}$ into a more tractable case, e.g., projecting each clause into a binary clause. Such an approach, however, does not preserve soundness – the returned solution may make use of constraints that do not hold – and neither does it preserve completeness – the problem may only be solvable under weaker constraints. In this subsection, we provide a first set of insights in this direction; not all details are fully worked out yet, but the results already show that this is an interesting direction.

It turns out one can preserve either of soundness or completeness by approximating dynamically instead of statically: *instead of approximating the input to the composition, one can approximate the update reasoning that it performs.*

Our algorithm maintains search states $s = (C_s, L_s^-, L_s^+)$ (in particular the search states s are now triples rather than pairs), where L_s^- under-approximates $Lits(b)$, and L_s^+ over-approximates $Lits(b)$. The main underlying observation is that Lemma 5.5 can be approximated using information about $Lits(b)$. The algorithm is shown in Figure 5.6.

procedure *reasoning-startstate*()
(1) $L := \{l \mid T \wedge \mathrm{pre}_{\mathcal{U}} \models l\}$
(2)   **if** ex. l s.t. $l \in L$ and $\neg l \in L$ **then return** (undefined)
(3)   **return** $(C_{\mathcal{U}}, L, L)$

procedure *reasoning-resultstate*(s, a)
(1−) **if** $\mathrm{pre}_a \not\subseteq L_s^-$, $C_a \not\subseteq C_s$, or $E_a \cap C_s \neq \emptyset$ **then**
          return (undefined)
(1+) **if** $\mathrm{pre}_a \not\subseteq L_s^+$, $C_a \not\subseteq C_s$, or $E_a \cap C_s \neq \emptyset$ **then**
          return (undefined)
(2) $L := \{l \mid T \wedge \mathrm{eff}_a \models l\}$
(3)   **if** ex. l s.t. $l \in L$ and $\neg l \in L$ **then return** (undefined)
(4) $L^- := L_s^- \setminus \neg L$
(5)   **for all** $l \in L^-$ **do**
(6)   **if** ex. $L_0 \subseteq \mathcal{L}^{C_s}$ s.t. $T \wedge \bigwedge L_s^- \wedge \bigwedge L_0 \not\equiv 0$ and
                      $T \wedge \mathrm{eff}_a \wedge \bigwedge L_0 \not\equiv 0$ and
                      $T \wedge \mathrm{eff}_a \wedge \bigwedge L_0 \wedge l \equiv 0$
          then $L^- := L^- \setminus \{l\}$
(7) $L^+ := L_s^+ \setminus \neg L$
(8)   **for all** $l \in L^+$ **do**
(9)   **if** ex. $L_0 \subseteq L_s^-$ s.t. $T \wedge \mathrm{eff}_a \wedge \bigwedge L_0 \not\equiv 0$ and
                      $T \wedge \mathrm{eff}_a \wedge \bigwedge L_0 \wedge l \equiv 0$
          then $L^+ := L^+ \setminus \{l\}$
(10) **return** $(C_s \cup E_a, L \cup L^-, L \cup L^+)$

Fig. 5.6. Approximate update reasoning

In the start state, no "update" is involved and so no approximate update is necessary. Note that we use deduction in T – e.g. for determining $\{l \mid T \wedge \mathrm{pre}_{\mathcal{U}} \models l\}$ – as a sub-procedure; if that deduction is hard (when T is not Horn), then this step, too, must be itself approximated to obtain a worst-case polynomial procedure.

Lines (1−) and (1+) denote alternative options: (1−) for L^- is pessimistic (sound but incomplete), whereas (1+) for L^+ is optimistic (complete but unsound), respectively. The key to the algorithm are lines (6) and (9). (6) is a *necessary* criterion for Lemma 5.5: if L_0 is satisfied by a model $m \in b$, then certainly $T \wedge \bigwedge Lits(b) \wedge \bigwedge L_0$ is consistent, and then certainly $T \wedge \bigwedge L_s^- \wedge \bigwedge L_0$ is consistent. Conversely, (9) is a *sufficient* criterion for Lemma 5.5: if $L_0 \subseteq L_s^-$, then certainly $L_0 \subseteq Lits(b)$, and then certainly L_0 is satisfied by a model $m \in b$. Note here that we must use the under-approximation as input to the over-approximation: if $L_0 \subseteq L_s^+$, then it may *not* be the case that $L_0 \subseteq Lits(b)$. We get:

Theorem 5.8. *Assume a WSC problem* $(\Omega, \mathcal{O}, \mathcal{U})$. *Assume b is a belief and s is the corresponding search state as computed by Figure 5.6. For option* $(-)$, *if s is defined, then b is defined and* $L_s^- \subseteq Lits(b)$. *For option* $(+)$, *if b is defined, then s is defined and* $Lits(b) \subseteq L_s^+$.

Proof Sketch: Follows by Lemma 5.5 and construction of Figure 5.6.   ∎

Theorem 5.8 allows us to choose between a sound but incomplete or a complete but unsound procedure for the general case, with the key feature that *the construction via states* (C_s, L_s^-, L_s^+) *gets us around having to maintain an exact representation of the beliefs b*. If deduction is easy, like in the Horn case, then the algorithm is efficient except for its quantification over sets L_0 in lines (6) and (9). To obtain efficient technology, these must themselves be approximated, by a necessary criterion for line (6) and a sufficient criterion for line (9). One possible approach for the former is to recognize easy cases where an appropriate set L_0 cannot exist, and to remove l unless one of those cases holds; the trivial instantiation of this is to always remove l. One simple approach for approximating (9) is to always try only a limited number of sets L_0, and remove l if one of those fires; the trivial instantiation is to never remove l. It remains to be seen in future work how approximations of this kind can be realized, and what their empirical performance (in terms of both runtime and solution quality) is.

5.5 Heuristic Function

We now present techniques to effectively navigate the forward search. For this purpose, we develop a heuristic function (the *heuristic-function* sub-procedure needed for the main forward search loop, Figure 5.3) that estimates the number of services still required to reach the goal ("h" in the main loop), as well as an indication of useful services to reach the goal that can be used for filtering ("H"). As mentioned earlier, heuristic functions are a way of dealing with exponentially large search spaces [227]. Our heuristic function is inspired by successful techniques from AI Planning [139]. The technical basis is an approximate composition problem, where the main approximation is to act as if both a literal and its negation could be true at the same time.[20] Given a state s, the approximate composition finds an approximate solution for s; h and H are then easily obtained from the approximate solution. We will see that the approximate WSC is computationally cheap enough to make its solution feasible in every s. Going beyond all previous approximations of its kind, we show how the approximate WSC can deal with ontologies, and with on-the-fly creation of new constants. We consider the general case, arbitrary T; our techniques for binary T are obtained from that in an obvious way.

---

[20] Note that this approximation is much more severe than approximate update reasoning as discussed in the previous section.

5.5.1 Main Approach of the Heuristic Function

In AI parlance, given a search problem, a heuristic function is defined as the solution to a *relaxation* of that search problem. The term "relaxation" here has the same meaning as the terms "optimistic" or "over-approximation". For every search state s that comes up during the search, the relaxed problem is solved starting from s; the size of the relaxed solution provides the distance estimate. A canonical example is the problem of finding a path from A to B on a map; a possible relaxation is to act as if one does not need any roads; and the heuristic function that arises as the solution of this relaxation is the straight-line distance. The question of course is, *what are useful relaxations of the problem at hand? And how do we solve these relaxations efficiently enough to do so in every search state?*

The art is in devising a heuristic function that is (mostly) optimistic (cf. the reasons for optimality of A* in obtaining the best solution, e.g., in [258]), but at the same time is as precise as possible. In other words, we want a *high* lower bound estimate. If the heuristic function delivers a low lower bound estimate, then this means that many more states will have the same heuristic value; for states with the same value, the main search algorithm from Fig. 5.3 degenerates to breadth-first or depth-first search[21].

As said, the primary relaxation we employ is that an interpretation may contain a literal *and* its negate. We thus assume the "principle of contradiction"[22], i.e., $\neg(l \wedge \neg l)$, no longer holds. A general intuition behind the relaxation in our context is that we "keep all old values when updating the state". The state can thus only grow monotonically. Recall the trouble related to the frame problem in the previous section. A crucial aspect of the relaxation we make is that, in the spirit of "keeping all old values", we just act as if all old intersection literals survive. This simple measure essentially removes the frame problem, and thus puts the reasoning back on the same level of complexity as the reasoning in the theory itself, c.f. Theorem 5.2.

None of the related heuristic functions based on ignoring negative effects (e.g. [197, 36, 139, 106, 52, 47, 137]) can deal with background theories. Further, ours is the first approach that can deal with on-the-fly creation of new constants. We remark that the latter is crucial, because a naïve solution to this problem generates exponentially many constants each time the approximated problem is solved.

To give an overview, the following is a rough description of our approximate WSC algorithm; for simplicity, we ignore the background theory for the moment. Figures 5.9 and 5.11 depict the procedures graphically, but since they make use of the formal symbols introduced below, they are positioned in the explanation of the formal presentation. First, a forward chaining step builds

---

[21] Depending on the exact insertion of states into the open list: inserting a new state *before* all states with the same h results in a depth-first sorting style; inserting the new state *after* all states with the same h results in breadth-first-like search.

[22] First mentioned in "Politeia" (The Republic) by Plato, approximately 380 B.C.

what we call an *approximated composition graph (ACG)*. When it starts, this step applies all services that are applicable in the current state, and accumulates their results. The result of the application is an enlarged state: those literals affected by the services accumulate new values. To that enlarged state, again all applicable services are applied – which may now be more than in the previous state – and we obtain an even larger state. This process is iterated as long as applying services yields new values, and the goal is not contained in the current state. If a fixpoint is reached that does not contain the goal, then it is proved that there is no solution. The heuristic estimate is then set to be infinite. Otherwise, if the goal is reached in one of the enlarged states, then the forward chaining step stops, and a backward chaining step is invoked. The latter step is called *approximated solution extraction*. This selects a subset of the services reached during the forward chaining. Namely, a subset is selected that is relevant to support the goal. The number of services in this subset yields the heuristic estimate. It is important to note here that the backward step is necessary to obtain a high-quality heuristic. The number of forward iterations until reaching the goal is typically, at least in AI Planning, a far too optimistic (under-estimating) heuristic.[23] On the other hand, the total number of services reached during the forward chaining is typically a far too pessimistic (over-estimating) heuristic function.

More formally:

procedure *heuristic-function(s)*
(1) $(t_{max}, C, L, A, S) := build\text{-}ACG(s)$
(2) **if** $t_{max} = \infty$ **then return** $(\infty, \emptyset)$
(3) $\langle A_0, \ldots, A_{t-1} \rangle := extract(t_{max}, C, L, A, S)$
(4) **return** $(\sum_{i=0}^{t_{max}-1} |A_i|, \{w \in \mathcal{O} \mid a \in A_0 \text{ is based on } w\})$

Fig. 5.7. Heuristic function main control

The approximate WSC consists of a forward step, *build-ACG*, and of a backward step, *extract*. Figure 5.7 shows how these are arranged. First, the forward step returns a tuple (t, C, L, A, S). The meaning of this tuple will become clear below; t is an estimation of how many steps it takes to achieve $eff_{\mathcal{U}}$, starting from s. If $t = \infty$ then we know that $eff_{\mathcal{U}}$ cannot be reached from s, and we can prune s from the search. Otherwise, the backward step, *extract*, is called, returning an approximate solution $\langle A_0, \ldots, A_{t-1} \rangle$ where each A_i is a set of services. The heuristic function returns the count of services as h, and the set of Web services participating in A_0 as H.

5.5.2 Building an Approximated Composition Graph

We now describe the function *build-ACG* in detail.

---

[23] This kind of heuristic function was used in the composition tool developed in [206].

procedure *build-ACG(s)*
/* s must contain information providing C and L */
(1) $t := 0;\ C_0 := C$ s.t. $C \supseteq C_b;\ L_0 := L$ s.t. $L \supseteq Lits(b)$
(2) **while** not ex. $C \subseteq C_t$ s.t. $\text{eff}_{\mathcal{U}}[C] \subseteq L_t$ **do**
(3)   create $\{e_{t+1}^1, \ldots, e_{t+1}^M\}$ s.t. $\{e_{t+1}^1, \ldots, e_{t+1}^M\} \cap C_t = \emptyset$
(4) $C_{t+1} := C_t \cup \{e_{t+1}^1, \ldots, e_{t+1}^M\};\ L_{t+1} := L_t$
(5) $A_t := \{w[C/X_w, (e_{t+1}^1, \ldots, e_{t+1}^{|Y_w|})/Y_w] \mid$
$$w \in \mathcal{O}, C \subseteq C_t, \text{pre}_w[C] \subseteq L_t\}$$
(6)   **for all** $a \in A_t$ **do**
(7)   **for all** $l \notin L_{t+1}$ s.t. $T \wedge \text{eff}_a \models l$ **do**
(8) $L_{t+1} := L_{t+1} \cup \{l\},\ S(l) := a$
(9)   **if** $\sigma_e(L_{t-K+1}) = \cdots = \sigma_e(L_{t+1})$ **then return** ∞
(10) $t := t + 1$
(11) $t_{max} := t$
(12) **return** (t_{max}, C, L, A, S)

Fig. 5.8. Building an ACG

Figure 5.8 shows pseudo-code for *build-ACG*, Figure 5.9 depicts a constructed ACG. The notations are as follows. C_b is the set of constants in the belief (recall that all models within a belief share the same constants, c.f. Section 5.4). M is the maximum number of outputs any Web service has. K is the maximum over: 1; the number of input variables of any Web service whose precondition contains inequality; and the number of variables in $\text{eff}_{\mathcal{U}}$ if that contains inequality. The σ_e function maps any e_t^i generated in any layer t to a constant e^i.

The algorithm builds a structure that we refer to as the *approximated composition graph* (ACG) for s. The ACG is a tuple (t_{max}, C, L, A, S) where:

- t_{max} is the number of *time steps* in the ACG. At each time step t between 0 and t_{max}, the ACG represents an approximation of what can be achieved within t steps. t_{max} is the index of the highest time step built by the algorithm. This either means that the ACG reached $\text{eff}_{\mathcal{U}}$ (the user requirement effect) for the first time at t_{max}; or that the ACG reached a fixpoint without reaching $\text{eff}_{\mathcal{U}}$, in which case $t_{max} = \infty$.
- C is a vector of sets of constants, indexed by time steps t. Each C_t contains the set of constants that is considered reachable by the ACG, within t steps.
- L is a vector of sets of literals, indexed by time steps t. Each L_t contains the set of literals that is considered reachable by the ACG, within t steps. If $l \in L_t$, then the interpretation is that l can become known (true in all models of a belief) within t steps. L_t *may contain both a literal and its negation; both are considered reached, i.e., there is no handling of conflicts.*
- A is a vector of sets of services, indexed by time steps t. Each A_t is the set of services that is considered reachable by the ACG, within t steps.
- S is a function from literals to services. The meaning of $S(l) = a$ is that, if t is the first time step where l is reached in the ACG, then a can be used at

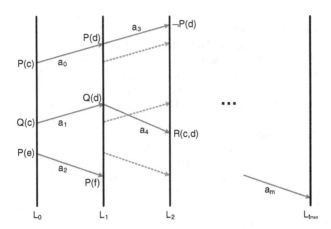

Fig. 5.9. Graphical representation of the *build-ACG* function. The strong gray arrows correspond to services a_i that can be applied on a layer L_j for the first time. The dashed arrows show schematically that repetitions of the a_i from previous layers are always possible on subsequent layers.

time $t - 1$ to achieve l at time t. S will be used to extract an approximate solution.

Line (1) of Figure 5.8 initializes the ACG, in an obvious way. Note that we do not require exact information as input to the heuristic function, but can make do with over-approximating information. That is, s is required to provide supersets of C_b and $Lits(b)$. The reason is that the heuristic function itself is by nature an over-approximating algorithm. With our techniques from Section 5.4, this will be C_s and L_s for the case of binary clauses, where we have $C_s = C_b$ and $L_s = Lits(b)$; it will be C_s and L_s^+ for the general case and approximate update reasoning, where we have $C_s = C_b$ and $L_s^+ \supseteq Lits(b)$. The ACG algorithm as specified works with any representation of search states, as long as appropriate $C \supseteq C_b$ and $L \supseteq Lits(b)$ can efficiently be extracted from it. In principle, it can be imagined to devise an under-approximating algorithm as the heuristic function instead, although this would be very unconventional; the entire vast literature on heuristic functions (see [227] as an entry point) is concerned with over-approximation. Part of the reason is that, because the heuristic functions influences only the order of search states, soundness can never be affected by it. However, the heuristic function may prune a search state if it comes to the conclusion that this node has no solution. Under-approximating heuristic functions may do so incorrectly, i.e., they may prune a search state even though it actually has a solution. So under-approximating heuristic functions may invalidate completeness of the search. Probably that may not matter when the search itself is under-approximating anyway. We leave this as a possible option for future research, and proceed with the more conventional over-approximation.

Lines (2) to (10) loop until the goal is reached in L_t, or until line (9) has stopped the algorithm. Each loop iteration extends the ACG by another time step, $t + 1$. Lines (3) to (5) set the constants at $t + 1$, and the services at t. This is straightforward; the only subtlety is the creation of new constants, which we discuss below. Lines (6) to (8) include all new literals that can be deduced from the effect of a service in A_t; the S function is set accordingly.

Line (9) is a fixpoint test. The test is non-trivial in that it takes the creation of new constants into account: since the ACG creates a set of new constants at every time step, it never reaches a fixpoint in the naïve sense. However, we *can* notice that all new constants behave exactly like the old constants. If that is the case, then extending the ACG further will not get us anywhere, unless some Web service (or the goal) requires several different constants with the same properties. The latter is captured by K as explained above; using the mapping σ_e, line (9) tests whether no relevant progress has been made in the last $K + 1$ steps. Lemma 5.10 below proves that this is correct.

A remarkable trick used in *build-ACG* is its handling of constants creation. We generate a fixed number of new constants – the maximum number of outputs of any Web service – per ACG layer, and let all services output *the same* constants. This saves us from exponential growth! If one allows different output constants for each service, then the number of constants may grow by a multiplicative factor in each time step, and the ACG size is exponential in t. A simple example: there are two Web services w_{GH} and w_{HG}, the former with input x of concept G and output y of concept H, the latter vice versa. There are 2 constants initially, one in G one in H. At $t = 0$ we get one service for each Web service, and hence at $t = 1$ we get 2 new constants. At $t = 1$ we get 2 services for each Web service, at $t = 2$ we get 4 new constants, etc. In this example the exponential growth is obviously redundant, but that redundancy is far from obvious in the general case. Our solution to this problem is best viewed as an additional relaxation, weakening the constraint that different services generate different outputs. In other words, the prize we pay for polynomial growth is a loss of precision. It is easy to construct examples that require a long solution, but that have illegal "short-cut" solutions where two different services create the same output. The ACG as per Figure 5.8 does not notice that the short-cuts are illegal, and hence the heuristic may be overly optimistic.

Our ACG algorithm has all the desirable properties of an over-approximation underlying a heuristic function:

Lemma 5.9. *Assume a WSC problem $(\Omega, \mathcal{O}, \mathcal{U})$. Assume a belief b and corresponding search state s; assume that $\langle a_0, \ldots, a_{n-1} \rangle$ is a solution for b. Then, executing build-ACG(s) without line (9) returns t_{max} so that $t_{max} \leq n$.*

Proof Sketch: Denote by b_t the belief after executing $\langle a_0, \ldots, a_{t-1} \rangle$ in b, and denote by C_t^b the set of constants shared by all models in b_t. One can prove by induction over t that, for every $0 \leq t \leq n$, there exists an injective $\sigma : C_t^b \mapsto C_t$ such that $Lits(b_t) \subseteq \sigma(L_t)$ where the extension of σ to sets of literals is per-constant as obvious. The claim follows directly from this. For $t = 0$, by construction we can choose σ to be the identity function. For $t \longrightarrow t + 1$, we apply Lemma 5.4, and get that $l \in Lits(b_{t+1})$ either follows from $\mathcal{T} \wedge \mathrm{eff}_t$, or is contained in $Lits(b_t)$. The latter is covered by induction assumption for a mapping σ_t; the former is covered by lines (6) to (8) when extending σ_t with $\sigma(c_i) := e_{t+1}^i$ where $E = (c_1, \ldots, c_k)$ is the output tuple of a_t. ∎

Lemma 5.10. *Assume a WSC problem $(\Omega, \mathcal{O}, \mathcal{U})$. Assume a belief b and corresponding search state s. If* build-ACG(s) *stops with $t = \infty$, then there is no solution for b.*

Proof Sketch: If the condition tested in line (9) holds in iteration t, then, continuing the algorithm, it will hold for all $t' > t$. This is because, with no changes in $K + 1$ steps, no further service preconditions, nor the goal, can become satisfied. The claim then follows with Lemma 5.9: assuming there is a solution of length n, *build-ACG* stops with $t < \infty$ in iteration n, which is a contradiction. ∎

Lemma 5.11. *Assume a WSC problem $(\Omega, \mathcal{O}, \mathcal{U})$ with fixed arity. Assume a search state s. If* build-ACG(s) *uses an oracle for SAT, then it terminates in time polynomial in the size of $(\Omega, \mathcal{O}, \mathcal{U})$ and s.*

Proof Sketch: Within each time step, the only exponential work is in deducing literals implied by $\mathcal{T}$ and effects; this can be performed by SAT testing. The claim then follows by a polynomial bound on the number of time steps. Such a bound follows from line (9). The number of constants distinct under σ_e is $|C_s| + M$. Line (9) operates only on literals based on these constants; the number of such literals is $\Sigma_{G[X] \in P}(|C_s| + M)^{|X|}$, where $|X|$ is fixed due to fixed arity. The algorithm terminates unless $\sigma_e(L_t)$ grows by at least one literal in every $K + 1$th iteration. Hence the number of iterations is bound by $(K + 1) * \Sigma_{G[X] \in P}(|C_s| + M)^{|X|}$. ∎

Taken together, all this means that the ACG computes what AI calls an *admissible heuristic function*, and that it does so in polynomial time provided deduction is tractable:

Theorem 5.12. *Assume a WSC problem $(\Omega, \mathcal{O}, \mathcal{U})$ with fixed arity. Assume a belief b and corresponding search state s. Let n be the length of a shortest solution for b, or $n = \infty$ if there is no such solution. Then* build-ACG(s) *returns t_{max} so that $t_{max} \leq n$; if* build-ACG(s) *uses an oracle for SAT, then it terminates in time polynomial in the size of $(\Omega, \mathcal{O}, \mathcal{U})$ and s.*

Proof. Immediate from Lemmas 5.9, 5.10 and 5.11.

Of course, we do not have an "oracle for SAT", as postulated here. However, we "only" need standard reasoning over $\mathcal{T}$, not the update reasoning from Section 5.4. If $\mathcal{T}$ consists of binary clauses, then, in line (7) of Figure 5.8, we can use standard machinery that efficiently decides whether $\mathcal{T} \wedge \text{eff}_a \models l$. Similarly, if $\mathcal{T}$ consists of Horn clauses, then we can use efficient standard machinery. If $\mathcal{T}$ does not fall into a tractable class, then an option is to map $\mathcal{T}$ into a stronger, tractable, formula: e.g. by removing all but 2 literals from each clause in case $\mathcal{T}$ is clausal. Such an approximation will preserve the stated property of t_{max}.

5.5.3 Extracting an Approximated Solution

By Theorem 5.12, we know that t_{max} is a lower bound on solution distance. This is nice because algorithms such as A* can use it to find provably shortest solutions [227]. However, we found that, using t_{max} as a heuristic function, A* fails to solve any but the tiniest examples. We address this problem by devising a different heuristic function: an additional *backward step* is performed on the ACG, to extract an approximated solution, which delivers much better search guidance in practice. See Figure 5.10.

procedure $extract(t_{max}, C, L, A, S)$
(1) **for** $t := 1, \ldots, t_{max}$ **do** $G_t := \emptyset$; $A_{t-1} := \emptyset$
(2) select $C \subseteq C_t$ s.t. $\text{eff}_\mathcal{U}[C] \subseteq L_{t_{max}}$
(3) $sub\text{-}goal(\text{eff}_\mathcal{U}[C])$
(4) **for** $t := t_{max}, \ldots, 1$ **do**
(5)   **for all** $l \in G_t$ **do**
(6) $A_{t-1} := A_{t-1} \cup \{S(l)\}$, $sub\text{-}goal(pre_{S(l)})$
(7) **return** $\langle A_0, \ldots, A_{t_{max}-1} \rangle$

procedure $sub\text{-}goal(L)$
(1) **for all** $l \in L$ **do** $t := min\{t \mid l \in L_t\}$; $G_t := G_t \cup \{l\}$

Fig. 5.10. Extracting an approximate solution

The approximate solution extraction chains backwards from the goal, using the S function to select supporting services for sub-goal literals. The sub-goals here are stored in the vector G of sets of literals, indexed by time steps t. The interpretation of $l \in G_t$ is that l should be made true at time t; by virtue of the $sub\text{-}goal$ function, we always have that t is the first ACG time step at which l is reachable. The main loop of the algorithm, lines (4) to (6), simply goes backwards over the time steps t in the ACG, selects a supporting service according to S, and marks the preconditions of that service as new sub-goals. Note here that, due to the way the ACG is built, we know that the preconditions will appear at time steps *below* t.

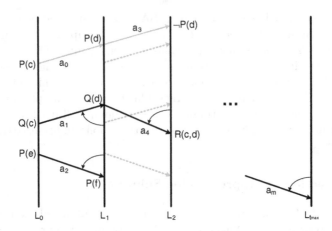

Fig. 5.11. Graphical representation of the *extract* function, applied to the ACG constructed in Fig. 5.9. The strong black arrows correspond to services a_i that are part of the extracted solution, the thin arcs sketch the workings of the support function $S(l)$.

In difference to t_{max}, $\sum_{i=0}^{t_{max}-1} |A_i|$ is *not* a lower bound: the function S commits to a particular choice how to support a sub-goal, although different combinations of such choices may result in different solutions. In fact, finding a shortest approximate solution can easily be shown to be **NP**-hard. However, our empirical results in the following confirm that $h := \sum_{i=0}^{t_{max}-1} |A_i|$ and $H := \{w \in \mathcal{O} \mid a \in A_0 \text{ is based on } w\}$) (c.f. Figure 5.7) deliver very useful search guidance in practice.

In certain situations, it can be helpful to enrich the support function with a cost function, such that it can distinguish between multiple services (including multiple instantiations of the same Web service) which support the same literal. Especially in settings where there are services with preconditions that require several other services' effects, this can be helpful in obtaining a lower heuristic value (corresponding to a shorter approximated solution). This is best explained with the following example.

Example 5.13. Consider the following scenario, as a motivation for the need for a cost function in the *extract function.*

Assume we have (in the notation pre → eff) the user goal: $A(c_0) \rightarrow F(x)$ as well as the following Web services:

- $w_B : A(x) \rightarrow B(o)$
- $w_C : B(x) \rightarrow C(o)$
- $w_D : E(x) \rightarrow D(o)$
- $w_E : A(x) \rightarrow E(o)$
- $w_F : B(x), C(y), D(z) \rightarrow F(o)$

The solution is depicted in Fig. 5.12, where one may note the synchronizing role of w_F.

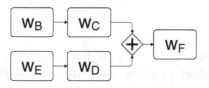

Fig. 5.12. Solution for Example 5.13

In the initial state s_0, the heuristic function estimates the correct distance of 5 services. Say the main loop picks an instance of w_B as a first service, yielding the state s with $C_s = \{c_0, c_1\}$ and $I_s = \{A(c_0), B(c_1)\}$. Then, executing the heuristic function for s yields the following service application layers (where s_X is an instantiation w_X, not showing the repetition of services, and omitting all but the s_F in A_2):

$A_0 = \{s_B : A(c_0) \rightarrow B(c_2);$
$\qquad s_C : B(c_1) \rightarrow C(c_2);$
$\qquad s_E : A(c_0) \rightarrow E(c_2)\}$
$A_1 = \{s_C : B(c_2) \rightarrow C(c_3);$
$\qquad s_D : E(c_2) \rightarrow D(c_3)\}$
$A_2 = \{s_F : B(c_1), C(c_2), D(c_3) \rightarrow F(c_4);$
$\qquad s_F : B(c_2), C(c_2), D(c_3) \rightarrow F(c_4);$
$\qquad s_F : B(c_1), C(c_3), D(c_3) \rightarrow F(c_4);$
$\qquad s_F : B(c_2), C(c_3), D(c_3) \rightarrow F(c_4); \}$

The interesting aspect in this example is, that A_2 contains four options to reach the goal, two of which use $C(c_2)$ and the other two $C(c_3)$. If one of the latter instantiations is be picked, then the precondition of s_C in A_1 becomes a subgoal, leading to the inclusion of s_B from A_0 in the approximated solution! The result is that executing w_B *again* is recommended by the heuristic function, and that heuristic value is then again 5. Note that this is actually *pessimistic*, since from s the goal can be reached in four steps.

The above example motivates why a cost function for supporting services is desirable. Fortunately, it is not hard to devise such a function. A simple cost function can be obtained by assigning to each ground literal in a fact layer the fact layer index in which the literal first appears. A cost for services can then be obtained as the sum over the precondition literals' costs. Keeping track of the cost of literals is very simple during *build-ACG*. We implemented this procedure in our prototype, with the result of significant speed-ups in scenarios similar to the example above.

With the description of the heuristic function in this section, we completed the explanation of the main parts of our composition approach: the formalism, the main loop, the reasoning, and the heuristics. We now shed some light on the peripheral parts of the approach.

5.6 Peripherals

As explained in Section 5.2.1, our overall approach has two pre-processing steps: information gathering and discovery. We now specify in detail how these two steps can be performed. Since the two steps happen outside our composition formalism, c.f. Figure 5.2, we choose a less formal presentation. We start with the information gathering approach in Section 5.6.1, then proceed to discovery in Section 5.6.2.

5.6.1 Information Gathering

In short, the technique we refer to as *Information Gathering* collects the information from the process context that is relevant for the task to be composed[24]. Information Gathering is very relevant in the context of using service composition to find task implementations; readers who are interested in service composition in general, but not this context, may safely skip this section and continue with Section 5.6.2. As depicted in Figures 3.9 and 5.2, and mentioned various times in this work, this step is thus done as a pre-process to task composition. Since this section is related to the previous chapter, we herein borrow some formal notation from there while generally remaining a rather informal presentation style.

Assume that information gathering would not be executed. Then, composition can only exploit the annotations explicitly attached to the tasks in the process. This may lead to cases where no solution can be found, possibly because none of the relevant services is applicable. If, however, the previous activity in the process has the effect of making a relevant service applicable, then it is clearly desirable to take this information into account: it may make the composition problem solvable. Further, task composition in this chapter is performed for a single task in the process in isolation, because process level composition is computationally prohibitive in practical settings. The orchestration that results from a task composition is locally consistent and correct. However, inconsistencies may be caused by a lack of information about dependencies to other tasks.

In this section we present a solution to the problems mentioned above. The rough outline of the approach is the following: (1) before starting task composition, all implicit information is derived from the process context; (2) based on this information we can potentially extend the precondition of the user goal; (3) also due to the context information, the user goal is enriched with a

---

[24] For the more general setting of the conceptual framework from Chapter 3, the same technique can be applied to service discovery and auto-completion.

constraint set. This constraint set is used to avoid the construction of a composition that is inconsistent with other parts of the process model. Given the extended precondition resulting from (1), composition can potentially start with more applicable services, which increases the chance that any solution is found. Further, the modeling overhead is reduced, since the precondition literals that stem from the process do not have to be redundantly annotated by the process modeler.

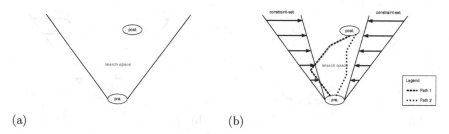

(a)   (b)

Fig. 5.13. Visualization of the composition search space. (a): the original search space. (b): alternative solution paths, one of which violates the constraint set.

In the remainder of this section we focus on the effects of these extensions on the search space in composition. In order to better explain the implications, we visualize the composition search space. Fig. 5.13 (a) shows an exemplary, unchanged search space, where the search starts from pre_i and tries to reach $post_i$. The funnel above pre_i then indicates the boundaries of the search space, which are essentially given by the applicability of services. Possible solutions can be depicted as paths from pre_i to $post_i$, as depicted in Figure 5.13 (b).

A solution path is only valid if it does not cross the boundaries of the search space. Note that Path 1 in Fig. 5.13 (b) leads through a region which is out of boundaries once the constraint set is taken into account. That is, Path 2 is valid with and without considering the constraint set, whereas Path 1 is only a valid solution when the constraint set is neglected. Below, we show how extending the precondition and the inclusion of constraint sets affects the shape of the search space.

First, we propose to expand the precondition of the user goal, i.e., the task n to be composed. For this purpose we merge pre_n with the logical facts which must always hold when this task may be executed. Given the process is executable (cf. Definition 4.10), which we require as per Chapter 3 as a pre-requisite, then this information can be obtained by computing $I^*(in(n))$ – see Section 4.6. Basically, those are the literals which were established at one point in the process before the current task, i.e., that were true from the start on, or that were made true as an effect of another task – and they cannot be made false before the task at hand is executed. As discussed in Section 4.5, the computation of this set of literals can be done in polynomial time for restricted classes of processes.

The effect of expanding the precondition pre_i is shown in Fig. 5.14 (a). In general, the extended precondition can make additional Web services applicable. This increases the choices to orchestrate Web services, and thus it becomes more likely to find a composition: a previously unsatisfiable goal may become satisfiable with the expanded precondition.

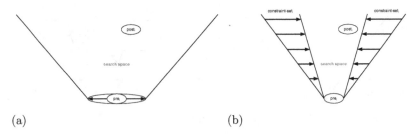

(a)   (b)

Fig. 5.14. Modifications of the search space. (a): expanded precondition. (b): constrained search space.

As a second extension, the constraint set may have an opposite effect. A constraint set is interpreted as a disjunctive formula of literals over the process variables, which expresses constraints on the states that may be reached during the execution of a task: if one of the literals from the constraint set appears in a state encountered by a composition, the constraint is violated. The constraint set is used to preemptively avoid precondition and effect conflicts, which result from parallelism of incompatible tasks in a process (cf. Definition 4.10). Thus, the constraint set is computed as the negated union of all preconditions and effects of the tasks that may be executed in parallel to the chosen task node n_i:

$$\text{constraint-set}(n_i) := \bigcup_{n_j \in N_T,\ n_j \| n_i} \{l \mid \neg l \in \text{pre}(n_j) \cup \text{eff}(n_j)\}$$

We can apply the M-propagation algorithm presented in Section 4.4 (or an alternative) to compute the set of parallel nodes for each task node. Given that, the computation of a constraint-set$_i$ is straight-forward. As above, this can be done in polynomial time. In principle, one could also allow the process modeler to explicitly model constraints; e.g., only services provided by preferred service providers may be considered. This is related to Requirement 14, protection scopes: the annotation could be made for parts of a process instead of single tasks.

As shown in Fig. 5.14 (b), constraint sets restrict the search space considered during service composition. As an important positive implication service composition avoids generating solutions that will conflict with tasks executed

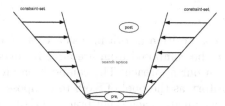

Fig. 5.15. Constrained search space with expanded precondition

in parallel. This can be achieved by filtering out services whose preconditions and effects would cause a conflict with the constraint set; in particular, this filtering can be included in the discovery pre-processing step that is described in the next section.

One problem may be that composition fails because a task in the process model cannot be composed without violating its constraint set. Then it may be useful to actually use the composition regardless of the violation, and change other parts of the process model to resolve the inconsistency. Thus, if no solution can be found, the composition of the task may be re-tried while ignoring the constraint set. The user can be asked for a decision whether to include the composition in the process (and thus to accept the violation); if so, or if the user approval is omitted, a subsequent verification step can highlight the violation – as foreseen in Sections 3.6 and 3.7.

By including both extensions (Fig. 5.15) we gain the best of both: while considering further relevant services we restrict the search space to compositions that do not cause process-level conflicts. However, note that the expanded precondition can actually be in conflict with the constraint set. Apparently, the respective goal is not satisfiable and should not be considered. While the conflict may be between the expanded precondition and constraint set, it can also be present with the original boundaries or the original precondition, respectively. The check in the second line of our main loop (Fig. 5.3) tests the presence of such conflicts, regardless of the origin.

In terms of runtime, the two extensions have contrary effects: On the one hand, the search space considered during composition is reduced through the constraint set, since it is used to prune away solutions which would lead to inconsistent states in the resulting orchestration anyhow. On the other hand, the extended preconditions may lead to a larger search space, if the composition is performed in the manner of a forward search (i.e., starting at the user goal's precondition, searching towards the user goal's effect); if, however, composition performed in a backward search manner (i.e., starting from the user goal's effect, searching towards the user goal's precondition), this downside can be avoided. We leave an according revision of the algorithms (main loop and heuristic function) for future work.

5.6.2 Discovery

Theoretically, if the composition algorithm has access to an SWS repository where all the SWS to be composed from are already collected, then discovery is not necessary in our approach. The composition algorithm could just take the entire repository as the pool of SWS to compose the solution from. However, of course such an approach is not practical if the repository contains several thousand Web services (which already is the case in some scenarios, cf. Section 6.3.2). Further, of course there may be situations where the available SWS are *not* conveniently placed in one central repository, and discovering them from multiple heterogeneous sources is actually a challenging task.

In that sense, discovery plays two roles in our approach. First, it serves as a relevance filter between the huge number of options offered by a large service repository (or the Web), and the necessities of the composition problem. In that way, as argued e.g., by [32], discovery is the first in a chain of steps iteratively addressing the complexity of Web service composition. Second, discovery can be used for filtering, as required by constraint sets from the above-described information gathering, or to filter out services with undesired annotations based on protection scopes (cf. Requirement 14). Third, discovery serves as the technical interface between the outside world and the inputs to our task composition algorithm, taking care of collecting a set of relevant SWS wherever they may originate from.

As stated in Section 5.2, it is a deliberate choice to perform the Discovery as a pre-process to composition, rather than interleaving the two processes. When doing the latter, meaningful heuristic functions cannot be defined. A heuristic function performs an estimation of the form "Given these available SWS, how many SWS will I approximately need to turn my current partial solution into a solution?" Obviously, this question is not applicable without the restriction on the available SWS: there could be a yet unknown SWS somewhere which turns any partial solution into a complete solution in a single step. At the other extreme, there may not be any SWS which can accomplish the composition problem.

Discovery in our sense can be implemented using standard discovery methods, e.g. [25, 117, 274], as the basic building block. The main difference between standard methods and what we need is that, in standard methods, it is assumed that a single SWS is sought which accomplishes the goal. By contrast, we need to discover any SWS that may become useful *at some point during the composition process*. In other words, for the composition a SWS may be useful even if it has no direct connection whatsoever to the user goal – it suffices if there is an *indirect* connection. Indirect connections can be detected via chaining methods. We present two variants, forward or backward chaining, in Figure 5.16.

Note that the pseudo-code in Figure 5.16 is more vague than the other pseudo-codes in this chapter; this is because discovery happens outside our composition formalism, c.f. Figure 5.2. The pseudo-code is written in a way

procedure *fwd-discovery*(user-goal)
(1) $P := \text{precondition}_D(\text{user-goal}); W := \emptyset$
(2)   **while** 1 **do**
(3)   *Discover* $W' :=$ all SWS w so that $P \supseteq_D \text{precondition}_D(w)$
(4)   **for all** $w \in W' \setminus W$ **do** $P := P \cup_D \text{postcondition}_D(w)$
(5)   **if** $W' \subseteq W$ **then return** W **else** $W := W'$

procedure *bwd-discovery*(user-goal)
(1) $G := \text{postcondition}_D(\text{user-goal}); W := \emptyset$
(2)   **while** 1 **do**
(3)   *Discover* $W' :=$ all SWS w so that $G \cap_D \text{postcondition}_D(w) \neq_D \emptyset_D$
(4)   **for all** $w \in W' \setminus W$ **do** $G' := G' \cup_D \text{precondition}_D(w)$
(5)   **if** $W' \subseteq W$ **then return** W **else** $W := W'$

Fig. 5.16. The discovery pre-process, in both variants, chaining forwards or backwards

so as to show up the main principles behind the chaining methods; the precise details on how to deal with preconditions and postconditions have to be filled in depending on the specifics of the underlying (standard) discovery method. Accordingly, the various set notations used for dealing preconditions and postconditions, $\supseteq$, $\cup$, $\cap$, $\neq$, and $\emptyset$, as well as the preconditions and postconditions themselves, are parametrized by the underlying discovery method; this is indicated by the subscript D.

By precondition_P we henceforth denote the set of predicate symbols in the precondition; similarly for postconditions. Let us assume a simple *set-based* instantiation of Figure 5.16 for the moment, where "precondition_D" is simply taken to be precondition_P, and similar for postconditions; accordingly, the notations $\supseteq_D$, $\cup_D$, $\cap_D$, $\neq_D$, and $\emptyset_D$ are the standard set notations. In this setting, it is quite easy to see what the algorithms do. The forward chaining starts with what is available in the user goal precondition, accordingly initializing the set P. Then, the algorithm discovers all SWS which are applicable to P. The postconditions of the new SWS are accumulated into P. If no new SWS were discovered, then the algorithm stops; otherwise, it iterates.

In a similar fashion, the backward chaining starts with what is relevant to the user goal postcondition, accordingly initializing the set G. (The naming G here is chosen to indicate that this set is "a goal", i.e., something we want to be achieved, rather than the set P in the forward chaining, which captures what we already did achieve.) Then, the algorithm discovers all SWS which may contribute to G. The preconditions of the new SWS are accumulated into G (this corresponds to the creation of new "sub-goals"). If no new SWS were discovered, then the algorithm stops; otherwise, it iterates.

It is easy to see that the set-based instantiation of Figure 5.16 is complete, in the sense that, if the underlying discovery method *can* discover the components of a solution, then it does so.

Observation 5.14. *Assume a user goal, and assume that discovery is performed by the set-based instantiation of* fwd-discovery *or* bwd-discovery *as per Figure 5.16. If there does not exist a solution to the WSC problem generated based on the discovered set W, then there does not exist any solution with SWS that are in reach of the underlying discovery method.*

Proof Sketch: By contraposition, making use of the exhaustiveness of the search up to the fixpoint. By construction, no Web service that becomes applicable at one point is not discovered by forward chaining; analogously, no Web service that can contribute to the goal (or the sub-goal after any number of iterations) is missed by backward chaining.   ∎

Note that Observation 5.14 holds only because the algorithms in Figure 5.16 keep iterating up to a fixpoint. Now, of course, going all the way up (or down, in the case of backward chaining) to a fixpoint may take significant time, and it may discover far too many, potentially irrelevant, SWS. One can trade some completeness for efficiency by stopping the chaining before a fixpoint is reached. In principle, the stopping criterion can be anything, as long as it keeps going at least until the *minimal stopping point*: before that point, the collection W of Web services does definitely not contain a solution. In the case of set-based forward chaining, the minimal stopping point is when $P \supseteq \text{postcondition}_P(\text{user-goal})$. In the case of set-based backward chaining, the minimal stopping point is when $G \cap \text{precondition}_P(\text{user-goal}) \neq \emptyset$.

While the set-based instantiation of Figure 5.16 has nice and obvious properties, one may wish to use more complex technology for the underlying discovery method, in order to gain precision. In particular, one may want to consider a *logic-based* instantiation. In that case, the subscript D on preconditions and postconditions is the identity function. Further, the operation $\supseteq_D$ is implication, and testing whether an intersection is non-empty is a consistency test. The adequate treatment of the $\cup_D$ operation depends on the direction of the chaining. In the forward chaining, the meaning of $P' := P' \cup_D \text{postcondition}_D(w)$ is that now we have achieved everything that we already had *and* the postcondition of w. Hence the interpretation of $\cup_D$ should be logical conjunction. Conversely, in the backward chaining, the meaning of $G' := G' \cup_D \text{precondition}_D(w)$ is that now a SWS can help us if it either achieves some of the things we had before *or* if it helps achieve the precondition of w. Hence the interpretation of $\cup_D$ should be logical disjunction.

It is pretty obvious that an equivalent of Observation 5.14 holds for this instantiation of Figure 5.16, if the algorithms are taken to iterate until a fixpoint. It is also obvious that the minimal stopping point for forward chaining is when $P \implies \text{postcondition}(\text{user-goal})$, and that the minimal stopping point for backward chaining is when the conjunction of G and precondition(user-goal) is satisfiable.

However, it should be noted that the logic-based instantiation of Figure 5.16 also has its imprecisions. Consider backward chaining first. In this algorithm, a SWS is considered relevant as soon as it does not contradict at least one of the goal postcondition or any of the preconditions of already collected SWS. While this – logical consistency – is the standard definition of what is usually called *intersection matches* (e.g. [274]), it would seem more desirable to have a test that tells us whether the SWS can actually *contribute* to the goal postcondition, or to any of the preconditions of already collected SWS. Note that the set-based instantiation of Figure 5.16 actually has such a notion, by postulating that the SWS mentions a predicate symbol that appears in the goal postcondition or in the preconditions of already collected SWS.

A possibly more important imprecision is inherent in the logic-based instantiation of forward chaining. The method simply conjoins P with all incoming postconditions. Chances are that this will pretty soon end up with a contradictory (non-satisfiable) P. This means that everything follows from P, and hence any SWS can be added. This difficulty can in principle be fixed by taking $\cup_D$ to be disjunction instead of conjunction, and by requiring not that P implies precondition(w), but only that the conjunction of P and precondition(w) can be satisfied. In this configuration, the forward chaining becomes rather similar in spirit to the backward chaining, using intersection matches to collect the SWS. The minimal stopping point for such a forward chaining is when the conjunction of P and postcondition(user-goal) is satisfiable.

A very common intuition in AI Planning is that backward chaining is more suitable to approximate relevance than forward chaining. When starting at the beginning, one can perform all sorts of actions, not many of which are related to what one actually wants to do (example: fly to China when the goal is to shop for groceries). By contrast, naturally the actions detected in backward chaining are relevant to the goal (flying to China would appear relevant only after many backward chaining steps). For this reason, our intuition is that backward chaining is the better choice than forward chaining. With the weakness of logic-based backward chaining mentioned above, the most promising method appears to be a combination of the set-based and logic-based backward chaining methods. Pseudo-code for that approach is given in Figure 5.17.

Note in Figure 5.17 that the test whether $\phi_G \wedge$ postcondition(w) is satisfiable can be done in the form of one separate test for each disjunct in ϕ_G; in other words, this test corresponds to testing intersection matches for the goal, and for all previously discovered Web services.

It is easy to see that the approach from Figure 5.17 is complete, in the same sense as before.

Observation 5.15. *Assume a user goal, and assume that discovery is performed by combined-bwd-discovery as per Figure 5.17. If there does not exist a solution to the WSC problem generated based on the discovered set W, then there does not exist any solution with SWS that are in reach of the underlying discovery method.*

procedure *combined-bwd-discovery*(user-goal)

(1) $G :=$ postcondition$_P$(user-goal); $\phi_G :=$ postcondition(user-goal); $W := \emptyset$

(2)   **while** 1 **do**

(3)   *Discover* $W' :=$ all SWS w so that $G \cap$ postcondition$_P(w) \neq \emptyset$ and

                                        $\phi_G \wedge$ postcondition(w) is satisfiable

(4)   **for all** $w \in W' \setminus W$ **do** $G := G \cup$ precondition$_P(w)$;

                                $\phi_G := \phi_G \vee$ precondition(w)

(5)   **if** $W' \subseteq W$ **then return** W **else** $W := W'$

Fig. 5.17. The best option for the discovery pre-process, combining set-based and logic-based elements in backwards chaining. By postcondition$_P$ we denote the set of predicate symbols in the postcondition; similarly for preconditions.

Proof Sketch: Straight-forward adaptation of the proof for Observation 5.14 to the combination of the set-based and the logic-based criteria.   ∎

Having presented all the pieces of our composition approach, we can now describe the connections between our and related work.

5.7 Related Work

As outlined in the beginning of Chapter 3, there are several meanings for the word "composition" in the service and business process context. From the perspective of service description and its usage in composition, [283] distinguishes two types of Web service composition: static and dynamic composition. Static composition there refers to WSDL Web services that do not have semantic descriptions. That is why there is no possibility to automate the composition process by applying the ontology reasoning techniques. Static composition has two main approaches: orchestration and choreography (cf. Section 2.2). The former combines available services by adding a central coordinator that is responsible for invoking and combining the single sub-activities. The latter defines complex tasks via the definition of the conversation that should be undertaken by each service participant. Consequently, the overall goal is obtained by the composition of peer-to-peer interactions among the collaborating services [169].

Automatic or dynamic service composition is the more challenging problem we address here. In the context of execution-level process design, we have essentially some aspects similar to orchestration, but are not concerned with technical details of service invocations. Instead, we remain at a conceptual level, where we are interested in finding an implementation, but leave the technical details to the person in charge of the configuration phase (cf. Section 3.6). The process context is taken into account via our information gathering technique, see Section 5.6.1.

Our underlying composition technology, as detailed in the beginning of this chapter, is most closely related to the usage of AI Planning in an automatic Web Service Composition. The key differences to previous work where outlined throughout the chapter already. Here we fill in more details, and give a broader overview of the related literature. The discussion is structured in three subsections, one for related work in the area of AI Planning, one for work in the area of update problems (which are related to our computation of search states during task composition), and one for related work in the area of automatic Web service composition.

5.7.1 AI Planning

Planning is a long-standing topic in AI, originally introduced having in mind the generation of action strategies for autonomous robots. Based on logical descriptions of an initial world state, a set of actions, and a goal, the planner should compose a (partially or totally ordered) set of actions – a *plan* – that transforms the initial state into a state satisfying the goal. Actions are described in terms of their *preconditions* and *effects*. By far the most popular logical framework, which has practically become a standard for more than two decades, is the so-called *propositional STRIPS* formalism [96, 196]. This is based on a restricted form of propositional logic, where formulas are conjunctions of positive atoms, and action effects are confined to sets of facts that are made true respectively false. Since the 90s, vast progress has been made. On the one hand, the discovery of a variety of automatically generated heuristic functions [34, 197, 36, 139, 128] and other heuristic methods [106, 140, 52] have boosted the scalability of planning tools. On the other hand, steady progress has been made in extending the language framework and algorithms to temporal and numerical constructs [272, 72, 124, 97, 78, 134, 138, 52, 107], as well as to dealing with user preferences [105].

STRIPS and related formalisms assume that the initial state of the world is fully known with no ambiguities, and that the action effects are deterministic. These assumptions are relaxed in *planning under uncertainty*. A variety of formalisms and solution algorithms have been developed, e.g. [271, 112, 109, 54, 35, 31, 232, 81, 55, 47, 44, 137]. In our context, *conformant planning* [271, 54, 81, 55, 47, 137] is particularly important. There, the initial state and action effects are ambiguous, and the plan is required to work for every possible initial state and effect outcome. This corresponds to a composed Web service that must work regardless of the ambiguities arising from incomplete descriptions of Web services and ontological information. Our non-deterministic algorithm, Fig. 5.5, is a variant of conformant planning: as argued in Section 5.2.3, we weaken the criterion of being "required to work for every possible initial state and effect outcome". This is done since it seems unreasonable in the Web service context: there can be goals where such a guarantee can simply not be made, e.g., when, regardless of the other choices, an approval or booking step is required, which always has the option of a negative outcome. Technically, our composition formalism is "conformant", in that we require the goal condition to hold in *all* possible worlds of the final belief.

One of the characteristic features of SWS composition that we address is that it happens in the context of a background ontology – the ontology in which the Web services are semantically annotated. Hence notions of background theories in planning are important in our context. There are such notions, and a few existing tools treat them. These approaches can be grouped into two classes: (1) Scalable tools incorporating the heuristic techniques, but with severely limited background theories. (2) Approaches with very general background theories, based on general deduction and lacking the planning-specific heuristic techniques. Examples of (2) are [81, 110]; examples of (1) are [285, 106, 52]. In the latter approaches, the main limitation is the requirement for a strict distinction between "basic" and "derived" predicates, where the actions are only allowed to affect basic predicates, and the background theory is only allowed to affect derived predicates [285]. Such a distinction is not possible in SWS composition; we circumvent it through focusing instead on commonly occurring (restricted) forms of the axioms in the background ontology. It is important to note here that the research in the area of the heuristic planning techniques has almost exclusively focused on temporal and numeric aspects of planning. The combination of the heuristic techniques with more general background theories has not been explored yet. One viewpoint on our proposed research is that it fills this gap, exploring interesting special cases – plug-in matches and restrictions on the background theory – to retain efficiency.

Finally, a certain relation exists of our work to formalisms from the actions and change literature, particularly works related to possible worlds semantics [322], planning with background theories [82], and description logics [17, 180, 179]. Like those works, we describe a formalism for state transitions in the presence of background theories (closely following [322] and [82]). Unlike those works, the main focus of our work is on scalable algorithms, not on different formalisms and their semantics/complexity. In particular, none of the mentioned works is concerned with identifying tractable special cases or the development of scalable tools.

5.7.2 Update Problems

Update problems, as discussed in Section 5.4, address the question how a belief (a set of possible world configurations) changes when a service's effect is applied to it. Variants of this problem have been known for a long time, under the name "database update" in the database community, e.g. [92, 323, 324], and under the name "belief update" in the AI community, e.g. [83, 131]. More recently, update problems have also been considered for Description Logics [17, 180, 179, 65]. Although the update problem may appear harmless at first sight, it actually poses a whole range of severe conceptual and computational challenges. The conceptual challenges essentially arise from the need to define which properties do *not* change when an update is applied [322, 131]. The computational challenges arise from the fact that, under most existing answers to the previous question, reasoning about the updated state is computationally harder than reasoning in the underlying logics itself [83, 176].

Abstractly speaking, these problems have the following form. We are given a description, Φ, of the current state of affairs, equivalently in terms of the set of possible world configurations or in terms of a logical formula defining those worlds. We are further given an update, ϕ, which specifies a change to the state of affairs. We want to obtain a description, Φ', of the state of affairs that results from updating Φ with ϕ.

An update problem of this form arises in dynamic Web service composition at the functional level, when considering Web service applications. Φ describes the set of possible configurations before that application; ϕ describes the effect of the Web service; Φ' describes the set of possible configurations after the application. This update problem is trivial in extremely simplified settings, e.g., the before-mentioned propositional STRIPS [196], where Φ describes a single world configuration (a value assignment to all propositional variables) and the updates ϕ are confined to conjunctions of ground literals. However, the update problem becomes very much non-trivial as soon as one allows uncertainty – Φ describes several possible world configurations – and/or background ontologies $\mathcal{T}$. In the latter case, the constraints of $\mathcal{T}$ hold in Φ, and they are required to still hold in Φ'; the latter means that $\mathcal{T}$ must be added conjunctively to the update ϕ, and hence the update becomes quite complex. Our Theorem 5.2, which we adapted from results by [83], testifies this complexity in the context of Web service composition (without DL constructors, in difference to [17, 180, 179]).

The correspondence of Web service applications to an update problem as above has previously been observed by [182, 17, 180, 179]. There is no work on Web service composition that disagrees with this observation. Most existing work makes severe simplifying assumptions trivialising the update problem. Often, the simplifying assumption is to ignore the ontology constraints, e.g. [237, 273, 263]. Sometimes, e.g., [58, 59, 60], the ontology constraints are restricted to subsumption hierarchies, where the update problem is also benign. Other works essentially base the composition on one or the other form of "input/output messages", e.g., [161, 135, 181]. The individual messages are independent from each other, and so one must reason in the ontology in order to determine the properties of the messages, but no update problem arises. In [267, 269], the difficulties in the absence of simplifying assumptions are observed, but the connection to the notion of update problems is not recognized. Finally, some works, e.g., [206], do deal with ontology constraints during composition, but do not define a formal semantics for that. We review all these approaches, including more algorithmic details, below in Section 5.7.3, when we overview the related literature on Web service composition. In the remainder of the section at hand, we briefly summarize the literature on update problems, and how it relates to our work on search states and search state transitions.

A fundamental difficulty in update problems is how to actually define the set of possible successor configurations, Φ'. As outlined in Section 5.4, this is non-trivial essentially because we must define what does *not* change as a result of the update. Most of the early works in this area, e.g. [93, 92, 108] addressed this issue by means of a notion of *minimal change with respect to Φ*, in one or the other sense. As stated various times, we follow the most popular approach of this kind, the *possible models approach (PMA)*, suggested in 1988 by Winslett [322]. Again, in this approach, Φ' consists of all worlds (all models) that satisfy the update ϕ, and that amongst such worlds are a minimal change with respect to at least one world of Φ. We adopt the PMA for our composition formalism $\mathcal{WSC}$.

It has been argued that the PMA exhibits unintuitive behavior in the case of disjunctive updates, and that the PMA lacks a notion of causality; various fixes for these shortcomings were suggested. For an excellent overview of these works, see [131]. With the exception of the non-deterministic services treated in Section 5.2.3, the problem of disjunctive updates is currently avoided in our Web service composition framework: if the action effects are not disjunctive, the only disjunctive part of the "update" is the ontology itself, which holds in Φ already. Causality is problematic because, to make use of such a notion, we would have to assume that the domain ontology is annotated in this regard; this may be an interesting topic for further research, but is currently not part our work. For this direction, it is helpful to view the ontology axioms as a set of *rules r* (e.g., as deductive rules in F-logic, cf. Section 2.3.2), which take the form $\phi_r \implies H_r$ where ϕ_r is the rule *body*, and H_r is the rule *head*. The body is a conjunction of logical *literals*, i.e., a list of positive or negated logical predicates. The rule head is a predicate. The intuitive meaning is that, whenever the rule body is true, the rule head is also true. For example, the rule may be $conn(x, y) \wedge conn(y, z) \implies conn(x, z)$, stating that the relation *conn* is transitive. The rule head may also be empty (false), in which case the rule body is not allowed to hold, and the rule is called an *integrity constraint*.[25] There are two simple options of basing causality on a $\mathcal{T}$ made up of rules, assuming a left-to-right causality meaning that the rule heads are affected by the rule bodies, but not vice versa. However, such approaches are powerless when the rule head is empty. Further, these approaches either require a distinction between extensional and intensional predicates, not allowing a Web service to affect any predicates appearing in rule heads; or, they run into the same computational problems as the non-causal approach, see the next paragraph.

The second major difficulty inherent in update problems is the computational complexity of computing Φ'. Most often, even deciding about basic

---

[25] Strictly speaking, one may also allow disjunction in the rule body, and conjunction and implication in the rule head; however, such rules can be rewritten to rules as above.

properties of Φ' is computationally hard. In fact, in most cases, reasoning about Φ' is computationally harder than reasoning in the class of formulas used for formulating the previous state of affairs Φ, and the update ϕ. Examples for this phenomenon are captured in our Theorem 5.2. It shows that reasoning about Φ' is hard even if Φ and ϕ are formulated in Horn logics, where reasoning is polynomial. These results were, as stated, adapted from [83] which provides very comprehensive results on the computational complexity of the various update semantics that were defined until 1991. Liberatore [176] does the same for the various new update semantics that were defined during the 90s.

Recently, the relevance of update problems in the Semantic Web context was recognized, and researched in the context of Description Logics [182, 17, 180, 179, 65] (cf. Section 2.3.3 for a general introduction to DL). All these works adopt the PMA for their update semantics. The work so far was mostly concerned with identifying under which conditions Φ' can or cannot be expressed in terms of a new DL ABox. By far the closest relative to our work on search states and their transitions is [65], which investigates restrictions to the underlying DL – "DL-Lite" – under which Φ' *can* be expressed as a new ABox, and under which that new ABox can be computed in polynomial time. We share with this work the emphasis on a polynomial-time computable update operation. We are not as much concerned with expressing Φ' as an ABox; while [65] target delivering that ABox to the human user, in our context Φ' corresponds to a new search state which is entirely internal to our composition algorithm. DL-Lite is more powerful than our binary clauses in some aspects, and less powerful in other aspects. All clauses ($\mathcal{T}$ statements) in DL-Lite are binary. However, [65] allow unqualified existential quantification, membership assertions (ABox literals) using variables, and updates involving general (constructed) DL concepts. On the other hand, DL-Lite does not allow clauses with two positive literals, DL-Lite TBoxes allow literals on roles only if one of the 2 variables is existentially quantified, and DL-Lite (like any DL) does not allow predicates of arity greater than 2. Also, in difference to us, [65] do not develop an actual WSC tool. Our heuristic techniques are certainly compatible with (a subset of) DL-Lite updates, and so an exciting topic remains to combine the two, yielding scalable WSC technology for an interesting fragment of DL.

5.7.3 Web Service Composition

The semantic annotation of Web services, and approaches for their automated composition, have emerged in the Semantic Web area over the last few years. Different annotation languages have been proposed [284, 70]; one thing they have in common is that they distinguish between at least two levels of abstraction, one defining just the service "profile" or "capability", and the other one defining in more detail the protocol that must be followed for communication with the service. Capability descriptions were initially motivated by planning formalisms, and hence it is no coincidence that there is some similarity; particularly, both formalisms share the notions of preconditions and effects.[26] The main difference, as pointed out above, lies in that the existing scalable planning tools developed in the last decade have no notion of a background ontology. Many of the existing works on automatic SWS composition compile the problem directly into an AI planning problem – in contrast to our approach of adapting a planning method to Web service composition, e.g., by adding a notion of constants creation. Also in difference to our work, most existing approaches assume that input/output types are matched exactly, ignoring the background ontology. Further, in difference to our work, none of the existing works allows the on-the-fly generation of new constants.

A brief survey of the existing works on SWS composition follows. There is a variety of works that compile composition into more or less standard deterministic planning formalisms, e.g. [237, 273, 263]; one branch of research additionally focuses on end-to-end integration of SWS composition in the larger context [5, 4]; another branch includes techniques to disambiguate concept names [7]; another achieves composition with simple forms of non-atomic services, by modeling the latter as atomic actions that take the meaning of a kind of macro-actions [198]; another obtains a simple composition ability as a side-effect of verifying SWS properties using Petri Nets [214]; another focuses on information gathering at composition time (rather than at plan execution time) [170, 15, 16].

Two approaches explore how to adapt formalisms from so-called "hand-tailored planning", namely Golog [199] respectively HTN [270] planning, for SWS composition. In such a framework, the provided mechanisms do not fully automate composition; rather, they provide convenient programming languages with powerful machine support. Both approaches are capable of handling control constructs (loops, branches). In Golog, the possible plans – the possible composition solutions – are described in a kind of logics where high-level instructions are given by the programmer, and the planner will bind these instructions to concrete actions as part of the execution. In HTN, the programmer supplies the planning algorithm with a set of so-called "decomposition methods". Such a method specifies how a certain task can be accomplished in terms of a combination of sub-tasks; recursively, there are decomposition methods for those sub-tasks. Hence the overall task can be decomposed in a step-wise fashion, until atomic actions are reached which resemble the implemented operations of the underlying IT structure. If no decomposition methods are provided, then the planning is exactly like non-HTN planning, and in that sense HTN planning is strictly more powerful than non-HTN planning. That said, the HTN literature, including [270], deals mostly with the handling of decomposition methods, rather than with techniques for search guidance or with belief update operations as we do herein. There is

---

[26] WSMO distinguishes between preconditions and assumptions, as well as between postconditions and effects. As discussed in in the beginning of this chapter, these distinctions are not (yet) relevant in our context.

synergetic potential in combining the two lines of research; we leave this for future work.

Another approach capable of handling control constructs is described in [234, 235, 233, 33], which implements what we have termed *behavioral composition* at the beginning of this chapter. There, BDD (Binary Decision Diagram) based search techniques are exploited to obtain complex solutions fully automatically; however, input/output type matches are assumed to be exact. A final approach based on planning treats the actual interaction (communication) with a Web service as a planning problem [195].

To the best of our knowledge, there are only three works where the requirements on the matches are relaxed. One of those is described in the papers by Sirin et al. [266, 268, 267, 269]. The other two were developed by Constantinescu et al., and Weske and Meyer, respectively. These are discussed below. In [266, 268], an SWS composition support tool for human programmers is proposed: at any stage during the composition process, the tool provides the user with a list of matching services. The matches are found by examining the subconcept relation; an output A is considered a match of input B if $A \subseteq B$. In [267, 269], the HTN approach [270] mentioned above is adapted to not work on the standard planning semantics, but on the description logics semantics of OWL-S. As we stated above in Section 5.7.2, the difficulties inherent in updating a belief are observed, but the connection to update problems as studied in the literature is not made; no solution to the difficulties is offered.

Constantinescu et al. [58, 59, 60] propose an approach to composition at the capability level, allowing partial matches. The main differences to our work lie in the more general notion of matches, in a much more restricted notion of background ontologies, and in a lack of heuristic information to guide the search. Specifically, in [60], the background ontology is a subsumption hierarchy. This is compiled into intervals, where each interval represents a concept and the contents are arranged to correspond to the hierarchy. The intervals are used for matching the Web services during composition, where a notion of "switches" is used to be able to construct solutions dealing with partial matches. Search proceeds in a depth-first fashion, with no heuristic information. Hence, by comparison to our work, [60] uses a more general notion of matches, but a more restrictive notion of ontologies, and lacks our techniques for search guidance. A combination of both techniques might be interesting to explore.

Weske and Meyer [206] is related to our work in that, like us, it is inspired by [139]. However: [206] do not provide a formal semantics and analysis, and the precise meaning of their techniques remains unclear; they do not take the ontology constraints $\mathcal{T}$ into account in the heuristic function, and they take the heuristic value to be the number of iterations until the abstract composition graph, c.f. Section 5.5, reaches the goal, which is typically much too optimistic; they use a worst-case exponential reasoner to determine their search states, and they explicitly enumerate the models in every belief, which is in itself exponential; they restrict the creation of new constants to a single one per ontology concept; and they show results only for a single small example composition problem.

5.8 Chapter Conclusion

Automatic WSC is a core feature of flexible service-oriented architectures – in the context of this work and beyond. In its full expressivity, WSC suffers both from a combinatorial explosion in possible compositions, and from the severe computational complexity inherent in the semantics of Web service applications in the presence of constraints imposed by an ontology. Our approach provides a uniquely strong trade-off between expressivity and scalability, in that it allows non-trivial ontologies without resorting to worst-case exponential reasoning, and in that it employs heuristic and filtering techniques. This is underlined with the empirical results provided in the next chapter. These show that the implementation of the approach can easily scale up to hundreds of services.

Our approximate reasoning techniques open up ways to obtain even better trade-offs in future work. In ongoing work that is not in the scope of this monograph, we extended our composition approach so as to (i) tackle temporal constraint rules that can, e.g., formalize business policies; and (ii) to take non-functional properties into account, to enable optimizing the composition not for the shortest orchestration, but for the one with a good trade-off between, say, price and execution time.

Following the contributions presented in this part, we now come to the final part.

Part III

Finale

6

Evaluation

In this chapter, we evaluate the contributions from Part II holistically. As various means of evaluation have already been taken within Part II, in this chapter there is an emphasis on giving an overview, a business-level evaluation, and a detailed evaluation of the task composition's performance. As we will see, the verification algorithms' performance is not a critical point.[1]

The chapter is structured in the following way. In Section 6.1, we repeat the hypotheses from the introduction and derive argumentatively the most relevant aspects from them; an overview of the evaluation measures taken throughout the work is given as well. As some of the evaluation measures depend on our prototypical implementations, Section 6.2 describes those: the algorithms of the two technical core topics have been implemented in back-end prototypes, which are used in several integrated prototypes for different scenarios and with different user interfaces. The mentioned evaluation of the performance of our task composition is described in Section 6.3. Several aspects on the business level remained open, such as usability and applicability of the whole approach taken herein. These aspects are investigated with a set of small case studies, as described in Section 6.4. With the case studies we essentially try out how well the approach can be used on real-life processes with real-life services, both from external sources.

6.1 Evaluation Overview

The presented work clearly falls into the broad category of design science, as classified, e.g., by Hevner et al. [132]. According to this source, "IT artifacts can be evaluated in terms of functionality, completeness, consistency, accuracy, performance, reliability, usability, fit with the organization, and other relevant

---

[1] Concepts, results, and prototypes from this chapter have been published or demonstrated: [41, 42, 143, 312, 319].

quality attributes."[132] They further emphasize that, in design science, repeated evaluation and design phases should alternate: a design is evaluated, and based on the evaluation's outcome the design is improved. However, according to Zobel [330], experiments must be clearly split into an *observation* and a *testing* phase. The differences are, that during observation one still learns about the object under study, whereas during testing one validates hypotheses. We followed this advice and clearly separate below which processes and testbeds have been used for observation and which for testing. Tichy [286] argues, that computer scientists should experiment more. "Experimentalists test theoretical predictions against reality."[286] However, "to paraphrase Dijkstra, an experiment can only show the presence of bugs in a theory, not their absence."[286] He continues: "Experiments probe the influence of assumptions, eliminate alternative explanations of phenomena, and unearth new phenomena in need of explanation."[286] Following Tichy, we complement the conceptual contributions made herein with the (partially experimental) evaluation described in this chapter. Fairness of the evaluation means must of course be given – in the words of Zobel [330]: "Tests should be fair rather than constructed to support the hypothesis."

The evaluation here aims at verifying or falsifying the hypotheses made in the introduction. We thus repeat those below, and subsequently derive the evaluation goals from them.

Main hypothesis:

H0. Execution-level process modeling can be supported by enriching the process models with formal change semantics at the level of process activities.

In the introduction we refined this main hypothesis into the following more concrete sub-hypotheses:

H1. Creating and adapting process implementations is a challenge for businesses today; reducing time and money needed for it is a relevant problem which can be addressed by support for execution-level process modeling.
H2. Many of the most common requirements of execution-level process modeling support can be fulfilled by a careful combination of few components.
H3. It is possible to algorithmically verify the consistency of semantically annotated process models.
H4. It is possible to find and compose pre-existing artifacts for the realization of process activities automatically.

H0 and H1 are focused around modeling support, i.e., in our context increased productivity and quality of models and easier transition to executable processes. We thus require (i) increased productivity of experienced modelers, (ii) enablement of new categories of modelers, (iii) increased quality of the created models with respect to execution, and (iv) ease of reuse of execution-level artifacts.

From this, we can derive the requirements for (a) scalable tools and fast algorithms on practical problems, (b) usability, i.e., an intuitive way of modeling and intuitive logics, such that a process modeler can understand the meaning without attending a logics training, (c) sufficient expressivity to model relevant aspects, and (d) usefulness with respect to productivity, i.e., that the form of support actually increases the productivity.

With respect to (a) - (c) we have a triangular trade-off between scalability, expressivity, and usability:

- Usability vs. expressivity is a trade-off, because if expressivity (in process modeling primitives or logical constructs) is increased above a certain point, the possibility to intuitively understand the constructs is exceeded and specialists knowledge is required.
- Scalability vs. expressivity is another trade-off, as argued multiple times throughout Chapters 4 and 5. We positioned the work herein at unique points in the trade-off between scalability and expressivity, usually such that the expressivity has been increased in comparison to other works, while remaining at a restricted level that still allows the construction of scalable algorithms.
- Usability demands scalability, i.e., the implementations have to be able to provide an answer for practical problems in a timely fashion. If a tool requires five minutes to perform an operation, the value of this feature must be perceived as high enough to wait five minutes for it – otherwise it is unlikely it will be used.

The concept pursued in this section is to evaluate each aspect of the presented work with appropriate means. In particular, we will use argumentative or formal methods where applicable, and prototypes for performance and use case coverage where possible. An overview of the measures taken is given in Table 6.1. In the following, we will discuss these evaluation measures and how they relate to the hypotheses and the points (a) - (d) above.

H1 addresses the relevance of the problem, which we showed in the general introduction, Chapter 1, and the introduction of Chapter 3. The means for this was the argumentative motivation based on the predictions and findings of the market analyst companies Gartner and Forester. Furthermore, the relevance of task composition can be underlined by a simple calculation: enterprises today have often more than 50, sometimes more than 100 enterprise application systems – and SAP systems alone offer thousands of services (in their most recent versions). Thus, dealing with the services manually is likely to become too complex, and the need for tool support becomes obvious. Time and money in H1 relate to the productivity of the modeler (d), as argued above.

The question whether execution-level process modeling is helpful by itself, and with our extensions in particular, can be answered by inverting the viewpoint: when a conceptual process is refined to a degree that is suitable for direct implementation in an executable process model, then it *is* what we here refer to as an execution-level model. Further, if an executable process can be

Table 6.1. Overview over the evaluation measures taken for the individual contributions

Hypothesis, topic	Type	Means
H1, Relevance	Argumentative	Market analyst's predictions.
H2, Conceptual Framework	Argumentative	Requirements coverage.
H3, Verification	Theoretical	Hardness for general process graphs, polynomial-time algorithms for basic annotated process graphs, correctness and uniqueness for the algorithms' outcomes.
H3, Verification	Prototypical	Proof-of-concept, performance.
H4, Composition	Theoretical	Hardness of general problem, correctness of the approximations, polynomial-time heuristic function.
H4, Composition	Prototypical	Proof-of-concept, performance.
H0, H1, Integration	Prototypical	Proof-of-concept, expressivity, usability.

directly translated out of the execution-level process model, then there is no overhead in creating the latter. By definition, execution-level process models are at the right level of granularity and quality. If the executable process model is only a refined model of the execution-level, then the conceptual (business) level and the implementation stay connected. However, whether BPM is the right vehicle for enabling faster and less costly changes in enterprises, and how many processes can be expressed as executable process models, remains yet to be determined. The assumption in this work is that the whole idea of flow-based process modeling and execution is in principle helpful – otherwise improving it makes little sense. While we believe this is the case, this question is not evaluated here.

The requirements analyzed in Chapter 3 are used for the evaluation of H2, and we showed how to satisfy them with the conceptual framework. The exact requirement coverage is discussed in Section 3.9.

As not all parts of the conceptual framework were available in sufficient quality, we devised techniques for verification (H3, Chapter 4) and composition (H4, Chapter 5). Both of them were treated at a formal level, so we gained a number of theoretical results, which were discussed throughout the respective chapters. The outcome of the theoretical analysis includes complexity results, proofs on the correctness and uniqueness of the algorithms' results or the approximations, and polynomial runtime for a set of our algorithms (the propagation techniques and the heuristic function with restricted ontology expressivity).

Further, for H3 and H4 as well as their integration with a process modeling tool, we developed proof-of-concept implementations. These prototypes first of all show that the algorithms based on the theoretical models actually have the expected outputs. Further, we used them for performance testing (scalability, (a)), as discussed in Sections 6.2 and 6.3. The integrated prototypes are used to demonstrate the potential of the developed techniques in various application scenarios (H0, H1, and points (b), (c), and (d) above). The prototypes further explore aspects that have been only discussed to a limited degree in this work: how relatively user-friendly modes of annotation can be constructed, and how the results can be presented to users. These aspects are not core aspects of the work, and it is furthermore hard to devise user-friendly annotation modes that are of general applicability. Finally, we used the prototypes to model the example processes and to evaluate the expressivity on this basis – as discussed in Section 6.4. According to the classification of experiments by Zelkowitz et al. [328], our proof-of-concept tests are *assertions*, the performance testing is either of *dynamic analysis* or *simulation*, and the set of processes with which we evaluate the expressivity are referred to as *case studies*[2].

6.2 Prototypes

The prototypes developed in the course of this work can be split into two categories: back-end and front-end components. The back-end components implement the algorithms devised in the body of this work and stay on a generic level, whereas the front-ends are integrated prototypes with user interfaces for specific scenarios.

6.2.1 Back-End Components

The two technical core parts of this work, the verification technique (Chapter 4) and the task composition (Chapter 5), have been implemented in back-end prototypes. In both cases, Java was used as a programming language, and unit testing was done with JUnit. Further, the back-end implementations are split up between a framework part and an algorithms part. The frameworks hereby are straight-forward implementations of our respective formalisms, and the algorithm parts implement the conceptual algorithms using the framework code.

The prototype for verification is comparatively simple: the main algorithms (M and I-propagation) each only have a few hundred lines of code. Without any code optimization, the execution can be said to perform well. E.g., a non-trivial process with 40 nodes and 46 edges has been processed in 0.2 s on a Pentium M CPU running at 1.6 GHz, and the main memory usage has been negligible. Since the worst-case behavior is roughly cubic in the number of nodes and edges, performance is unlikely to be problematic in typical

---

[2] According to [328], those are *not* assertions, since we do not have control over the experimental conditions: the processes are received from external units or, in one case, the literature.

real-world settings. We thus found a further evaluation of the performance unnecessary.

In contrast, the prototype for task composition is rather complex, including a total of around 13,000 lines of code. It handles three of the alternatives of the forward search given in Section 5.2, namely greedy best-first search, weighted A*, and best-first AO*. Different parsers were developed to translate from the Web service descriptions used in the different scenarios into the framework code. Numerous switches for optimizations (heuristics, sorting style of the open list, using cost in the *extract* function, etc.) exist. The scalability of our approach has been evaluated (described in Section 6.3 below), and shows that the implementation scales up well in terms of the services that have to be considered.

6.2.2 Integrated Prototypes

The above back-end components have been used in five integrated prototypes, which we describe shortly below. Different forms of semantic annotations were used for services, and different means to specify the user goals were implemented. From this wide-spread and broad use, several requirements for specific features emerged, most of which we managed to incorporate in the solutions presented in Part II. Further, we used the prototypes for our process case studies, which we describe along with the resulting findings in Section 6.4.

- The *BPMO editor*, an extension to WSMO Studio[3] which was developed in the SUPER project [71], is integrated with the task composition component. The prototype offers task composition for single tasks in a process model, triggered by right-clicking on a task which has previously been semantically annotated with a WSMO goal (selecting a pre-defined goal and attaching it to the task), and by selecting "Compose" from the context menu. The composer is called with the goal attached to the task. The composition component then accesses the SWS Repository through the SWS discovery component provided by the Semantic Execution Environment (SEE) – cf. the SUPER architecture [327] for details. This discovery component receives a query with a WSMO goal from the composition's internal discovery (cf. Section 5.6.2), in order to retrieve all SWSs which need to be considered by the composition to achieve its original goal (in the simple case: all services annotated with the same ontology as the goal). After composing a subset of the discovered services, the component provides the composed solution to the BPMO Editor as a partial BPMO process. The BPMO Editor in turn asks for approval by the modeler, and in the case of a positive response updates the original process model. The update is performed by replacing the previously selected task with the partial process that forms its implementation.

---

[3] http://www.wsmostudio.org

- The SAP demonstrator on the European Union (EU) *Services Directive* which was shown at the *CeBIT* trade fair 2008 also featured our composition component. It was shown as a research prototype at the regular SAP booth, and was demonstrated to potential customers by the SAP sales team. The EU Services Directive aims at easing the burdens for the EU's citizens to open up new businesses by providing a single-point-of-contact for the complete business lifecycle. It has to be implemented by all EU member states by the end of 2009. The key challenge from a technical perspective is the strong dependency between the individual situation of each citizen and the underlying business process, which makes it difficult to pre-configure all possible processes due to the large variability. To overcome this bottleneck we presented a vision and prototype for automatic service composition, visualization, monitoring, and execution based on Semantic Web services. The focus thus was not on *task* composition in the sense presented here, but on the composition of a process model *for* an instance of a particular request – i.e., a specialized usage of service composition in the environment of public administration. The concept and architecture have been published [319].

- Another scenario, the *Automatic Configuration for Service Brokers* which we explain below, also differs from the BPM scenarios for which the works here were created. However, it uses the technical components from this work, namely the verification for information gathering, cf. Section 5.6.1, and the task composition component. The scenario addresses service marketplaces, which are steadily gaining momentum nowadays. In a service marketplace services from a variety of service providers can be registered, published, advertised, discovered, and brokered. Marketplace brokers, as such, manage the "front-desk" of services to be the point for collecting payments from consumers and disbursing transaction fees to the service providers involved in a consumed service - along agreed upon shared revenue arrangements. The work on automatic configuration of brokered processes proposes a model-based technique to lower the entrance barrier of service providers for registering services with a marketplace broker. The aim is that the service is rapidly configured to utilize the broker's "local" service delivery management components. The service provider can easily out-source functionality, such as payment handling, to platform services offered by the broker. The problem of intertwining the provider's behavioral service interface with the usage of the platform services is handled via simple annotations. The resulting configuration is automatically derived using the back-end components developed in this work: information gathering determines the "current" status of the platform service, and composition fills in the necessary service calls to achieve the desired state. The Web browser-based process modeling tool *Oryx* [67] serves as a user interface. The concept and architecture behind this prototype have been published [312].

- *Maestro for BPMN* is a process modeling tool for the BPMN notation that is developed at SAP Research. It is part of the Maestro tools family that is mainly used for early prototyping. The tool has been extended to allow for semantic annotation, as proposed in [40], and has been integrated with the service discovery from [188] as well as the task composition and verification functionality described herein. A screenshot is shown in Fig. 6.1. In the screenshot, the way in which the annotation is displayed can be seen at the example of the "Sales Order" document, which is shown as a BPMN data object on the upper edge of the modeling pane. The association with the "Create sales order..." task is annotated with "> received (Sales Order)", where the ">" sign denotes that the following part is an effect of the task (in contrast to "<" for preconditions). Further, "received" is the status in which the sales order object will be after the task has been executed.[4] We interpret these annotations as preconditions and effects for discovery [188], verification, and task composition. The dialog window for discovery / composition can be seen in the screenshot (Fig. 6.1), where a composition of two services is proposed. Two different versions of the tool have been demonstrated at conferences [41, 42].

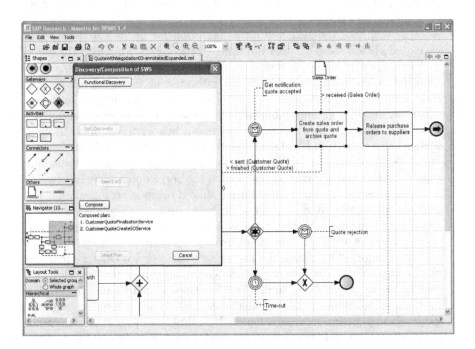

Fig. 6.1. Screenshot of Maestro for BPMN with extensions for semantic annotation, discovery, composition, and verification. Dialog window showing the suggested composition for the selected activity ("Create sales order...").

---

[4] Note that the task here is "Create sales order...", i.e., "receive" and "create" here are synonyms. The tool can detect synonyms during annotation, as proposed in [40].

- *SAP NetWeaver BPM Process Composer* is the modeling part of SAPs future product for Business Process Management: "SAP NetWeaver BPM delivers a suite of state-of-the-art, standards-based tools that enable customers to quickly and efficiently model processes and execute them without time-consuming, error-prone coding. It leverages the service-enabled functionality of SAP Business Suite applications, and of third-party software, to create and modify processes. This ultimately leads to significant increases in speed, flexibility, quality and time to value."
  The tool suite has different parts for process modeling and execution. The process modeling is done in the BPMN notation, with a concrete (partially proprietary) execution semantics, according to which the execution engine tool can execute BPMN processes directly, i.e., without translation to another language like BPEL. Therefore, the Process Composer can be used for process modeling on any of the conceptual, execution-level, and executable process modeling layers, and fits the theme of this work rather well.

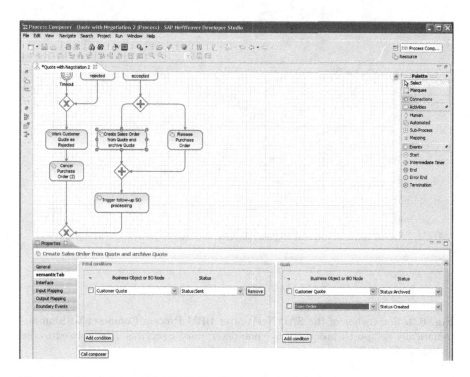

Fig. 6.2. Screenshot of the SAP NetWeaver BPM Process Composer with extensions for semantic annotation. Within the "semanticTab" on the bottom, the precondition for the selected activity ("Create Sales Order...") can be entered on the left-hand side ("Initial Conditions"), the effect on the right-hand side ("Goals"). The annotation is specialized for status changes of business objects.

Our extensions cater for specialized semantic annotations, based on business objects and their respective states. A screenshot is shown in Fig. 6.2. Based on these annotations, verification and task composition as described herein can be invoked. Fig. 6.3 shows the outcome[5] of a non-deterministic composition of five services. Note in particular the side effect of the create operation (top): approval can be either necessary or not; depending on the actual outcome, an additional approval step must be executed or not; this approval step can have a positive or a negative outcome (not obvious from the composition), and only in the positive outcome, the process can proceed with submitting the quote – cf. Section 5.2.3 for the details. The extensions are scheduled for a pilot customer evaluation project at SAP.[6]

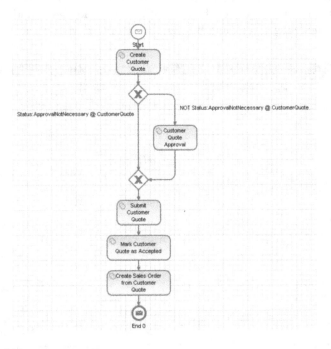

Fig. 6.3. Screenshot of the SAP NetWeaver BPM Process Composer with an automatically composed process of five non-deterministic services. (Not related to the process in Fig. 6.2).

---

[5] The graph layout has been slightly improved manually from the default automatic layout.

[6] At the time of writing, the author and other persons involved in this project left SAP and cannot further see through the developments in this organization. For this and various other reasons, neither the commitment of the pilot customer nor of SAP can be guaranteed.

We next describe the empirical evaluation of the task composition, which is based on the respective back-end prototype.

6.3 Empirical Results for Task Composition

In order to evaluate the performance of the task composition approach, we implemented a tool handling binary clauses as per Theorem 5.7, and computing heuristic (h) and filtering (H) information as per Section 5.5. Further, the implementation switches automatically between the implementation for services with fully deterministic effects and the one handling non-deterministic effects[7] (cf. Section 5.2.3): if a single service with non-deterministic effects has to be considered, the non-deterministic variant is used. Finally, we implemented the discovery technique discussed in Section 5.6.2, which can filter the pool of services prior to the actual composition.

The tool accepts a set of Semantic Web service (SWS) and user requirement descriptions in either a proprietary XML format or the WSMO formalism, specified in a subset of the WSML language. Our experiments ran on a laptop computer with a Pentium M CPU running at 2.0 GHz, reserving up to 1GB of main memory for the tool. To assess the benefits of both heuristic techniques – h and H – we experimented with all possible configurations: **Blind** uses neither h nor H; **Heuristic** uses only h; **Filtering** uses only H; **Full** uses both. To evaluate the usefulness of the discovery technique, we also test the configuration **Discovery**, which runs **Full** subsequent to an up-front discovery.

Tichy states, that "[...] benchmarking can be used for many questions in computer science. The subjective and therefore weakest part in a benchmark test is the composition of the benchmark."[286] Due to the limited public availability of real-world services with semantic annotations[8], we pursue two strategies: we simulate the worst case for the deterministic composition variant and we evaluate the discovery and the non-deterministic variant on real-world SAP-internal services. Our testbeds resemble the expected surrounding conditions of WSC in practice: we keep the size of the solutions moderate; the parameter we scale is *the size of the SWS pool*. This corresponds to the common intuition about WSC, that solutions tend to be simple but finding the right services to incorporate is difficult.

---

[7] A simple example for non-deterministic effects is ordering goods: if the goods are available, the order succeeds, otherwise it fails; however, the decision is non-deterministic for the consumer of the service, so we model multiple mutually exclusive outcomes as non-deterministic effects.

[8] Recently, the Online Portal for Semantic Services (OPOSSum) [168] has been created. Unfortunately, at the time of writing there were no SWS available in an input format supported by our tools – in particular, there was not a single service in any variant of WSML.

6.3.1 Performance with Deterministic Simulated Services

For the deterministic part, we simulated the expected situation when more services become available publicly. Note that the SWS pool here corresponds to the *outcome* of discovery. Hence our deterministic scaling scenario addresses the case where many SWS can be found and, without performing the actual composition, it is not feasible to filter out those few SWS that are actually needed. When discovering in a large environment, one can expect that, for some of the required functionality, many alternative implementations can be found; the alternative implementations are similar but not identical – like different SWS offering flight connections. At the time of writing, the offerings of Web services in public marketplaces have not grown to significant numbers (yet). Thus, it is hard to make predictions on the distribution of service functionalities. One basis for predictions that seems reasonable is that of Web sites: the continuum ranges from niche Web sites that are only of interest to a fairly small number of users to large numbers of Web sites with very similar functionality, which do or do not differentiate themselves via other means (quality, price, location-bound, language, etc.). The market for Web services in the Web might take a similar turn. In fact, one may view Web sites as a specialized form of Web services. In contrast, when using exclusively Web service interfaces that are exposed by a single application software in an organization's IT application landscape, it is rather unlikely to see many implementations of the same functionality. This is of course the case in the SAP scenario.

Since the case where many services implement the same functionality is the worst case for our approach, we simulate this situation for the deterministic variant as follows. In addition to the SWS that are needed for the solution, we add N additional "randomized" SWS into the pool. All randomized SWS use (only) the original ontology, and we generate them by randomly modifying the original SWS. Say *max* is the maximum number of literals appearing in the precondition/effect of any original SWS. Then each of the N randomized SWS is generated by, uniformly: choosing one of the original SWS; choosing numbers $0 \leq k, l \leq max$; choosing k literals to add to the precondition; and choosing l literals to add to the effect. Care had to be taken such that the resulting SWS preconditions and effects did not contradict themselves, and that no "shortcuts" in the solution were created with the randomization. Tichy continues: "[...] the composition of the benchmark is always hotly debated (is it representative enough?), and benchmarks must evolve over time to get them closer to what one wants to test." [286] The described solution evolved over multiple iterations of testbed generations. When more Web services become available in future, the assumptions should be checked and, if required, the testbeds should be further evolved.

We designed two test cases, called TPSA and VTA. The latter is a variant of the well-known virtual travel agency (VTA), where transport and accommodation etc. need to be booked based on a trip request. TPSA comes from a use case in the telecommunications sector[9] and describes a scenario in which a client requests a Voice over IP (VoIP) service. The WSC problem is to automatically compose a process for setting up the VoIP in the TP system. This process involves identifying the required hardware, setting up the contract, saving the contract within the CRM system, etc. The user requirement is to obtain an invoice confirming the activation of the VOIP. In both VTA and TPSA, the shortest solution contains 7 Web services. In all cases, a correct composition of 7 Web services was found, there are no differences in the solution quality for the runs in these testbeds.

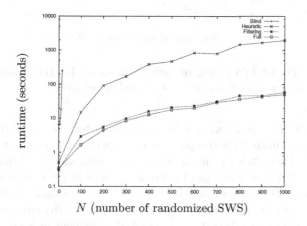

Fig. 6.4. Results for VTA, deterministic composition. Runtime (y-axis, seconds) plotted over N (x-axis), i.e., the number of randomized SWS. Note the logarithmic runtime scale.

Figures 6.4 and 6.5 show our results for VTA and TPSA, respectively, plotting runtime for the four configurations over N, for one instance per each setting of N. Note that the scale for VTA is logarithmic to improve readability. We applied a runtime cut-off of 10000 seconds. (**Blind** actually ran overnight on VTA with 20 randomized SWS, without finding a solution). Note that the runtime sometimes does not grow monotonically over N; this is just due to the randomization, and would disappear when taking mean values over several runs.

The data clearly show that the heuristic techniques bring a vast advantage over the blind search. We can also see that the importance of the different techniques, solution distance estimation, h, or filtering, H, depends on the domain.

---

[9] This use case stems from Telekomunikacja Polska Spółka Akcyjna (TPSA), where the "SA" refers to the legal entity type (incorporated). The testbed is a part of the SUPER Integrated Project mentioned earlier. To avoid confusion, we refer to the testbed as TPSA and to the company as TP.

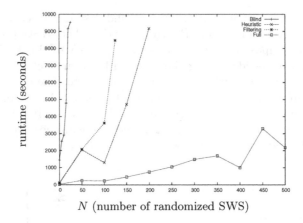

N (number of randomized SWS)

Fig. 6.5. Results for TPSA, deterministic composition. Runtime (y-axis, seconds) plotted over N (x-axis), i.e., the number of randomized SWS.

In VTA, if H is used, we get linear runtime behavior and the effect of applying h in addition is, in comparison, only cosmetic. In contrast, for TPSA, using only h (**Heuristic**) is much better than using only H (**Filtering**). We also see in TPSA that there can be strong synergy in the combination of the two techniques: **Full** works vastly better than any other configuration. In fact, this configuration is significantly more effective than **Filtering** in the TPSA scenario, as opposed to the rather minimal improvement in VTA. This is due to the more parallel nature of the solution of the TPSA setting, in contrast to the more sequential VTA solution, where the difference between **Filtering** and **Full** is not so significant. That is, there are several SWS in TPSA which could be executed in parallel, resulting in more actions which are still to be considered after **Filtering**. Looking at the numbers of states explored by the various configurations, we see that for TPSA with $N = 0$ – when the pool contains only the original SWS – **Blind** already needs to look at 15596 states (different possible compositions) before finding a solution. By contrast, **Heuristic** looks only at 29 states, **Filtering** looks only at 13, and **Full** looks only at 8. For VTA, these numbers are 11659 (**Blind**), 33 (**Heuristic**), 85 (**Filtering**), and 13 (**Full**).

Due to the artificial nature of our randomized SWS, the observed advantage of the heuristic techniques over blind search might be more extreme than what one would get with real publicly available large SWS pools (which do not yet exist). However, one can reasonably expect that the overall patterns of behavior will be similar.

A sensible comparison to alternate WSC tools is difficult due to their widely disparate nature (besides the technical challenge arising from widely disparate input languages). We ran tests with the DLVK tool [81], which is based on general reasoning (answer set programming). We chose DLVK because it is publicly available, and its language is expressive enough to handle our test cases. In fact, DLVK allows more general $\mathcal{T}$ than our tool; so the question answered by the experiment is whether performance gains can be realized with our tool, by giving up some expressivity. It turns out that DLVK is much slower even than **Blind**. With $N = 0$, DLVK takes 12 minutes for VTA and 2 hours for TPSA. In both test cases, DLVK runs out of time for $N \geq 5$. These results should not be over-interpreted, since a direct comparison between DLVK and our tool is unfair. But the results certainly show that the trade-off between expressivity and scalability is important.

6.3.2 Performance with Non-deterministic Real-World Services

For the evaluation of the non-deterministic composition variant (cf. Section 5.2.3) we used a repository of services from SAP. As part of the model-driven software development of SAP, a large number of models has been created. A subset of these models describe how services manipulate business objects (such as supplier invoices) in terms of state models (e.g., the approval service marks a supplier invoice as approved). These models have been translated into an XML format which can be parsed by our composer. Hereby we interpret the pre-states and post-states as preconditions and effects. A service can result in several post-states, which then are mutually exclusive. Therefore, the non-deterministic variant of our composer had to be used with these services.

To vary the size of the SAP service pool, we excluded services from the pool of all modeled services. That is, the test considering $N = 100$ services contains: the services that are necessary to find a solution; the services which discovery does not remove; and around 80 more services, chosen at random. The test considering $N = 200$ services contains the 100 services as above, plus 100 more services chosen at random, and so forth. Thus, the set of services grows monotonically, and always contains the services that were part of the smaller service pools already. The maximal number contains all available services from the SAP repository, slightly more than 2700 in total. The correct composition contains five services, and is in its structure similar to the process shown in Fig. 6.3.

Figure 6.6 shows the results of our experiments on the SAP testbed, both for **Full** and **Discovery**. First it should be noted that the absolute numbers in Figure 6.6 cannot be compared to the ones in Figures 6.4 and 6.5: different parsers are used on different inputs, the non-deterministic algorithm differs from the deterministic one in many points, the services differ in the number of preconditions and effects, and the services which are added to the pool in the non-deterministic case are, indeed, useless for the composition – in stark contrast to the deterministic testbeds. Due to the latter point, we observe the following. Firstly, **Full** shows a linear behavior. Secondly, **Discovery** offers a strong performance increase: while the discovery loop itself takes near to no time, it cuts the service pool down to the 22 services which cannot be excluded

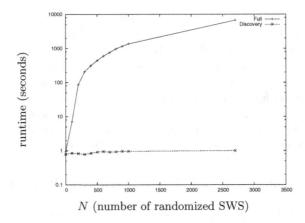

N (number of randomized SWS)

Fig. 6.6. Results for the SAP testbed, non-deterministic composition. Runtime (y-axis, seconds) plotted over N (x-axis), i.e., the number of SWS. Note the logarithmic runtime scale.

before performing the actual composition. This number is independent of the input size. Therefore **Discovery** scales up extremely well, with near to constant time. These results have also been published [143].

6.4 Process Case Studies

The remaining point out of the measures described in Table 6.1 is the evaluation of the main contributions' integration from the perspective of the applicability to the business level: *do the proposed techniques actually provide modeling support?* We address this question by trying out whether this is the case when modeling a set of processes. In this section we first outline a few general observations, then describe the processes that were used on an abstract level. One of them has been used for the purpose of what Zobel refers to as observation [330] as mentioned – i.e., the observations made with this process were used to improve the solution approaches. In contrast, the other processes were solely used for testing [330], i.e., the findings from these processes did *not* influence the solutions. The findings obtained in this way are summarized at the end of the section.

6.4.1 General Observations

When working with the concrete tools, we tried to analyze how the *procedure* of modeling executable processes changes with our extensions. However, this procedure is very much dependent on the specific tool at hand. A few observations seem to hold in general, and we describe them in the following.

It should be noted that these observations were made in the context of the process case studies described below. There is a subjective element to them which may hamper generalization, and they are thus of a partially speculative nature.

When it comes to selecting an executable artifact, then the potential advantage of discovery and composition depends mainly on three factors: the experience of the modeler with the service repository, the number of available services, and the suitability of the tooling. There is an apparent advantage if the level of granularity differs, i.e., when one business-level task is implemented by multiple services, composition often is helpful.

Although not implemented yet in the prototypes, it can be foreseen that the auto-completion feature (cf. Section 3.5.4) will be of great help – given its results are relevant. This way, the right services are included in a matter of seconds, as opposed to creating a task, manually searching for a fitting service; or annotating it with preconditions and effect and performing discovery/composition. However, the great advantage of composition in combination with information gathering is, that specifying a desired effect may be sufficient, and that non-obvious service chains for achieving this effect are created. Using auto-completion, the modeler has to find out about the service chain for herself: auto-completion is not driven by a goal, but only by the current status.

While finding the right services can be of quite some help, another big advantage is in the verification. Hidden dependencies can lead to inconsistent behavior. Without our verification techniques the problem may only surface during testing, or, worse, after deployment when the process is used. Again, information gathering takes a central point in avoiding incorrect outcomes of discovery, composition, and auto-completion.

6.4.2 Overview of the Process Case Studies

The techniques were tested with five process case studies, i.e., real-world processes from different sources, namely three different departments within SAP, IBM, and the before-mentioned Telekomunikacja Polska (TP). In this subsection we give an overview of these case studies, including the one which was used in the observation phase (Quote with Negotiation). We shortly mention the main challenges in each of the processes, but present the overall findings in a combined view in the next subsection.

- Supplier invoicing with 3rd party duplicate detection (source: SAP). The task here is to create a variant of the existing implemented process for supplier invoicing. This existing process is not available as a process model, but implemented in a procedural programming language. However, the building blocks are available as Web services in addition. The new variant should orchestrate these and a third party service for duplicate detection. The service descriptions derived from model-driven software development at SAP (cf. Section 6.3.2) were used. These models have been translated into an XML format which can be parsed by the SAP NW Process Composer extension described above. With this input, the skeleton process for supplier invoice handling was created by task composition – similar to the skeleton shown in Fig. 6.3 for a customer quote. A particular challenge was posed by the third-party service which was not described in the same terminology.

- Quote with Negotiation (source: SAP). When receiving a request for quotation, the usual behavior is to look up prices and stock levels and answer with a quote. However, when some required items are not on stock (or even need to be tailor-made by suppliers), an enterprise first needs to negotiate about price, timing, specification and the like with its suppliers. Only when all prices are known, the quote can be submitted. A process model for this complex behavior is depicted in Fig. 6.7. Further, once the quote has been accepted by the customer, the purchase orders for the previously negotiated items must be released, i.e., sent to the suppliers. In contrast, if the quote is rejected or remains unanswered for some time, the respective purchase orders are canceled.

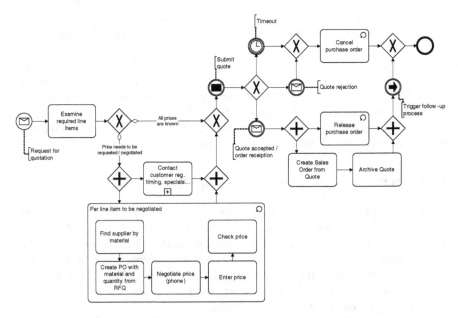

Fig. 6.7. Example process: quote with negotiation

As in the above supplier invoice process, we used the SAP services with preconditions and effects derived from software development models. The particular challenges in this process arise from the cross-departmental behavior of the process (sales and procurement of a single enterprise) as well as the different levels of details that must be handled: business objects such as purchase order and customer quote along with the individual line items.

- Customer returns handling with / without prior approval (source: SAP). When a customer wants to return goods (e.g., due to damages from transport, deviation from the specification, etc.), depending on the contract the supplier's approval for the return has to be requested before returning the goods. Dealing with customer returns is a challenge for some enterprises today, and streamlining the process can save time and money and result in higher quality of problem resolution in the production process. For the evaluation here, we attempted to implement the process with the same Web services mentioned in the above supplier invoicing process, where we derived preconditions and effects from software development models. Since the process model has been designed independently from the services (and this work), there was a partial mismatch between the services at hand and the process' expectations. This challenge arose from the fact that a detailed execution-level process had to be implemented with other services than intended by the original modeler.

- Insurance claims handling (source: IBM [154, 165]). In contrast to the other sample processes, this process was taken from the literature [165]. It has already been used in Chapter 4 as a running example, cf. Examples 4.2 and 4.7. The particular challenge with this process were the conditions for loop repetition and edges. Since no Web services were available for this process, composition has not been evaluated on it.

- Quad-play in telecommunications (source: TP). Quad-play in the telecoms domain refers to a combination of four different services, namely fixed-line phone, broadband Internet connection, Voice over IP (VoIP), and Video on Demand (VoD) over the broadband connection. The process deals with receiving an order, communication with the customer relationship management (CRM) system, configuring the respective provisioning systems, and billing activation. The TeleManagement Forum, an inter-trade organization for the telecoms industry, started the NGOSS [280] initiative to standardize processes and terminology in telecommunications. This initiative has two parts that are of relevance to us: the enhanced Telecom Operations Map (eTOM) [279] as a high-level view on the process landscape, and the Shared Information / Data model (SID) [281] as the standardized business terminology, containing also the relations between the terms. For both of these two parts, SID and eTOM, ontological representations have been created in the SUPER project. The challenge in this particular process was on using the SID / eTOM ontologies for annotation of services and processes.

6.4.3 Findings

In the following, we describe the findings obtained by experimenting with the process case-studies. While the set of processes is an arguably small and not necessarily representative sample, the experiments have been conducted in a fair way and with great care. Subsequent to the list of outcomes below, we provide a short discussion of how these outcomes will impact future work.

- Services often *do* have preconditions and effects, even if they are not explicitly or formally described. In several cases (from SAP and other sources) we saw documents in which preconditions and effects were captured – however in natural language, and not in a formal way. We further found that the presentation of preconditions and effects in terms of state changes of objects (states in life-cycles of objects) can be intuitively understood and meaningfully express what an activity does. However, it became clear that life-cycle states *cannot* capture everything. This has been observed with the SAP models from software development mentioned above, where a minority, but still a significant percentage of the operations, is not part of the life-cycles. For these, we found that expressing their meaning in life-cycles is either difficult or would lead to rather artificial constructs, and an intuitive understanding would be hampered. A generic logics framework, as the one proposed in this work, can capture life-cycle states and many other forms of states and change semantics.

- Change semantics in general have certain weaknesses in expressing semantics. A simple example in our context which is hard to model with preconditions and effects is arbitrarily updating the value of a certain field: how can we adequately and unambiguously model the behavior of this operation with preconditions and effects? Further, if we apply the approach to individual data fields, then we leave the conceptual level of modeling the semantics; instead, we then have to generally consider the values / states of individual fields. For common business objects in SAP systems, the number of fields can easily be in the thousands, some of which may be instantiated more than once. Another example is when no supplier invoice exists in a process context, but one is needed. How do we express with preconditions and effects that we want to find an existing supplier invoice from the database, vs. creating a new invoice object? One approach may be to construct specialized techniques for handling a number of special cases. E.g., for the latter case, one may analyze the task's textual label: if it starts with "Find" or "Retrieve" or another synonym, then use a find operation; if the task label is "Create" or contains the words "new supplier invoice", then use the create operation; otherwise ask the modeler. If there is a fixed set of such themes of operations which cannot be expressed well with preconditions and effects, then specialized ways of dealing with them (as in the above example) may be found.

- Services must be truthfully represented, and their preconditions and effects must be in line with the implementation. If there are hidden dependencies, e.g., such that the execution of one service may trigger another one, then this breaks the assumption of the tools designed in this work. According to the Principles of Service-Orientation Design (cf. Section 2.2.3), this should not be the case; however, not all actual SOA implementations take them into account. In case such hidden dependencies exist, they should be modeled and can then be taken into account – e.g., as non-deterministic effects.

- Non-deterministic task effects, XOR and loop conditions, which are not parts of basic processes (cf. Chapter 4), form a practical restriction. These constructs are not required for all processes, and it is, in part, possible to model around them. But in the latter case the model is influenced by the restrictions of our approach which is in general undesirable. It remains to be determined if an automatic semantics-preserving translation from the more general way of modeling to our formalism can be designed.

  This is the point where future work seems most relevant for practical applications. E.g., in specialized cases it may be possible to further restrict the expressivity of the annotations, but devise a complete approximation of the logical state summaries. That is, in contrast to $I(e)$ which contains any literal that always holds when edge e carries a token, we may be able to compute a set of all those literals that *may* be true when e carries a token. Another possible direction would be to not propagate individual literals, but minimal clauses that will hold when e is activated. This may be particular useful in being able to adequately deal with non-deterministic task effects. We will come back to this point in the next chapter.

- The relations between different objects should be made clear. This is in particular true for the above-mentioned relation of item level status values which are aggregated to a header object status value. E.g., if all line items of a purchase order are in stock, then the purchase order is said to be in stock: $\forall x : [\text{PurchaseOrder}(x) \land (\forall y : \text{LineItem}(y, x) \land \text{inStock}(y))] \Rightarrow \text{inStock}(x)$. If these relations are modeled, then they may be used in specific process constructs, such as a parallel-for-each construct (a subprocess is executed in parallel for each object belonging to a certain group). The parallel-for-each can then have an aggregated effect on the header object.

- If the starting point for annotation and discovery / composition is a detailed execution-level process model that does not take into account the available services, mapping the modeled tasks to these available services can be very hard. In extreme cases, many of the process activities and the whole structure of the model need to be changed – it might even be easier to start over from scratch. Thus, the value added by the proposed techniques is particularly high if the process model in the beginning contains tasks that are on a higher level of abstraction than the services.

- Especially when a process is larger than a handful of activities, the verification was found to be helpful in unveiling hidden problems. While a superficial view on process modeling may leave the impression that the execution models are simple, intricate problems can come into being with a small number of activities, even without annotations. When the combination of control flow and annotations needs to be consistent, then the complexity of modeling correctly increases. Again, the preconditions and effects do exist in reality – even if they are not modeled explicitly. By requiring them to be explicit, we simply create the basis for a solution to the underlying problem. Further, the secondary purpose of the verification technique, the information gathering, can have the effect of drastically reducing the necessary modeling effort for annotations.

• Task composition proved quite helpful in finding correct service chains for achieving a certain goal. Instead of having to manually find out from documentation in which order certain actions need to be performed, it suffices to state the desired outcome. Together with the information gathering technique for providing (parts of) the precondition and the constraints, the task composition can be very helpful, especially when the process modeler is not intimately familiar with the available Web services. To give an example: in our process case studies, a quite common case was that the consistency and/or the data completeness needed to be determined before another activity could be executed. When designing the process manually, the modeler has to know about these constraints, otherwise the execution will fail. In contrast, our task composition automatically takes the constraints into account and orchestrates the service calls accordingly.

Herein, we did experiments based on the input of various sources (different departments of SAP, a process from the literature, and a process from TP), all of which were developed independently of this work. The main objective was to evaluate the practicability and usefulness of the techniques proposed in this work, with respect to usability, scalability, and expressivity. The scalability of the back-ends was easily sufficient in the case studies. While the evidence provided by this small sample of processes can hardly be conclusive as to the overall usefulness and applicability, it represents a number of hints in this direction. The findings lead to requirements for future work on how the techniques should be extended, such that industrial applicability becomes interesting in general. The strongest weakness is related to the restrictions made in verification, but some points also have an impact on composition. When the assumptions (such as adequate annotation of services) are met, and when the provided expressivity is sufficient, then the techniques *are* indeed helpful.

6.5 Chapter Summary

In this chapter, we provided a holistic evaluation of the presented work. Starting from the hypotheses of this work, we derived more tangible evaluation criteria. We then related these and the hypotheses to various means of evaluation. Some of these means are embedded in the previous chapters, the others are included in this chapter. Based on a number of prototypes, we evaluated (i) the performance of our task composition approach, both for simulated (worst-case) situations and with a large service pool of real services from SAP; and (ii) the applicability of our techniques when modeling business processes from practice. While the findings with respect to the task composition are very encouraging, the expressivity test resulted in a mixed picture: the restrictions made for verification exclude exact handling of a portion of processes that are encountered in practice. Most of the weaknesses can be addressed by specialized methods that depend on the exact set of scenarios to be supported in a concrete application – but the expressivity weakness brings us to the borders of what can be dealt with efficiently. The conclusion in the next chapter discusses the outcome in more depth and describes directions of future work.

7

Conclusions and Outlook

In the following, we conclude the monograph by first providing a summary of the contributions and the main results. Subsequently, we describe open points in the presented work as well as further research topics that can be investigated based on this work. The chapter ends with a short reflection on the structure of the work.

7.1 Summary

In this work we investigate the problem of providing support for execution-level process modeling by means of semantic technologies. Some of the limitations in process modeling seemed to stem from the fact that the traditional BPM tools have little insight into the content of the process that is being modeled. We thus put an emphasis on the question how annotations of change semantics (preconditions and effects) can be used to construct a more informed guidance of modelers. We started by broadly analyzing the requirements of this problem on the business level. For example, it should be possible to analyze whether the sequencing of tasks in a process is correct; or to find multiple services which together implement a process activity; or to detect non-compliance in a process model at design time. Our analysis yielded 19 such requirements.

Subsequently, we constructed a conceptual framework with the goal of catering for a majority of those requirements. The conceptual framework forms a business-level solution to this problem, and abstractly specifies a structural architecture of a number of components, along with a manual and an automated methodology for using the components to provide modeling support. While the abstract architecture and most of the high-level components are part of the state of the art, the methodologies form contributions. The components cater for discovery and composition of executable artifacts, auto-completion as the suggestion of subsequent process tasks, data mediation, and validation with respect to various criteria. Out of the components, solutions for the task composition component and the default validator were not provided in sufficient quality and posed interesting research problems. The default validator poses the problem of verifying annotated process models. We investigated these two problems in depth on a formal level.

For the verification we adapted a formalism for processes with a token passing-based execution semantics from the BPM literature, extended it with change semantics from the AI actions and change community, and defined a combined execution semantics. We then defined the verification problems addressed in this work, namely the questions of conflicting parallel process activities, the reachability, and the executability of tasks. After analyzing the computational complexity, we found that in general those questions cannot be answered efficiently. Therefore, we defined a restricted class of annotated processes, called basic processes, in which we showed that the verification questions can be answered in low-order polynomial time over the input size. The proof is constructive, i.e., we devised algorithms answering the verification questions in polynomial time and proved their correctness.

For task composition, we adapted an AI planning formalism to the problem of Web Service Composition. The goal here is to construct combinations of services on the functional level which can implement given process activities. Similarly to the verification problem, we first analyzed the problem, which has two main sources of complexity: the combinatorial explosion and the reasoning about changes. We addressed the prior by guiding the search for a solution with a novel heuristic function that can take ontology axioms into account, and the latter by restricting the expressivity of the ontology. We then devised an exact solution for binary axioms, and an approximate solution, if the ontology contains axioms in the form of Horn clauses. Our composition approach can handle services with deterministic and non-deterministic (alternative) outcomes.

Finally, we evaluated the work. For the verification and the composition we implemented technical back-end prototypes. Due to their nature, the verification algorithms perform very well. In contrast, the scalability of the composition approach is less obvious. We thus examined the performance by simulating worst case composition problems and by using a real-world service repository from SAP, and found the approach to be very well-behaved with respect to scalability. The two back-end prototypes were used in various scenarios for which integrated prototypes were implemented. With two of them we examined (on the business level) the fit of the designed solutions to real-world business processes that were obtained from external sources. In general, the result is a positive one: we found that, indeed, *semantic technologies can be used to support the modeling of execution-level processes*. One of the integrated prototypes is therefore scheduled for a customer pilot evaluation within SAP. However, a number of points remain open. These are described next.

7.2 Open Problems

In future work, we plan on exploring further alternatives, as mentioned throughout the work. Can we find other trade-offs with respect to expressivity, such that efficient techniques can be designed? Can we reduce the problem using our efficient techniques – i.e., can average-case processes be reduced efficiently to a size which can be verified using model checking techniques in acceptable time frames? Or can we devise a heuristic function for task composition which estimates the distance to the nearest solution more precisely in the presence of non-deterministic effects? Basically, we want to apply the lessons learned from the evaluation in this work to further develop the techniques; note however that it remains unclear to which degree this can be achieved without changing the direction of the work completely.

While we were able to achieve scalability and have shown in various prototypes how usable tools can be engineered for a given scenario, the allowed expressivity for the verification proved to be restrictive for a set of scenarios. With the presented techniques, a subset of the processes in reality can be represented and verified exactly; for most of the remaining processes, the verification questions can still be answered approximatively. There are scenarios where the restrictions do not play a role: e.g., it is unlikely that behavioral interfaces of services will express their decision conditions, and are thus best modeled with non-deterministic decisions (as handled by our basic processes). However, for a significant portion of processes, dealing more precisely with XOR and loop conditions seems desirable.

There are a number of ways in which the expressivity can be increased. As mentioned in Chapter 4, we attempted to use model checking techniques to answer the verification questions. Our initial results are rather discouraging in terms of performance and/or memory consumption. However, it may be possible to adapt reduction techniques such that, on average, the process that needs to be checked can be reduced to a size for which the computation only takes an acceptable amount of time. More specifically, it may be possible to use the verification techniques developed herein for this reduction.

Another approach includes approximating the logical states a process can encounter from the opposite side: instead of computing all literals that *must* be true, we may be able to compute which literals *may* be true. A simple form of this information is already used in one of our approaches to compliance checking [313]. However, there the approximation is likely to be impractically conservative. When further restricting the expressivity, in particular the uncertainty about the initial state, it may become possible to compute a less conservative (but still accurate) approximation in the mentioned form. We plan on addressing these questions in the mid-term future.

7.3 Future Research Topics

Besides the immediate open points in this work, there are also a few larger or separate research topics that may be addressed based on the presented work.

As stated previously, a number of extensions were already developed on the basis on this work. Since these extensions do not belong to the core of this work, we did not discuss them in detail here. To mention some of them: task composition has been extended to take non-functional properties into account, thus searching for the *best* solution instead of the shortest; task composition has further been extended so as to deal with temporal constraint rules, which may be used to specify compliance requirements, organizational policies, or the like; and the verification algorithms can be used as a basis for approximate compliance checking of modeled processes [115, 313]. Further, the techniques have been found to support various scenarios other than process design, some of which have been shortly described in the prototypes section (6.2).

A number of the requirements from Chapter 3 were not addressed in this work and in the extensions. Three of those deal with resources. In [252], we looked at the relation of process activities, Web services, workflow tasks, and task patterns. Future work could address a more detailed investigation, taking into account that resources can also be machines or could be used to model organizational entities, such as business partners, departments, or the like. We further believe that the idea of a context-based configuration of complex services (Requirement 18) is a very interesting problem; however, a practical solution can most likely only be designed for specific settings where a strong link to the development of the services can be established.

Another larger point of interest to us would be to adapt the techniques described herein to the problem of business-to-business integration or choreography settings in general. Research questions could then include: Can we determine the fitness of (annotated) process interfaces of various participants in a choreography with respect to the collaboration? Can we automatically compose mediator processes when the fit is not perfect? Can we determine compliance from an annotated choreography?

7.4 Reflection

Taking an abstract perspective, the presented work has the following shape: while the requirements analysis and the conceptual framework took a rather broad form on the business level, the work on composition and verification delved into rather deep formal detail.

The goal of this work as a piece of applied research was to create a value proposition on the business level while making contributions to the respective scientific communities. The scheduled pilot customer evaluation for one of the integrated prototypes is going to investigate in depth in how far composition and verification are ready for productive use within a specific setting. From our observations so far, it seems that a likely result is that composition will be usable as-is, whereas the verification techniques require further work with respect to the expressivity. It comes with little surprise that we were able to solve the composition problem to a higher degree than the verification problem: for composition, we were able to build on the vast experience of decades of research in AI planning – in contrast to the work on verification, where we take more of a pioneering role.

We hope that some of the results will come to productive use, and that the publications out of this work stimulate further relevant research.

Appendix: A

Proofs

A.1 Proofs for the Verification Technique

A.1.1 Correctness of M-Propagation

Lemma A.1. *Let $\mathcal{P} = (N, E, \lambda)$ be a process graph. There exists exactly one M-propagation result M^*. The time required to compute M^* is $O(|E^{\mathcal{Q}}|^2 + |N^{\mathcal{Q}}| * |E^{\mathcal{Q}}| * max^{\mathcal{Q}})$, where $max^{\mathcal{Q}}$ is the maximum number of incoming or outgoing edges any node in $\mathcal{Q}$ has.*

Proof: First, we show uniqueness. Assume to the contrary of the claim that $(M_1^*)_j^i \neq (M_2^*)_j^i$, for M-propagation results M_1^*, M_2^*. Let $n \in N$ so that $e \in out(n)$ with $\#(e) = i$. Since M-propagation sets the value of each matrix cell exactly once, and since the value is a function of the cells for edges with lower $\#$ values, we can conclude that we have $(M_1^*)_j^l \neq (M_2^*)_j^l$ for some $l < i$. Obviously, we can iterate this argument. Since the graph is acyclic, we hence obtain $(M_1^*)_0^0 \neq (M_2^*)_0^0$, which is clearly wrong and disproves the assumption.

As for computation time, we take look-ups of values in the matrix, as well as setting a value in the matrix, as atomic operations. Initialization of M^* obviously takes time $O(|E^{\mathcal{Q}}|^2)$. Then the propagation performs one propagation step for every $n \in N^{\mathcal{Q}}$. The requirements 1 and 2 can be accounted for simply by ordering the propagation steps according to the enumeration function, so this requires constant time per step. Denote by $max^{\mathcal{Q}}$ the maximum number of incoming or outgoing edges any node in $\mathcal{Q}$ has. The propagation steps 3 to 5 can be implemented in time $O(|E^{\mathcal{Q}}| * max^{\mathcal{Q}})$, affecting one row and column of the matrix, for every outgoing edge. Propagation steps 6 and 7 do the same, within a loop over all ingoing edges, also resulting in time $O(|E^{\mathcal{Q}}| * max^{\mathcal{Q}})$. Hence, overall, we get a runtime behavior in $O(|E^{\mathcal{Q}}|^2 + |N^{\mathcal{Q}}| * |E^{\mathcal{Q}}| * max^{\mathcal{Q}})$. ∎

If two edges are parallel, then, in particular situations, we can "choose" which one to activate last:

Lemma A.2. *Let $\mathcal{P} = (N, E, \lambda)$ be a sound process graph. Let $e \neq e' \in \mathcal{E}$ so that $e \parallel e'$, and $e \in out(n)$ where $n \notin \mathcal{N}_{PS}$. Let t' be a token-reachable token marking where $t'(e) > 0$ and $t'(e') > 0$. Then there exists a token-reachable token marking t so that $t \xrightarrow{n} t'$.*

Proof: Since $e \parallel e'$, we know that t' as claimed exists. Say t' is reached on the execution path $\vec{p} = \langle t_0 \xrightarrow{n_0} t_1 \xrightarrow{n_1} \ldots \xrightarrow{n_{k-1}} t_k \rangle$ where t_0 is the start state and $t_k = t'$. By prerequisite we have $t_k(e) > 0$. Define i to be the highest index of a state that activates e, i.e., $n_{i-1} = n$ and consequently $t_i(e) > 0$, such that e remains activated until t_k. That is, we have: (*) *for all $i \leq j \leq k : t_j(e) > 0$.*

Now, consider the token markings t_{i-1} and t_i, as well as the nodes $n_{i-1} = n$ and n_i. We know that n is executable in t_{i-1}, and that n_i is executable in t_i. We prove that we can re-order n and n_i in $\vec{p}$, and still obtain a valid execution path. Once this is proved, we are done: iterating the argument, we can move n upwards in $\vec{p}$ and, ultimately, execute it last.

Consider the re-ordered sequence $\langle t_0 \xrightarrow{n_0} \ldots \xrightarrow{n_{i-2}} t_{i-1} \xrightarrow{n_i} t'_i \xrightarrow{n_{i-1}} t'_{i+1} \rangle$. It suffices to show that:

1. n_i is token-executable in t_{i-1},
2. $n_{i-1} = n$ is token-executable in t'_i, and
3. $t'_{i+1} = t_{i+1}$.

As for 1., we know that n_i is token-executable in t_i, which differs from t_{i-1} only in that n is executed beforehand. Observe that executing n puts a token only on e. This is obvious for non-split nodes, which have only a single outgoing edge. For XOR splits it is clear because otherwise we would not have $t_i(e) > 0$, in contradiction to (*). This covers all cases because by prerequisite n is not a parallel split. Now, n_i cannot have e as an ingoing edge: tokens from ingoing edges are always removed by definition, except for XOR joins. But ingoing edges of XOR joins cannot be parallel: the process is assumed to be sound so that would be a contradiction to Proposition 4.4. Thus, if n_i had e as an ingoing edge, then we would not have $t_{i+1}(e) > 0$, in contradiction to (*). Hence n_i must be executable in t_{i-1} already, as desired.

As for 2., we know that n is token-executable in t_{i-1}. This differs from t'_i only in that n_i is not executed beforehand. Now, token-executability of n (of any node) depends of course only on the activation of n's ingoing edges, and execution of n_i (of any node) removes tokens only from its ingoing edges. Hence, if n is not executable in t'_i, then we can derive that $in(n) \cap in(n_i) \neq \emptyset$, which is of course not possible since every edge has exactly one target node.

As for 3., we have already seen that n_i does not consume any tokens set by n. Likewise, it is obvious that n does not consume any tokens set by n_i, or else n could not be executed prior to n_i in $\vec{p}$. Hence the effects of the nodes on the token structure are mutually independent, from which the claimed property follows. This concludes the argument.   ∎

In the next lemma, and at some points further below, we will make use of *flow orderings*. Given a process graph, a flow ordering is a bijective function

$\#: E \mapsto \{0, \ldots |E| - 1\}$, numbering the edges such that (i) every incoming edge of a node has a lower number than any of the node's outgoing edges, and (ii) all outgoing edges of a split node are consecutively enumerated. Flow orderings obviously exist, since (N, E) is acyclic. For example, a flow ordering results from a breadth-first traversal of the process graph. We assume in the rest of the work that, for every process graph under consideration, a flow ordering $\#$ is fixed. This is just a simple device to be able to more conveniently state certain proof arguments. We use the following helper notations. $\#^{-1}$ is the inverse function of $\#$, i.e., $\#^{-1}(i) = e$ iff $\#(e) = i$. If E is a set of edges, then $\#E_{max} := max\{\#(e) \mid e \in E\}$ is the maximum number of any edge in E, and analogously for $\#E_{min}$. For example, given a node n, $\#in(n)_{max} = max\{\#(e) \mid e \in in(n)\}$ is the maximum number of any incoming edge.

Lemma A.3. *Let* $\mathcal{P} = (N, E, \lambda)$ *be a sound process graph, and let* $\mathcal{Q} \in Sub(\mathcal{P})$. *Let* $e \neq e' \in E^{\mathcal{Q}}$ *so that* $e \parallel e'$, $e \in out(n)$ *where* $n \in N_{PS}^{\mathcal{Q}}$, *and* $\#^{\mathcal{Q}}(e') < \#out(n)_{min}$. *Let* t' *be a token-reachable token marking where* $t'(e) > 0$ *and* $t'(e') > 0$. *Then there exist token-reachable token markings* t, t'' *so that* $t \xrightarrow{n} t''$ *where* $t''(e) > 0$ *and* $t''(e') > 0$.

Proof: Since $e \parallel e'$, we know that t' as claimed exists. Say t' is reached on the execution path $\vec{p} = \langle t_0 \xrightarrow{n_0} t_1 \xrightarrow{n_1} \ldots \xrightarrow{n_{k-1}} t_k \rangle$ as in the proof to Lemma A.2. Since, obviously, parts of the path outside the subprocess $\mathcal{Q}$ in question do not matter, and $\vec{p}$ ends within $\mathcal{Q}$, in the following we will ignore the part of $\vec{p}$ outside $\mathcal{Q}$, i..e., we act as if the path was completely contained within $\mathcal{Q}$.

Virtually all arguments in the proof to Lemma A.2 remain intact, with a single exception, namely the proof that n_i is token-executable in t_{i-1}. Precisely, the only part of the proof of Lemma A.2 that makes use of the prerequisite $n \notin \mathcal{N}_{PS}$, is the argument given here to show that execution of n does not put a token on any edge $e'' \in in(n_i)$. We need to find a different argument for this.

Such an argument can be based on the new prerequisite of our claim here, namely that $\#^{\mathcal{Q}}(e') < \#out(n)_{min}$. What we prove is that: (*) *a suitable* $\vec{p'}$ *can be constructed so that, for all nodes* n_j *in* $\vec{p'}$, $\#in(n_j)_{max} < \#out(n)_{min}$. This immediately proves the claim: if $e'' \in out(n) \cap in(n_i)$, then, by construction of $\#$, it follows that $\#^{\mathcal{Q}}(e'') \geq \#out(n)_{min}$ in contradiction to (*).

Say $n_j \neq n$ is the node in $\vec{p}$ with maximal $\#in(n_j)_{max}$. If $\#in(n_j)_{max} < \#out(n)_{min}$, there is nothing to prove. Else, construct $\vec{p'}$ by removing n_j, i.e., set $\vec{p'} := \langle t_0 \xrightarrow{n_0} \ldots \xrightarrow{n_{j-1}} t_j \xrightarrow{n_{j+1}} t'_{j+2} \xrightarrow{n_{j+2}} \ldots \xrightarrow{n_{k-1}} t'_k \rangle$.

First, observe that $\vec{p'}$ is still a valid execution path, i.e., for $j+2 \leq l \leq k-1$, we have that n_l is executable in t'_l. If that were not the case, then obviously there would exist an l so that $in(n_l) \cap out(n_j) \neq \emptyset$, i.e., n_j produces a token needed by n_l. However, by construction of $\#$, $\#in(n_j)_{max} < \#out(n_j)_{min}$. So, if $e'' \in in(n_l) \cap out(n_j)$, then $\#in(n_l)_{max} \geq \#^{\mathcal{Q}}(e'') > \#in(n_j)_{max}$ which is a contradiction since $\#in(n_j)_{max}$ is assumed to be maximal.

Second, observe that $t'_k(e) > 0$ and $t'_k(e') > 0$. Obviously, the only chance for that not to happen is if e, respectively e', is contained in $out(n_j)$. So $t'_k(e) > 0$ is obvious since $n_j \neq n$. As for $t'_k(e') > 0$, assume that $e' \in out(n_j)$. Then, by construction of #, we have $\#^{\mathcal{Q}}(e') > \#in(n_j)_{max}$. Further, by assumption we have $\#in(n_j)_{max} \geq \#out(n)_{min}$. Finally, by prerequisite we have $\#out(n)_{min} > \#^{\mathcal{Q}}(e')$. We can conclude that $\#^{\mathcal{Q}}(e') > \#^{\mathcal{Q}}(e')$ which is of course a contradiction.

Iterating the argument, we can remove from $\vec{p}$ all nodes where $\#in(n_j)_{max} \geq \#out(n)_{min}$, and still obtain an execution path at whose end both e and e' are active. This proves (*) and hence concludes the argument.   ∎

Henceforth, if E is a set of edges, then we write $\parallel E$ iff all pairs of edges in E are parallel. In that case, we can activate all edges in E at the same time:

Lemma A.4. *Let $\mathcal{P} = (N, E, \lambda)$ be a sound process graph, let $\mathcal{Q} \in Sub(\mathcal{P})$, and let $E' \subseteq E^{\mathcal{Q}}$ with $\parallel E'$. Then there exists a token-reachable token marking t such that $t(e) > 0$ for all $e \in E'$.*

Proof: The proof is by induction over the process structure, as reflected in the enumeration function $\#^{\mathcal{Q}}$. The base case refers to all E' where $\#E'_{max} \leq 0$. The inductive case considers individual nodes n in the graph. The induction hypothesis is that the claim holds for all E' where $\#E'_{max} \leq \#out(n)_{min} - 1$. It is proved that the claim then holds also for all E' where $\#E'_{max} \leq \#out(n)_{max}$. Note that this induction stops at $\mathcal{Q}$'s end node. The execution paths constructed do not include repetitions of $\mathcal{Q}$, i.e., we show that we can reach the desired t within a single iteration of $\mathcal{Q}$.

Base case. There exists exactly one edge with $\#^{\mathcal{Q}}$ value 0, namely the start edge $e_0^{\mathcal{Q}}$. Hence the only set E' is the singleton $\{e_0^{\mathcal{Q}}\}$ for which the claim holds trivially – since $\mathcal{P}$ is assumed sound, at least one token execution reaches $e_0^{\mathcal{Q}}$.

Inductive case. Let $n \in N^{\mathcal{Q}}$. Stated formally, the induction hypothesis is that, for every $E' \subseteq E^{\mathcal{Q}}$ where $\parallel E'$ and $\#E'_{max} \leq \#out(n)_{min} - 1$, there exists a token-reachable token marking t' such that $t'(e') > 0$ for all $e' \in E'$. We prove that, for every $E'' \subseteq E^{\mathcal{Q}}$ where $\parallel E''$ and $\#E''_{max} \leq \#out(n)_{max}$, there exists a token-reachable token marking t'' such that $t''(e'') > 0$ for all $e'' \in E''$. Since the induction hypothesis already accounts for all E'' where $\#E''_{max} \leq \#out(n)_{min} - 1$, it suffices to consider sets E'' where $\#E''_{max} > \#out(n)_{min} - 1$, i.e., $out(n) \cap E'' \neq \emptyset$. We distinguish the different kinds of nodes n:

1. $n \in N_T^{\mathcal{Q}} \cup N_L^{\mathcal{Q}}$. Let $E'' \subseteq E^{\mathcal{Q}}$ be arbitrary so that $\parallel E''$, $\#E''_{max} \leq \#out(n)_{max}$, and $out(n) \in E''$. If E'' has only one element, there is nothing to show. Else, let $out(n) \neq e'' \in E''$ be arbitrary. We know that $out(n) \parallel e''$, and hence there exists a token-reachable token marking t where $t(out(n)) > 0$ and $t(e'') > 0$. We can apply Lemma A.2 and get that t can be reached on a path $\vec{p}$ where n is executed last, i.e., we

have a token-reachable token marking t_0 so that $t_0 \overset{n}{\rightarrow} t$. Obviously, we have $t_0(in(n)) > 0$ and $t_0(e'') > 0$. Hence $in(n) \parallel e''$. Construct E' as $E' := E'' \setminus out(n) \cup in(n)$. With what we have just proved, we have that $\parallel E'$. Clearly, $\#E'_{max} \leq \#out(n)_{min} - 1$. Hence we can apply the induction hypothesis and get that there exists a token-reachable token marking t' such that $t'(e') > 0$ for all $e' \in E'$. If we apply n in t', then we get a token marking t'' as claimed.

2. $n \in N^{\mathcal{Q}}_{XJ}$. Let $E'' \subseteq E^{\mathcal{Q}}$ be arbitrary so that $\parallel E''$, $\#E''_{max} \leq \#out(n)_{max}$, and $out(n) \in E''$. The proof goes almost exactly as for task nodes above. For $out(n) \neq e'' \in E''$, we get a token-reachable token marking t where $t(out(n)) > 0$ and $t(e'') > 0$, and with Lemma A.2 n is executed last. Say the predecessor t_0 activates $e' \in in(n)$. Then we know that $e' \parallel e''$, and hence $\parallel E'$ where $E' := E'' \setminus out(n) \cup \{e'\}$. We can apply the induction hypothesis and get a token-reachable token marking t' which activates all of E'; applying n here yields t'' as claimed.

3. $n \in N^{\mathcal{Q}}_{PJ}$. This is proved exactly like the case of XOR joins, except that t_0 activates all edges in $in(n)$ and hence E' is defined as $E' := E'' \setminus out(n) \cup in(n)$.

4. $n \in N^{\mathcal{Q}}_{XS}$. This is proved exactly like the case of task nodes, except that we focus on one particular $e \in out(n)$. The only important observation here is that it never happens that $e_1, e_2 \in out(n) \cap E''$, with $e_1 \neq e_2$. This would require that $e_1 \parallel e_2$. Since the process is assumed to be sound, that would be a contradiction to Proposition 4.4.

5. $n \in N^{\mathcal{Q}}_{PS}$. This case requires a different proof because Lemma A.2 is not applicable to parallel splits. We instead use Lemma A.3. Let $E'' \subseteq E^{\mathcal{Q}}$ be arbitrary so that $\parallel E''$, $\#E''_{max} \leq \#out(n)_{max}$, and $out(n) \cap E'' \neq \emptyset$. The latter two prerequisites imply that E'' consists of a (non-empty) subset E_{out} of $out(n)$, plus a set of edges e'' for which we have $\#(e'') < \#out(n)_{min}$. If no such edge e'' is contained in E'', then there is nothing to prove – since the process is assumed sound, there exists a token execution on which n is executed; in the outcome state, all the edges in $out(n)$ carry a token, in particular those in E_{out}. So, let e'' be arbitrary with $e'' \in E'' \setminus out(n)$. Further, let $e \in E_{out}$. We know that $e \parallel e''$, and hence there exists a token-reachable token marking t where $t(e) > 0$ and $t(e'') > 0$. We can apply Lemma A.3 and get token-reachable token markings t_1, t_2 so that $t_1 \overset{n}{\rightarrow} t_2$ where $t_2(e) > 0$ and $t_2(e'') > 0$. Obviously, we have $t_1(in(n)) > 0$ and $t_1(e'') > 0$. Hence $in(n) \parallel e''$. Construct E' as $E' := E'' \setminus E_{out} \cup in(n)$. With what we have just proved, we have that $\parallel E'$. Obviously, $\#E'_{max} \leq \#out(n)_{min} - 1$. Hence we can apply the induction hypothesis and get that there exists a token-reachable token marking t' such that $t'(e') > 0$ for all $e' \in E'$. If we apply n in t', then obviously we get a token marking t'' as claimed. This concludes the argument. ∎

Lemma A.5. *Let* $\mathcal{P} = (N, E, \lambda)$ *be a sound process graph, let* $\mathcal{Q} \in Sub(\mathcal{P})$, *and let* M^* *be the M-propagation result for* $\mathcal{Q}$. *Let* $e_1 \neq e_2 \in E^{\mathcal{Q}}$ *be arbitrary. Then* $e_1 \parallel e_2$ *iff* $M^{*\mathcal{Q}}{}^{\#^{\mathcal{Q}}(e_2)}_{\#^{\mathcal{Q}}(e_1)} = 1$.

Proof: For the rest of this proof, to avoid clumsy notation we skip the $\mathcal{Q}$ superscript. In particular, whenever we write M^* we mean $M^{*\mathcal{Q}}$, whenever we write $\#$ we mean $\#^{\mathcal{Q}}$, whenever we write N we mean $N^{\mathcal{Q}}$, and whenever we write E we mean $E^{\mathcal{Q}}$.

The proof is by induction over the process structure, as reflected in the enumeration function $\#^{\mathcal{Q}}$. The base case refers to all pairs $e_1 \neq e_2$ where $\#(e_1), \#(e_2) \leq 0$ (no such pair exists and hence the base case is trivial). The inductive case considers individual nodes n in the graph. The induction hypothesis is that the claim holds for all pairs $e_1 \neq e_2$ where $\#(e_1), \#(e_2) \leq \#out(n)_{min} - 1$. It is proved that the claim then holds also for all pairs $e_1' \neq e_2'$ where $\#(e_1'), \#(e_2') \leq \#out(n)_{max}$.

Base case. There exists exactly one edge with $\#$ value 0, namely the start edge. Hence no pairs of edges as claimed exist, so the claim is void and trivially true.

Inductive case. Let $n \in N$. Stated formally, the induction hypothesis is that, for all $e_1 \neq e_2 \in E$ where $\#(e_1), \#(e_2) \leq \#out(n)_{min} - 1$, we have that $e_1 \parallel e_2$ iff $M^{*}{}^{\#(e_2)}_{\#(e_1)} = 1$. We prove that, for all $e_1' \neq e_2' \in E$ where $\#(e_1'), \#(e_2') \leq \#out(n)_{max}$, we have that $e_1' \parallel e_2'$ iff $M^{*}{}^{\#(e_2')}_{\#(e_1')} = 1$.

In the following, we usually show this separately for the two directions: $e_1' \parallel e_2'$ "$\Rightarrow$" $M^{*}{}^{\#(e_2')}_{\#(e_1')} = 1$ and $e_1' \parallel e_2'$ "$\Leftarrow$" $M^{*}{}^{\#(e_2')}_{\#(e_1')} = 1$. Note that the propagation rules of Definition 4.13 never overwrite a field M_j^i that is already specified, i.e., where $M_j^i \neq \perp$. Thus, we only need to consider pairs e_1', e_2' where (without loss of generality) $e_1' \in out(n)$. We distinguish the different kinds of nodes n:

1. $n \in N_T \cup N_L$.
   "$\Leftarrow$": According to Definition 4.13, $M^{*}{}^{\#(e_2')}_{\#(out(n))} = 1$ iff $M^{*}{}^{\#(e_2')}_{\#(in(n))} = 1$. By induction hypothesis we know that this implies $in(n) \parallel e_2'$, i.e., there exists a token-reachable t such that $t(in(n)) > 0, t(e_2') > 0$. Since the token-execution of n depends on nothing but $t(in(n)) > 0$, there exists a t' such that $t \xrightarrow{n} t'$, and in t' we thus have $t(out(n)) > 0, t(e_2') > 0$, which is what we needed to show.
   "$\Rightarrow$": $out(n) \parallel e_2'$ means by definition that there exists a token-reachable t' with $t'(out(n)) > 0, t'(e_2') > 0$. According to Lemma A.2, there must exist a token-reachable t so that $t \xrightarrow{n} t'$. Obviously, we have $t(in(n)) >$

$0, t(e_2') > 0$. By induction hypothesis we thus have $M^*{}^{\#(e_2')}_{\#(in(n))} = 1$, which, by definition, implies $M^*{}^{\#(e_2')}_{\#(out(n))} = 1$.

2. $n \in N_{PS}$. For any $e_1' \in out(n)$ and $e_2' \notin out(n)$ we can apply the exact same arguments as for task nodes above, with a single difference. We apply Lemma A.3 instead of Lemma A.2, and obtain a token-reachable t so that $t \xrightarrow{n} t''$ where $t(in(n)) > 0, t(e_2') > 0$; the rest of the argument remains the same. Hence it remains only to show the claim for $e_1', e_2' \in out(n)$. But that is trivial. We obviously have $e_1' \parallel e_2'$, and by definition we have $M^*{}^{\#(e_2')}_{\#(e_1')} = 1$.

3. $n \in N_{XS}$. Again, for any $e_1' \in out(n)$ and $e_2' \notin out(n)$ we can apply the same arguments as for task nodes above. For $e_1', e_2' \in out(n)$ the proof is, again, trivial. We obviously have $e_1' \not\parallel e_2'$, and by definition we have $M^*{}^{\#(e_2')}_{\#(e_1')} = 0$.

4. $n \in N_{PJ}$.

"$\Leftarrow$": By definition, $M^*{}^{\#(e_2')}_{\#(out(n))} = 1$ implies that $M^*{}^{\#(e_2')}_{\#(e_i)} = 1$ for all $e_i \in in(n)$. By induction hypothesis we thus have that, for all such e_i, $e_i \parallel e_2'$. We can apply Lemma A.4 and conclude that there exists a token-reachable t with $t(e_2') > 0$ and $t(e_i) > 0$ for all e_i. In t, n can be executed, yielding a token marking t'. Clearly, $t'(e_2') > 0, t'(out(n)) > 0$, which is what we needed to show.

"$\Rightarrow$": This is analogous to the same direction for task nodes, the only difference being that the token marking t derived from Lemma A.2 has $t(e_i) > 0$ for all $e_i \in in(n)$.

5. $n \in N_{XJ}$.

"$\Leftarrow$": According to Definition 4.13, $M^*{}^{\#(e_2')}_{\#(out(n))} = 1$ iff there exists $e_i \in in(n)$ such that $M^*{}^{\#(e_2')}_{\#(e_i)} = 1$. By induction hypothesis, this implies $e_i \parallel e_2'$, i.e., there exists a token-reachable t such that $t(e_i) > 0, t(e_2') > 0$. Since the token execution of n depends on nothing but $t(e_j) > 0$ for some $e_j \in in(n)$, with $e_i = e_j$ we can execute n in t, obtaining a token marking t'. Obviously, $t(out(n)) > 0, t(e_2') > 0$ and hence $out(n) \parallel e_2'$.

"$\Rightarrow$": Again, this is analogous to the same direction for task nodes. The only difference is that the token marking t derived from Lemma A.2 has $t(e_i) > 0$ for one of the $e_i \in in(n)$.   ∎

Theorem 4.14. *Let* $\mathcal{P} = (N, E, \lambda)$ *be a sound process graph, and let* $\mathcal{Q} \in Sub(\mathcal{P})$. *There exists exactly one M-propagation result M^* for* $\mathcal{Q}$. *For all* $n_1, n_2 \in N_T^{\mathcal{Q}}$ *we have* $n_1 \parallel n_2$ *iff* $M^*{}^{\#(in(n_2))}_{\#(in(n_1))} = 1$. *The time required to compute M^* is* $O(|E^{\mathcal{Q}}|^2 + |N^{\mathcal{Q}}| * |E^{\mathcal{Q}}| * max^{\mathcal{Q}})$, *where $max^{\mathcal{Q}}$ is the maximum number of incoming or outgoing edges any node in $\mathcal{Q}$ has.*

Proof: Follows immediately from Lemmas A.1 and A.5.   ∎

A.1.2 Binary Theories Can Be Compiled Away

We sometimes need to distinguish the state spaces of different processes. We then indicate the process as a superscript. That is, $\bigcap^{\mathcal{Q}} e$ denotes the set of literals that are always true when e is activated, in an execution path of $\mathcal{Q}$.

Lemma A.6. Let $\mathcal{Q} = (N, E, \lambda, \Omega, \alpha)$, $\Omega = (P, T)$, be an executable basic annotated process graph. Denote by C the set of all constants appearing in any of the annotated $pre(n)$, $eff(n)$. Let $\mathcal{Q}' = (N, E, \lambda, \Omega', \alpha')$ be the modification of $\mathcal{Q}$ where $\Omega' = (P, 1)$ and $\alpha' \equiv \alpha$ except that, for all $n \in N_T$, $eff'(n) := \{l \in P[C] \mid T[C] \land eff(n) \models l\}$ if $eff(n)$ is defined, and $eff'(n) := \{l \in P[C] \mid T[C] \models l\}$ otherwise. Then, for every $e \in \mathcal{E}$, we have: $\bigcap^{\mathcal{Q}} e = \bigcap^{\mathcal{Q}'} e$.

Proof: In what follows, we denote a state by the set of literals it makes true. We first prove the following: given a reachable state s with a token on $in(n)$ for a task node n, in $\mathcal{Q}$ exactly one state s' can be reached by executing n in s, namely the state $s' := (s \setminus \neg eff'(n)) \cup eff'(n)$.

Recall that, by definition, the states s' reachable by executing n in s are all those where $s' \in min(s, T[C] \land eff(n))$, which is defined to be the set of all states that satisfy $T[C] \land eff(n)$ and that differ in a set-inclusion minimal set of values from s.

First, for any $s' \in min(s, T[C] \land eff(n))$ it is clear by definition that $eff'(n) \subseteq s'$. The definition of s' as given above changes $only$ those values. It suffices to show that $s' \models T[C]$: then, we have $s' \models T[C] \land eff(n)$, and clearly the set of changed values is a proper subset of any other state with the same property. Assume to the contrary of the claim that $(l \lor l') \in T[C]$ and $s' \not\models l \lor l'$, i.e., $\neg l \in s'$ and $\neg l' \in s'$; note here that T is binary and hence every clause has at most two literals. If $\neg l \in eff'(n)$, then $l' \in eff'(n)$ – because, given the clause $l \lor l'$, l' is a logical consequence of $\neg l$. With $eff'(n) \subseteq s'$ we obtain a contradiction, proving that $\neg l$ cannot be contained in $eff'(n)$. Similarly, we can disprove $\neg l' \in eff'(n)$. Hence, by construction of s', $\{\neg l, \neg l'\} \subseteq s$. But then, $s \not\models T[C]$ which is a contradiction because s is reachable.

With the above, we know that, for any reachable state s and any task node n, the (single) transition induced in $\mathcal{Q}$ is exactly the same as the transition induced in $\mathcal{Q}'$. Hence, obviously since the graph structure is not changed in any other way, any possible difference in the sets $\bigcap e$ would have to be due to different start states. So let us consider the start states in $\mathcal{Q}$ and $\mathcal{Q}'$.

The start states in $\mathcal{Q}$ are all those with $s_0 \models T[C]$, and $s_0 \models T[C] \land eff(n_0)$ in case $\alpha(n_0)$ is defined. In $\mathcal{Q}'$, by construction the start states are all those where $s_0 \models 1 \land eff'(n_0)$, with $eff'(n_0) = \{l \in P[C] \mid T[C] \models l\}$ in case $\alpha(n_0)$ is undefined, and $eff'(n_0) = \{l \in P[C] \mid T[C] \land eff(n_0) \models l\}$ in case $\alpha(n_0)$ is defined.

Obviously, this means that the set of start states of $\mathcal{Q}'$ is a superset of the set of start states of $\mathcal{Q}$ – any start state of $\mathcal{Q}$ is a start state of $\mathcal{Q}'$, but not vice versa. However, likewise obviously, the set of literals true in all start states is the same in both cases, i.e., we have $\bigcap^{\mathcal{Q}} e_0 = \bigcap^{\mathcal{Q}'} e_0$.

Let e be any edge in the graph. Consider, for the moment, only the workflow structure of the graphs, i.e., the token executions. Since Q' does not change the graph structure, the set of token execution paths leading from (a state with a token on) e_0 to (a state with a token on) e is the same in both Q and Q'. Let's call this set of paths $\vec{P}$. By prerequisite, every task node is executable, there are no conditions at the outgoing edges of XOR splits, and there are no conditions at loop nodes. Thus we know that every path $\vec{p} \in \vec{P}$ can be executed from every possible start state s_0, in both Q and Q'. The change that $\vec{p}$ makes to s_0 is the accumulated effect of the task nodes executed on $\vec{P}$. From the above, we know that this is the same in both Q and Q'. We can write the resulting state s as $s = (s_0 \setminus \neg\text{eff}(\vec{p})) \cup \text{eff}(\vec{p})$, where $\text{eff}(\vec{p})$ denotes the accumulated effect of $\vec{p}$ – what exactly that latter effect is does not play a role in our argument below. The important point is that $\text{eff}(\vec{p})$ is a function, i.e., is well-defined.

Consider now the sets $\bigcap^Q e$ and $\bigcap^{Q'} e$. With the above, we know that

$$\bigcap_{s_0,\vec{p}}^{Q} e = \bigcap ((s_0 \setminus \neg\text{eff}(\vec{p})) \cup \text{eff}(\vec{p})),$$

where s_0 ranges over the start states of Q and $\vec{p}$ ranges over $\vec{P}$. Now, first, we can separate the "positive effects" – which occur irrespectively of the start state – out and get

$$\bigcap_{s_0,\vec{p}}^{Q} e = (\bigcap (s_0 \setminus \neg\text{eff}(\vec{p}))) \cup (\bigcap_{\vec{p}} \text{eff}(\vec{p})).$$

Further, we can re-write $\bigcap_{s_0,\vec{p}}(s_0 \setminus \neg\text{eff}(\vec{p}))$ to $\bigcap_{s_0,\vec{p}}(s_0 \cap L(\vec{p}))$ where $L(\vec{p})$ is the complement of $\neg\text{eff}(\vec{p})$. We can re-write $\bigcap_{s_0,\vec{p}}(s_0 \cap L(\vec{p}))$ to $(\bigcap_{s_0} s_0) \cap (\bigcap_{\vec{p}} L(\vec{p}))$. Hence, overall, we have derived that

$$\bigcap_{s_0}^{Q} e = ((\bigcap s_0) \cap (\bigcap_{\vec{p}} L(\vec{p}))) \cup (\bigcap_{\vec{p}} \text{eff}(\vec{p})).$$

In the same way, we can derive

$$\bigcap_{s_0'}^{Q'} e = ((\bigcap s_0') \cap (\bigcap_{\vec{p}} L(\vec{p}))) \cup (\bigcap_{\vec{p}} \text{eff}(\vec{p})),$$

where s_0' ranges over the start states of Q'. We need to prove that $\bigcap^Q e = \bigcap^{Q'} e$. Replacing both sides of the equation with the expressions we have just derived, the terms concerning $\vec{p}$ occur on both sides and can be removed. Thus we find that our desired equality is equivalent to $\bigcap_{s_0} s_0 = \bigcap_{s_0'} s_0'$, which we have already proved above. This concludes the argument. ∎

A.1.3 Correctness of I-Propagation

We define aggregate-eff($\mathcal{Q}$), the aggregated effect literals of a sub-graph $\mathcal{Q}$, as follows:

$$\text{aggregate-eff}(\mathcal{Q}) := \bigcup_{n \in N_T^{\mathcal{Q}}} \text{eff}(n) \cup \bigcup_{n \in N_L^{\mathcal{Q}}} \text{aggregate-eff}(\lambda^{\mathcal{Q}}(n))$$

Lemma A.7. *Let $\mathcal{Q} = (N, E, \lambda, \Omega, \alpha)$ be an executable basic sound annotated process graph without effect conflicts, and let $t \geq 0$. Let $E^0 \subseteq E$ be a set of edges so that there exists a state $s \in \mathcal{S}$ where, for all $e \in E^0$, $t_s(e) > 0$. Let l be a literal so that, for each $e \in E^0$, there exists a state $s' \in \mathcal{S}$ where $s' \not\models l$ and $t_{s'}(e) > 0$. Then, there exists a state $s_0 \in \mathcal{S}$ where $s_0 \not\models l$ and, for all $e \in E^0$, $t_{s_0}(e) > 0$.*

Proof: Let l be an arbitrary literal, and let $t \geq 0$ be arbitrary. We prove that the claim holds for all possible E^0, by induction over the process structure, as reflected in the enumeration function $\#$. As the induction base case, we prove that the claim holds for every set E^0 where $\#E^0_{max} \leq 0$. As the inductive step, we prove that, for every node n, if the claim holds for every E^0 where $\#E^0_{max} \leq \#out(n)_{min} - 1$, then the claim holds for every E^0 where $\#E^0_{max} \leq \#out(n)_{max}$.

Base case. Since e_0 is not parallel to any other edge (no edge can carry a token at the same time as e_0 does), the only set E^0 containing e_0 is the singleton $\{e_0\}$, for which the claim holds trivially.

Inductive case. Let $n \in N$. As stated, the induction hypothesis is that the claim holds for every E^0 where $\#E^0_{max} \leq \#out(n)_{min} - 1$. We prove that, under this hypothesis, the claim holds for every E^0 where $\#E^0_{max} \leq \#out(n)_{max}$.

To avoid clumsiness of language, we will use the following conventions. Whenever we write "E^0", we mean a set of edges with $\#E^0_{max} \leq \#out(n)_{min} - 1$ for which the prerequisite of the claim holds: there exists a state $s \in \mathcal{S}$ where, for all $e \in E^0$, $t_s(e) > 0$; and, for each single $e \in E^0$, there exists a state $s' \in \mathcal{S}$ where $s' \not\models l$ and $t_{s'}(e) > 0$. Similarly, whenever we write "$E^{0'}$", we mean a set of edges with $\#E^{0'}_{max} \leq \#out(n)_{max}$ for which the prerequisite of the claim holds. Further, since the induction hypothesis covers all other cases, we assume that $E^{0'} \cap out(n) \neq \emptyset$. Finally, since the case of $E^{0'} \subseteq out(n)$ is trivial for all kinds of nodes n, we assume that $E^{0'} \not\subseteq out(n)$. We distinguish the different kinds of nodes n:

1. $n \in N_T$. We distinguish three cases:
   1.1. $l \in \overline{\text{eff}(n)}$. This case is trivial because no $E^{0'}$ exists. Assume the opposite was the case. Then there exists a state $s' \in \mathcal{S}$ where $t_{s'}(out(n)) > 0$ and $s' \not\models l$. Since, directly after executing n, l is true, this means that a task node parallel to n has made l false. Hence we have an effect conflict, in contradiction to the prerequisite.

1.2. $\neg l \in \overline{\text{eff}(n)}$. Let $E^{0'}$ be an arbitrary set of edges, with $out(n) \in E^{0'}$ and so that there exists a state $s \in \mathcal{S}$ where $t_s(e) > 0$ for every $e \in E^{0'}$. In order to reach s, n must be executed. Since n is not a parallel split, we can apply Lemma A.2 to any pair of $out(n)$ and $out(n) \neq e \in E^{0'}$. Hence there exists an execution path to s on which n comes *last*. By prerequisite, n is executable, and so we can execute it at this point. Obviously, and $s_0 \not\models l$. Hence the claim holds for $E^{0'}$, and we are done.

1.3. $\{l, \neg l\} \cap \overline{\text{eff}(n)} = \emptyset$. For this case, we prove that there is a mapping from sets E^0 to sets $E^{0'}$. Precisely, we prove that we can construct each set $E^{0'}$ as $E^{0'} = E^0 \setminus \{in(n)\} \cup \{out(n)\}$ where E^0 is a set satisfying the prerequisite of the claim. Once this is proved, the claim follows easily: by induction hypothesis, we know that there exists a state $s_0 \in \mathcal{S}$ where $s_0 \not\models l$ and $t_{s_0}(e) > 0$ for all $e \in E^0$; in that state, we can execute n; the resulting state obviously satisfies the requirements of the claim.

It remains to prove the desired mapping. Let $E^{0'}$ be a set of edges with $E^{0'} \cap out(n) \neq \emptyset$ so that: there exists a state $s \in \mathcal{S}$ where, for all $e \in E^{0'}$, $t_s(e) > 0$; and, for each single $e \in E^{0'}$, there exists a state $s' \in \mathcal{S}$ where $s' \not\models l$ and $t_{s'}(e) > 0$. We need to prove that $E^0 := E^{0'} \setminus \{out(n)\} \cup \{in(n)\}$ has the same properties. The existence of the desired state $s \in \mathcal{S}$ follows by application of Lemma A.2 to $E^{0'}$ and s: we get a path to s on which n is applied last; the predecessor state activates all edges in E^0 and hence serves as the desired state s for E^0. Regarding the existence of the state $s' \in \mathcal{S}$ with $s' \not\models l$ and $t_{s'}(out(n)) > 0$, there are two possible reasons for that. First, there exists a state $s'' \in \mathcal{S}$ with $s'' \not\models l$ and $t_{s'}(in(n)) > 0$; in that case there is nothing to prove. Second, there exists a task node n' parallel to n that falsifies l in its effect. But then, n' can be executed directly before n, and hence we are back in the first case, i.e., we can construct a state $s'' \in \mathcal{S}$ as appropriate.

2. $n \in N_L$. We distinguish three cases similar as for task nodes; the respective proofs are similar as well:

2.1. On every path through $\lambda(n)$, the last change to l makes l true; in particular, $l \in \overline{\text{aggregate-eff}(\lambda(n))}$. This case is trivial because no $E^{0'}$ exists. Assume the opposite was the case. Then there exists a state $s' \in \mathcal{S}$ where $t_{s'}(out(n)) > 0$ and $s' \not\models l$. Since, directly after executing $\lambda(n)$, l is true, this means that a task node parallel to n has made l false. Hence we have an effect conflict, in contradiction to the prerequisite.

2.2. There exists a path $\vec{p}$ through $\lambda(n)$ where the last change makes l false; in particular, $\neg l \in \overline{\text{aggregate-eff}(\lambda(n))}$. Let $E^{0'}$ be an arbitrary set of edges, with $out(n) \in E^{0'}$ and so that there exists a state $s \in \mathcal{S}$ where $t_s(e) > 0$ for every $e \in E^{0'}$. In order to reach s, n must be executed. Since n is not a parallel split, we can apply Lemma A.2 to any pair of

$out(n)$ and $out(n) \neq e \in E^{0'}$. Hence there exists an execution path to s on which n comes *last*. By prerequisite, $\lambda(n)$ is executable, and so we can execute $\vec{p}$ at this point. Obviously, the resulting state s_0 has $s_0 \not\models l$. Hence the claim holds for $E^{0'}$, and we are done.

  2.3. $\{l, \neg l\} \cap \overline{\text{aggregate-eff}(\lambda(n))} = \emptyset$. This case is proved exactly as for task nodes. The only difference is that, rather than executing just n without affecting the value of l, we execute some path through $\lambda(n)$ without affecting the value of l. This does not affect the proof arguments.

3. $n \in N_{XS}$. There is a mapping from sets $E^{0'}$ to sets E^0. Namely, we can construct each $E^{0'}$ respectively as $E^{0'} = E^0 \setminus \{in(n)\} \cup \{e'\}$, where $e' \in out(n)$. This, like above, follows from Lemma A.2 regarding parallelism, i.e., the existence of the state s in the prerequisite of the claim. Regarding the existence of the states s' in the prerequisite of the claim, the argument is the same as before: a state s' which falsifies l and activates one of the outgoing edges can always be constructed from a state which falsifies l and activates the incoming edge.

   By induction hypothesis we know that there exists a reachable state $s_0 \in \mathcal{S}$ where $s_0 \not\models l$ and, for all $e \in E^0$, $t_{s_0}(e) > 0$. In that state, we can execute n. Because, by prerequisite, the process graph is basic, in particular no conditions are annotated at the outgoing edges of any XOR split. Hence, regardless of how s_0 interprets the logical propositions, we can choose to execute n in a way so that a token is put on e'. The resulting state obviously satisfies the requirements of the claim.

4. $n \in N_{XJ}$. Like for XOR splits, we have a mapping from sets $E^{0'}$ to sets E^0: every set $E^{0'}$ can be constructed from a set E^0 as $E^{0'} = E^0 \setminus \{e\} \cup \{out(n)\}$, where $e \in in(n)$. The proof for that is as before, and the claim follows as before.

5. $n \in N_{PJ}$. This case is also handled analogously: every set $E^{0'}$ can be constructed from a set E^0 as $E^{0'} = E^0 \setminus in(n) \cup \{out(n)\}$. That correspondence is proved as before, and the claim follows as before.

6. $n \in N_{PS}$. In this case, every set $E^{0'}$ can be constructed from a set E^0 as $E^{0'} = E^0 \setminus \{in(n)\} \cup E'$, where $E' \subseteq out(n)$; we argue this mapping below. With this mapping, the proof proceeds as before. By induction hypothesis we know that there exists a reachable state $s_0 \in \mathcal{S}$ where $s_0 \not\models l$ and, for all $e \in E^0$, $t_{s_0}(e) > 0$. In that state, we can execute n and put a token on every edge in E'. The resulting state obviously satisfies the requirements of the claim.

   It remains to prove that every set $E^{0'}$ can be constructed from a set E^0 as $E^{0'} = E^0 \setminus \{in(n)\} \cup E'$, where $E' \subseteq out(n)$. Let $E^{0'}$ be any set of edges with $E^{0'} \cap out(n) \neq \emptyset$ and $\#E^{0'}_{max} \leq \#out(n)_{max}$ so that: there exists a state $s \in \mathcal{S}$ where, for all $e \in E^{0'}$, $t_s(e) > 0$; and, for each single $e \in E^{0'}$, there exists a state $s' \in \mathcal{S}$ where $s' \not\models l$ and $t_{s'}(e) > 0$. We prove that $E^0 := E^{0'} \setminus out(n) \cup in(n)$ has the same properties. The existence of the state $s \in \mathcal{S}$ follows by application of Lemma A.3 to $\mathcal{Q}$, $E^{0'}$, and s: we get a path on which n is applied last and whose end state activates all edges in $E^{0'}$; the predecessor state activates all edges in E^0. Regarding the existence of the state $s' \in S$ with $s' \not\models l$ which activates the edges in E', there are two possible reasons for that. First, there exists a state $s'' \in S$ with $s'' \not\models l$ and $t_{s'}(in(n)) > 0$; in that case there is nothing to prove. Second, there exists a task node n' parallel to n that falsifies l in its effect. But then, n' can be executed directly before n, and hence we are back in the first case, i.e., we can construct a state s'' as appropriate. This concludes the argument.   ∎

Lemma A.8. *Let $\mathcal{P} = (N, E, \lambda, \Omega, \alpha)$ be an executable basic annotated process graph. Say we run I-propagation on $\mathcal{P}$, and I^* is an I-propagation result. Then, for all $e \in \mathcal{E}$, $\bigcap e \supseteq I^*(e)$.*

Proof: Since $\mathcal{P}$ is executable and basic, we can apply Lemma A.6. That is, we can compile the binary ontology into extended action effects without affecting the sets $\bigcap e$. Hence in what follows we can assume without loss of generality that the ontology is empty.

Let $e \in \mathcal{E}$ and let $l \in P[C]$, where C are the constants used by α. Assume that there exists an execution path $s_0 \overset{n_1}{\rightarrow} s_1 \overset{n_2}{\rightarrow} s_2 \ldots s_{k-1} \overset{n_k}{\rightarrow} s_k = s$ so that $t_s(e) > 0$ and $i_s \not\models l$. We show that, then, there exists an I-propagation path $I_0 \overset{n'_1}{\rightarrow} I'_1 \overset{n'_2}{\rightarrow} I'_2 \ldots I'_{l-1} \overset{n'_l}{\rightarrow} I_l = I'$ so that $l \notin I(e)$.

Note first that, given a function $I : E \mapsto 2^{P[C]}$ and a node n, there exists at most one I' so that I' is the propagation of I at n, i.e., I' is completely determined; I' exists iff propagating I at n results in any changes.

Consider now the sequence of nodes $n_1, \ldots, n_k$. We construct a sequence $I_0, I_1, \ldots, I_k$ as follows. For all $0 \leq j < k$, if propagating I_j at n_j results in changes, then set I_{j+1} to the outcome of that propagation; else, set $I_{j+1} := I_j$. Obviously, we get an I-propagation path $I_0 \overset{n'_1}{\rightarrow} I'_1 \overset{n'_2}{\rightarrow} I'_2 \ldots I'_{l-1} \overset{n'_l}{\rightarrow} I'_l = I$ by removing from $I_0, I_1, \ldots, I_k$ those steps where no changes occur. We then have $I_k = I$, and hence it suffices to prove that $l \notin I_k(e)$.

In what follows, we denote $t_j := t_{s_j}$ and $i_j := i_{s_j}$. We prove by induction that, for all $0 \leq j \leq k$: for all e where $t_j(e) > 0$, we have $i_j \models I_j(e)$.

Base case, $j = 0$. The only e' with $t_j(e') > 0$ is the start edge e_0. Since $I_0(e_0) = \text{eff}(n_0)$, the claim follows.

Inductive case, $j \rightarrow j + 1$. We distinguish the different kinds of executions of the node $n := n_{j+1}$:

1. $n \in N_{PS} \cup N_{XS}$. Consider the edges e' where $t_{j+1}(e') > 0$. We either have (a) $t_j(e') > 0$, or (b) $e' \in out(n)$. In case (a), the claim follows immediately from the induction hypothesis because $i_{j+1} = i_j$ and $I_{j+1}(e') = I_j(e')$. As for case (b), since n can be executed in s_j, we have that $t_j(in(n)) > 0$, and hence by induction assumption we know that $i_j \models I_j(in(n))$. The claim then follows because $i_{j+1} = i_j$ and, for all $e' \in out(n)$, $I_{j+1}(e') \subseteq I_j(in(n))$.

2. $n \in N_T$. Consider the edges e' where $t_{j+1}(e') > 0$. We either have (a) $t_j(e') > 0$, or (b) $e' = out(n)$. In case (a), the claim follows immediately from the induction hypothesis because $i_{j+1} = \text{eff}(n) \cup (i_j \setminus \neg\text{eff}(n))$, writing an interpretation as the set of literals it satisfies; and $I_{j+1}(e') = I_j(e') \setminus \neg\text{eff}(n)$ because, with $t_j(e') > 0$ and $t_j(in(n)) > 0$, we have $e' \parallel in(n)$. As for case (b), since $t_j(in(n)) > 0$ by induction assumption we know that $i_j \models I_j(in(n))$. The claim then follows because $i_{j+1} = \text{eff}(n) \cup (i_j \setminus \neg\text{eff}(n))$ and $I_{j+1}(out(n)) \subseteq \text{eff}(n) \cup (I_j(in(n)) \setminus \neg\text{eff}(n))$.

3. $n \in N_{PJ}$. Consider the edges e' where $t_{j+1}(e') > 0$. We either have (a) $e' \neq out(n)$ and $t_j(e') > 0$, or (b) $e' = out(n)$. In case (a), $I_{j+1}(e') = I_j(e')$ and hence the claim follows from the induction hypothesis and $i_{j+1} = i_j$. As for case (b), since n can be executed in s_j, we have that $t_j(e') > 0$ for all $e' \in in(n)$. Hence by induction assumption we know that $i_j \models I_j(e')$ for all $e' \in in(n)$. The claim then follows because $i_{j+1} = i_j$ and $I_{j+1}(out(n)) \subseteq \bigcup_{e' \in in(n)} I_j(e')$.

4. $n \in N_{XJ}$. Consider the edges e' where $t_{j+1}(e') > 0$. We either have (a) $e' \neq out(n)$ and $t_j(e') > 0$, or (b) $e' = out(n)$. In case (a), $I_{j+1}(e') = I_j(e')$ and hence the claim follows from the induction hypothesis and $i_{j+1} = i_j$. As for case (b), since n can be executed in s_j, we have that $t_j(e') > 0$ for at least one $e' \in in(n)$. By induction assumption we know that $i_j \models I_j(e')$ for that e'. The claim then follows because $i_{j+1} = i_j$ and $I_{j+1}(out(n)) \subseteq \bigcap_{e' \in in(n)} I_j(e')$.

5. $n \in N_L^Q$ with $\lambda^Q(n) = Q'$. Consider the edges e' where $t_{j+1}(e') > 0$. We either have (a) $t_j(e') > 0$, or (b) $e' = e_0^{Q'}$. In case (a), the claim follows immediately from the induction hypothesis because $i_{j+1} = i_j$ and $I_{j+1}(e') = I_j(e')$. As for case (b), since n can be executed in s_j, we have that $t_j(in(n)) > 0$, and hence by induction assumption we know that $i_j \models I_j(in(n))$. The claim then follows because $i_{j+1} = i_j$ and $I_{j+1}(e_0^{Q'}) \subseteq I_j(in(n))$.

6. $n = n_+^Q$ and $t_{j+1}(e_0^Q) > t_j(e_0^Q)$. Consider the edges e' where $t_{j+1}(e') > 0$. We either have (a) $t_j(e') > 0$, or (b) $e' = e_0^Q$. In case (a), the claim follows immediately from the induction hypothesis because $i_{j+1} = i_j$ and $I_{j+1}(e') = I_j(e')$. As for case (b), since n can be executed in s_j, we have that $t_j(in(n)) > 0$, and hence by induction assumption we know that $i_j \models I_j(in(n))$. The claim then follows because $i_{j+1} = i_j$ and $I_{j+1}(e_0^Q) \subseteq I_j(in(n))$.

7. $n = n_+^Q$ with $Q = \lambda^{Q'}(n')$ and $t_{j+1}(out(n')) > t_j(out(n'))$. Consider the edges e' where $t_{j+1}(e') > 0$. We either have (a) $t_j(e') > 0$, or (b) $e' = out(n')$. In case (a), the claim follows immediately from the induction hypothesis because $i_{j+1} = i_j$ and $I_{j+1}(e') = I_j(e')$. As for case (b), since n can be executed in s_j, we have that $t_j(in(n)) > 0$, and hence by induction assumption we know that $i_j \models I_j(in(n))$. The claim then follows because $i_{j+1} = i_j$ and $I_{j+1}(out(n')) \subseteq I_j(in(n))$. ∎

Lemma A.9. *Let $\mathcal{P} = (N, E, \lambda, \Omega, \alpha)$ be an executable basic sound annotated process graph without effect conflicts. Say we run I-propagation on $\mathcal{P}$, and I^* is an I-propagation result. Then, for all $e \in \mathcal{E}$, $\bigcap e \subseteq I^*(e)$.*

Proof: Since $\mathcal{P}$ is executable and basic, we can apply Lemma A.6. That is, we can compile the binary ontology into extended action effects without affecting the sets $\bigcap e$. Hence in what follows we can assume without loss of generality that the ontology is empty.

Assume an I-propagation path $I_0 \xrightarrow{n_1} I_1 \xrightarrow{n_2} I_2 \ldots I_{k-1} \xrightarrow{n_k} I_k$. We prove the following. For every $0 \leq j \leq k$ and for every edge $e \in \mathcal{E}$ and literal $l \in P[C]$ where $l \notin I_j(e)$, there exists an execution path ending in a state s so that $t_s(e) > 0$ and $s \not\models l$. The proof is by induction over j.

Base case, $j = 0$. By definition, $I_0(e) = P[C]$ except for $e = e_0$, where $I_0(e_0) = \text{eff}(n_0)$. Hence the only pairs e, l with $l \notin I_0(e)$ are those where $e = e_0$ and $l \notin \text{eff}(n_0)$. Obviously, every start state s_0 has $t_{s_0}(e_0) > 0$. If $l \notin \text{eff}(n_0)$ then by definition at least one start state s_0 exists where $s_0 \not\models l$. This shows the claim.

Inductive case, $j \rightarrow j+1$. By induction hypothesis, we know that, for every edge $e \in \mathcal{E}$ and literal $l \in P[C]$ where $l \notin I_j(e)$, there exists an execution path ending in a state s so that $t_s(e) > 0$ and $s \not\models l$. We distinguish the different kinds of nodes $n := n_{j+1}$:

1. $n \in N_{PS} \cup N_{XS}$. Say that $e \in \mathcal{E}$ and $l \in P[C]$ where $l \notin I_{j+1}(e)$. By the definition of I-propagation over split nodes, we either have (a) $l \notin I_j(e)$ or (b) $e \in out(n)$ and $l \notin I_j(in(n))$. In case (a), the induction hypothesis shows the existence of an execution path as desired, so there is nothing to prove. As for case (b), by induction hypothesis there exists an execution path ending in a state s so that $t_s(in(n)) > 0$ and $s \not\models l$. We can execute n in s. Since there are no conditions at the outgoing edges of XOR splits, if n is an XOR split then we can choose to put a token on e; if n is a parallel split then tokens are put on all outgoing edges, in particular on e. Hence we can construct an execution path ending in a state s' where $t_{s'}(e) > 0$ and $s' \not\models l$. This concludes the argument.

2. $n \in N_T$. Say that $e \in \mathcal{E}$ and $l \in P[C]$ where $l \notin I_{j+1}(e)$. By the definition of I-propagation over task nodes, we have one of the following cases: (a) $l \notin I_j(e)$; or (b) $e \parallel out(n)$ and $l \in \neg\text{eff}(n)$; or (c) $e = out(n)$ and $l \in \neg\text{eff}(n)$; or (d) $e = out(n)$ and $l \notin I_j(in(n))$. In case (a), the induction hypothesis proves the claim. In case (b), we construct some execution path that activates both e and $out(n)$, and which executes n last. A token execution path of $\mathcal{P}$ doing so exists by Lemma A.2; any token execution of $\mathcal{P}$ corresponds directly to an execution path because by prerequisite there are no conditions at the outgoing edges of XOR splits, there are no conditions at loop nodes, and all task nodes are executable. In case (c), we simply construct some execution path that executes n last; at least one such path exists because by prerequisite $\mathcal{P}$ is sound, all task nodes are executable, there are no conditions at the outgoing edges of XOR

splits, and there are no conditions at loop nodes. In case (d), finally, by induction hypothesis there exists an execution path ending in a state s so that $t_s(in(n)) > 0$ and $s \not\models l$. Since n is executable by prerequisite, we can execute n in s, getting to a state s' where $t_{s'}(e) > 0$ and $s' \not\models l$. This concludes the argument.

3. $n \in N_{PJ}$. Say that $e \in \mathcal{E}$ and $l \in P[C]$ where $l \notin I_{j+1}(e)$. By the definition of I-propagation over parallel join nodes, we either have (a) $l \notin I_j(e)$ or (b) $e = out(n)$ and for every $e_i \in in(n) : l \notin I_j(e_i)$. In case (a), the induction hypothesis shows the existence of an execution path as desired, so there is nothing to prove. As for case (b), by induction hypothesis for every $e_i \in in(n)$ there exists an execution path ending in a state s_i so that $t_{s_i}(e_i) > 0$ and $s_i \not\models l$. We can thus apply Lemma A.7, and obtain an execution path to a state s with $s \not\models l$ and $t_s(e_i) > 0$ for all $e_i \in in(n)$. We can execute n in s, getting to a state s' where $t_{s'}(e) > 0$ and $s' \not\models l$. This concludes the argument.

4. $n \in N_{XJ}$. Say that $e \in \mathcal{E}$ and $l \in P[C]$ where $l \notin I_{j+1}(e)$. By the definition of I-propagation over XOR join nodes, we either have (a) $l \notin I_j(e)$ or (b) $e = out(n)$ and for at least one $e' \in in(n) : l \notin I_j(e')$. In case (a), the induction hypothesis shows the existence of an execution path as desired, so there is nothing to prove. As for case (b), by induction hypothesis there exists an execution path ending in a state s so that $t_s(e') > 0$ and $s \not\models l$. We can execute n in s, getting to a state s' where $t_{s'}(e) > 0$ and $s' \not\models l$. This concludes the argument.

5. $n \in N_L^{\mathcal{Q}}$ with $\lambda^{\mathcal{Q}}(n) = \mathcal{Q}'$. Say that $e \in \mathcal{E}$ and $l \in P[C]$ where $l \notin I_{j+1}(e)$. By the definition of I-propagation over loop nodes, we either have (a) $l \notin I_j(e)$ or (b) $e = e_0^{\mathcal{Q}'}$ and $l \notin I_j(in(n))$. In case (a), the induction hypothesis shows the existence of an execution path as desired, so there is nothing to prove. As for case (b), by induction hypothesis there exists an execution path ending in a state s so that $t_s(in(n)) > 0$ and $s \not\models l$. We can execute n in s, getting to a state s' where $t_{s'}(e) > 0$ and $s' \not\models l$. This concludes the argument.

6. $n = n_+^{\mathcal{Q}}$ with $\mathcal{Q} = \lambda^{\mathcal{Q}'}(n')$. Say that $e \in \mathcal{E}$ and $l \in P[C]$ where $l \notin I_{j+1}(e)$. By the definition of I-propagation over end nodes, we have one of the following cases: (a) $l \notin I_j(e)$; or (b) $e = e_0^{\mathcal{Q}}$ and $l \notin I_j(in(n))$; or (c) $e = out(n')$ and $l \notin I_j(in(n))$. In case (a), the induction hypothesis shows the existence of an execution path as desired, so there is nothing to prove. As for cases (b) and (c), by induction hypothesis there exists an execution path ending in a state s so that $t_s(in(n)) > 0$ and $s \not\models l$. Since n is executable by prerequisite, we can execute n in s. Since by prerequisite there are no conditions at loop nodes, we can choose to repeat the loop or exit the loop, i.e., we can put a token on $e_0^{\mathcal{Q}}$ or $out(n')$ as desired for case (b) respectively for case (c). We hence, in both cases, get to a state s' where $t_{s'}(e) > 0$ and $s' \not\models l$. This concludes the argument. ∎

Theorem 4.21. *Let* $\mathcal{P} = (N, E, \lambda, \Omega, \alpha)$ *be an executable basic sound anno-tated process graph without effect conflicts. Say we run I-propagation on* $\mathcal{P}$. *There exists exactly one I-propagation result* I^*. *For all* $e \in \mathcal{E}$, $\bigcap e = I^*(e)$. *With fixed arity, the time required to compute* I^* *is polynomial in the size of* $\mathcal{P}$.

Proof: First, it is a direct consequence of Lemmas A.8 and A.9 that, for all $e \in \mathcal{E}$, $\bigcap e = I^*(e)$, for any I-propagation result I^*. From this it follows directly that there exists exactly one such I^*.

For time complexity, there are three issues to consider: (1) the time taken for compiling binary clauses away, (2) the time taken within any single propagation step, and (3) the maximal number of propagation steps performed. (1) consists of computing, for every task node n, the set $\overline{\text{eff}(n)}$ of literals that are implied by $\text{eff}(n) \wedge \mathcal{T}$. This can be done as follows. We view $\mathcal{T}$ as a directed graph whose nodes are literals and whose edges correspond to the clauses. The number of nodes of the graph is the number of literals $|P[C]|$, where C is the set of constants mentioned by α. We compute the transitive closure of that graph, in time $O(|P[C]|^3)$. Then, for every effect $\text{eff}(n)$ and for every literal l, we ask whether there is an edge $(\neg l, l)$ in the transitive closure, or whether for any literal $l' \in \text{eff}(n)$ there is an edge (l', l) in the transitive closure. This is done in time $O(|\mathcal{N}| * |P[C]| * max_{\text{eff}})$, where max_{eff} is the maximum number of effect literals any task node has.

As for (2), loop nodes and end nodes take time $O(|P[C]|)$ since sets can be intersected in linear time using, e.g., a bitvector representation. Parallel and XOR joins/splits, accordingly, take time $O(|P[C]| * max_E)$, where max_E is the maximum number of incoming or outgoing edges any node has. Task nodes take time $O(|\mathcal{E}| * |P[C]|)$.

As for (3), define, for any funtion $I : \mathcal{E} \mapsto 2^{P[C]}$, $|I| := \sum_{e \in \mathcal{E}} |I(e)|$. That is, $|I|$ counts the total number of literals annotated by I, at any edge in the process. I-propagation admits a propagation step from I to I' only if $I \neq I'$. Since we always have, for all $e \in \mathcal{E}$, that $I(e) \supseteq I'(e)$, this means that $|I'| \leq |I| - 1$. If $|I'| = 0$, then certainly a fixpoint is reached. Now, obviously $|I_0| \leq |\mathcal{E}| * |P[C]|$. Hence $|\mathcal{E}| * |P[C]|$ is an upper bound on the number of propagation steps performed.

Overall, we get that the runtime is in $O(|P[C]|^3 + |\mathcal{N}| * |P[C]| * max_{\text{eff}} + (|P[C]| * max_E + |\mathcal{E}| * |P[C]|) * |\mathcal{E}| * |P[C]|)$. With fixed arity, $|P[C]|$ is $O(|P| * |C|)$, which concludes the argument.   ∎

A.1.4 I-Propagation Can Be Used for Executability Checking

Lemma 4.22. *Let* $\mathcal{P} = (N, E, \lambda, \Omega, \alpha)$ *be an annotated process graph without effect conflicts, which is basic except that* α *may be defined for edges and loop nodes. Say we run I-propagation on* $\mathcal{P}$, *and* I^* *is an I-propagation result. Then, for all* $e \in \mathcal{E}$, $\bigcap e \supseteq I^*(e)$.

Proof: The only differences of this claim compared to Lemma A.8 is that we do not require $\mathcal{P}$ to be executable, and that conditions may be annotated at XOR splits and loops.

Let $\mathcal{P}_0 = N, E, \lambda, \Omega, \alpha_0)$ be like $\mathcal{P}$ except that $\mathrm{pre}_0(n)$ has been set to $\emptyset$ for all $n \in \mathcal{N}_T$, and that α_0 is undefined on all XOR edges and loop nodes. Obviously, $\mathcal{P}_0$ is executable and basic. Hence we can apply Lemma A.8, and get that $\bigcap^{\mathcal{P}_0} e \supseteq I_0^*(e)$ where I_0^* is an I-propagation result for $\mathcal{P}_0$. Since $\mathcal{P}_0$ differs from $\mathcal{P}$ only in terms of the task node preconditions and the XOR/loop conditions, which are not considered by I-propagation, we have $I_0^* = I^*$ where I^* is an I-propagation result for $\mathcal{P}$, and hence $\bigcap^{\mathcal{P}_0} e \supseteq I^*(e)$. In what follows, we show that $\bigcap^{\mathcal{P}_0} e \subseteq \bigcap^{\mathcal{P}} e$. Obviously, this proves the claim.

Consider the execution paths through $\mathcal{P}$ and $\mathcal{P}_0$. Let us denote the set of these paths with $\vec{P}$ and $\vec{P}_0$, respectively. $\mathcal{P}_0$ does not alter the structure of $\mathcal{P}$ in any way other than removing preconditions and XOR/loop conditions. So the only difference is that some paths are disallowed in $\mathcal{P}$ – but are allowed in $\mathcal{P}_0$ – due to preconditions or conditions that are not satisfied along the path. Hence we have $\vec{P} \subseteq \vec{P}_0$. Consider now a particular edge $e \in \mathcal{E}$, and consider the sets of states

(A) $\{s \mid s \in \mathcal{S}^{\mathcal{P}}, t_s(e) > 0\}$
(B) $\{s \mid s \in \mathcal{S}^{\mathcal{P}_0}, t_s(e) > 0\}$

With what we just said about paths, we have that (B) is a superset of (A). Now, by definition, $\bigcap^{\mathcal{P}} e$ is the set of literals satisfied by all states in (A), and $\bigcap^{\mathcal{P}_0} e$ is the set of literals satisfied by all states in (B). Since (B) is a supserset of (A), this means that $\bigcap^{\mathcal{P}_0} e \subseteq \bigcap^{\mathcal{P}} e$, which is what we needed to show. This concludes the argument.   ∎

Theorem 4.23. *Let $\mathcal{P} = (N, E, \lambda, \Omega, \alpha)$ be a basic annotated process graph without effect conflicts. Say we run I-propagation on $\mathcal{P}$, and I^* is an I-propagation result. Then $\mathcal{P}$ is executable iff for all $n \in \mathcal{N}_T \cup \{n_+^{\mathcal{P}}\}$: $\mathrm{pre}(n) \subseteq I^*(\mathrm{in}(n))$.*

Proof: Recall that a task node $n \in \mathcal{N}_T$ is executable iff, for all reachable states s so that $t_s(\mathrm{in}(n)) > 0$, we have $s \models \mathrm{pre}(n)$. In other words, whenever a path of transitions reaches n with a token, n's precondition is satisfied. $\mathcal{P}$ is executable if all its nodes are executable. Obviously, a node n is executable iff $\mathrm{pre}(n) \subseteq \bigcap \mathrm{in}(n)$.

First, consider the direction from left to right. $\mathcal{P}$ is executable, so we can apply Lemma A.9 and get that $I^*(e) \supseteq \bigcap e$ for all $e \in \mathcal{E}$. Let $n \in \mathcal{N}_T \cup \{n_+^{\mathcal{P}}\}$ be arbitrary. We have $\bigcap \mathrm{in}(n) \subseteq I^*(\mathrm{in}(n))$. Since n is executable, we have $\mathrm{pre}(n) \subseteq \bigcap \mathrm{in}(n)$. Hence $\mathrm{pre}(n) \subseteq I^*(\mathrm{in}(n))$ as desired.

Now, consider the direction from right to left. We can apply Lemma 4.22, and get that $I^*(e) \subseteq \bigcap e$ for all $e \in \mathcal{E}$. Assume to the contrary of the claim that $n \in \mathcal{N}_T \cup \{n_+^{\mathcal{P}}\}$ so that $\mathrm{pre}(n) \subseteq I^*(\mathrm{in}(n))$, but n is not executable, i.e., ex. $l \in \mathrm{pre}(n) \backslash \bigcap \mathrm{in}(n)$. We have that $l \in \mathrm{pre}(n)$ and hence $l \in I^*(\mathrm{in}(n))$. With the above, this implies that $l \in \bigcap e$, in contradiction. Hence all $n \in \mathcal{N}_T \cup \{n_+^{\mathcal{P}}\}$ are executable, which concludes the proof. ∎

Theorem 4.24. *Let $\mathcal{P} = (N, E, \lambda, \Omega, \alpha)$ be an annotated process graph without effect conflicts, which is basic except that α may be defined for edges and loop nodes. Say we run I-propagation on $\mathcal{P}$, and I^* is an I-propagation result. If, for all $n \in \mathcal{N}_T \cup \{n_+^{\mathcal{P}}\} : pre(n) \subseteq I^*(in(n))$, then $\mathcal{P}$ is executable.*

Proof: Recall that a task node $n \in \mathcal{N}_T$ is executable iff, for all reachable states s so that $t_s(in(n)) > 0$, we have $s \models pre(n)$. In other words, whenever a path of transitions reaches n with a token, n's precondition is satisfied. $\mathcal{P}$ is executable if all its nodes are executable. Obviously, a node n is executable iff $pre(n) \subseteq \bigcap in(n)$.

We can apply Lemma 4.22, and get that $I^*(e) \subseteq \bigcap e$ for all $e \in \mathcal{E}$. Assume to the contrary of the claim that $n \in \mathcal{N}_T \cup \{n_+^{\mathcal{P}}\}$ so that $pre(n) \subseteq I^*(in(n))$, but n is not executable, i.e., ex. $l \in pre(n) \setminus \bigcap in(n)$. We have that $l \in pre(n)$ and hence $l \in I^*(in(n))$. With the above, this implies that $l \in \bigcap e$, in contradiction. Hence all $n \in \mathcal{N}_T \cup \{n_+^{\mathcal{P}}\}$ are executable, which concludes the proof. ∎

A.1.5 Complexity Results

Lemma A.10. *Assume a sound atomic annotated process graph $\mathcal{P} = (N, E, \lambda, \Omega, \alpha)$ without effect conflicts, where $N \setminus \{n_0, n_+\} \subseteq \mathcal{N}_T$, eff$(n_0)$ is a complete assignment, all predicates have arity 0, and $\mathcal{P}$ is basic except that T is not binary. Even if $\mathcal{P}$ is known to be reachable, deciding whether $\mathcal{P}$ is executable, or whether some $n \in N$ is executable, is $\mathbf{\Pi_2^P}$-hard for general T, and $\mathbf{coNP}$-hard if T is Horn. Deciding whether $\mathcal{P}$ is reachable, or whether some $n \in N$ is reachable, is $\mathbf{\Sigma_2^P}$-hard for general T, and $\mathbf{NP}$-hard if T is Horn.*

Proof: Let us first consider the general case, with no restrictions on T. The proofs are by reduction of validity of a QBF formula $\forall X. \exists Y. \phi[X, Y]$, where ϕ is in CNF. The process graphs $\mathcal{P}$ in our construction are very similar for reachability and executability; we first consider the common parts, then explain the details below.

We have a node $n_t \in N$ which is connected to the start node n_0 via an edge $(n_0, n_t) \in E$. We set $pre(n_t) = \emptyset$. The main trick of the proof lies in the definitions of Ω, eff(n_0), and eff(n_t). Those are adapted from the constructions used in the proof of Lemma 6.2 from [83]. The predicates P of Ω are all 0-ary, i.e., they have no arguments and are hence logical propositions. Precisely, we have the predicates $X = \{x_1, \ldots, x_m\}$ and $Y = \{y_1, \ldots, y_n\}$ from the formula $\forall X. \exists Y. \phi[X, Y]$, as well as new predicates $\{z_1, \ldots, z_m, q, t\}$. We define eff$(n_0)$ to contain all x_i, all y_i, all z_i, q, and $\neg t$. So all facts except t are made true by the start state s_0; note that the start state is complete. We define eff(n_t)

to be $\{t\}$. The complex part of the construction lies in the theory T of Ω. We define $T :=$

$$(\bigwedge_{i=1}^{m}(\neg t \vee x_i \vee z_i)) \wedge (\bigwedge_{i=1}^{m}(\neg t \vee \neg x_i \vee \neg z_i)) \wedge (\bigwedge_{C \in \phi}(\neg t \vee \neg q \vee C)) \wedge (\bigwedge_{i=1}^{n}(\neg t \vee \neg y_i \vee q))$$

where ϕ is viewed as a set of clauses C. More readably, the theory is equivalent to:

$$t \Rightarrow [(\bigwedge_{i=1}^{m} x_i \equiv \neg z_i) \wedge (q \Rightarrow \phi) \wedge ((\bigvee_{i=1}^{n} y_i) \Rightarrow q)]$$

Note that $\mathrm{eff}(n_t)$ is consistent with the theory: any interpretation that sets r and all y_i to 0 satisfies $T \wedge \mathrm{eff}(n_t)$. Hence n_t complies with Definition 4.5.

We now prove that *(*) $\forall X.\exists Y.\phi[X, Y]$ is valid iff q is true in any state s that results from executing n_t.* From this, the desired hardness results will be easy to obtain. We denote with S the set of states s that may be reached by executing n_t.

The theory conjuncts $x_i \equiv \neg z_i$ make sure that each $s \in S$ makes exactly one of x_i, z_i true. In particular, the different assignments to X are incomparable with respect to set inclusion. Hence, we have that for every assignment a_X of truth values to X, there exists a state $s \in S$ that complies with a_X: a_X is satisfiable together with $T \wedge \mathrm{eff}(n_t)$, and any other assignment a'_X is more distant from s_0 in at least one proposition (e.g., if $a'_X(x_i) = 1$ and $a_X(x_i) = 0$ then a_X is closer to s_0 than a'_X regarding the interpretation of z_i).

We first prove that, if q is true in any state s that results from executing n_t, then $\forall X.\exists Y.\phi[X, Y]$ is valid. Let a_X be a truth value assignment to X. With the above, we have a state $s \in S$ that complies with a_X. By assumption, s makes q true. Therefore, due to the theory conjunct $q \Rightarrow \phi$, we have $i_s \models \phi$. Obviously, the values assigned to Y by i_s satisfy ϕ for a_X.

For the other direction, say $\forall X.\exists Y.\phi[X, Y]$ is valid. Assume that, to the contrary of the claim, there exists a $s \in S$ so that $i_s \not\models q$. But then, due to the theory conjunct $(\bigvee_{i=1}^{n} y_i) \Rightarrow q$, we have that s sets all y_i to false. Now, because $\forall X.\exists Y.\phi[X, Y]$ is valid, there exists a truth value assignment a_Y to Y that complies with the setting of all x_i and z_i in s. Obtain s' by modifying s to comply with a_Y, and setting q to 1. We have that $i_{s'} \models T \wedge \mathrm{eff}(n_t)$. But then, s' is closer to s_0 than s, and hence $s \notin S$ in contradiction. This concludes the argument for (*).

To prove $\mathbf{\Pi_2^P}$-hardness of deciding executability, we now simply connect n_t via an edge (n_t, n_+) to the stop node, and set $\mathrm{pre}(n_+) = \{q\}$. By (*), n_+ is executable iff $\forall X.\exists Y.\phi[X, Y]$ is valid; since the other nodes have no preconditions and are trivially executable, and since all nodes are trivially reachable, the claim follows.

To prove $\mathbf{\Sigma_2^P}$-hardness of deciding reachability, an only slightly more complex construction is required. We introduce another node $n_{\neg q} \in N$, and connect $(n_t, n_{\neg q})$ as well as $(n_{\neg q}, n_+)$. We set $\mathrm{pre}(n_{\neg q}) = \{\neg q\}$, and $\mathrm{eff}(n_{\neg q}) = \mathrm{pre}(n_+) = \emptyset$. Then, by (*), n_+ is reachable iff $\forall X.\exists Y.\phi[X, Y]$ is *not* valid; the other nodes are trivially reachable; this concludes the argument.

Let's consider now the case where $\mathcal{T}$ is restricted to be Horn. The graphs (N, E) that we use for reachability/executability remain exactly the same. What changes is the semantic annotation. The latter is obtained by the following adaptation of the proof of Lemma 7.1 from [83]. The proof works by a reduction of satisfiability of a CNF formula $\phi[X]$. We use the 0-ary predicates $X = \{x_1, \ldots, x_m\}$, and new 0-ary predicates $Y = \{y_1, \ldots, y_n, z_1, \ldots, z_n, q, t\}$. As before, $\text{pre}(n_t) = \emptyset$ and $\text{eff}(n_t) = \{t\}$. We define $\text{eff}(n_0)$ to contain all x_i, all y_i, all $\neg z_i$, $\neg q$, and $\neg t$; note that this is a complete assignment. The theory is:

$$(\neg t \vee (\textstyle\bigvee_{i=1}^{n} \neg z_i) \vee q) \wedge$$
$$(\textstyle\bigwedge_{i=1}^{n}((\neg t \vee \neg x_i \vee \neg y_i) \wedge (\neg t \vee \neg x_i \vee z_i) \wedge (\neg t \vee \neg y_i \vee z_i))) \wedge$$
$$(\textstyle\bigwedge_{C \in \phi}(\neg t \vee C[-Y/ + X]))$$

where ϕ is viewed as a set of clauses C, and $C[-Y/ + X]$ for a clause C denotes the modification of C where every occurrence of a positive literal x_i is replaced with $\neg y_i$. More readably, the theory is equivalent to:

$$t \Rightarrow [((\bigwedge_{i=1}^{n} z_i) \Rightarrow q) \wedge (\bigwedge_{i=1}^{n}((\neg x_i \vee \neg y_i) \wedge (x_i \Rightarrow z_i) \wedge (y_i \Rightarrow z_i))) \wedge (\bigwedge_{C \in \phi} C[-Y/+X])]$$

Obviously, this theory is in Horn format: every clause contains at most one positive literal. Note that $\text{eff}(n_t)$ is consistent with the theory: e.g., the interpretation that sets all propositions except t to 0 satisfies $\mathcal{T} \wedge \text{eff}(n_t)$. Hence n_t complies with Definition 4.5.

The key in this transformation is that ϕ is made Horn by replacing positive occurrences of x_i with $\neg y_i$. If the truth value of y_i is different from the value of x_i, for each i, then $C[-Y/ + X]$ is satisfied by this assignment iff C is satisfied. The role of z_i is to indicate whether x_i and y_i are indeed different. The role of q is to indicate whether the latter is the case for all i.

We now prove that $(**)$ $\phi[X]$ is unsatisfiable iff $\neg q$ is true in any state s that results from executing n_t. From this, the desired hardness results will be easy to obtain. We denote with S the set of states s that may be reached by executing n_t.

We first prove that, if there exists $s \in S$ so that $i_s \models \neg q$, then ϕ is satisfiable. Let L_0 be the set of literals on whose interpretation s agrees with s_0. We can conclude that $\mathcal{T} \wedge \text{eff}(n_t) \wedge \bigwedge_{l \in L_0} l \wedge \neg q$ is unsatisfiable, since otherwise we can construct a state s' that has $s' \models L_0 \wedge \neg q$ and that is hence closer to s_0 than s. The only part of $\mathcal{T} \wedge \text{eff}(n_t)$ that forces implication of q is $(\bigwedge_{i=1}^{n} z_i) \Rightarrow q$. Thus we infer that $\mathcal{T} \wedge \text{eff}(n_t) \wedge \bigwedge_{l \in L_0} l \models \bigwedge_{i=1}^{n} z_i$. The only part of $\mathcal{T} \wedge \text{eff}(n_t)$ that forces implication of z_i is if either x_i or y_i are true. Hence, for all i, either x_i or y_i are implied by $\mathcal{T} \wedge \text{eff}(n_t) \wedge \bigwedge_{l \in L_0} l$. Hence, in particular s satisfies, for all i, either $i_s \models x_i$ or $i_s \models y_i$. Hence the value of x_i and y_i is different for all i, and hence, with the above, the assignment that s makes to X satisfies ϕ.

For the other direction, assume that ϕ is satisfiable, by the truth value assignment a_X. We construct a state s so that $s \models q$ and $s \in S$. First, we set that for all x_i, $i_s \models x_i$ iff $a_X(x_i) = 1$. Then, we set that for all y_i, $i_s \models y_i$ iff

$a_X(x_i) = 0$. We set that for all z_i, $i_s \models z_i$. Finally, we set $i_s \models q$ and $i_s \models t$. It is easily verified that $i_s \models \mathcal{T} \wedge \text{eff}(n_t)$: ϕ is satisfied because the values of x_i and y_i are different, for each i. Further, s is maximally close to s_0. This can be seen as follows. First, we cannot change any of the values of a z_i or of q, because those are implied by the distinct values of each x_i and y_i. Second, we cannot set any x_i or y_i to true in isolation, because that would be in conflict with the respective other value. So any change we make to the setting of x_i and y_i would involve switching one x_i or y_i to false, and hence being further away from s_0 in that proposition. This concludes the argument for (**).

To prove $\mathbf{\Pi_2^P}$-hardness of deciding executability, as before connect n_t via an edge (n_t, n_+) to the stop node. We set $\text{pre}(n_+) = \{\neg q\}$. By (**), n_+ is executable iff $\phi[X]$ is unsatisfiable; since the other nodes have no preconditions and are trivially executable, and since all nodes are trivially reachable, the claim follows.

To prove $\mathbf{\Sigma_2^P}$-hardness of deciding reachability, we introduce another node $n_q \in N$, and connect (n_t, n_q) as well as (n_q, n_+). We set $\text{pre}(n_q) = \{q\}$, and $\text{eff}(n_q) = \text{pre}(n_+) = \emptyset$. Then, by (*), n_+ is reachable iff $\phi[X]$ is satisfiable; the other nodes are trivially reachable; this concludes the argument.   ■

Lemma A.11. *Assume a sound atomic annotated process graph* $\mathcal{P} = (N, E, \lambda, \Omega, \alpha)$ *without effect conflicts, where* $N \setminus \{n_0, n_+\} \subseteq N_T \cup N_{XS} \cup N_{XJ}$, *eff*$(n_0)$ *is a complete assignment, all predicates have arity 0, and* $\mathcal{P}$ *is basic except that con*(e) *may be defined for some* $e \in E$. *Even if* $\mathcal{P}$ *is known to be reachable, deciding whether* $\mathcal{P}$ *is executable, or whether some* $n \in N$ *is executable, is* **coNP***-hard. Even if* $\mathcal{P}$ *is known to be executable, deciding whether* $\mathcal{P}$ *is reachable, or whether some* $n \in N$ *is reachable.*

Proof: The proof for reachability checking is by the following reduction from 3SAT. Assume a CNF ϕ with n propositions $p_1, \ldots, p_n$, and k clauses $c_1, \ldots, c_k$ where $c_i = l_{i1} \vee l_{i2} \vee l_{i3}$. We obtain an atomic basic annotated process graph with some annotated edges, $(N, E, \lambda, \Omega, \alpha)$, as follows. The ontology contains only 0-ary predicates, namely $P := \{p_1, notp_1, \ldots, p_n, notp_n\}$; we identify literal $\neg p_i$ with proposition $notp_i$. The construction is illustrated in Figure A.1.

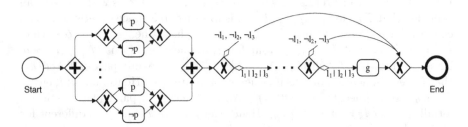

Fig. A.1. Schematic illustration of 3SAT reduction for Lemma A.11, reachability checking

The set of nodes N and their annotation (of which we show only the non-empty ones) is:

1. start node n_0; $\text{eff}(n_0) = \emptyset$
2. parallel split node nps
3. XOR-split nodes $nxs_1 \ldots nxs_n$
4. for $1 \leq i \leq n$: task nodes np_i and $nnotp_i$; $\text{eff}(np_i) = \{p_i\}$, $\text{eff}(np_i) = \{notp_i\}$
5. XOR-join nodes $nxj_1 \ldots nxj_n$
6. parallel join node npj
7. for $1 \leq i \leq k$: XOR-split node nxs_i'
8. for $1 \leq i \leq k-1$: XOR-join node nxj_i'
9. task node ng
10. XOR-join node nxj'
11. stop node n_+

The set of edges E and their annotation is given below. Again, empty annotation is not shown; also, the position of the annotated edges does not matter and is hence not specified.

1. (n_0, nps)
2. for $1 \leq i \leq n$: (nps, nxs_i)
3. for $1 \leq i \leq n$: (nxs_i, np_i) and $(nxs_i, nnotp_i)$
4. for $1 \leq i \leq n$: (np_i, nxj_i) and $(nnotp_i, nxj_i)$
5. for $1 \leq i \leq n$: (nxj_i, npj)
6. (npj, nxs_1)
7. for $1 \leq i \leq k$: (nxs_i', nxj'); $\text{con}((nxs_i', nxj')) = \{\neg l_{i1}, \neg l_{i2}, \neg l_{i3}\}$
8. for $1 \leq i \leq k-1$: for $1 \leq j \leq 3$: (nxs_i', nxj_i'); $\text{con}((nxs_i', nxj_i')) = \{l_{ij}\}$
9. for $1 \leq i \leq k-1$: (nxj_i', nxs_{i+1}')
10. for $1 \leq j \leq 3$: (nxs_k', ng); $\text{con}((nxs_k', ng)) = \{l_{kj}\}$
11. (ng, nxj')
12. (nxj', n_+)

Since all preconditions are empty, it is obvious that $\mathcal{P}$ is executable. By construction, $\mathcal{P}$ is reachable iff ng is reachable. The latter is the case iff ϕ is satisfiable. The annotation of the start node can be set to be $\text{eff}(n_0) = \{\neg p_1, \neg notp_1, \ldots, \neg p_n, \neg notp_n\}$, and hence to be complete. The parallel split/join can be replaced by a simple sequencing of all the XORs setting proposition values.

For executability checking, we can use a similar reduction. Given a CNF ϕ, let p be a new proposition; obtain ϕ' by inserting p into every clause of ϕ. Then construct, for ϕ', the process graph as above, with the only difference being that ng has the annotation $\text{pre}(ng) = \{p\}$. With this construction, we have that (1) ng is reachable (trivially, by making p true and choosing the p-branch for every clause); (2) with that, clearly all nodes are reachable; and (3) ng is executable iff every satisfying assignment to ϕ' makes p true. The latter is, obviously, the case iff ϕ is unsatisfiable. Since ng is the only node with a precondition, all other nodes are trivially executable and hence the claim follows.   ∎

Lemma A.12. *Assume a sound annotated process graph $\mathcal{P} = (N, E, \lambda, \Omega, \alpha)$ without effect conflicts, where $N \setminus \{n_0, n_+\} \subseteq N_T \cup N_{XS} \cup N_{XJ}$, for all $n \in N_L$ we have $N^{\lambda(n)} = \{n_0^{\lambda(n)}, n_+^{\lambda(n)}\}$, eff($n_0$) is a complete assignment, all predicates have arity 0, and $\mathcal{P}$ is basic except that con(n) may be defined for some $n \in N_L$. Even if $\mathcal{P}$ is known to be reachable, deciding whether $\mathcal{P}$ is executable, or whether some $n \in N$ is executable, is coNP-hard. Even if $\mathcal{P}$ is known to be executable, deciding whether $\mathcal{P}$ is reachable, or whether some $n \in N$ is reachable.*

Proof: This can be proved via a 3SAT reduction very similar to that used for proving Lemma A.11. We simply replace each edge condition with a loop node n where $\lambda(n)$ points to an empty subprocess – consisting only of start and end node. The idea is to only allow exiting the loop if the edge condition holds true. The only tricky bit here lies in the interpretation of edge conditions and repetition conditions. An edge condition con(e) means that the edge can be taken when con(e) is true. A repetition condition con(n) means that the loop is repeated if con(n) is true. Our construction necessitates us to say the opposite, i.e., we want to state a condition under which the loop may be exited. The solution is, of course, to use $\neg$con(e) as the repetition condition. If con(e) contains several literals, then $\neg$con(e) is a disjunction, which is not supported by repetition conditions. However, we can obtain the desired effect by creating, in this case, one loop node for every literal in con(e).

In detail, the reduction works as follows. We assume a CNF ϕ with n propositions $p_1, \ldots, p_n$, and k clauses $c_1, \ldots, c_k$ where $c_i = l_{i1} \vee l_{i2} \vee l_{i3}$. The construction follows the same scheme as depicted in Figure A.1, and the reader is advised to consider this figure when reading the following. The set of nodes N and their annotation (of which we show only the non-empty ones) is:

1. start node n_0; eff(n_0) = $\emptyset$
2. parallel split node nps
3. XOR-split nodes $nxs_1 \ldots nxs_n$
4. for $1 \leq i \leq n$: task nodes np_i and $nnotp_i$; eff(np_i) = $\{p_i\}$, eff(np_i) = $\{notp_i\}$
5. XOR-join nodes $nxj_1 \ldots nxj_n$
6. parallel join node npj
7. for $1 \leq i \leq k$: XOR-split node nxs_i'
8. for $1 \leq i \leq k$: loop node nl_i with con(nl_i) = $\{\neg l_{i1}, \neg l_{i2}, \neg l_{i3}\}$; for $1 \leq j \leq 3$: loop node nl_i^j with con(nl_i^j) = $\{l_{ij}\}$
9. for $1 \leq i \leq k - 1$: XOR-join node nxj_i'
10. task node ng
11. XOR-join node nxj'
12. stop node n_+

As stated, λ points to an empty subprocess for every loop node. The set of edges E is:

1. (n_0, nps)
2. for $1 \le i \le n$: (nps, nxs_i)
3. for $1 \le i \le n$: (nxs_i, np_i) and $(nxs_i, nnotp_i)$
4. for $1 \le i \le n$: (np_i, nxj_i) and $(nnotp_i, nxj_i)$
5. for $1 \le i \le n$: (nxj_i, npj)
6. (npj, nxs_1)
7. for $1 \le i \le k - 1$: (nxs_i', nl_i) and (nl_i, nxj_i')
8. for $1 \le i \le k$: (nxj_i', nl_i^1), (nl_i^1, nl_i^2), (nl_i^2, nl_i^3), (nl_i^3, nxj')
9. for $1 \le i \le k - 1$: (nxj_i', nxs_{i+1}')
10. (nxs_k', nl_k) and (nl_k, ng)
11. (ng, nxj')
12. (nxj', n_+)

Since all preconditions are empty, it is obvious that $\mathcal{P}$ is executable. By construction, $\mathcal{P}$ is reachable iff ng is reachable. The repetition conditions at nodes nl_i ensure that one can exit the loop iff clause i is satisfied. The repetition conditions at the sequenced nodes nl_i^1, nl_i^2, nl_i^3 ensure that one can traverse the entire sequence iff clause i is violated. Hence ng is reachable iff ϕ is satisfiable. The annotation of the start node can be set to be $\text{eff}(n_0) = \{\neg p_1,$ $\neg notp_1, \ldots, \neg p_n, \neg notp_n\}$, and hence to be complete. The parallel split/join can be replaced by a simple sequencing of all the XORs setting proposition values.

For executability checking, we can use a similar reduction. Given a CNF ϕ, let p be a new proposition; obtain ϕ' by inserting p into every clause of ϕ. Then construct, for ϕ', the process graph as above, with the only difference being that ng has the annotation $\text{pre}(ng) = \{p\}$. With this construction, we have that (1) ng is reachable (trivially, by making p true and choosing the p-branch for every clause); (2) with that, clearly all nodes are reachable; and (3) ng is executable iff every satisfying assignment to ϕ' makes p true. The latter is, obviously, the case iff ϕ is unsatisfiable. Since ng is the only node with a precondition, all other nodes are trivially executable and hence the claim follows.   ∎

Lemma A.13. *Assume a basic sound atomic annotated process graph $\mathcal{P} = (N, E, \lambda, \Omega, \alpha)$ without effect conflicts, where $N \setminus \{n_0, n_+\} \subseteq N_T \cup N_{XS} \cup N_{XJ}$, $\text{eff}(n_0)$ is a complete assignment, and all predicates have arity 0. Even if $\mathcal{P}$ is known to be reachable, deciding whether $n \in N$ is executable is coNP-hard. Deciding whether $\mathcal{P}$ is reachable, or whether $n \in N$ is reachable, is NP-hard.*

Proof: This can be proved via a 3SAT reduction very similar to that used for proving Lemma A.11. The difference to that lemma is that $\mathcal{P}$ is basic, so we cannot make use of edge conditions or of repetition conditions. The main property underlying the situations considered is that non-executable task nodes are allowed. We can simply use those just like edge conditions, to filter the set of execution paths that may traverse a certain branch of the process. Note here that, for executability, we consider only the decision problem asking whether *a particular node* (rather than the entire process) is executable. For reachability, it is noteable that we can not restrict consideration to executable processes – if the process is executable then it is also reachable, c.f. Proposition 4.11.

In detail, the reduction works as follows. We assume a CNF ϕ with n propositions $p_1, \ldots, p_n$, and k clauses $c_1, \ldots, c_k$ where $c_i = l_{i1} \vee l_{i2} \vee l_{i3}$. The construction follows the same scheme as depicted in Figure A.1, and the reader is advised to consider this figure when reading the following.

The set of nodes N and their annotation (of which we show only the non-empty ones) is:

1. start node n_0; eff$(n_0) = \emptyset$
2. parallel split node nps
3. XOR-split nodes $nxs_1 \ldots nxs_n$
4. for $1 \leq i \leq n$: task nodes np_i and $nnotp_i$; eff$(np_i) = \{p_i\}$, eff$(np_i) = \{notp_i\}$
5. XOR-join nodes $nxj_1 \ldots nxj_n$
6. parallel join node npj
7. for $1 \leq i \leq k$: XOR-split node nxs'_i
8. for $1 \leq i \leq k$: for $1 \leq j \leq 3$: task node $nxst_{ij}$; pre$(nxst_{ij}) = \{l_{ij}\}$
9. for $1 \leq i \leq k$: task node $nxst'_i$; pre$(nxst'_i) = \{\neg l_{i1}, \neg l_{i2}, \neg l_{i3}\}$
10. for $1 \leq i \leq k - 1$: XOR-join node nxj'_i
11. task node ng
12. XOR-join node nxj'
13. stop node n_+

The set of edges E and their annotation is:

1. (n_0, nps)
2. for $1 \leq i \leq n$: (nps, nxs_i)
3. for $1 \leq i \leq n$: (nxs_i, np_i) and $(nxs_i, nnotp_i)$
4. for $1 \leq i \leq n$: (np_i, nxj_i) and $(nnotp_i, nxj_i)$
5. for $1 \leq i \leq n$: (nxj_i, npj)
6. (npj, nxs_1)
7. for $1 \leq i \leq k$: $(nxs'_i, nxst'_i)$ and $(nxst'_i, nxj')$
8. for $1 \leq i \leq k - 1$: for $1 \leq j \leq 3$: $(nxs'_i, nxst_{ij})$ and $(nxst_{ij}, nxj'_i)$
9. for $1 \leq i \leq k - 1$: (nxj'_i, nxs'_{i+1})
10. for $1 \leq j \leq 3$: $(nxs'_k, nxst_{kj})$ and $(nxst_{kj}, ng)$
11. (ng, nxj')
12. (nxj', n_+)

Obviously, $\mathcal{P}$ is reachable iff ng is reachable iff ϕ is satisfiable. The annotation of the start node can be set to be eff$(n_0) = \{\neg p_1, \neg notp_1, \ldots, \neg p_n, \neg notp_n\}$, and hence to be complete. The parallel split/join can be replaced by a simple sequencing of all the XORs setting proposition values.

For executability checking, we use a similar reduction. Given a CNF ϕ, let p be a new proposition; obtain ϕ' by inserting p into every clause of ϕ. Then construct, for ϕ', the process graph as above, with the only difference being that ng has the annotation $pre(ng) = \{p\}$. With this construction, ng is executable iff every satisfying assignment to ϕ' makes p true. The latter is, obviously, the case iff ϕ is unsatisfiable. Since all nodes are reachable (ng can be reached by setting p to be true), this proves the claim.　■

Theorem 4.18. *Assume a sound annotated process graph* $\mathcal{P} = (N, E, \lambda, \Omega, \alpha)$ *without effect conflicts, where* $N \setminus \{n_0, n_+\} \subseteq N_T \cup N_{XS} \cup N_{XJ} \cup N_L$, $\mathit{eff}(n_0)$ *is a complete assignment, all predicates have arity 0, and either* $\mathcal{P}$ *is atomic or for all* $n \in N_L$ *we have* $N^{\lambda(n)} = \{n_0^{\lambda(n)}, n_+^{\lambda(n)}\}$. *The following problem is* Π_2^p*-hard even if* $\mathcal{P}$ *is known to be reachable:*

- *Is* $\mathcal{P}$ *executable, or is* $n \in N$ *executable, given that* $\mathcal{P}$ *is basic except that* $\mathcal{T}$ *may involve arbitrary clauses?*

The following problems are **coNP**-*hard even if* $\mathcal{P}$ *is known to be reachable:*

- *Is* $\mathcal{P}$ *executable, or is* $n \in N$ *executable, given that* $\mathcal{P}$ *is basic except that* $\mathcal{T}$ *may involve arbitrary Horn clauses?*
- *Is* $\mathcal{P}$ *executable, or is* $n \in N$ *executable, given that* $\mathcal{P}$ *is basic except that* $con(e)$ *may be defined for some* $e \in E$?
- *Is* $\mathcal{P}$ *executable, or is* $n \in N$ *executable, given that* $\mathcal{P}$ *is basic except that* $con(n)$ *may be defined for some* $n \in N_L$?
- *Is* $n \in N$ *executable, given that* $\mathcal{P}$ *is basic?*

Proof: Follows directly from Lemmas A.10, A.11, A.12, and A.13.　■

Theorem 4.19. *Assume a sound annotated process graph* $\mathcal{P} = (N, E, \lambda, \Omega, \alpha)$ *without effect conflicts, where* $N \setminus \{n_0, n_+\} \subseteq N_T \cup N_{XS} \cup N_{XJ} \cup N_L$, $\mathit{eff}(n_0)$ *is a complete assignment, all predicates have arity 0, and either* $\mathcal{P}$ *is atomic or for all* $n \in N_L$ *we have* $N^{\lambda(n)} = \{n_0^{\lambda(n)}, n_+^{\lambda(n)}\}$. *The following problem is* Σ_2^p*-hard:*

- *Is* $\mathcal{P}$ *reachable, or is* $n \in N$ *reachable, given that* $\mathcal{P}$ *is basic except that* $\mathcal{T}$ *may involve arbitrary clauses?*

The following problems are **NP**-*hard:*

- *Is* $\mathcal{P}$ *reachable, or is* $n \in N$ *reachable, given that* $\mathcal{P}$ *is basic except that* $\mathcal{T}$ *may involve arbitrary Horn clauses?*
- *Is* $\mathcal{P}$ *reachable, or is* $n \in N$ *reachable, given that* $\mathcal{P}$ *is executable, and basic except that* $con(e)$ *may be defined for some* $e \in E$?
- *Is* $\mathcal{P}$ *reachable, or is* $n \in N$ *reachable, given that* $\mathcal{P}$ *is executable, and basic except that* $con(n)$ *may be defined for some* $n \in N_L$?
- *Is* $\mathcal{P}$ *reachable, or is* $n \in N$ *reachable, given that* $\mathcal{P}$ *is basic?*

Proof: Follows directly from Lemmas A.10, A.11, A.12, and A.13.　■

A.2 Proofs for Task Composition

Theorem 5.2. *Assume a* $\mathcal{WSC}$ *task* $(\Omega, \mathcal{O}, \mathcal{U})$ *with fixed arity. Assume a model* m, *a service* a, *and a literal* l *such that* $m \models l$. *It is* Π_2^p-*complete to decide whether* $l \in Lits(res(m, a))$. *If* $\mathcal{T}$ *is Horn, then the same decision is* **coNP**-*complete.*

Proof: We first consider the general case, where $\mathcal{T}$ is arbitrary. Membership follows by a guess-and-check argument. First, observe that transformation into fully grounded (propositional) format is polynomial time with fixed arity. Second, observe that testing, for any m', whether $m' \in res(m, a)$ is in **coNP**: one can guess any m'' and test in polynomial time whether it satisfies $\mathcal{T} \wedge \text{eff}_a$ and whether it is closer to m than m'; $m' \in res(m, a)$ holds iff no m'' succeeds. Now, to decide whether $l \in Lits(res(m, a))$, guess a state m'. Test in constant time whether $m' \not\models l$. If yes, test with an **NP** oracle whether $m' \in res(m, a)$. We have $l \in Lits(res(m, a))$ if and only if no guess succeeds.

Hardness follows by the following adaptation of the proof of Lemma 6.2 from [83]. The proof works by a reduction of validity of a QBF formula $\forall X.\exists Y.\phi[X, Y]$, where ϕ is in CNF. We use the 0-ary predicates $X = \{x_1, \ldots, x_m\}$, $Y = \{y_1, \ldots, y_n\}$, and new 0-ary predicates $\{z_1, \ldots, z_m, q, t\}$. The set of Web services contains the single Web service w with empty in/out parameters, empty precondition, and effect t. The initial constants $C_{\mathcal{U}}$ are empty; $\text{pre}_{\mathcal{U}}$ is the conjunction of all x_i, all y_i, all z_i, q, and $\neg t$; $\text{eff}_{\mathcal{U}}$ does not matter for our purposes. The theory is:

$$(\bigwedge_{i=1}^{m}(\neg t \vee x_i \vee z_i)) \wedge (\bigwedge_{i=1}^{m}(\neg t \vee \neg x_i \vee \neg z_i)) \wedge$$

$$(\bigwedge_{C \in \phi}(\neg t \vee \neg q \vee C)) \wedge (\bigwedge_{i=1}^{n}(\neg t \vee \neg y_i \vee q))$$

where ϕ is viewed as a set of clauses C. More readably, the theory is equivalent to:

$$t \Rightarrow [(\bigwedge_{i=1}^{m} x_i \equiv \neg z_i) \wedge (q \Rightarrow \phi) \wedge ((\bigvee_{i=1}^{n} y_i) \Rightarrow q)]$$

Obviously, the initial belief b_0 contains a single model, where everything except t is true; we take this to be our model m. We take the single service based on (equal to, in fact) w to be our service a. Note that a is consistent with the theory: any interpretation that sets r and all y_i to 0 satisfies $\mathcal{T} \wedge \text{eff}_a$. We denote $b' := res(m, a)$. We set $l := q$, posing the problem of testing whether $q \in Lits(b')$.

The theory conjuncts $x_i \equiv \neg z_i$ make sure that each $m' \in b'$ makes exactly one of x_i, z_i true. In particular, the different assignments to X are incomparable with respect to set inclusion. Hence, we have that for every assignment a_X of truth values to X, there exists a model $m' \in b'$ that complies with a_X:

a_X is satisfiable together with $\mathcal{T} \wedge \text{eff}_a$, and any other assignment a'_X is more distant from m in at least one variable (e.g., if $a'_X(x_i) = 1$ and $a_X(x_i) = 0$ then a_X is closer to m than a'_X regarding the interpretation of z_i).

We now prove that, if $q \in Lits(b')$, then $\forall X.\exists Y.\phi[X, Y]$ is valid. Let a_X be a truth value assignment to X. With the above, we have a model $m' \in b'$ that complies with a_X. Since $q \in Lits(b')$, we have $m' \models q$. Therefore, due to the theory conjunct $q \Rightarrow \phi$, we have $m' \models \phi$. Obviously, the values assigned to Y by m' satisfy ϕ for a_X.

For the other direction, say $\forall X.\exists Y.\phi[X, Y]$ is valid. Assume that, to the contrary of the claim, $q \notin Lits(b')$. Then we have $m' \in b'$ so that $m' \not\models q$. But then, due to the theory conjunct $(\bigvee_{i=1}^n y_i) \Rightarrow q$, we have that m sets all y_i to false. Now, because $\forall X.\exists Y.\phi[X, Y]$ is valid, there exists a truth value assignment a_Y to Y that complies with the setting of all x_i and z_i in m'. Obtain m'' by modifying m' to comply with a_Y, and setting q to 1. We have that $m'' \models \mathcal{T} \wedge \text{eff}_a$. But then, m'' is closer to m than m', and hence $m' \notin b'$ in contradiction. This concludes the argument.

We now consider the case where $\mathcal{T}$ is Horn. Membership follows by a guess-and-check argument. First, observe that transformation into fully grounded (propositional) format is polynomial time with fixed arity. Guess a state m'. Test in polynomial time whether $m' \not\models l$, and whether $m \models \mathcal{T} \wedge \text{eff}_a$. If yes, test whether m' is a minimal change of m. Then, $l \in Lits(res(m, a))$ holds iff no guess succeeds. Testing whether m' is a minimal change of m can be done as follows. Let L_0 be the set of literals on whose interpretation m' agrees with m. Test, for all other literals l' with $m' \models l'$, whether $\mathcal{T} \wedge \text{eff}_a \wedge \bigwedge_{l_0 \in L_0} l_0 \wedge \overline{l'}$ is satisfiable. Each such test can be done in polynomial time because $\mathcal{T}$ is Horn. Clearly, m' is a minimal change of m iff no test succeeds. This concludes the argument.

Hardness follows by the following adaptation of the proof of Lemma 7.1 from [83]. The proof works by a reduction of satisfiability of a CNF formula $\phi[X]$. We use the 0-ary predicates $X = \{x_1, \ldots, x_m\}$, and new 0-ary predicates $Y = \{y_1, \ldots, y_n, z_1, \ldots, z_n, q, t\}$. The set of Web services contains the single Web service w with empty in/out parameters, empty precondition, and effect t. The initial constants $C_\mathcal{U}$ are empty; $\text{pre}_\mathcal{U}$ is the conjunction of all x_i, all y_i, all $\neg z_i$, $\neg q$, and $\neg t$; $\text{eff}_\mathcal{U}$ does not matter for our purposes. The theory is:

$$(\neg t \vee (\bigvee_{i=1}^n \neg z_i) \vee q) \wedge$$
$$(\bigwedge_{i=1}^n ((\neg t \vee \neg x_i \vee \neg y_i) \wedge (\neg t \vee \neg x_i \vee z_i) \wedge (\neg t \vee \neg y_i \vee z_i))) \wedge$$
$$(\bigwedge_{C \in \phi} (\neg t \vee C[-Y/ + X]))$$

where ϕ is viewed as a set of clauses C, and $C[-Y/ + X]$ for a clause C denotes the modification of C where every occurrence of a positive literal x_i is replaced with $\neg y_i$. More readably, the theory is equivalent to:

$$t \Rightarrow [((\bigwedge_{i=1}^n z_i) \Rightarrow q) \wedge$$

$$(\bigwedge_{i=1}^{n} ((\neg x_i \vee \neg y_i) \wedge (x_i \Rightarrow z_i) \wedge (y_i \Rightarrow z_i))) \wedge$$

$$(\bigwedge_{C \in \phi} C[-Y/ + X])]$$

Obviously, this theory is in Horn format: every clause contains at most one positive literal. Likewise obviously, the initial belief b_0 contains a single model where all x_i and y_i are true, while all z_i, q, and t are false; we take this to be our model m. We take the single service based on (equal to, in fact) w to be our service a. Note that a is consistent with the theory: e.g., the interpretation that sets all variables except t to 0 satisfies $\mathcal{T} \wedge \text{eff}_a$. We denote $b' := res(m, a)$. We set $l := \neg q$, posing the problem of testing whether testing whether $\neg q \in Lits(b')$.

The key in this transformation is that ϕ is made Horn by replacing positive occurrences of x_i with $\neg y_i$. If the truth value of y_i is different from the value of x_i, for each i, then $C[-Y/ + X]$ is satisfied by this assignment iff C is satisfied. The role of z_i is to indicate whether x_i and y_i are indeed different. The role of q is to indicate whether the latter is the case for all i.

We now prove that, if $\neg q \notin Lits(b')$, then ϕ is satisfiable. Say $m' \in b'$ so that $m' \models q$. Let L_0 be the set of literals on whose interpretation m' agrees with m. We can conclude that $\mathcal{T} \wedge \text{eff}_a \wedge \bigwedge_{l \in L_0} l \wedge \neg q$ is unsatisfiable, since otherwise we can construct a model m'' that has $m'' \models L_0 \wedge \neg q$ and that is hence closer to m than m'. The only part of $\mathcal{T} \wedge \text{eff}_a$ that forces implication of q is $(\bigwedge_{i=1}^{n} z_i) \Rightarrow q$. Thus we infer that $\mathcal{T} \wedge \text{eff}_a \wedge \bigwedge_{l \in L_0} l \models \bigwedge_{i=1}^{n} z_i$. The only part of $\mathcal{T} \wedge \text{eff}_a$ that forces implication of z_i is if either x_i or y_i are true. Hence, for all i, either x_i or y_i are implied by $\mathcal{T} \wedge \text{eff}_a \wedge \bigwedge_{l \in L_0} l$. Hence, in particular m' satisfies, for all i, either $m' \models x_i$ or $m' \models y_i$. Hence the value of x_i and y_i is different for all i, and hence, with the above, the assignment that m' makes to X satisfies ϕ.

For the other direction, assume that ϕ is satisfiable, by the truth value assignment a_X. We construct a model m' so that $m' \models q$ and $m' \in b'$, and hence we prove that $\neg q \notin Lits(b')$. First, we set that for all x_i, $m' \models x_i$ iff $a_X(x_i) = 1$. Then, we set that for all y_i, $m' \models y_i$ iff $a_X(x_i) = 0$. We set that for all z_i, $m' \models z_i$. Finally, we set $m' \models q$ and $m' \models t$. It is easily verified that $m' \models \mathcal{T} \wedge \text{eff}_a$: ϕ is satisfied because the values of x_i and y_i are different, for each i. Further, m' is maximally close to m. This can be seen as follows. First, we cannot change any of the values of a z_i or of q, because those are implied by the distinct values of each x_i and y_i. Second, we cannot set any x_i or y_i to true in isolation, because that would be in conflict with the respective other value. So any change we make to the setting of x_i and y_i would involve switching one x_i or y_i to false, and hence being further away from m in that variable. This concludes the argument. ∎

Theorem 5.3. *There exist a WSC task $(\Omega, \mathcal{O}, \mathcal{U})$ where T is Horn, a service a, and two beliefs b and b' so that $Lits(b) = Lits(b')$, but $Lits(res(b, a)) \neq Lits(res(b', a))$.*

Proof: An example where the situation occurs is the following:

- $P = \{G, H, I, J, K\}$
- T contains the clauses:
  - $\forall x.(\neg G(x) \vee \neg H(x) \vee \neg I(x) \vee \neg J(x))$
  - $\forall x.(\neg H(x) \vee \neg I(x) \vee \neg K(x))$
- $\mathcal{O}$ contains the Web services:
  - $w_1 = (\{x\}, G(x), \emptyset, K(x))$
  - $w_2 = (\{x\}, G(x), \emptyset, \neg K(x))$
  - $w_3 = (\{x\}, G(x), \emptyset, J(x))$
- $C_\mathcal{U} = \{c\}$
- $pre_\mathcal{U} = G(c) \wedge \neg J(c) \wedge \neg K(c)$

The user goal does not matter for our purposes. We consider the situation where $a = w_3(c)$ is applied to the two beliefs $b := b_0$ and $b' := res(b_0, \langle w_1(c), w_2(c) \rangle)$. As we will see, $Lits(b) = Lits(b')$ but $Lits(res(b, \langle w_3(c) \rangle)) \neq Lits(res(b', \langle w_3(c) \rangle))$.

In what follows, we denote models by the list of literals they satisfy; we omit the constants since these always consist only of c. We have $b = b_0 =$

$$\{(G, \neg H, \neg I, \neg J, \neg K), (G, \neg H, I, \neg J, \neg K),$$
$$(G, H, \neg I, \neg J, \neg K), (G, H, I, \neg J, \neg K)\}$$

This is because, with J and K being false, H and I can take on arbitrary values. We get $res(b_0, \langle w_1(c) \rangle) =$

$$\{(G, \neg H, \neg I, \neg J, K), (G, \neg H, I, \neg J, K),$$
$$(G, H, \neg I, \neg J, K)\}$$

This is because, with K being true, H and I cannot be both true, so the last of the models in b_0 is mapped onto two models were either H or I is inverted – which are two models we already have. We get $b' = res(b_0, \langle w_1(c), w_2(c) \rangle) =$

$$\{(G, \neg H, \neg I, \neg J, \neg K), (G, \neg H, I, \neg J, \neg K),$$
$$(G, H, \neg I, \neg J, \neg K)\}$$

Namely, $w_2(c)$ has no effect other than making K false again (this satisfies one of the theory clauses; the other clause is satisfied because J is false). We have $Lits(b) = Lits(b') = \{G, \neg J, \neg K\}$.

Further, we have $res(b', \langle \{w_3(c)\} \rangle) =$

$$\{(G, \neg H, \neg I, J, \neg K), (G, \neg H, I, J, \neg K),$$
$$(G, H, \neg I, J, \neg K)\}$$

because J is set to true, which does not have any further effect since the theory clauses are satisfied by all resulting models. We have $Lits(res(b', \langle w_3(c) \rangle)) = \{G, J, \neg K\}$. However, we get $res(b, \langle w_3(c) \rangle) =$

$$\{(G, \neg H, \neg I, J, \neg K), (G, \neg H, I, J, \neg K),$$

$$(G, H, \neg I, J, \neg K), (\neg G, H, I, J, \neg K)\}$$

Namely, the last of the models in $b = b_0$ has both H and I true, which is why all ways of fixing the theory clause $\forall x.(\neg G(x) \lor \neg H(x) \lor \neg I(x) \lor \neg J(x))$ are produced; one of them (the only one that is not already present in the result belief) is $(\neg G, H, I, J, \neg K)$. We hence get $Lits(res(b, \langle w_3(c) \rangle)) = \{J, \neg K\}$. Thus G disappears in b, but not in b'. ∎

Lemma 5.4. *Assume a WSC task* $(\Omega, \mathcal{O}, \mathcal{U})$. *Assume a belief b and a service a. Then* $Lits(res(b, a)) \subseteq \{l \mid \mathcal{T} \land eff_a \models l\} \cup Lits(b)$.

Proof: We must prove that every literal $l \in Lits(res(b, A))$ either follows logically from $\mathcal{T} \land eff_a$, or is contained in $Lits(b)$. We show this by contraposition, i.e., we show that, if $l \notin Lits(b)$ and $\mathcal{T} \land eff_a \not\models l$, then $l \notin Lits(res(b, a))$. This can be seen as follows. For any literal l, if $l \notin Lits(b)$, then there exists $m \in b$ so that $m \not\models l$. Since res collects *all* possible outcomes with minimal changes, this will lead to a model with the same property in $res(b, a)$, unless l follows from $\mathcal{T} \land eff_a$. To prove the latter, we consider $res(m, a)$, and show that this contains a model that does not satisfy l. The computation of $res(m, a)$ can be characterised as follows. First, m is modified with eff_a, i.e., the respective proposition values are changed accordingly. If the resulting model m_1 satisfies $\mathcal{T}$, then nothing happens, i.e., m_1 is included into $res(b, a)$. If m_1 does not satisfy $\mathcal{T}$, then one model m_2 is put into $res(b, a)$ for every possibility to accordingly modify "old" values in m_1, i.e., values not set by eff_a. Now, say all of the generated m_2 model l. This means that, in order to satisfy eff_a and $\mathcal{T}$, no matter how one changes the values of the other propositions, l must be set to true – in other words, l follows from $\mathcal{T} \land eff_a$. This is a contradiction to the assumption, which concludes the argument. ∎

Lemma 5.5. *Assume a WSC task* $(\Omega, \mathcal{O}, \mathcal{U})$. *Assume a belief b, a service a, and a literal $l \in Lits(b)$. Then, $l \notin Lits(res(b, a))$ iff there exists a set L_0 of literals satisfied by a model $m \in b$, such that $\mathcal{T} \land eff_a \land \bigwedge L_0$ is satisfiable and $\mathcal{T} \land eff_a \land \bigwedge L_0 \land l$ is unsatisfiable.*

Proof: *From right to left:* Let $m \in b$ with $m \models \bigwedge_{l_0 \in L_0} l_0$. Consider $res(m, a)$. This contains all models m' satisfying $\mathcal{T} \land eff_a$ and differing minimally from m. We construct such a model m' as follows. First, we set the values following logically from $\mathcal{T} \land eff_a$. Then, we fill in the remaining values according to m. If the resulting model does not satisfy $\mathcal{T} \land eff_a$, then we have to "repair" the model by switching a minimal subset of the m values. By prerequisite, $\mathcal{T} \land eff_a \land \bigwedge_{l_0 \in L_0} l_0$ is satisfiable. Hence the repair can be done without affecting any of the values dictated by L_0. The resulting repaired model m' is contained in $res(m, a)$. It satisfies $\mathcal{T} \wedge \text{eff}_a \wedge \bigwedge_{l_0 \in L_0} l_0$. Hence by prerequisite it cannot satisfy l. This concludes the argument.

From left to right: For any l, if $l \notin Lits(res(b, a))$, then there exists $m' \in res(b, a)$ so that $m' \not\models l$. Consider an arbitrary $m \in b$ so that $m' \in res(m, a)$. By prerequisite, $m \models l$. We construct our set L_0 as $L_0 := \{l_0 \mid m \models l_0, m' \models l_0\}$. Clearly, $\mathcal{T} \wedge \text{eff}_a \wedge \bigwedge_{l_0 \in L_0} l_0$ is satisfiable. Assume to the contrary of the claim that $\mathcal{T} \wedge \text{eff}_a \wedge \bigwedge_{l_0 \in L_0} l_0 \wedge l$ is also satisfiable. Then, from that satisfying assignment, similar to the above, we can construct a model $m'' \in res(m, a)$ which satisfies $m'' \models l$ and is hence closer to m than m'. This is a contradiction and concludes the argument. ∎

Lemma 5.6. *Assume a WSC task $(\Omega, \mathcal{O}, \mathcal{U})$ where $\mathcal{T}$ is binary. Assume a belief b, a service a, and a literal $l \in Lits(b)$. If $l \notin Lits(res(b, a))$, then $\mathcal{T} \wedge \text{eff}_a \wedge l$ is unsatisfiable.*

Proof: By Lemma 5.5, there exists a set L_0 of literals such that, in particular:

- (1) Exists $m \in b$ so that $m \models \bigwedge_{l_0 \in L_0} l_0$.
- (2) $\mathcal{T} \wedge \text{eff}_a \wedge \bigwedge_{l_0 \in L_0} l_0 \wedge l$ is unsatisfiable.

From (1) we get that:

- (3) $\mathcal{T} \wedge \bigwedge_{l_0 \in L_0} l_0 \wedge l$ is satisfiable.

Simply because, by prerequisite, $l \in Lits(b)$.

Because every clause in $\mathcal{T}$ has at most two literals, we get from (2) and (3) that, as required,

- (4) $\mathcal{T} \wedge \text{eff}_a \wedge l$ is unsatisfiable.

This is due to the nature of 2-clauses. Consider that a 2-CNF can be characterised by a directed graph, where the nodes are all literals, and each clause $l \vee l'$ corresponds to two edges, namely $\bar{l} \to l'$ and $\bar{l'} \to l$. Compute the transitive closure over this graph. Say L is, as in our case L_0, a set of literals so that $\mathcal{T} \wedge \bigwedge_{l' \in L} l'$ is satisfiable. Say further that l'' is, as in our case l, a literal so that $\mathcal{T} \wedge \bar{l''}$ is satisfiable. Then, an implication $\mathcal{T} \wedge \bigwedge_{l' \in L} l' \models l''$ holds iff there exists $l' \in L$ so that, in the closed graph, l' has an edge to l''.

In (2), the role of L is taken by eff_a combined with L_0. In (3), the role of L is taken by L_0 alone. We see that the former implies $\bar{l}$, but the latter does not. The only difference is eff_a. Hence it must be the case that one literal in eff_a has, in the closed graph, an edge to $\bar{l}$, and hence we have that $\text{theory} \wedge \text{eff}_a$ implies $\bar{l}$. ∎

Theorem 5.7. *Assume a WSC task $(\Omega, \mathcal{O}, \mathcal{U})$ with fixed arity, where $\mathcal{T}$ is binary. Assume a belief b, and a service a; let $L := \{l \mid \mathcal{T} \wedge \text{eff}_a \models l\}$. Then $Lits(res(b, a)) = L \cup (Lits(b) \setminus \bar{L})$. Given $Lits(b)$, this can be computed in time polynomial in the size of $(\Omega, \mathcal{O}, \mathcal{U})$.*

Proof: Follows directly from Lemmas 5.4 and 5.6, with the fact that reasoning in propositional binary theories is polynomial.   ∎

Theorem 5.8. *Assume a WSC task* $(\Omega, \mathcal{O}, \mathcal{U})$. *Assume b is a belief and s is the corresponding search state as computed by Figure 5.6. For option* $(-)$, *if s is defined, then b is defined and* $L_s^- \subseteq Lits(b)$. *For option* $(+)$, *if b is defined, then s is defined and* $Lits(b) \subseteq L_s^+$.

Proof: This can be proved by induction over the number of services applied to reach s. If that number is 0, then s is computed by *reasoning-startstate()* and the claim obviously holds. Assume for the inductive step that s' is obtained from a state s, where by induction hypothesis the claim holds for s. We prove that the claim then also holds for s'. Let b be the belief corresponding to s, and let b' be the belief corresponding to s'. First, by induction hypothesis the lines $(1-)$ and $(1+)$ obviously under-approximate respectively over-approximate definedness of b' as required. The claim then follows from Lemma 5.5 and the following two observations.

First, the condition tested in line (6) of Figure 5.6 is a necessary criterion for Lemma 5.5: if L_0 is satisfied by a model $m \in b$, then certainly $\mathcal{T} \wedge \bigwedge Lits(b) \wedge \bigwedge L_0$ is consistent, and then by induction hypothesis $\mathcal{T} \wedge \bigwedge L_s^- \wedge \bigwedge L_0$ is consistent. Hence, whenever $l \in Lits(b)$ but $l \notin Lits(b')$, we have $l \notin L_{s'}^-$. It follows by construction of Figure 5.6 and with Lemma 5.4 that $L_{s'}^- \subseteq Lits(b')$.

Second, the condition tested in line (9) is a sufficient criterion for Lemma 5.5: if $L_0 \subseteq L_s^-$, then by induction hypothesis $L_0 \subseteq Lits(b)$, and then certainly L_0 is satisfied by a model $m \in b$. Hence, whenever $l \in L_s^+$ but $l \notin L_{s'}^+$, we have $l \notin Lits(b')$. It follows by construction of Figure 5.6 and with Lemma 5.4 that $Lits(b') \subseteq L_{s'}^+$.   ∎

Lemma 5.9. *Assume a WSC task* $(\Omega, \mathcal{O}, \mathcal{U})$. *Assume a belief b and corresponding search state s; assume that* $\langle a_0, \ldots, a_{n-1} \rangle$ *is a solution for b. Then* build-ACG(s) *run without line (9) returns t_{max} so that $t_{max} \leq n$.*

Proof: We use the notations from Figure 5.8, i.e., the data structures underlying *build-ACG*. Further, denote by b_t the belief we get after applying the services up to a_t, i.e., $b_t := res(b, \langle \{a_0\}, \ldots, \{a_{t-1}\} \rangle)$. Denote by C_t^b the set of constants shared by all models in b_t (note that the set of constants created by *build-ACG* at layer t is named C_t). To deal with newly generated constants, we need a notation for renaming of constants. If σ is a function from a set of constants C into another set of constants C', and $p = G(c_1, \ldots, c_k)$ is a proposition over P and C, then we denote $\sigma(p) := G(\sigma(c_1), \ldots, \sigma(c_k))$. If *build-ACG* stops successfully at an iteration $t < n$, there is nothing to prove. Assuming that the latter is not the case, we now prove, by induction over t, that for every $0 \leq t \leq n$ there exists an injective $\sigma : C_t^b \mapsto C_t$ such that:

(*) For all literals l over P and C_t^b, if $m \models l$ for all $m \in b_t$, then we have
$$\sigma(l) \in L_t.$$

From this property, for $t = n$, the claim follows. Namely, since $\langle\{a_0\}, \ldots,$ $\{a_{n-1}\}\rangle$ is a solution for b, there exists a tuple C of constants from C_n so that, for all $m \in b_n$, $m \models \text{eff}_{\mathcal{U}}[C]$. In other words, for every literal l in $\text{eff}_{\mathcal{U}}[C]$ we have that $m \models l$ for all $m \in b_n$. With (*), we have $\text{eff}_{\mathcal{U}}[\sigma(C)] \subseteq L_t$. Hence, in iteration n, the goal test in line (2) of *build-ACG* succeeds, and we are done.

It remains to show (*). Base case, $t = 0$. By assumption of the algorithm, the search state delivers C so that $C \supseteq C_0^b$, and L so that $L \supseteq Lits(b_0)$; then, $C_0 := C$ and $L_0 := L$ are set. Hence, taking σ to be the identity function (*) holds simply by definition. Inductive case, $t \longrightarrow t+1$. Assume that σ_t is the renaming for which (*) holds at t. Denote by $E = (c_1, \ldots, c_k)$ the output tuple of a_t. We have $k \leq M$ (where M is as in Figure 5.8), and we define our new $\sigma : C_{t+1} \mapsto C_{t+1}$ by $\sigma(c) := \sigma_t(c)$ if $c \in C_t$, and otherwise $\sigma(c_i) := e_{t+1}^i$ (where e_{t+1}^i is generated for C_{t+1} as specified in Figure 5.8). Now, say we have a literal $l \in P_{t+1}$ so that $m \models l$ for all $m \in b_{t+1}$. With Lemma 5.4, we have that either (a) we had $m \models p$ for all $m \in b_t$ already, or (b) $\mathcal{T} \wedge \text{eff}_{a_t} \models l$. Case (a) is covered by line (4) of *build-ACG*, since, by induction assumption, L_t contains all literals that are true in all $m \in b_t$. As for case (b), by induction assumption and line (5), a_t is contained in A_t. Hence the respective iteration of the loops in lines (6) – (10) will add l into L_{t+1}. This concludes the argument. ∎

Lemma 5.10. *Assume a* $\mathcal{WSC}$ *task* $(\Omega, \mathcal{O}, \mathcal{U})$. *Assume a belief b and corresponding search state s. If* build-ACG(s) *stops with $t = \infty$, then there is no solution for b.*

Proof: We prove that

(*) If the condition tested in line (9) of Figure 5.8 holds true in iteration t, then, continuing the algorithm, it will hold true for all iterations $t' > t$.

With Lemma 5.9, this proves the claim: if there was a solution of length n, *build-ACG* would stop with $t < \infty$ in iteration n.

First, assume that $\neq$ does not appear anywhere in the Web services or the goal. Then the condition in line (9) of Figure 5.8 simplifies to $\sigma_e(L_t) = \sigma_e(L_{t+1})$. Note that the renaming σ_e just removes the distinctions between the new constants generated at each layer, so literals involving (corresponding) new constants are mapped onto each other. Hence this condition means that the reached literals at $t + 1$ are exactly the same as at t, except that L_{t+1} contains copies of the literals involving new constants at L_t. Obviously, creating copies of literals does not do anything to satisfy an (as yet unsatisfied) service precondition, nor the goal – unless those require that some of their variables are instantiated with distinct constants. Since we excluded the latter case, we have that $\sigma_e(L_{t+1}) = \sigma_e(L_{t+2})$, and so on.

Say now that $\neq$ does appear in some Web service preconditions, or in the goal. Then an obvious upper bound on the maximum number of distinct constants needed is K as defined for Figure 5.8. So, if nothing changed for more than K layers – except the addition of copied literals – then we can be sure that no further service precondition, nor the goal, will become satisfied in the next iteration. This proves the claim since the condition $\sigma_e(L_{t-K+1}) = \cdots = \sigma_e(L_{t+1})$ compares $K+1$ layers.   ∎

Lemma 5.11. *Assume a WSC task* $(\Omega, \mathcal{O}, \mathcal{U})$ *with fixed arity. Assume a search state* s. *If* build-ACG(s) *uses an oracle for SAT, then it terminates in time polynomial in the size of* $(\Omega, \mathcal{O}, \mathcal{U})$ *and* s.

Proof: The size of the set of constants at layer t is $|C_s| + t * M$, which is polynomial in t and the size of s – M comes from the output parameters and is hence fixed. Also, for each t, the number of services (Web service instantiations) is polynomial in $|\mathcal{O}|$ and $|C_t|$, because the number of input parameters is assumed fixed. Further, the number of literals for any t is polynomial in $|P|$ because predicate arity is fixed, and the size of the grounded theory is polynomial in $|\mathcal{T}|$ and $|C_t|$ because the maximal nesting depth is fixed as well. Finally, note that deduction in the grounded theory, i.e., the question whether some literal follows from $\mathcal{T} \wedge \mathrm{eff}_a$, can be reduced to SAT, and hence line (8) of the algorithm can be realized by the oracle. Putting all this together, we have that, for each t, the time spent is polynomial in the size of $(P, \mathcal{T}, \mathcal{O}, C_{\mathcal{U}}, \mathrm{pre}_{\mathcal{U}}, \mathrm{eff}_{\mathcal{U}})$ and s.

It remains to show that the number of iterations until termination is polynomial in the size of $(P, \mathcal{T}, \mathcal{O}, C_{\mathcal{U}}, \mathrm{pre}_{\mathcal{U}}, \mathrm{eff}_{\mathcal{U}})$ and s. Consider that the number of constants distinct under σ_e is $|C_s| + M$, which is polynomial in the size of s. Consider further that the condition in line (9) operates only on literals based on these constants. The number of such literals is $\Sigma_{G[X] \in P}(|C_s| + M)^{|X|}$. Since the maximum predicate arity is assumed fixed, this is polynomial in the size of $(P, \mathcal{T}, \mathcal{O}, C_{\mathcal{U}}, \mathrm{pre}_{\mathcal{U}}, \mathrm{eff}_{\mathcal{U}})$ and s. Now, the algorithm terminates unless $\sigma_e(L_t)$ grows by at least one literal in every $K + 1$th iteration. Hence the number of iterations is bound by $(K+1) * \Sigma_{G[X] \in P}(|C_s| + M)^{|X|}$. Since K comes from the input and goal arity, it is also assumed fixed, and the number of iterations is polynomial in the size of $(P, \mathcal{T}, \mathcal{O}, C_{\mathcal{U}}, \mathrm{pre}_{\mathcal{U}}, \mathrm{eff}_{\mathcal{U}})$ and s.   ∎

Observation 5.14. *Assume a user goal, and assume that discovery is performed by the set-based instantiation of* fwd-discovery *or* bwd-discovery *as per Figure 5.16. If there does not exist a solution to the WSC task generated based on the discovered set* W, *then there does not exist any solution with SWS that are in reach of the underlying discovery method.*

Proof. Assume to the contrary of the claim that there does exist a solution with SWS that are in reach of the underlying discovery method. Say the solution consists of $w_1, \ldots, w_n$, where there is at least one w_i so that w_i is not contained in W. Say that W' are those w_i that are contained in W, and W'' are those w_i that are not contained in W. We know that, without the w_i in W'', the solution is not valid.

For forward chaining, we know that precondition$_P$(user-goal) $\cup \bigcup_{w_i \in W'}$ postcondition$_P(w_i)$ does not contain precondition$_P(w_i)$ for any of the $w_i \in$

W'': otherwise, since the algorithm keeps collecting SWS up to a fixpoint, the w_i in W'' would have been collected. But then, obviously, the w_i in W'' are not applicable in the solution, which is a contradiction.

For backward chaining, we know that postcondition$_P$(user-goal) $\cup \bigcup_{w_i \in W'}$ precondition$_P(w_i)$ has an empty intersection with postcondition$_P(w_i)$ for every $w_i \in W''$: otherwise, since the algorithm keeps collecting SWS up to a fixpoint, the w_i in W'' would have been collected. But then, obviously, the w_i in W'' cannot contribute anything to the solution, which is a contradiction.

Observation 5.15. *Assume a user goal, and assume that discovery is performed by* combined-bwd-discovery *as per Figure 5.17. If there does not exist a solution to the WSC task generated based on the discovered set W, then there does not exist any solution with SWS that are in reach of the underlying discovery method.*

Proof. Assume to the contrary of the claim that there does exist a solution with SWS in reach of the underlying discovery method. Say the solution consists of $w_1, \ldots, w_n$, where there is at least one w_i so that w_i is not contained in W. Say that W' are those w_i that are contained in W, and W'' are those w_i that are not contained in W. We know that, without the w_i in W'', the solution is not valid.

By construction of the algorithm as per Figure 5.17, we know that, for every $w_i \in W''$, either

$$(\text{postcondition}_P(\text{user-goal}) \cup \bigcup_{w_j \in W'} \text{precondition}_P(w_j)) \cap \text{postcondition}_P(w_i) = \emptyset$$

or

$$(\text{postcondition}(\text{user-goal}) \vee \bigvee_{w_j \in W'} \text{precondition}(w_j)) \wedge \text{postcondition}(w_i)$$

is unsatisfiable: otherwise, since the algorithm keeps collecting SWS up to a fixpoint, w_i would have been collected.

With the above, obviously, none of the w_i can contribute anything to the solution, in contradiction to the assumption.

References

1. Adam, N.R., Atluri, V., Huang, W.-K.: Modeling and analysis of workflows using petri nets. Journal of Intelligent Information Systems 10(2), 131–158 (1998)
2. Agarwal, S.: A goal specification language for automated discovery and composition of web services. In: WI 2007, International Conference on Web Intelligence, pp. 528–534 (2007)
3. Agarwal, S., Rudolph, S., Abecker, A.: Semantic description of distributed business processes. In: AAAI Spring Symposium – AI Meets Business Rules and Process Management (2008)
4. Agarwal, V., Chafle, G., Dasgupta, K., Karnik, N., Kumar, A., Mittal, S., Srivastava, B.: Synthy: A system for end to end composition of web services. Journal of Web Semantics 3(4), 311–339 (2005)
5. Agarwal, V., Dasgupta, K., Karnik, N., Kumar, A., Kundu, A., Mittal, S., Srivastava, B.: A service creation environment based on end to end composition of web services. In: WWW 2005, 14th International Conference on the World Wide Web, pp. 128–137 (2005)
6. Aho, A.V., Sethi, R., Ullman, J.D.: Compilers: principles, techniques, and tools. Addison-Wesley Longman Publishing Co., Inc., Boston (1986)
7. Akkiraju, R., Srivastava, B., Anca-Andreea, I., Goodwin, R., Syeda-Mahmood, T.: SEMAPLAN, Combining planning with semantic matching to achieve web service composition. In: ICWS 2006, 4th IEEE International Conference on Web Services (2006)
8. Alves, A., Arkin, A., Askary, S., Barreto, C., Bloch, B., Curbera, F., Ford, M., Goland, Y., Guzar, A., Kartha, N., Liu, C.K., Khalaf, R., König, D., Marin, M., Mehta, V., Thatte, S., van der Rijn, D., Yendluri, P., Yiu, A.: Web Services Business Process Execution Language. OASIS, Version 2.0, Committee specification (January 2007)
9. Alves de Medeiros, A., Pedrinaci, C., van der Aalst, W.: Semantic process mining tools: Core building blocks. In: ECIS 2008, 16th European Conference on Information Systems (2008)
10. Alves de Medeiros, A., Pedrinaci, C., van der Aalst, W., Domingue, J., Song, M., Rozinat, A., Norton, B., Cabral, L.: An outlook on semantic business process mining and monitoring. In: On The Move (OTM) Workshops (2007)

11. Andrews, T., Curbera, F., Dholakia, H., Goland, Y., Klein, J., Leymann, F., Liu, K., Roller, D., Smith, D., Thatte, S., Trickovic, I., Weerawarana, S.: Business Process Execution Language for Web Services. 2nd public draft release, Version 1.1 (May 2003)

12. Ankolekar, A., Burstein, M., Hobbs, J.R., Lassila, O., Martin, D.L., McDermott, D., McIlraith, S.A., Narayanan, S., Paolucci, M., Payne, T.R., Sycara, K.: DAML-S: Web service description for the semantic web. In: Horrocks, I., Hendler, J. (eds.) ISWC 2002. LNCS, vol. 2342, p. 348. Springer, Heidelberg (2002)

13. Ankolekar, A., Paolucci, M., Sycara, K.: Towards a formal verification of OWL-S process models. In: Gil, Y., Motta, E., Benjamins, V.R., Musen, M.A. (eds.) ISWC 2005. LNCS, vol. 3729, pp. 37–51. Springer, Heidelberg (2005)

14. Aspvall, B., Plass, M., Tarjan, R.: A linear-time algorithm for testing the truth of certain quantified boolean formulas. Information Processing Letters 8, 121–123 (1979)

15. Au, T.-C., Kuter, U., Nau, D.: Web service composition with volatile information. In: Gil, Y., Motta, E., Benjamins, V.R., Musen, M.A. (eds.) ISWC 2005. LNCS, vol. 3729, pp. 52–66. Springer, Heidelberg (2005)

16. Au, T.-C., Nau, D.: The incompleteness of planning with volatile external information. In: ECAI 2006, 17th European Conference on Artificial Intelligence (2006)

17. Baader, F., Lutz, C., Milicic, M., Sattler, U., Wolter, F.: Integrating description logics and action formalisms: First results. In: AAAI 2005, 20th National Conference on Artificial Intelligence (2005)

18. Baader, F., McGuinness, D.L., Nardi, D., Patel-Schneider, P.F. (eds.): The Description Logic Handbook: Theory, Implementation, and Applications. Cambridge University Press, Cambridge (2003)

19. Backstrom, C.: Computational aspects of reordering plans. Journal of Artificial Intelligence Research 9, 99–137 (1998)

20. Bandara, W., Indulska, M., Chong, S., Sadiq, S.: Major issues in business process management: An expert perspective. BPTrends Article (2007), http://www.bptrends.com

21. Barros, A., Dumas, M., Hofstede, A.H.M.T.: Service interaction patterns. In: van der Aalst, W.M.P., Benatallah, B., Casati, F., Curbera, F. (eds.) BPM 2005. LNCS, vol. 3649, pp. 302–318. Springer, Heidelberg (2005)

22. Becker, J., Kugeler, M., Rosemann, M. (eds.): Process Management: A Guide for the Design of Business Processes, Preparation of Process Modeling, pp. 41–78. Springer, Heidelberg (2003)

23. Behrmann, G., Bengtsson, J., David, A., Larsen, K.G., Pettersson, P., Yi, W.: UPPAAL implementation secrets. In: Damm, W., Olderog, E.-R. (eds.) FTRTFT 2002. LNCS, vol. 2469, pp. 3–22. Springer, Heidelberg (2002)

24. Benatallah, B., Dumas, M., Sheng, Q., Ngu, A.: Declarative composition and peer-to-peer provisioning of dynamic web services. In: ICDE 2002, Proceedings of the 18th IEEE International Conference on Data Engineering (2002)

25. Benatallah, B., Hacid, M., Leger, A., Rey, C., Toumani, F.: On automating web services discovery. VLDB Journal 14(1), 84–96 (2005)

26. Benazera, E., Brafman, R., Meuleau, N., Mausam, Hansen., E.: An AO* algorithm for planning with continuous resources. In: International Workshop on Planning under Uncertainty for Autonomous Systems (2005)

27. Berardi, D., Calvanese, D., Giacomo, G.D., Hull, R., Mecella, M.: Automatic composition of transition-based semantic web services with messaging. In: VLDB 2005, 31st International Conference on Very Large Data Bases, pp. 613–624 (2005)
28. Berners-Lee, T., Hendler, J., Lassila, O.: The semantic web. Scientific American 284(5), 34–43 (2001)
29. Berthelot, G.: Transformations and Decompositions of Nets. In: Brauer, W., Reisig, W., Rozenberg, G. (eds.) APN 1986. LNCS, vol. 254, pp. 360–376. Springer, Heidelberg (1987)
30. Bertino, E., Ferrari, E., Atluri, V.: The specification and enforcement of authorization constraints in workflow management systems. ACM Transactions on Information System Security 2(1), 65–104 (1999)
31. Bertoli, P., Cimatti, A., Roveri, M., Traverso, P.: Planning in nondeterministic domains under partial observability via symbolic model checking. In: IJCAI 2001, 17th International Joint Conference on Artificial Intelligence, pp. 473–478 (2001)
32. Bertoli, P., Hoffmann, J., Lecue, F., Pistore, M.: Integrating discovery and automated composition: From semantic requirements to executable code. In: ICWS 2007, 5th IEEE International Conference on Web Services (2007)
33. Bertoli, P., Pistore, M., Traverso, P.: Automated web service composition by on-the-fly belief space search. In: ICAPS 2006, 16th International Conference on Automated Planning and Scheduling (2006)
34. Blum, A.L., Furst, M.L.: Fast planning through planning graph analysis. Artificial Intelligence 90(1-2), 279–298 (1997)
35. Bonet, B., Geffner, H.: Planning with incomplete information as heuristic search in belief space. In: AIPS 2000, 5th International Conference on Artificial Intelligence Planning Systems, pp. 52–61 (2000)
36. Bonet, B., Geffner, H.: Planning as heuristic search. Artificial Intelligence 129(1-2), 5–33 (2001)
37. Borges, B., Holley, K., Arsanjani, A.: Delving into service-oriented architecture (2004), http://www.developer.com/java/ent/article.php/3409221 (accessed September 19, 2008)
38. Borgida, A.: On the relative expressiveness of description logics and predicate logics. Artificial Intelligence 82(1-2), 353–367 (1996)
39. Born, M., Brelage, C., Markovic, I., Pfeiffer, D., Weber, I.: Auto-completion of executable business process models. In: Semantics4WS 2008, 3rd International Workshop Semantics for Web services at BPM 2008, Milano, Italy, September 2008, pp. 510–515 (2008)
40. Born, M., Dörr, F., Weber, I.: User-friendly semantic annotation in business process modeling. In: Hf-SDDM 2007, Workshop on Human-friendly Service Description, Discovery and Matchmaking at WISE 2007, Nancy, France, December 2007, pp. 260–271 (2007)
41. Born, M., Hoffmann, J., Kaczmarek, T., Kowalkiewicz, M., Markovic, I., Scicluna, J., Weber, I., Zhou, X.: Semantic annotation and composition of business processes with Maestro. In: Bechhofer, S., Hauswirth, M., Hoffmann, J., Koubarakis, M. (eds.) ESWC 2008. LNCS, vol. 5021, pp. 772–776. Springer, Heidelberg (2008)

42. Born, M., Hoffmann, J., Kaczmarek, T., Kowalkiewicz, M., Markovic, I., Scicluna, J., Weber, I., Zhou, X.: Supporting execution-level business process modeling with semantic technologies. In: Demonstrations at DASFAA 2009, Database Systems for Advanced Applications, Brisbane, Australia, April 2009, pp. 759–763 (2009)
43. Brachman, R.J., Schmolze, J.G.: An overview of the KL-ONE knowledge representation system. Cognitive Science 9(2), 171–216 (1985)
44. Brafman, R., Hoffmann, J.: Conformant planning via heuristic forward search: A new approach. In: ICAPS 2004, 14th International Conference on Automated Planning and Scheduling, pp. 355–364 (2004)
45. Brewka, G., Hertzberg, J.: How to do things with worlds: On formalizing actions and plans. Journal of Logic and Computation 3(5), 517–532 (1993)
46. Bryant, R.: Graph-based algorithms for boolean function manipulation. IEEE Transactions on Computers 35, 677–691 (1986)
47. Bryce, D., Kambhampati, S., Smith, D.E.: Planning graph heuristics for belief space search. Journal of Artificial Intelligence Research 26, 35–99 (2006)
48. Burch, J., Clarke, E., Mcmillan, K., Dill, D., Hwang, L.: Symbolic model checking: 10^{20} states and beyond. In: 5th IEEE Symposium on Logic in Computer Science, pp. 1–33 (1990)
49. Cabral, L., Drumm, C., Domingue, J., Pedrinaci, C., Goyal, A.: DIP Deliverable D5.6: Mediator Library (July 2006)
50. Cardoso, J., Sheth, A.P. (eds.): Semantic Web Services, Processes and Applications. Semantic Web And Beyond Computing for Human Experience, vol. 3. Springer, Heidelberg (2006)
51. Chappell, D.A.: Enterprise Service Bus. O'Reilly, Sebastopol (2004)
52. Chen, Y., Wah, B., Hsu, C.: Temporal planning using subgoal partitioning and resolution in SGPlan. Journal of Artificial Intelligence Research 26, 323–369 (2006)
53. Christensen, E., Curbera, F., Meredith, G., Weerawarana, S.: Web Services Description Language (WSDL) 1.1 (2001)
54. Cimatti, A., Roveri, M.: Conformant planning via symbolic model checking. Journal of Artificial Intelligence Research 13, 305–338 (2000)
55. Cimatti, A., Roveri, M., Bertoli, P.: Conformant planning via symbolic model checking and heuristic search. Artificial Intelligence 159(1–2), 127–206 (2004)
56. Clarke, E., Biere, A., Raimi, R., Zhu, Y.: Bounded model checking using satisfiability solving. Formal Methods in System Design 19(1), 7–34 (2001)
57. Clarke, E., Grumberg, O., Peled, D.: Model Checking. The MIT Press, Cambridge (2000)
58. Constantinescu, I., Faltings, B.: Efficient matchmaking and directory services. In: WI 2003, 2nd International Conference on Web Intelligence (2003)
59. Constantinescu, I., Faltings, B., Binder, W.: Type based service composition. In: Posters at WWW 2004, 13th International Conference on the World Wide Web, pp. 268–269 (2003)
60. Constantinescu, I., Faltings, B., Binder, W.: Large scale, type-compatible service composition. In: ICWS 2004, 2nd IEEE International Conference on Web Services, pp. 506–513 (2004)
61. Fensel, D., et al.: Enabling Semantic Web Services: The Web Service Modeling Ontology. Springer, Heidelberg (2006)
62. Da Rold, C.: European IT services survey signals irreversible changes. Technical Report Markets Note, M-20-0616, Gartner Research (June 19, 2003)

63. Davenport, T.H., Short, J.E.: The new industrial engineering: Information technology and business process redesign. MIT Sloan Management Review 31(4), 11–27 (1990)
64. Davenport, T.H., Stoddard, D.B.: Reengineering: Business change of mythic proportions? MIS Quarterly 18(2), 121–127 (1994)
65. De Giacomo, G., Lenzerini, M., Poggi, A., Rosati, R.: On the update of description logic ontologies at the instance level. In: AAAI 2006, 21st National Conference on Artificial Intelligence (2006)
66. De Giacomo, G., Lenzerini, M., Poggi, A., Rosati, R.: On the approximation of instance level update and erasure in description logics. In: AAAI 2007, 22nd Natl. Conf. of the Association for the Advancement of Artificial Intelligence (2007)
67. Decker, G., Overdick, H., Weske, M.: Oryx – an open modeling platform for the BPM community. In: Dumas, M., Reichert, M., Shan, M.-C. (eds.) BPM 2008. LNCS, vol. 5240, pp. 382–385. Springer, Heidelberg (2008)
68. Dehnert, J., van der Aalst, W.: Bridging the gap between business models and workflow specifications. International Journal of Cooperative Information Systems 13(3), 289–332 (2004)
69. Desel, J., Esparza, J.: Free choice Petri nets. Cambridge University Press, New York (1995)
70. Digital Enterprise Research Institute (DERI). Web Service Modelling Ontology, WSMO (2004), http://www.wsmo.org/
71. Dimitrov, M., Simov, A., Stein, S., Konstantinov, M.: SUPER Deliverable D5.1: Semantic Process Modelling Environment (September 2007), http://www.ip-super.org
72. Do, M.B., Kambhampati, S.: Sapa: A domain-independent heuristic metric temporal planner. In: ECP 2001, 6th European Conference on Planning, pp. 109–120 (2001)
73. Do, M.B., Kambhampati, S.: Improving the temporal flexibility of position constrained metric temporal plans. In: ICAPS 2003, 13th International Conference on Automated Planning and Scheduling, pp. 42–51 (2003)
74. Drumm, C., Filipowska, A., Hoffmann, J., Kaczmarek, M., Kaczmarek, T., Kowalkiewicz, M., Markovic, I., Scicluna, J., Vanhatalo, J., Völzer, H., Weber, I., Wieloch, K., Zyskowski, D.: SUPER Deliverable D3.2: Dynamic Composition Reasoning Framework and Prototype (September 2007), http://www.ip-super.org
75. Drumm, C., Schmitt, M., Do, H.-H., Rahm, E.: Quickmig - automatic schema matching for data migration projects. In: CIKM 2007, 16th ACM Conference on Information and Knowledge Management (2007)
76. Dumas, M., ter Hofstede, A., van der Aalst, W. (eds.): Process Aware Information Systems: Bridging People and Software Through Process Technology. Wiley Publishing, Chichester (2005)
77. Dustdar, S., Schreiner, W.: A survey on web services composition. International Journal on Web and Grid Services 1(1), 1–30 (2005)
78. Edelkamp, S.: Taming numbers and durations in the model checking integrated planning system. Journal of Artificial Intelligence Research 20, 195–238 (2003)
79. Edelkamp, S., Lluch-Lafuente, A., Leue, S.: Directed explicit-state model checking in the validation of communication protocols. International Journal on Software Tools for Technology (2004)

80. Een, N., Sörensson, N.: An extensible SAT solver. In: Giunchiglia, E., Tacchella, A. (eds.) SAT 2003. LNCS, vol. 2919, pp. 502–518. Springer, Heidelberg (2004)

81. Eiter, T., Faber, W., Leone, N., Pfeifer, G., Polleres, A.: A logic programming approach to knowledge-state planning, II: The DLV$^{\mathcal{K}}$ system. Artificial Intelligence 144(1-2), 157–211 (2003)

82. Eiter, T., Faber, W., Leone, N., Pfeifer, G., Polleres, A.: A logic programming approach to knowledge-state planning: Semantics and complexity. Transactions on Computational Logics 5(2), 206–263 (2004)

83. Eiter, T., Gottlob, G.: On the complexity of propositional knowledge base revision, updates, and counterfactuals. Artificial Intelligence 57(2-3), 227–270 (1992)

84. El Kharbili, M., Alves de Medeiros, A., Stein, S., van der Aalst, W.: Business process compliance checking: Current state and future challenges. In: MobIS 2008, Modellierung betrieblicher Informationssysteme, November 2008, pp. 107–113 (2008)

85. El Kharbili, M., Stein, S., Markovic, I., Pulvermüller, E.: Towards a framework for semantic business process compliance management. In: GRCIS 2008, International Workshop on Governance, Risk, and Compliance in Information Systems at CAiSE 2008, Montepellier, France (June 2008)

86. Ellis, C.A., Nutt, G.J.: Office information systems and computer science. ACM Computing Surveys 12(1), 27–60 (1980)

87. Ellis, C.A., Nutt, G.J.: Modeling and enactment of workflow systems. In: ATPN 1993, 14th International Conference on Application and Theory of Petri Nets, London, UK, pp. 1–16. Springer, Heidelberg (1993)

88. Erl, T.: Service-Oriented Architecture: Concepts, Technology, and Design. Prentice-Hall, Englewood Cliffs (2006)

89. Erl, T.: Service-Oriented Architecture: Principles of Service Design. Prentice-Hall, Englewood Cliffs (2007)

90. Esfandiari, B., Tosic, V.: Requirements for web service composition management. In: 11th Workshop of the HP OpenView University Association (HPOVUA) (June 2004)

91. Euzenat, J., Shvaiko, P.: Ontology Matching. Springer, Heidelberg (2007)

92. Fagin, R., Kuper, G., Ullman, J., Vardi, M.: Updating logical databases. Advances in Computing Research 3, 1–18 (1986)

93. Fagin, R., Ullman, J.D., Vardi, M.Y.: On the semantics of updates in databases. In: PODS 1983, 2nd ACM SIGACT-SIGMOD Symposium on Principles of Database Systems, pp. 352–365 (1983)

94. Fantini, P., Savoldelli, A., Milanesi, M., Carizzoni, G., Koehler, J., Stein, S., Angeli, R., Hepp, M., Roman, D., Brelage, C., Born, M.: SUPER Deliverable D2.2: Semantic Business Process Life Cycle (May 2007), http://www.ip-super.org

95. Fensel, D., Decker, S., Erdmann, M., Studer, R.: Ontobroker in a nutshell. In: Nikolaou, C., Stephanidis, C. (eds.) ECDL 1998. LNCS, vol. 1513, pp. 663–664. Springer, Heidelberg (1998)

96. Fikes, R.E., Nilsson, N.: STRIPS: A new approach to the application of theorem proving to problem solving. Artificial Intelligence 2, 189–208 (1971)

97. Fox, M., Long, D.: PDDL2.1: An extension to PDDL for expressing temporal planning domains. Journal of Artificial Intelligence Research 20, 61–124 (2003)

98. Frederiks, P., Weide, T.: Information modeling: The process and the required competencies of its participants. Data & Knowledge Engineering 58(1), 4–20 (2006)

99. Friesen, A.: Semantic web service discovery and selection in B2B integration scenarios. In: Reasoning Web, 3rd Intl. Summer School, Tutorial Lectures, September 2007, pp. 338–343 (2007)

100. Friesen, A., Lemcke, J.: Composing web-service-like abstract state machines (ASMs). In: WSCA 2007, Workshop on Web Service Composition and Adaptation at ICWS (2007)

101. Friesen, A., Namiri, K.: Towards semantic service selection for B2B integration. In: Workshops at ICWE 2006, 6th International Conference on Web Engineering, July 11-14 (2006)

102. Garcia-Valles, F., Colom, J.: Implicit places in net systems. In: 8th International Workshop on Petri Nets and Performance Models, pp. 104–113 (1999)

103. Genovese, Y., Hayward, S., Phifer, G., Plummer, D., Comport, J., Smith, D.: Flexibility drives the emergence of the business process platform. Technical Report G00126854, Gartner Research, (April 26, 2005)

104. Gerevini, A., Dimopoulos, Y., Haslum, P., Saetti, A. (eds.): 5th International Planning Competition – Deterministic Part. At ICAPS 2006, 16th International Conference on Automated Planning and Scheduling (2006)

105. Gerevini, A., Long, D.: Preferences and soft constraints in PDDL3. In: Workshop on Preferences and Soft Constraints in Planning at ICAPS 2006 (2006)

106. Gerevini, A., Saetti, A., Serina, I.: Planning through stochastic local search and temporal action graphs. Journal of Artificial Intelligence Research 20, 239–290 (2003)

107. Gerevini, A., Saetti, A., Serina, I.: An approach to temporal planning and scheduling in domains with predictable exogenous events. Journal of Artificial Intelligence Research 25, 187–231 (2006)

108. Ginsberg, M., Smith, D.: Reasoning about action I: A possible worlds approach. Artificial Intelligence 35(2), 165–195 (1988)

109. Giunchiglia, E.: Planning as satisfiability with expressive action languages: Concurrency, constraints, and nondeterminism. In: KR 2000, 7th International Conference on Principles of Knowledge Representation and Reasoning (2000)

110. Giunchiglia, E., Lee, J., Lifschitz, V., McCain, N., Turner, H.: Nonmonotonic causal theories. Artificial Intelligence 153(1-2), 49–104 (2004)

111. Giunchiglia, E., Muscettola, N., Nau, D. (eds.): ICAPS 2003, Proceedings of the 13th International Conference on Automated Planning and Scheduling. Morgan Kaufmann, Trento (2003)

112. Giunchiglia, F., Traverso, P.: Planning as model checking. In: Biundo, S., Fox, M. (eds.) ECP 1999. LNCS, vol. 1809, pp. 1–20. Springer, Heidelberg (2000)

113. Goasduff, L., Forsling, C.: Business process management suites (BPMS) will be among the fastest growing software markets through 2011, says Gartner, Gartner Press Release (March 27, 2007),
http://www.gartner.com/it/page.jsp?id=502645 (accessed: December 12, 2008)

114. Governatori, G.: Representing business contracts in RuleML. International Journal of Cooperative Information Systems 14, 181–216 (2005)

115. Governatori, G., Hoffmann, J., Sadiq, S., Weber, I.: Detecting regulatory compliance for business process models through semantic annotations. In: BPD 2008, 4th International Workshop on Business Process Design, Milano, Italy, September 2008, pp. 5–17 (2008)
116. Grimm, S.: Intersection-based matchmaking for semantic web service discovery. In: ICIW 2007, International Conference on Internet and Web Applications and Services (2007)
117. Grimm, S.: Discovery. In: Studer, R., Grimm, S., Abecker, A. (eds.) Semantic Web Services Concepts, Technologies and Applications, ch. 8, pp. 211–244. Springer, Heidelberg (2007)
118. Gruber, T.: A translation approach to portable ontology specifications. Knowledge Acquisition 5(2), 199–220 (1993)
119. Gruber, T.: Toward principles for the design of ontologies used for knowledge sharing. International Journal of Human Computer Studies 43(5-6), 907–928 (1995)
120. Haller, A., Cimpian, E., Mocan, A., Oren, E., Bussler, C.: WSMX – a semantic service-oriented architecture. In: ICWS 2005, 3rd IEEE International Conference on Web Services (July 2005)
121. Hammer, M.: Reengineering work: Don't automate, obliterate. Harvard Business Review 68(4), 104–112 (1990)
122. Hammer, M., Champy, J.: Reengineering the Corporation: A Manifesto for Business Revolution. HarperBusiness (1993)
123. Hansen, E.A., Zilberstein, S.: LAO *: A heuristic search algorithm that finds solutions with loops. Artificial Intelligence 129(1-2), 35–62 (2001)
124. Haslum, P., Geffner, H.: Heuristic planning with time and resources. In: ECP 2001, 6th European Conference on Planning, pp. 121–132 (2001)
125. Havey, M.: Essential Business Process Modeling. O'Reilly Media, Inc., Sebastopol (2005)
126. Hee, K., Sidorova, N., Somers, L., Voorhoeve, M.: Consistency in model integration. Data & Knowledge Engineering 56, 4–22 (2006)
127. Heffner, R., Cameron, B., Dowling, K.: Your strategic SOA platform vision crafting your architectural evolution to service-oriented architecture. Technical report, Forrester Research, Trends, (March 29, 2005)
128. Helmert, M.: A planning heuristic based on causal graph analysis. In: ICAPS 2004, 14th International Conference on Automated Planning and Scheduling, pp. 161–170 (2004)
129. Hepp, M., Hinkelmann, K., Karagiannis, D., Klein, R., Stojanovic, N. (eds.): Proceedings of the Workshop on Semantic Business Process and Product Lifecycle Management (SBPM 2007), Innsbruck, Austria (June 2007)
130. Hepp, M., Leymann, F., Domingue, J., Wahler, A., Fensel, D.: Semantic business process management: A vision towards using semantic web services for business process management. In: ICEBE 2005, IEEE International Conference on e-Business Engineering, October 2005, pp. 535–540 (2005)
131. Herzig, A., Rifi, O.: Propositional belief base update and minimal change. Artificial Intelligence 115(1), 107–138 (1999)
132. Hevner, A.R., March, S.T., Park, J., Ram, S.: Design science in information systems research. MIS Quarterly 28(1), 75–105 (2004)
133. Hoffmann, J.: FF: The fast-forward planning system. AI Magazine 22(3), 57–62 (2001)

134. Hoffmann, J.: The Metric-FF planning system: Translating ignoring delete lists to numeric state variables. Journal of Artificial Intelligence Research 20, 291–341 (2003)

135. Hoffmann, J., Bertoli, P., Pistore, M.: Web service composition as planning, revisited: In between background theories and initial state uncertainty. In: AAAI 2007, 22nd Natl. Conf. of the Association for the Advancement of Artificial Intelligence (2007)

136. Hoffmann, J., Brafman, R.: Contingent planning via heuristic forward search with implicit belief states. In: ICAPS 2005, 15th International Conference on Automated Planning and Scheduling, pp. 71–80 (2005)

137. Hoffmann, J., Brafman, R.: Conformant planning via heuristic forward search: A new approach. Artificial Intelligence 170(6–7), 507–541 (2006)

138. Hoffmann, J., Edelkamp, S.: The deterministic part of IPC-4: An overview. Journal of Artificial Intelligence Research 24, 519–579 (2005)

139. Hoffmann, J., Nebel, B.: The FF planning system: Fast plan generation through heuristic search. Journal of Artificial Intelligence Research 14, 253–302 (2001)

140. Hoffmann, J., Porteous, J., Sebastia, L.: Ordered landmarks in planning. Journal of Artificial Intelligence Research 22, 215–278 (2004)

141. Hoffmann, J., Scicluna, J., Kaczmarek, T., Weber, I.: Polynomial-time reasoning for semantic web service composition. In: WSCA 2007, Workshop on Web Service Composition and Adaptation at ICWS 2007, Salt Lake City, UT, USA, July 2007, pp. 229–236 (2007)

142. Hoffmann, J., Weber, I., Governatori, G.: On compliance checking for clausal constraints in annotated process models. Information Systems Frontiers, Special Issue on Governance, Risk, and Compliance (2009)

143. Hoffmann, J., Weber, I., Kraft, F.M.: Planning@SAP: An application in business process management. In: SPARK 2009, Scheduling and Planning Applications woRKshop at ICAPS 2009 (2009)

144. Hoffmann, J., Weber, I., Scicluna, J., Kaczmarek, T., Ankolekar, A.: Combining scalability and expressivity in the automatic composition of semantic web services. In: ICWE 2008, 8th International Conference on Web Engineering, Yorktown Heights, NY, USA, July 2008, pp. 98–107 (2008)

145. Holzmann, G.: The Spin Model Checker - Primer and Reference Manual. Addison-Wesley, Reading (2003)

146. Holzmann, G., Peled, D.: An improvement in formal verification. In: FORTE 1994, 7th International Conference on Formal Description Techniques for Distributed Systems and Communication Protocols, pp. 197–211 (1994)

147. Horn, A.: On sentences which are true of direct unions of algebras. Journal of Symbolic Logic 16(1), 14–21 (1951)

148. Hornung, T., Koschmider, A., Lausen, G.: Recommendation based process modeling support: Method and user experience. In: Li, Q., Spaccapietra, S., Yu, E., Olivé, A. (eds.) ER 2008. LNCS, vol. 5231, pp. 265–278. Springer, Heidelberg (2008)

149. Hornung, T., Koschmider, A., Oberweis, A.: Rule-based autocompletion of business process models. In: Forum at CAiSE 2007, 19th Conference on Advanced Information Systems Engineering (2007)

150. Horrocks, I., Patel-Schneider, P.F.: Reducing OWL entailment to description logic satisfiability. Journal of Web Semantics 1(4), 345–357 (2004)

151. Howell, R., Rosier, L.: Problems concerning fairness and temporal logic for conflict-free petri nets. Theoretical Computer Science 64(3), 305–329 (1989)

152. Hull, D., Zolin, E., Bovykin, A., Horrocks, I., Sattler, U., Stevens, R.: Deciding semantic matching of stateless services. In: AAAI 2006, 21st National Conference on Artificial Intelligence (2006)

153. Humphrey, W.S.: Managing the Software Process. Addison-Wesley, Reading (1989)

154. IBM. Insurance Application Architecture (IAA), v 7.1, (2004), http://www-03.ibm.com/industries/financialservices/doc/content/solution/278918103.html, (accessed: 28 October 2008)

155. Jablonski, S., Bussler, C.: Workflow Management: Modeling Concepts, Architecture and Implementation. International Thomson Computer Press, London (1996)

156. Kaplan, R.S., Atkinson, A.A.: Advanced management accounting, 2nd edn. Prentice-Hall, Englewood Cliffs (1989)

157. Keller, G., Nüttgens, M., Scheer, A.-W.: Semantische Prozessmodellierung auf der Grundlage Ereignisgesteuerter Prozessketten (EPK). In: Veröffentlichungen des Instituts für Wirtschaftsinformatik, Heft, Saarbrücken, Germany, January 1992, vol. 89 (1992), http://www.iwi.uni-sb.de/iwi-hefte/heft089.pdf

158. Kifer, M., Lausen, G., Wu, J.: Logical foundations of object-oriented and frame-based languages. Journal of the ACM 42, 741–843 (1995)

159. Koehler, J., Hauser, R., Küster, J., Ryndina, K., Vanhatalo, J., Wahler, M.: The role of visual modeling and model transformations in business-driven development. In: 5th International Workshop on Graph Transformation and Visual Modeling Techniques (April 2006)

160. Koliadis, G., Ghose, A.: Verifying semantic business process models in interoperation. In: SCC 2007, IEEE International Conference on Services Computing, pp. 731–738 (2007)

161. Kona, S., Bansal, A., Gupta, G., Hite, D.: Automatic composition of semantic web services. In: ICWS 2007, 5th IEEE International Conference on Web Services (2007)

162. Koschmider, A.: Ähnlichkeitsbasierte Modellierungsunterstützung für Geschäftsprozesse. PhD thesis, Universität Karlsruhe (TH), Germany (November 2007)

163. Koschmider, A., Ried, D.: Semantische Annotation von Petri-Netzen. In: AWPN 2005, 12. Workshop Algorithmen und Werkzeuge für Petrinetze, September 2005, pp. 66–71 (2005)

164. Kovalyov, A., Esparza, J.: A polynomial algorithm to compute the concurrency relation of free-choice signal transition graphs. In: WODES 1996, International Workshop on Discrete Event Systems, pp. 1–6 (1996)

165. Kumaran, S., Liu, R., Wu, F.Y.: On the duality of information centric and activity-centric models of business processes. In: Bellahsène, Z., Léonard, M. (eds.) CAiSE 2008. LNCS, vol. 5074, pp. 32–47. Springer, Heidelberg (2008)

166. Küngas, P., Matskin, M.: Detection of missing web services: The partial deduction approach. International Journal of Web Services Practices 1(1-2), 133–141 (2005)

167. Küster, J., Koehler, J., Ryndina, K.: Improving business process models with reference models in business-driven development. In: BPD 2006, 2nd Workshop on Business Processes Design (2006)

168. Küster, U., König-Ries, B., Krug, A.: OPOSSum - an online portal to collect and share SWS descriptions. In: Demonstrations at ICSC 2008, 2nd IEEE International Conference on Semantic Computing (August 2008)

169. Küster, U., Stern, M., König-Ries, B.: A classification of issues and approaches in automatic service composition. In: WESC 2005, 1st International Workshop on Engineering Service Compositions, December 2005, pp. 25–33 (2005)

170. Kuter, U., Sirin, E., Nau, D., Parsia, B., Hendler, J.: Information gathering during planning for web service composition. Journal of Web Semantics 3(2-3), 183–205 (2005)

171. Lamparter, S.: Policy-based Contracting in Semantic Web Service Markets. PhD thesis, Universität Karlsruhe (TH), Fakultät für Wirtschaftwissenschaften (2007)

172. Lawrence, P. (ed.): Workflow Handbook. Workflow Management Coalition. John Wiley Publishing, New York (1997)

173. Leymann, F., Roller, D.: Production Workflow - Concepts and Techniques. Prentice-Hall, Englewood Cliffs (2000)

174. Li, L., Horrocks, I.: A software framework for matchmaking based on semantic web technology. In: WWW 2003, 12th International Conference on the World Wide Web (2003)

175. Li, Z., Sun, W., Du, B.: BPEL4WS unit testing: Framework and implementation. International Journal of Business Process Integration and Management 2(4), 131–143 (2007)

176. Liberatore, P.: The complexity of belief update. Artificial Intelligence 119(1-2), 141–190 (2000)

177. Lin, F., Reiter, R.: State constraints revisited. Journal of Logic and Computation 4(5), 655–678 (1994)

178. List, B., Korherr, B.: An evaluation of conceptual business process modelling languages. In: SAC 2006, pp. 1532–1539 (2006)

179. Liu, H., Lutz, C., Miličić, M., Wolter, F.: Reasoning about actions using description logics with general TBoxes. In: Fisher, M., van der Hoek, W., Konev, B., Lisitsa, A. (eds.) JELIA 2006. LNCS (LNAI), vol. 4160, pp. 266–279. Springer, Heidelberg (2006)

180. Liu, H., Lutz, C., Milicic, M., Wolter, F.: Updating description logic ABoxes. In: KR 2006, 10th International Conference on Principles of Knowledge Representation and Reasoning, pp. 46–56 (2006)

181. Liu, Z., Ranganathan, A., Riabov, A.: A planning approach for message-oriented semantic web service composition. In: AAAI 2007, 22nd Natl. Conf. of the Association for the Advancement of Artificial Intelligence (2007)

182. Lutz, C., Sattler, U.: A proposal for describing services with DLs. In: DL 2002, International Workshop on Description Logics (2002)

183. Ly, L.T., Rinderle, S., Dadam, P.: Semantic correctness in adaptive process management systems. In: Dustdar, S., Fiadeiro, J.L., Sheth, A.P. (eds.) BPM 2006. LNCS, vol. 4102, pp. 193–208. Springer, Heidelberg (2006)

184. Ly, L.T., Rinderle, S., Dadam, P.: Integration and verification of semantic constraints in adaptive process management systems. Data & Knowledge Engineering 64(1), 3–23 (2008)

185. Malhotra, Y.: Business process redesign: An overview. IEEE Engineering Management Review 26(3), 27–31 (1998)

186. Markovic, I., Costa Pereira, A., de Francisco, D., Munoz, H.: Querying in business process modeling. In: SeMSoC 2007, 2nd International Workshop on Business Oriented Aspects concerning Semantics and Methodologies in Service-oriented Computing (September 2007)

187. Markovic, I., Costa Pereira, A., Stojanovic, N.: A framework for querying in business process modeling. In: MKWI 2008, Multikonferenz Wirtschaftsinformatik, Munich, Germany (March 2008)

188. Markovic, I., Karrenbrock, M.: Semantic web service discovery for business process models. In: Hf-SDDM 2007, Workshop on Human-friendly Service Description, Discovery and Matchmaking at WISE 2007 (December 2007)

189. Markovic, I., Kowalkiewicz, M.: Linking business goals to process models in semantic business process modeling. In: 12th IEEE International EDOC Conference (September 2008)

190. Markovic, I., Pereira, A.C.: Towards a formal framework for reuse in business process modeling. In: Semantics4WS 2007, 2nd International Workshop Semantics for Web services at BPM 2007 (September 2007)

191. Marques-Silva, J., Sakallah, K.A.: GRASP – a search algorithm for propositional satisfiability. IEEE Transactions on Computers 48(5), 506–521 (1999)

192. Martelli, A., Montanari, U.: Additive AND/OR graphs. In: IJCAI 1973, International Joint Conference on Artificial Intelligence, pp. 1–11 (1973)

193. Martelli, A., Montanari, U.: Optimizing decision trees through heuristically guided search. Communications of the ACM 21(12), 1025–1039 (1978)

194. May, N., Weber, I.: Information gathering for semantic service discovery and composition in business process modeling. In: CIAO! 2008, Workshop on Cooperation & Interoperability - Architecture & Ontology at CAiSE 2008. LNBIP, vol. 10, pp. 46–60 (2008)

195. McDermott, D.: Estimated-regression planning for interactions with web services. In: AIPS 2002, 6th International Conference on Artificial Intelligence Planning Systems (2002)

196. McDermott, D., et al.: The PDDL Planning Domain Definition Language. In: The AIPS 1998 Planning Competition Committee (1998)

197. McDermott, D.V.: Using regression match graphs to control search in planning. Artificial Intelligence 109(1-2), 111–159 (1999)

198. McIlraith, S., Fadel, R.: Planning with complex actions. In: NMR 2002, 9th International Workshop on Non-Monotonic Reasoning, pp. 356–364 (2002)

199. McIlraith, S., Son, T.C.: Adapting Golog for composition of semantic web services. In: KR 2002, 8th International Conference on Principles of Knowledge Representation and Reasoning (2002)

200. Mehrotra, S., Rastogi, R., Korth, H.F., Silberschatz, A.: A transaction model for multidatabase systems. In: Workshops at NODe 2002, Web, Web-Services, and Database Systems, pp. 59–72 (2002)

201. Mendling, J.: Detection and Prediction of Errors in EPC Business Process Models. PhD thesis, Vienna University of Economics and Business Administration, Vienna, Austria (May 2007)

202. Mendling, J., Lassen, K., Zdun, U.: On the transformation of control flow between block-oriented and graph-oriented process modeling languages. International Journal of Business Process Integration and Management 2(4), 96–108 (2007)

203. Mendling, J., van der Aalst, W.M.P.: Formalization and verification of EPCs with OR-joins based on state and context. In: Krogstie, J., Opdahl, A.L., Sindre, G. (eds.) CAiSE 2007 and WES 2007. LNCS, vol. 4495, pp. 439–453. Springer, Heidelberg (2007)

204. Meyer, H.: On the semantics of service compositions. In: Marchiori, M., Pan, J.Z., de Marie, C.S. (eds.) RR 2007. LNCS, vol. 4524, pp. 31–42. Springer, Heidelberg (2007)

205. Meyer, H., Kuropka, D.: Requirements for service composition. Technical report, Universität Potsdam, Hasso-Plattner-Instituts für Softwaresystemtechnik, Technische Berichte Nr. 11, Univ.-Verlag Potsdam (2005)

206. Meyer, H., Weske, M.: Automated service composition using heuristic search. In: Dustdar, S., Fiadeiro, J.L., Sheth, A.P. (eds.) BPM 2006. LNCS, vol. 4102, pp. 81–96. Springer, Heidelberg (2006)

207. Milner, R.: Functions as processes. In: 17th International Colloquium on Automata, Languages and Programming, pp. 167–180 (1990)

208. Milner, R.: The polyadic π-calculus. In: Cleaveland, W.R. (ed.) CONCUR 1992. LNCS, vol. 630, Springer, Heidelberg (1992)

209. Minsky, M.: A framework for representing knowledge. In: Mind Design: Philosophy, Psychology, Artificial Intelligence, pp. 95–128. MIT Press, Cambridge (1981)

210. Moskewicz, M., Madigan, C., Zhao, Y., Zhang, L., Malik, S.: Chaff: Engineering an efficient SAT solver. In: DAC 2001, 38th Conference on Design Automation (2001)

211. Namiri, K., Kuegler, M.-M., Stojanovic, N.: A static business level verification framework for cross-organizational business process models using swrl. In: AST 2007, Proc. 2nd Intl. Workshop on Applications of Semantic Technologies (September 2007)

212. Namiri, K., Stojanovic, N.: A semantic-driven approach for internal controls compliance in business processes. In: SBPM 2007, Workshop on Semantic Business Process and Product Lifecycle Management, June 2007 (2007) ISSN 1613-0073

213. Namiri, K., Stojanovic, N.: Towards a formal framework for business process compliance. In: MKWI 2008, Multikonferenz Wirtschaftsinformatik (2008)

214. Narayanan, S., McIlraith, S.: Simulation, verification and automated composition of web services. In: WWW 2002, 11th International Conference on the World Wide Web, pp. 77–88 (2002)

215. Nilsson, N.J.: Searching problem-solving and game-playing trees for minimal cost solutions. Information Processing 68(2), 1556–1562 (1969)

216. Nilsson, N.J.: Principles of Artificial Intelligence. Tioga Publishing, Palo Alto (1980)

217. Nitzsche, J., van Lessen, T., Karastoyanova, D., Leymann, F.: BPEL for semantic web services. In: AWeSome 2007, 3rd International Workshop on Agents and Web Services in Distributed Environments (November 2007)

218. Nitzsche, J., van Lessen, T., Karastoyanova, D., Leymann, F.: WSMO/X in the context of business processes: Improvement recommendations. International Journal of Web Information Systems (2007)

219. Nitzsche, J., Wutke, D., van Lessen, T.: An ontology for executable business processes. In: SBPM 2007, Workshop on Semantic Business Process and Product Lifecycle Management (June 2007)

220. OASIS. UDDI Version 3.0.2. OASIS Standard (October 19, 2004),
     http://uddi.org/pubs/uddi-v3.0.2-20041019.htm
221. Oberweis, A., Sander, P.: Information system behavior specification by high
     level petri nets. ACM Transactions on Information Systems 14(4), 380–420
     (1996)
222. O.: Business Process Modeling Notation, V1.1. OMG Available Specification,
     Document Number: formal/2008-01-17 (January 2008),
     http://www.bpmn.org/
223. Orriëns, B., Yang, J., Papazoglou, M.P.: A framework for business rule driven
     service composition. In: Benatallah, B., Shan, M.-C. (eds.) TES 2003. LNCS,
     vol. 2819, pp. 14–27. Springer, Heidelberg (2003)
224. Ouyang, C., Dumas, M., Breutel, S., ter Hofstede, A.H.M.: Translating stan-
     dard process models to BPEL. In: Dubois, E., Pohl, K. (eds.) CAiSE 2006.
     LNCS, vol. 4001, pp. 417–432. Springer, Heidelberg (2006)
225. Paolucci, M., Kawamura, T., Payne, T.R., Sycara, K.: Semantic matching of
     web services capabilities. In: Horrocks, I., Hendler, J. (eds.) ISWC 2002. LNCS,
     vol. 2342, p. 333. Springer, Heidelberg (2002)
226. Papazoglou, M.: Web Services: Principles and Technology. Prentice-Hall, En-
     glewood Cliffs (2007)
227. Pearl, J.: Heuristics. Morgan Kaufmann, San Francisco (1983)
228. Peer, J.: Web service composition as AI planning - a survey. Technical report,
     Univ. of St. Gallen, Switzerland (2005)
229. Peltz, C.: Web services orchestration and choreography. Computer 36(10), 46–
     52 (2003)
230. Penberthy, J.S., Weld, D.S.: UCPOP: A sound, complete, partial order planner
     for ADL. In: KR 1992, International Conference on Principles of Knowledge
     Representation and Reasoning, pp. 103–114 (1992)
231. Peterson, J.L.: Petri Net Theory and the Modeling of Systems. Prentice Hall,
     Englewood Cliffs (1981)
232. Petrick, R.P.A., Bacchus, F.: A knowledge-based approach to planning with in-
     complete information and sensing. In: AIPS 2002, 6th International Conference
     on Artificial Intelligence Planning Systems, pp. 212–221 (2002)
233. Pistore, M., Marconi, A., Bertoli, P., Traverso, P.: Automated composition of
     web services by planning at the knowledge level. In: IJCAI 2005, 19th Inter-
     national Joint Conference on Artificial Intelligence (2005)
234. Pistore, M., Traverso, P., Bertoli, P.: Automated composition of web services
     by planning in asynchronous domains. In: ICAPS 2005, 15th International
     Conference on Automated Planning and Scheduling (2005)
235. Pistore, M., Traverso, P., Bertoli, P., Marconi, A.: Automated synthesis of
     composite BPEL4WS web services. In: ICWS 2005, 3rd IEEE International
     Conference on Web Services (2005)
236. Pnueli, A.: The temporal logic of programs. In: 18th IEEE Symposium on the
     Foundations of Computer Science, pp. 46–57 (1977)
237. Ponnekanti, S., Fox, A.: SWORD: A developer toolkit for web services com-
     position. In: WWW 2002, 11th International Conference on the World Wide
     Web (2002)
238. Preist, C.: A conceptual architecture for semantic web services. In: McIlraith,
     S.A., Plexousakis, D., van Harmelen, F. (eds.) ISWC 2004. LNCS, vol. 3298,
     pp. 395–409. Springer, Heidelberg (2004)

239. Puhlmann, F., Weske, M.: Investigations on soundness regarding lazy activities. In: Dustdar, S., Fiadeiro, J.L., Sheth, A.P. (eds.) BPM 2006. LNCS, vol. 4102, pp. 145–160. Springer, Heidelberg (2006)

240. Quillian, M.R.: Word concepts: A theorey and simulation of some basic capabilities. Behavioral Science 12, 410–430 (1967)

241. Rao, J.: Semantic Web Service Composition via Logic-based Program Synthesis. PhD thesis, Norwegian University of Science and Technology (2004)

242. Rao, J., Dimitrov, D., Hofmann, P., Sadeh, N.: A mixed initiative approach to semantic web service discovery and composition: SAP's guided procedures framework. In: ICWS 2006, 4th IEEE International Conference on Web Services (2006)

243. Rao, J., Su, X.: A survey of automated web service composition methods. In: Cardoso, J., Sheth, A.P. (eds.) SWSWPC 2004. LNCS, vol. 3387, pp. 43–54. Springer, Heidelberg (2005)

244. Recker, J., Mendling, J.: On the translation between BPMN and BPEL: Conceptual mismatch between process modeling languages. In: Dubois, E., Pohl, K. (eds.) CAiSE 2006. LNCS, vol. 4001, pp. 521–532. Springer, Heidelberg (2006)

245. Reichert, M., Rinderle, S., Dadam, P.: ADEPT workflow management system: Flexible support for enterprise-wide business processes. In: van der Aalst, W.M.P., ter Hofstede, A.H.M., Weske, M. (eds.) BPM 2003. LNCS, vol. 2678, pp. 370–379. Springer, Heidelberg (2003)

246. Reichert, M., Rinderle, S., Kreher, U., Dadam, P.: Adaptive process management with ADEPT2. In: ICDE 2005, Proceedings of the 21st International Conference on Data Engineering, pp. 1113–1114 (2005)

247. Reijers, H.A.: Design and Control of Workflow Processes: Business Process Management for the Service Industry. LNCS, vol. 2617. Springer, Heidelberg (2003)

248. Reisig, W.: Petri Nets: an Introduction. Springer, Heidelberg (1985)

249. Reisig, W.: A Primer in Petri Net Design. Springer Compass International, Heidelberg (1992)

250. Reisig, W., Rozenberg, G. (eds.): APN 1998. LNCS, vol. 1491. Springer, Heidelberg (1998)

251. Reisig, W., Rozenberg, G. (eds.): APN 1998. LNCS, vol. 1492. Springer, Heidelberg (1998)

252. Riss, U., Weber, I., Grebner, O.: Business process modeling, task management, and the semantic link. In: AAAI Spring Symposium – AI Meets Business Rules and Process Management, Palo Alto, CA, USA, April 2008, pp. 99–104 (2008)

253. Roman, D., Keller, U., Lausen, H., de Bruijn, J., Lara, R., Stollberg, M., Polleres, A., Feier, C., Bussler, C., Fensel, D.: Web service modeling ontology. Applied Ontology 1(1), 77–106 (2005)

254. Russell, N., Hofstede, A.H.M.T., Edmond, D.: Workflow data patterns. Technical report, QUT Technical report, FIT-TR-2004-01, Queensland University of Technology, Brisbane (2004)

255. Russell, N., ter Hofstede, A.H.M., Edmond, D.: Workflow resource patterns. In: Pastor, Ó., Falcão e Cunha, J. (eds.) CAiSE 2005. LNCS, vol. 3520, pp. 216–232. Springer, Heidelberg (2005)

256. Russell, N., ter Hofstede, A.H.M., Edmond, D.: Workflow exception patterns. In: Dubois, E., Pohl, K. (eds.) CAiSE 2006. LNCS, vol. 4001, pp. 288–302. Springer, Heidelberg (2006)

257. Russell, N., Hofstede, A.H.M.T., Mulyar, N.: Workflow control-flow patterns: A revised view. Technical report, BPM Center Report BPM-06-22, BPMcenter.org (2006)
258. Russell, S., Norvig, P.: Artificial Intelligence: A Modern Approach, 2nd edn. Prentice-Hall, Englewood Cliffs (2002)
259. Ryndina, K., Küster, J.M., Gall, H.C.: Consistency of business process models and object life cycles. In: Kühne, T. (ed.) MoDELS 2006. LNCS, vol. 4364, pp. 80–90. Springer, Heidelberg (2007)
260. Sadiq, S.W., Orlowska, M.E., Sadiq, W.: Specification and validation of process constraints for flexible workflows. Journal of Information Systems 30(5), 349–378 (2005)
261. Schaffner, J., Meyer, H., Tosun, C.: A semi-automated orchestration tool for service-based business processes. In: 2nd International Workshop on Engineering Service-Oriented Applications: Design and Composition, Chicago, USA (2006)
262. Schmidt-Schauß, M., Smolka, G.: Attributive concept descriptions with complements. Artificial Intelligence 48, 1–26 (1991)
263. Sheshagiri, M.: desJardins, M., Finin, T.: A planner for composing services described in DAML-S. In: AAMAS 2003, 2nd International Joint Conference on Autonomous Agents and Multiagent Systems (2003)
264. Shvaiko, P., Euzenat, J., Giunchiglia, F., He, B. (eds.): OM 2007, 2nd Intl. Workshop on Ontology Matching; Co-located with ISWC 2007, 6th International Semantic Web Conference (November 2007)
265. Sinur, J., Hill, J.B.: Align BPM and SOA initiatives now to increase chances of becoming a leader by 2010. Gartner Predicts 2007 (November 10, 2006)
266. Sirin, E., Hendler, J., Parsia, B.: Semi-automatic composition of web services using semantic descriptions. In: Workshop Web Services: Modeling, Architecture and Infrastructure at ICEIS 2003 (2003)
267. Sirin, E., Parsia, B.: Planning for semantic web services. In: Workshop on Semantic Web Services at ISWC 2004 (2004)
268. Sirin, E., Parsia, B., Hendler, J.: Composition-driven filtering and selection of semantic web services. In: AAAI Fall Symposium – Semantic Web Services (2004)
269. Sirin, E., Parsia, B., Hendler, J.: Template-based composition of semantic web services. In: AAAI Fall Symposium – Agents and Search (2006)
270. Sirin, E., Parsia, B., Wu, D., Hendler, J., Nau, D.: HTN planning for web service composition using SHOP2. Journal of Web Semantics 1(4), 377–396 (2004)
271. Smith, D.E., Weld, D.: Conformant Graphplan. In: AAAI 1998, 15th National Conference on Artificial Intelligence, pp. 889–896 (1998)
272. Smith, D.E., Weld, D.S.: Temporal planning with mutual exclusion reasoning. In: IJCAI 1999, 16th International Joint Conference on Artificial Intelligence, pp. 326–337 (1999)
273. Srivastava, B.: Automatic web services composition using planning. In: KBCS 2002, Knowledge Based Computer Systems, pp. 467–477 (2002)
274. Stollberg, M., Keller, U., Lausen, H., Heymans, S.: Two-phase web service discovery based on rich functional descriptions. In: Franconi, E., Kifer, M., May, W. (eds.) ESWC 2007. LNCS, vol. 4519, pp. 99–113. Springer, Heidelberg (2007)

275. Strichman, O.: Accelerating bounded model checking of safety formulas. Formal Methods in System Design 24(1), 5–24 (2004)

276. Studer, R., Benjamins, V.R., Fensel, D.: Knowledge engineering: Principles and methods. Data & Knowledge Engineering 25(1-2), 161–197 (1998)

277. Sycara, K., Paolucci, M., Ankolekar, A., Srinivasan, N.: Automated discovery, interaction and composition of semantic web services. Journal of Web Semantics 1(1), 27–46 (2003)

278. Tai, S., Mikalsen, T., Wohlstadter, E., Desai, N., Rouvellou, I.: Transaction policies for service-oriented computing. Data & Knowledge Engineering 51(1), 59–79 (2004)

279. TeleManagement Forum. Enhaced Telecom Operations Map (eTOM) (November 2004)

280. TeleManagement Forum. New Generation Operations Systems and Software (NGOSS) (July 2004)

281. TeleManagement Forum. Shared Information / Data model (SID) (November 2004)

282. Teng, J.T.C., Grover, V., Fiedler, K.D.: Business process re-engineering: Charting a strategic path for the information age. California Management Review 37(3), 9–31 (1994)

283. ter Beek, M., Bucchiarone, A., Gnesi, S.: Web service composition approaches: From industrial standards to formal methods. In: ICIW 2007, 2nd International Conference on Internet and Web Applications and Services (2007)

284. The OWL Services Coalition, Burstein, M., Hobbs, J., Lassila, O., McDermott, D., McIlraith, S., Narayanan, S., Paolucci, M., Parsia, B., Payne, T., Sirin, E., Srinivasan, N., Sycara, K. (eds.): OWL-S: Semantic Markup for Web Services. OWL-S 1.1 (November 2004), http://www.daml.org/services/owl-s/1.1/

285. Thiébaux, S., Hoffmann, J., Nebel, B.: In defense of PDDL axioms. Artificial Intelligence 168(1–2), 38–69 (2005)

286. Tichy, W.F.: Should computer scientists experiment more? – 16 excuses to avoid experimentation. IEEE Computer 31(5), 32–40 (1998)

287. Tobies, S.: Complexity Results and Practical Algorithms for Logics in Knowledge Representation. PhD thesis, RWTH Aachen, Germany (2001)

288. Toma, I., Iqbal, K., Moran, M., Roman, D., Strang, T., Fensel, D.: An evaluation of discovery approaches in grid and web services environments. In: NODe/GSEM 2005, Net.ObjectDays / Grid Services Engineering and Management (2005)

289. Tut, M.T., Edmond, D.: The use of patterns in service composition. In: AiSE 2002/ WES 2002: Revised Papers from the International Workshop on Web Services, E-Business, and the Semantic Web, pp. 28–40 (2002)

290. US Dept. of the Treasury, CIO Council. Treasury Enterprise Architecture Framework Version 1.0 (July 2000), http://www.eaframeworks.com/TEAF/teaf.doc (accessed September 4, 2007)

291. Valmari, A.: A stubborn attack on state explosion. In: Clarke, E., Kurshan, R.P. (eds.) CAV 1990. LNCS, vol. 531, pp. 156–165. Springer, Heidelberg (1991)

292. van der Aalst, W.: Verification of workflow nets. In: ATPN 1997: International Conference on Application and Theory of Petri Nets, London, UK, pp. 407–426. Springer, Heidelberg (1997)

293. van der Aalst, W.: The application of petri nets to workflow management. The Journal of Circuits, Systems and Computers 8(1), 21–66 (1998)

294. van der Aalst, W.: Formalization and verification of event-driven process chains. Information and Software Technology 41(10), 639–650 (1999)
295. van der Aalst, W.: Interorganizational workflows: An approach based on message sequence charts and petri nets. Systems Analysis - Modelling - Simulation 34(3), 335–367 (1999)
296. van der Aalst, W.: Business process management demystified: A tutorial on models, systems and standards for workflow management. In: Lectures on Concurrency and Petri Nets in ACPN 2004, Advanced Courses in Petri Nets, pp. 1–65 (2003)
297. van der Aalst, W.: Pi calculus versus petri nets: Let us eat "humble pie" rather than further inflate the "pi hype" (2003), http://is.tm.tue.nl/research/patterns/download/pi-hype.pdf (unpublished discussion paper, accessed April 2, 2009)
298. van der Aalst, W., de Beer, H.T., van Dongen, B.F.: Process mining and verification of properties: An approach based on temporal logic. In: On The Move (OTM) Conferences, pp. 130–147 (2005)
299. van der Aalst, W., Hirnschall, A., Verbeek, H.: An alternative way to analyze workflow graphs. In: Pidduck, A.B., Mylopoulos, J., Woo, C.C., Ozsu, M.T. (eds.) CAiSE 2002. LNCS, vol. 2348, pp. 535–552. Springer, Heidelberg (2002)
300. van der Aalst, W., ter Hofstede, A.H.M., Kiepuszewski, B., Barros, A.P.: Workflow Patterns. Distributed Parallel Databases 14(1), 5–51 (2003)
301. van der Aalst, W., van Hee, K.: Workflow Management: Models, Methods, and Systems (Cooperative Information Systems). MIT Press, Cambridge (2002)
302. van Lessen, T., Nitzsche, J., Dimitrov, M., Konstantinov, M., Karastoyanova, D., Cekov, L., Leymann, F.: An execution engine for semantic business processes. In: SeMSoC 2007, 2nd International Workshop on Business Oriented Aspects concerning Semantics and Methodologies in Service-oriented Computing (September 2007)
303. Vanhatalo, J., Völzer, H., Koehler, J.: The refined process structure tree. In: Dumas, M., Reichert, M., Shan, M.-C. (eds.) BPM 2008. LNCS, vol. 5240, pp. 100–115. Springer, Heidelberg (2008)
304. Vanhatalo, J., Völzer, H., Leymann, F.: Faster and more focused control-flow analysis for business process models through SESE decomposition. In: Krämer, B.J., Lin, K.-J., Narasimhan, P. (eds.) ICSOC 2007. LNCS, vol. 4749, pp. 43–55. Springer, Heidelberg (2007)
305. Verbeek, H., Basten, T., van der Aalst, W.: Diagnosing workflow processes using Woflan. The Computer Journal 44(4), 246–279 (2001)
306. Vernadat, F.: Enterprise Modeling and Integration: Principles and Applications. Springer, Heidelberg (1996)
307. Vu, L.-H., Hauswirth, M., Porto, F., Aberer, K.: A search engine for QoS-enabled discovery of semantic web services. International Journal on Business Process Integration and Management 1(4), 244–255 (2006)
308. W3C. SOAP Version 1.2. W3C Recommendation (June 24, 2003)
309. W3C. Web Services Architecture. W3C Working Group Note (Febuary 11, 2004), http://www.w3.org/TR/2004/NOTE-ws-arch-20040211/
310. W3C. Web Services Description Language (WSDL) 1.1. W3C Note (March 15, 2001)

311. Weber, I.: Requirements for implementing business process models through composition of semantic web services. In: I-ESA 2007, 3rd International Conference Interoperability for Enterprise Software and Applications, Funchal, Madeira, Portugal, March 2007, pp. 3–14 (2007)

312. Weber, I., Barros, A., May, N., Hoffmann, J., Kaczmarek, T.: Composing services for third-party service delivery. In: ICWS 2009, 7th IEEE International Conference on Web Services, Application and Industry Track, Los Angeles, CA, USA (July 2009)

313. Weber, I., Governatori, G., Hoffmann, J.: Approximate compliance checking for annotated process models. In: GRCIS 2008, International Workshop on Governance, Risk, and Compliance in Information Systems at CAiSE 2008, Montpellier, France, June 2008, pp. 46–60 (2008)

314. Weber, I., Hoffmann, J., Mendling, J.: Beyond soundness: On the semantic consistency of executable process models. In: ECOWS 2008, 6th IEEE European Conference on Web Services, Dublin, Ireland, November 2008, pp. 102–111 (2008)

315. Weber, I., Hoffmann, J., Mendling, J.: Semantic business process validation. In: SBPM 2008, 3rd International Workshop on Semantic Business Process Management at ESWC 2008, Tenerife, Spain (June 2008)

316. Weber, I., Hoffmann, J., Mendling, J., Nitzsche, J.: Towards a methodology for semantic business process modeling and configuration. In: SeMSoC 2007, 2nd International Workshop on Business Oriented Aspects concerning Semantics and Methodologies in Service-oriented Computing, Vienna, Austria, September 2007, pp. 176–187 (2007)

317. Weber, I., Markovic, I., Drumm, C.: A conceptual framework for composition in business process management. In: Abramowicz, W. (ed.) BIS 2007. LNCS, vol. 4439, pp. 54–66. Springer, Heidelberg (2007)

318. Weber, I., Markovic, I., Drumm, C.: A conceptual framework for semantic business process configuration. Journal of Information Science and Technology 5(2), 3–20 (2008)

319. Weber, I., Sure, Y.: Towards an implementation of the EU services directive. In: BIS 2009, 12th International Conference on Business Information Systems, Poznan, Poland, April 2009, pp. 217–227 (2009)

320. Weske, M.: Business process management: concepts, languages, architectures. Springer, Heidelberg (2007)

321. Weske, M., van der Aalst, W., Verbeek, H.M.W.E.: Advances in business process management. Data & Knowledge Engineering 50(1), 1–8 (2004)

322. Winslett, M.: Reasoning about actions using a possible models approach. In: AAAI 1988, National Conference on Artificial Intelligence (1988)

323. Winslett, M.: Updating Logical Databases. Cambridge University Press, Cambridge (1990)

324. Winslett, M.: Circumscriptive semantics for updating databases. Annals of Mathematics and Artificial Intelligence 3, 429–450 (1991)

325. World Wide Web Consortium (W3C). Web Ontology Language (OWL). W3C Recommendation (February 10, 2004)

326. Wynn, M.T., Edmond, D., van der Aalst, W.M.P., ter Hofstede, A.H.M.: Achieving a general, formal and decidable approach to the OR-join in workflow using reset nets. In: Ciardo, G., Darondeau, P. (eds.) ICATPN 2005. LNCS, vol. 3536, pp. 423–443. Springer, Heidelberg (2005)

327. Zaremba, M., Bhiri, S., Hauswirth, M., Gaaloul, W., Wetzstein, B., van Lessen, T., Weber, I., Markovic, I., Drumm, C., Kowalkiewicz, M., Filipowska, A., Wisniewski, M., Hench, G., Simov, A., Schreder, B., Stein, S.: SUPER Deliverable D7.2: Semantic Web Services-based Business Process Architecture (September 2007), http://www.ip-super.org
328. Zelkowitz, M., Wallace, D.: Experimental models for validating technology. IEEE Computer 31(5), 23–31 (1998)
329. Zhao, W., Hauser, R., Bhattacharya, K., Bryant, B., Cao, F.: Compiling business processes: Untangling unstructured loops in irreducible flow graphs. International Journal of Web and Grid Services 2(1), 68–91 (2006)
330. Zobel, J.: Writing for Computer Science, 2nd edn. Springer, Heidelberg (2004)
331. zur Muehlen, M.: Workflow-based Process Controlling – Foundation, Design, and Application of Workflow-driven Process Information Systems. PhD thesis, ERCIS, University of Muenster (2004)
332. zur Muehlen, M., Rosemann, M.: Multi-paradigm process management. In: Persson, A., Stirna, J. (eds.) CAiSE 2004. LNCS, vol. 3084, pp. 169–175. Springer, Heidelberg (2004)

Index